20TH CENTURY PERSONALITIES

20TH CENTURY PERSONALITIES

Martin Howard and Eleanor Stillwell

PARKGATE
BOOKS

Contains revised & updated text from Who's Who in the 20th Century, published in 1993

The publisher gratefully acknowledges all the organisations and photographers who contributed photography for the following pages:

Corbis/Bettmann for front cover (top left, bottom right), pages 2 (left and right), 3 (right), 6, 11, 14 (bottom), 19, 22 (top), 23, 24-25, 26 (middle), 28 (top), 28 (bottom), 29, 30 (top and bottom), 34 (top), 34 (middle and bottom), 35, 42 (top and bottom), 46 (top and middle), 49, 52, 53, 54 (top), 55 (all), 56 (middle and bottom), 57, 60 (top and middle), 65, 66 (middle and bottom), 70 (middle and bottom), 71, 72 (top and middle), 73, 74 (top), 76 (top and middle), 77, 78, 79, 81, 84 (top), 85, 86 (top and middle), 87, 88-89, 90 (top), 95, 97 (main), 98 (all), 102 (top and bottom), 104 (middle), 105, 110 (top and bottom), 111, 113, 114 (top and middle), 115, 116 (bottom), 117, 120 (top and middle), 122-123, 125, 126 (top), 127, 128 (top), 130 (top and middle), 133, 134 (all), 135, 138 (top), 139, 141, 144 (top and middle), 146-147, 148 (all), 149, 151, 153, 154-155 (main), 157, 158 (middle and bottom), 160, 162 (top), 166 (top and bottom), 167, 168, 169, 170 (top and middle), 171, 172 (top), 176 (middle), 177, 178 (all), 184, 186 (bottom), 187, 190 (top and middle), 191, 193, 207, 208 (bottom), 211 and back cover (middle right and bottom left);
Corbis for front cover (top right), pages 16,

17, 18 (middle), 20, 21, 46 (bottom), 70 (top), 97 (inset), 110 (middle), 128 (bottom), 138 (middle), 143, 176 (bottom) and 208 (top);
Illustrated London News for front cover (middle left), pages 2 (middle), 3 (left and middle), 7, 37, 40 (middle), 43, 47, 51, 54 (bottom), 58, 59, 61, 66 (top), 67, 80 (top), 80 (middle), 82, 83, 84 (middle), 102 (middle), 103, 108, 119, 124 (middle), 126 (bottom), 137, 142 (middle), 172 (middle), 175, 175 (top), 182, 183, 203, 205, 209 and back cover (bottom right);
Sportsphoto for front cover (middle, middle left, bottom left), pages 8 (all), 9 (all), 12, 13, 14 (top and middle), 15, 22 (middle), 26 (top), 27 (both), 38 (both), 39, 40 (all), 41, 45, 54 (middle), 62, 63, 74 (middle), 75, 76 (bottom), 80 (bottom), 84 (bottom), 90 (bottom(, 91, 92, 93 (both), 99 (both), 104 (bottom), 106, 120 (bottom), 128 (top), 154 (inset), 162 (bottom), 164, 165, 170 (bottom), 172 (bottom), 173 (top and bottom), 179, 186 (middle), 189 and back cover (top left and right, middle left);
Corbis/Neal Preston for pages 18 (top) and 121;
Corbis/Underwood & Underwood for pages 18 (bottom) and 158 (top);
Corbis/Robert Maass for page 22 (bottom);
Corbis/Wally McNamee for page 26 (bottom);
Corbis/Paul Almasy for page 28 (middle);
Corbis/Hulton-Deutsch Collection for pages

30 (middle), 69, 94 (top), 114 (bottom), 116 (top), 124 (bottom), 129, 130 (bottom), 138 (bottom), 142 (bottom), 162 (middle), 163, 185 and 186 (top);
Corbis/Henry Diltz for page 31;
Corbis/Nik Wheeler for page 33;
Corbis/Dave Rubinger for pages 42 (middle) and 94 (bottom);
Corbis/Bob Krist for page 56 (top);
Corbis/Colita for page 60 (bottom);
Corbis/Michael S Yamashita for page 70 (bottom) and 90 (bottom);
Corbis/Oscar White for page 74 (bottom);
Corbis/Francoise de Mulder for page 86 (bottom);
Corbis/Roger Ressmeyer for pages 90 (middle) and 124 (top);
Corbis/Shelley Gazin for page 94 (middle);
Corbis/Flip Schulke for page 101;
Corbis/Ted Streshinsky for page 104 (top);
Corbis/Bryn Colton; Assignments Photography for page 116 (middle);
Corbis/Francesco Venturi; Kea Publishing Service for page 128 (middle);
The Hulton Getty Picture Collection for page 142 (top);
Corbis/Jonathan Blair for page 144 (bottom);
Corbis/Michael Nicholson for page 145;
Corbis/Kevin Fleming for page 159;
Corbis/Barnabas Bosshart for page 166 (middle);
Corbis/Lynn Goldsmith for pages 180 and 181;
Corbis/E O Hoppé for page 190 (bottom).

First published in 1999 by
PRC Publishing Ltd,
Kiln House, 210 New Kings Road, London SW6 4NZ

This edition published in 1999 by
London House
Great Eastern Wharf
Parkgate Road
London
SW11 4NQ

© 1999 PRC Publishing Ltd

British Library Cataloguing in Publication Data:
A catalogue record for this book is available from the British Library.

ISBN 1 902616 33 2

Printed and bound in China

CONTENTS

INTRODUCTION

At the end of the century, looking back, the extent of human development is breathtaking. In these mere hundred years the human race has achieved feats and undertaken ventures that would have staggered belief at the beginning of the 1900s.

While it most certainly has not been the most peaceful of centuries — indeed it has been plagued by tyrants, madmen, and despots who have had wreaked damage on an unprecedented scale — human enterprise has flourished. At no other time have so many people made such a difference to the way that we live our lives. Every arena of human endeavor — science, the arts, politics and sport — has witnessed the ascent of people who have changed society and culture forever. And as well as the obvious luminaries — people who are household names the world over — there are others, the less well-known heroes and heroines who though their inventions and interventions effect us in ways that we may not even notice.

Technologically, we have passed from the age of steam to walking on the moon and beyond — planning missions to the remotest parts of our solar system while each day seems to bring fresh data from the furthest reaches of space that sheds more light on the universe and our place within it. Computers, unheard of in 1900, are now ubiquitous, and the mass media has invaded even the remotest parts of the globe. Each one of us, in the "Global Village," is aware of other cultures and has an ability to communicate, through the telephone and, more recently, the internet, that our grandparents could not have dreamed of. It has been said that science has become the new religion and as the new millennium dawns it promises to bring even more innovations and discoveries that will help in the war against disease and push the limits of understanding still further.

The arts too have experienced a revolution. Film, a medium in its infancy at the turn of the century, is now a huge industry, and one that has colored each of our lives. From the groundbreaking comedies of Charlie Chaplin and the on-screen charisma of stars such as Rudolph Valentino and Marilyn Monroe, to the technological wizardry of Steven Spielberg, the movies enjoy a popularity that has eclipsed every other form of narrative and entertain us on a scale that could never have been suspected. The 20th century has had more than its fair share of literary and artistic genius also. Ernest Hemingway, T.S. Eliot, Toni Morrison, Pablo Picasso, and Andy Warhol, are just a few who have given a commentary on the passage of the century that reminds us of its scope — its successes and its failures and the vast array of cultures and lifestyles that now form society.

The world of politics has been fraught. The two most disastrous wars in terms of human carnage have been fought in a century that can be characterized by political uncertainty and tension. In spite of ongoing atrocities however, there has been a great movement toward peace though tyrants and oppressors are not tolerated by the international community and we continue to wage war against those who would murder and dispossess. Men like Ghandi and Martin Luther King have forced a recognition of the rights of different cultures while women such as Emily Pankhurst have changed the female political standing irrevocably. The political sphere at the beginning of the century was an exclusively white male domain. That is slowly changing and perhaps true equality and justice for all is the noblest of challenges that the human race has assigned itself.

Sir Charles Spencer Chaplin

Marilyn Monroe

In every realm of activity, men and women have pushed forward the boundaries of human accomplishment and have worked tirelessly to provide knowledge, understanding, entertainment, and freedom. As a result, we now know little of the trials of our ancestors. While the world is still less than perfect, in the West extreme poverty has been virtually banished and people now live longer, healthier lives with generally more education and leisure. Who can say if our lives are better than those of our forebears? The only thing that is for certain is that ours are very, very different.

Unraveling and interpreting the 20th century is a task that will concern historians and social scientists for many years to come for it is an era that is richly complex and fascinating. The intention of this book is to capture the zeitgeist of this most incredible century. It details the geniuses, visionaries and the truly talented that have had a deep impact on our culture — from the megalomaniacal charisma of Adolf Hitler, to the lasting allure of Marilyn Monroe and the transcendent music of the Beatles. Figures as diverse as Margaret Thatcher, Stephen Hawking, Bill Clinton, Steven Spielberg, Bill

Gates, Princess Diana and Madonna, as well as lesser known personalities from fields as diverse as architecture, transport, fashion, technology, the media and academia. The only criteria for entrance into this account is that the person has made a fundamental impression on society and the way that we live. With the end of the millennium fast approaching, it is a timely celebration of the achievements of the past hundred years and a tribute to those people who with intelligence, determination, luck and willpower have left the world in a different state to that in which they found it.

A-

OF PERSO

-Z

NALITIES

A

Adams, Ansel
1902–1984
American photographer

Born in San Francisco on February 20, 1902, Adams became an influential leader of modern photography. His landscape photography of the American West is a groundbreaking and poetic testament to his art; the clarity of the pictures that he took etch a stark, yet grandiose, landscape of an undisturbed country, presided over by mountains and a wide sky. His portfolios include a comprehensive study of the landscape of Yosemite National Park, the Big Sur Coast, the Sierra Nevada, the American Southwest, and America's National Parks. In addition, Adams excelled in portraiture, architectural studies, and commercial illustration. His prolific output, the artistic quality of his work, its evolution in style, and its historical context confirm Adams's position as the most significant photographer of the 20th century.

In 1916, as a boy, he visited Yosemite Valley, California, with his first camera and the experience effected him deeply. It led him to join the Sierra Club in 1920, a society formed to protect the wilderness environment and to organize activities such as mountain climbing, orienteering, and camping. This was to be an association to which Adams would remain loyal throughout his life and from 1916 he would visit Yosemite at least once a year until his death.

Originally Adams was trained as a pianist, and he excelled in music while also devoting much time to his other passion – photography – in which he had developed a keen interest following that first vacation in Yosemite. His life was divided between the two arts until 1930, when he saw an exhibition of the work of Paul Strand, a great talent in early 20th century photography whose work was marked by a blend of formalism and humanism. After a meeting with Strand, he decided to forget his musical aspirations in order to concentrate his energies on photography. So enthused was he that he built his own workshop

and studio adjoining his parents home. Commercial assignments soon followed and provided a source of revenue that allowed Adams to explore his work and themes. The following year he exhibited at the Smithsonian Institution, Washington D.C.

In 1932 with Edward Weston and Imogen Cunningham, among others, he founded the f/64 group, dedicated to the promotion of pure photography. The aim of this group was to produce "straight" – unmanipulated – photography. As the technology of photography had improved, so it increased the artists' ability to produce images which were closer in form, light, and detail to the subject. Where previously photographers had attempted to control and formulate pictures in the same way that an artist would create a picture, the members of f/64 were dedicated to realism, obtaining the "fingerprint" of reality. In retrospect this can be seen as a turning point in the evolution of the art.

During the year 1932 Adams also enjoyed his own first solo exhibition which was well received and consolidated his growing reputation. His work soon caught the attention of Alfred Stieglitz who became an admirer and exhibited Adams photography at An American Place in 1936. This was a milestone in Adams' career — Stieglitz was a famous and respected photographer and leader of the Photo-Secession movement that had flourished in New York at the turn of the century.

In 1937 Adams moved to Yosemite, the source of his inspiration and took long photography treks in the company of Edward Weston through the High Sierra and with Georgia O'Keeffe and David McAlphin through the Southwest. In 1940, he was also instrumental in setting up the first department of photography as a fine art, at the Museum of Modern Art in New York. From this time onwards Adams photographed more and more

extensively in the national parks across America. Using naturally brilliant light and his 1941 innovation, the Zone system, Adams's pictures are intensely sharp, detailed images which contrast with the work of previous photographers and which lead a revolution in the field.

Over the next four decades a large volume of Adams' photography was published including; *My Camera in Yosemite Valley* (1949); *Portfolio Two: The National Parks* (1950); *This Is the American Earth* (1960); *Ansel Adams, Images 1923–1974* (1975); and *The Portfolios of Ansel Adams* (1977). He received an honorary Doctor of Fine Arts degree from the University of California, Berkeley in 1961, a Progress Medal from the Photographic Society of America in 1969. By 1975 such was the magnitude of back orders for his work that he was forced to stop taking individual orders: to print those already taken took a further three years. In 1980, President Carter awarded Adams the highest civilian honor –the Presidential Medal of Freedom – and from The Wilderness Society, he received the first Ansel Adams Award for Conservation. Further awards were heaped on him throughout the remainder of his life including the decoration of Commander of the Order of the Arts and Letters, the highest cultural award given by the French government to a foreigner. He was also elected an honorary member in the American Academy and Institute of Arts and Letters and California State Legislature proclaimed Ansel Adams Day. He also continued to work, exhibit, and publish some of the most memorable and important photography of the century and took a politically active role in conservation movements throughout the United States.

Ansel Adams died in 1984, his passing was commemorated with the designation of over 100,000 acres of land in Yosemite National Park as the Ansel Adams Wilderness Area.

A

Muhammad Ali (b. Cassius Clay) 1942–

American boxer

A poet and a pounder, Ali captured the imagination of people across the globe with his wicked charm, his fierce bravado, and his masterful boxing. He held at least a piece of the world heavyweight championship on several occasions, most impressively from 1964 to 1967 and from 1974 to 1978.

He was born in Louisville, Kentucky, on January 17, 1942 as Cassius Clay and started boxing at the age of 12. He first gained acclaim in the 1960 Olympics in Rome, capturing the gold medal in the light heavyweight division. Following this triumph he set out to win the heavyweight title and soon found national notoriety, scoring victories over legends such as Sonny Banks and Archie Moore.

In 1963, he traveled to England to fight the British heavyweight Henry Cooper. The match was set for June 18, and became known as one of the most legendary in the history of boxing. Cooper floored Ali in the fourth round and seemed set for victory. However, with an incredible flurry of combination punches, Ali came back and cut Cooper's face so badly that the fight was stopped in the fifth. Though Cooper was a national hero in Britain, Ali's charisma and great sportsmanship ensured that his popularity remained undiminished.

In 1964 Ali engineered a stunning upset victory by knocking out heavyweight champion Sonny Liston. However, the fight caused controversy as Ali (then still Clay) appeared to be on the verge of quitting before the match had finished. A second match with Liston was no less fraught as Liston went down and stayed down in the first round. Contention was soon quieted, however, as Ali proved himself a sporting champion, accepting the challenges of every heavyweight boxer with ranking credentials. His rhyming prediction of victory, "Float like a butterfly, sting like a bee," his graceful "Ali Shuffle," and his vicious punching

power made him a charismatic champion and his public visibility also benefited from the first successful television broadcasts by satellite, which brought him international celebrity. Soon after winning the title from Liston, Cassius Clay became a Black Muslim and changed his name — he was determined now to fight not only for himself but for his people to whom he became an idol.

His beliefs, however, were to cause problems. Ali was stripped of his title in 1967 when he refused to enter the US military because of religious convictions.

It was to be three years until Ali was to be allowed back in the ring and a further year before his appeal was honored by the Supreme Court in 1971 and he could resume his career. Despite a few encouraging victories Ali lost his championship bid to the reigning champ, Joe Frazier — though it was a hard won success for Frazier. By 1973 it looked like Ali's career was finished when Ken Norton broke his jaw. Always persistent though, he fought Norton again six months later and on this

occasion won on points. Another match with Frazier was scheduled for January 28, 1974, but by then Frazier had lost the championship to George Foreman. However, Ali won, beating his opponent, again on points, and was determined to make another bid at the championship. The match between Ali and Foreman was convened for October 30, 1974 and Ali stunned his rival with his "rope-a-dope" tactics, dodging Foreman's heavy blows with typical grace before knocking him out with a stunning right hook to the jaw in the seventh round.

Ali successfully defended the title until a surprise victory, on points, for the 1976 Olympic gold medallist, Leon Spinks, took it from him again in 1978. However, a rematch later in the year taught the usurper a lesson though the fight went to the full 15 rounds and was won on points. Ali had regained the championship, the first boxer to do so three times, and he retired soon after. This match boasted the biggest attendance in boxing history and the box office sold tickets worth $4,806,275. Ali attempted a couple of comebacks in 1980 and 1981, but lost his final title bid to Larry Holmes.

Ali deserves a place in history as perhaps the greatest sportsman of the 20th century, a vivacious celebrity, and an effective spokesman for America's black community. His staying power is legendary and the skill, athleticism, and elegance that he displayed in the ring at the height of his career have made a deep mark on the world of boxing. His record of 61 fights, of which he lost only five, is an outstanding achievement in itself. More importantly however, he showed the courage and strength of character of a truly great man. Currently fighting the Parkinson's disease, which is the legacy of so many blows to the head, Ali campaigns for the alleviation of poverty in the Third World with his characteristic tenacity and sense of purpose.

A

Amin, Idi
1928–
Ugandan politician

President of Uganda (1971–1979) Amin is remembered as a bloodthirsty buffoon who tyrannized his country for eight years and who was responsible for the murder of an estimated 300,000 people. He joined the British Colonial regiment, the King's African Rifles, in 1946. He was one of two African officers in Uganda's Military forces at Independence in 1962. He rose through the ranks and in 1968 was a major general and commander of the forces. He overthrew Milton Obote and expelled Uganda's 70,000 Asians in 1971. His reign as President was erratic, and left the country in confusion, with a collapsed economy. In 1979 Amin was overthrown by an invasion of forces from Tanzania: supported by Ugandan rebels he fled to exile in Saudi Arabia where he still resides.

Arafat, Yasser
1929–
Palestinian nationalist

Arafat was 19 years old when his homeland was split into Arab and Jewish areas. In 1955 he helped to found the guerrilla group *al-fatah*, later absorbed into the Palestine Liberation Organization (PLO), of which he became chairman in 1969. He has been an effective leader of the Palestinian people, gaining international credibility and recognition despite a series of political and military setbacks. Realizing that political dialogue was potentially more productive than armed confrontation, he renounced terrorism in 1985 and supported peace initiatives in the aftermath of the Gulf War in 1991. On September 13, 1993, in Washington, D.C., Arafat and Israeli Prime Minister Yitzhak Rabin witnessed the signing of a peace agreement. In 1994 Arafat, Rabin, and Shimon Peres shared the Nobel Peace Prize. He has been president of the Palestinian Authority (PA) since 1996.

Armstrong, Louis
1900–1971
American jazz trumpeter and singer

After gaining early experience in Joe (King) Oliver's band, Armstrong worked with the best outfits in Chicago by 1926, and was soon recording. For his warmth of tone and inventiveness of technique he was in great demand, first as a soloist and then as a bandleader. Fronting "Chocolates", a band for a Broadway Revue, he was at home in a big-band context. He toured Europe in the early 1930s, changing to popular tunes from the blues numbers that had been his staple fare. In the mid-1940s he began to use smaller ensembles, and was seen as a key figure in the American jazz establishment. His distinctive voice lacked the traditional qualities, but it had the same warmth, which characterized his tone on the trumpet. His sense of rhythm and early pioneering work earned him a place in the annals of jazz, but by the 1950s he was more of a popular entertainer than an innovator.

A

Allen, Woody [Allen Stewart Konigsberg]
1935–
American film director, actor and writer

Allen is America's most original movie actor, writer, and director all rolled into one. On screen, he is the epitome of the modern bungler, tormented by self-doubt, neurosis, and unswervable lust. He began using the name Woody Allen at 15, while writing jokes for newspaper columnists. He went on to write for radio and television performers, including Sid Caesar whose staff he joined in 1957. From 1961–64 Allen worked as a comedian in nightclubs, eventually being noticed by a film producer. He was hired and co-wrote, as well as acted in, *What's New Pussycat?* (1965). His first movie was *What's up Tiger Lily?* (1966), a Japanese spy thriller, dubbed in absurd English. His directing career began with *Take the Money and Run* (1969), followed by *Bananas* (1971), *Everything You Always Wanted to Know About Sex* (1972), and *Sleeper* (1975). Allen is renowned for producing funny pictures with a serious side, such as *Annie Hall* (1977) which won three Oscars. His later work such as *Crimes and Misdemeanors* (1989) is a little more thoughtful.

He won the Academy Award for best screenplay for *Hannah and her Sisters* (1986) and received Academy Award nominations in various categories for many of his movies. Allen's other movies include *Zelig* (1983), *Broadway Danny Rose* (1984), *Purple Rose of Cairo* (1985), *Radio Days* (1987), *Crimes and Misdemeanors* (1989), *Alice* (1990), *Shadows and Fog* (1992), *Husbands and Wives* (1992), *Bullets over Broadway* (1994), *Mighty Aphrodite* (1995), and the musical *Everyone Says I Love You* (1997). Allen has also written and starred in two plays, *Don't Drink the Water* (1966, filmed 1969) and *Play It Again, Sam* (1969, film 1972). *Play It Again, Sam* was the melancholy cry of a man who never got the girl and a tribute to Humphrey Bogart, who usually did. A 1994 film version of *Don't Drink the Water* was Allen's first made-for-television movie. Allen has published collections of short humorous writings, including *Getting Even* (1971), *Without Feathers* (1976), and *Side Effects* (1980).

Armstrong, Neil
1933–
American astronaut

As the commander of *Apollo 11*, Armstrong became the first human being to walk on the moon and this incredible feat, more than any other achievement this century, symbolized the dawning of the space age and captured the imagination of the world. Though somewhat eclipsed by the moon landing, Armstrong's life has been full of adventure and throughout some hair-raising experiences he has consistently distinguished himself as a man of courage and good humor.

Born in Wapakoneta, Ohio, on August 5,1930, Armstrong developed a passion for aviation as a young boy. His interest in aircraft was first aroused by a visit with his father to the National Air Races in Cleveland, Ohio, at the age of two. At six he had his first ride in a plane, a Ford Tri-Motor, "Tin Goose," in Warren, Ohio, and his interest in flight intensified. By the time he was 15, Armstrong was working in various part time jobs around town and at the airport to fund flying lessons in an Aeronca Champion aircraft which, at the time, cost $9 per hour. So enthusiastic was he that, at the age of 16 he had a student pilot's license even before he had a driver's license.

Following graduation from High School, Armstrong won a scholarship from the U.S. Navy and in 1947 began a course in aeronautical engineering at Purdue University. His education was disturbed by the advent of the Korean War (1950–1953) and he was called to active duty by the Navy as a pilot and shipped out to Korea where he was stationed on the aircraft carrier USS *Essex*. During the conflict Armstrong flew Navy Panther jets on 78 combat missions. During one of these his aircraft struck a cable which was strung across a valley and intended to bring down American planes. Though a part of one wing was torn off, Armstrong managed to pilot his Panther back to friendly territory where he parachuted to safety.

Following the war, Armstrong returned to Purdue University and in 1955 received his Bachelor of Science degree in aerospace engineering. For the next seven years he was stationed at Edwards Airforce base in California where he served as a test pilot for the pioneering X-15 which could attain speeds of up to 4,000 mph (6,000 km/h). In 1962 following the total failure of the Bay of Pigs invasion of Cuba, President Kennedy was in need of some policy which might gain him some much needed popularity. In a momentous speech to the nation he stated that it was his intention to land a man on the moon before the decade was over. In the same year Neil Armstrong was one of nine men accepted by NASA as an astronaut and he moved to El Lago in Texas to be close to the NASA Manned Spacecraft Center in Houston where he was to be trained.

His first space mission took place on March 16, 1966 — Armstrong was chosen as command pilot of the spacecraft *Gemini 8* which was to dock with the already orbiting *Agena*. The docking was successful but the two crafts soon became unstable as they orbited together. With calm professionalism Armstrong managed to undock his ship and fired the retrorockets to regain control of the *Gemini*. Despite being forced to make an emergency splashdown in the Pacific Ocean, Armstrong's presence of mind averted disaster.

On July 16, 1969, Armstrong, Michael Collins, and Edwin "Buzz" Aldrin began the *Apollo 11* trip to the moon. Armstrong was chosen to command the mission and would pilot the lunar module to the surface; the command module pilot and navigator was Collins; Aldrin was the second pilot of the lunar module the *Eagle*. On July 20, 1969, at 10:56 p.m. EDT, having made a safe touchdown. Neil Armstrong stepped out of the *Eagle* and onto the surface of the moon. At that time he made his famous statement, "That's one small step for man, one giant leap for mankind." Watched by the world on television, Armstrong and Aldrin spent 2 hours on the lunar surface, photographing, taking samples, and performing experiments. On July 24, 1969, the three men re-entered the earth's atmosphere and splashed down in the Pacific to instant fame and adulation from around the world. The module was retrieved by USS *Hornet*.

Honors heaped upon the three *Apollo 11* astronauts: a triumphant ticker-tape parade through New York City was followed by the presentation of the Presidential Medal of Freedom. Armstrong also received the NASA Distinguished Service Medal, the NASA Exceptional Service Medal, the Congressional Space Medal of Honor as well as 17 other awards from other countries.

Armstrong left NASA in 1971 to teach Aerospace engineering at the University of Cincinnati, a post he held until 1979. Currently, he is the chairman of an electronics company in New York and lives on his farm in Ohio.

A

Ashe, Arthur
1943–1993
American tennis player

Born in Richmond, Virginia, Arthur Ashe became a tennis pioneer and a moral force in the world of sports. With class and dignity Ashe played in an almost completely white game, winning 33 tournaments, including the US Open (1965), the Australian Open (1970), and Wimbledon (1975). At UCLA he won the NCAA singles title in 1966. Ashe underwent heart surgery in 1979 and announced his retirement from competition in 1980. He served as non-playing captain of the U.S. Davis Cup team from 1981–1984. He had a second bypass operation in 1983, during which it seems that he was given blood infected with HIV, which causes AIDS. After publicly confirming his infection, he became an active fundraiser and speaker on behalf of AIDS research. In 1988 Ashe published *A Hard Road to Glory: A History of the Afro-American Athlete* (3 volumes). He also wrote *Days of Grace: A Memoir* (1993).

Astaire, Fred
1899–1987
American dancer, actor, and choreographer

Astaire's early career began with his sister Adele, as a child vaudeville act, which toured the US until 1916. They danced together in various musicals until *The Band Wagon (*1931), after which Adele retired to marry. Astaire's first movie appearance was in *Dancing Lady* (1933), briefly partnering Joan Crawford. The same year he made his first movie for RKO, *Flying Down to Rio* in which he partnered Ginger Rogers. Their partnership became one of Hollywood's most popular and they made ten movies together. Astaire arranged all of his own dances in tandem with dance director, Hermes Pan. Astaire always maintained that his favorite partner was Gene Kelly. In 1949 he received a special Academy Award for his outstanding contribution to the technique of film musicals. In later years, he wrote an autobiography *Steps in Time*, and appeared in movies in acting roles, such as in *The Towering Inferno* (1974).

Baekeland, Leo Hendrik
1863–1944
Belgian-born American chemist

Baekeland, a Belgian-American contributed to the development of photography by inventing the first photographic paper – which he named Velox – that could be developed in artificial light. However Baekeland is really the father of modern plastics. In 1909, while looking for a substitute for shellac he produced a synthetic resin-like substance which, under certain conditions of temperature and pressure, would flow into a mould and set hard. Once set, this substance could not be reformed. It was the first artificially produced thermosetting plastic and he named it Bakelite. Its lightness, strength, durability and electrical resistance made it the basis of the earliest plastics industry. In recognition he received the Nichols Medal of the American Chemical Society in 1909 and the Franklin Medal of the Franklin Institute in 1940.

Bardot, Brigitte
1934–
French actress

Born Camille Javal to wealthy parents, Bardot began modeling at the age of 15 and was spotted by Roger Vadim (who she later married) on the cover of *Elle* magazine in 1950. She made her first movie *Le Trou Normand* (*Crazy for Love*) in 1952, and then acted in a series of supporting roles before her first starring role in Vadim's *Et Dieu créa la femme* (*And God Created Woman*, 1956) brought her international recognition. The movie created a sensation, particularly in the United States, where cinema-goers saw nudity in movie for the first time since the advent of the Production Code (imposed in 1934 and dissolved in the 1950s, it had strictly regulated the moral values of movies). Vadim had total control of Bardot's public image: carefully manipulated, she was seen as a blond erotic, amoral child of nature. Around this time she was also the model for a bust of the symbol of France, Marianne.

She starred in several minor French and Italian comedies, all showing her in various stages of undress. Bardot won critical acclaim for *The Truth* (1961) by French director Henri-Georges Clouzot, and *Le mepris* (*Contempt*, 1963), by French director Jean Luc Godard. Renowned as an international sex symbol throughout the western word Bardot retired from acting in 1973 having become more and more interested in animal welfare. In recent years she has used her time to help a variety of worthy causes, primarily related to animal rights. In 1976 she established a foundation for the protection of animals and she was awarded the Legion of Honor in 1985. Early in her career, Bardot was seen as a symbol of the ingenuous scorn for conventional morality by French leftists. In later years, she has continued to make headlines in Europe due to outspoken remarks in favor of far right groups.

Berlin, Irving
1888–1989
American composer

Irving Berlin, one of America's most gifted and prolific songwriters was born Israel Baline in Tyumen, in Siberian Russia, on May 11, 1888. His life was a truly American tale of rags to riches. By the time of his death in 1989 he had written the music and lyrics for an astonishing 1,500 songs, and his reign as the most popular of American songwriters had lasted for over half of the century. Though he was born a Russian Jew, his music captures a uniquely American flavor and among his songs are several classics including "God Bless America," "White Christmas," "All Alone," and "Alexander's Ragtime Band."

While Berlin was still a young boy a Russian pogrom victimizing the Jews forced his family to flee their home. They emigrated across the Atlantic and settled in New York City, on the South Side. Here, extreme poverty following the death of his father, forced the 13-year-old Berlin out onto the streets in order to make enough to feed himself. It was a Dickensian lifestyle which saw Berlin, accompanied by a blind musician, literally singing for his supper, on the Lower East Side and in cafes. He ate if he did well and starved if not. This dreadful hardship lasted for four or five years until, having taught himself the basics of the piano (it is rumored that he could only ever play the black keys) and while working as a singing waiter, he started writing songs. When his first tune was published, the name on the score was misprinted as I. Berlin and after this he always called himself Irving Berlin.

Writing under his new name, Berlin started to experience a small success with a few of his songs, with vocals from then minor celebrities such as Eddie Cantor and Fanny Brice. Nevertheless, it was not until 1916, when Berlin was 28-years-old that he

reached national popularity with his song "Alexander's Ragtime Band."

While doing service in the US army in 1918, Berlin wrote a musical to be staged by soldiers for benefit performances, "Yip, Yip Yaphank" was an instant success and paved the way for an incredible career that would continue over the next four decades. Screen musicals such as *Top Hat* (1935), starring Ginger Rogers and Fred Astaire and including the chic and zingy tune of "Cheek to Cheek," as well as *Easter Parade* (1948), *Blue Skies* (1946), and *White Christmas* (1954) were all box office smashes. He was also a prolific writer of Broadway musicals such as the *Music Box Revues* (1921–24), *As Thousands Cheer* (1933), and *Annie Get Your Gun* (1946). Berlin wrote hit song after hit song for the biggest names in show business. Frank Sinatra, Bing Crosby, Ella Fitzgerald, Billie Holliday, and other such luminaries lined up to record his numbers. For some, his tunes helped shape a career; for example Bing Crosby's rendition of *White Christmas*, written for the 1942 movie *Holiday Inn* was so successful for the singer that it became his signature song.

In 1942, on the eve of America's

entry into World War II, Berlin wrote *God Bless America*, the song was so popular that it became unofficially recognized as a second national anthem. Later in the year he produced the musical *This is the Army*, another show to be produced and staged by the forces. He donated the proceeds, which amounted to over $10 million, to government charities. In recognition of his contribution during both wars, Berlin was awarded the Presidential Medal of Freedom by President Ford in 1977.

Berlin's private life seems to have been generally happy, though as a very private man few details are known. He married the love of his life (and second wife) Catholic New York heiress Ellin Mackay in January 1926 – despite her father's objections to Berlin being of poor background, Jewish, and in show business – and the couple brought up three children as Protestants due to Ellin's desire for religious tolerance. They remained a happy and devoted couple by all accounts right up to Ellin's death in 1988.

In 1977, the increasingly reclusive Berlin presented his piano to the Smithsonian as a token of his retirement and there are very few reports of any public sightings after a public appearance at his 80th birthday party in 1968. However, a charming story relates that during the Christmas of 1983, a band of fans who were serenading his house with "White Christmas" were invited in and greeted in the kitchen by Berlin who was wearing pajamas. Cocoa was served and each well-wishers received a hug and a kiss from the grateful songwriter.

Irving Berlin died on September 22, 1989 at the age of 101. Outside his house a gathering of fans started to sing "God Bless America" as the announcement was made —a fitting tribute to a man who had entertained generations of Americans.

B

B

Barnard, Christiaan
1922–
South African surgeon

As a student, Christiaan Barnard was a well-liked man, but not an academic or surgical star. Graduating from Cape Town University, he went to Minneapolis in the 1940s to train under Walter Lillehei, the foremost American heart surgeon. On his return to South Africa, Barnard experimented on transplanting hearts into dogs, which reject transplanted tissues less readily than humans. Barnard soon established the necessary surgical principles, including keeping the patient's tissues supplied with oxygen during the period when the old heart had been removed and before the new heart was plumbed in. Hearing that Shumway (a rival surgeon) was to perform a heart transplant Barnard, decided to attempt it first, on December 3, 1967. That patient died after a few days, but his second patient lived for nearly two years. Barnard performed other transplants, but international fame and rheumatoid arthritis have combined to alter his career to that of medical guru and jetsetting playboy.

Blair, Tony, (Anthony Charles Lynton)
1953–
British politician and Prime Minister (1997–)

Tony Blair studied Law at St. John's College Oxford before becoming a lawyer specializing in trade union and industrial law in 1976. He became a Member of Parliament in 1983, for the Labour Party. Blair advanced to the party's front rank rapidly. He was opposition spokesman for various posts between 1984–92 and in 1992 he was promoted, to take charge of domestic issues in the Labour Party's shadow (opposition) cabinet. On the death of John Smith in 1994, Blair was elected as Labour Party leader. He worked to make the party more appealing to the mainstream voter, loosening ties with the trade unions and successfully broadening its membership. "New Labour" gained in popularity as the Conservative Government suffered from a series of scandals, and won a landslide victory at the 1997 General Election. Tony Blair became Britain's youngest Prime Minister in 200 years.

Brandt, Willy
1913–1992
German politician

Willy Brandt, originally named Herbert Ernst Karl Frahm, changed his name in 1933 when he fled to Norway to escape arrest by the Nazis. Brandt returned to Germany after working with the Norwegian Resistance during World War II and entered politics. He served in the Lower House of the first legislature of the Federal Republic of Germany until 1957. He was mayor of West Berlin from 1957–1966. A principal exponent of postwar *Ostpolitik* (reconciliation with the Eastern bloc), he served as Chancellor from 1969–74. He backed integration into NATO and the EEC, while his efforts for détente with the East brought him the Nobel Peace Prize in 1971. West Germany was brought into full participation in the community of nations by Brandt's administration. After he left office, he was active as president of the Socialist International and he later chaired the Brandt Commission, which reported on the world economy in 1980.

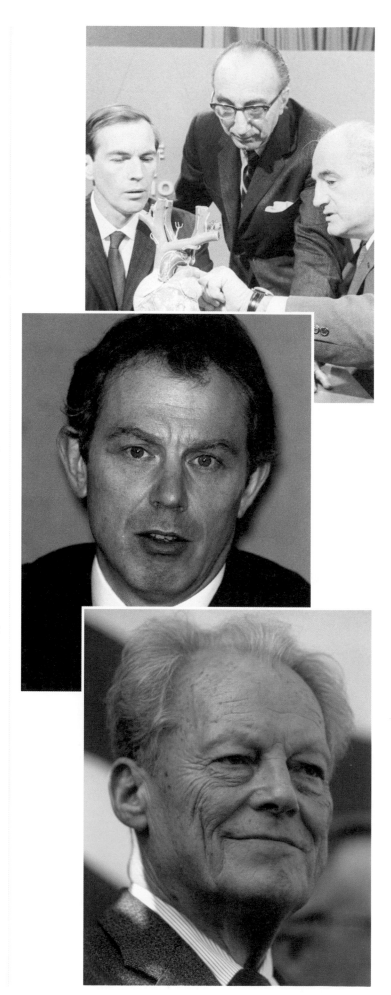

B

Brando, Marlon
1924–
American actor

Expelled from military school, the young Brando headed for New York and become a pupil of Stella Adler at the Actors' Studio; he became the first "Stanislavsky" method actor to make an impression in movies. A versatile actor, he first created the role of Stanley Kowalski in Tennessee William's play *A Streetcar named Desire* (1947) on Broadway. It made him a star and brought him to the attention of the Hollywood producers and he recreated the role for the movie in 1951. He played the role of Mark Anthony in *Julius Caesar* in 1953. *On the Waterfront* (1954) brought him an Academy Award, and he began to emerge as the image of non-conformity when this was still a rare commodity. But in the 1960s his movies went downhill amid a stormy personal life and a reputation for being temperamental; his own attempts at producing and directing led to financial disaster. He then made a brilliant comeback in *The Godfather* (1972). He was chosen to receive the Academy Award for Best Actor for his performance in *The Godfather* (1972), but he refused it, on the grounds of the movie industry's representation and exploitation of Native Americans. He created a stir in the bold and sexually explicit *Last Tango Paris* (1972) and played the cruel Commander Kurtz in *Apocalypse Now* (1979). For his first role in years as an African lawyer in *A Dry White Season* (1989) he was nominated for another Academy Award as Best Supporting Actor.

Brando's other movies include *Viva Zapata!* (1952), *The Wild One* (1954), *Guys and Dolls* (1955), *The Teahouse of the August Moon* (1956), *The Young Lions* (1958), *One-Eyed Jacks* (1961), which he also directed, *Mutiny on the Bounty* (1962), *Reflections in a Golden Eye* (1967), *Burn!* (1969), *The Freshman* (1990), and *Don Juan de Marco* (1995). Since 1966 Brando has lived on his privately owned island, Tetiaroa, in the Pacific Ocean.

The Beatles
British Rock Group

George Harrison, 1943–
John Lennon, 1940–1980
Paul McCartney, 1942–
Ringo Starr (Richard Starkey), 1940–

The biggest single influence on sixties' rock and pop, the Beatles, led by the songwriting team of Lennon and McCartney had a profound effect on the course of popular culture during the decade. Their innovation led a revolution in music, fashion, and youth culture the ramifications of which are still apparent.

The group came together in Liverpool, England, in the late 1950s, and soon found an enthusiastic audience — most notably in the Cavern Club where they were a regular booking. Originally, Lennon on guitar and McCartney playing bass, were in a group known as The Quarrymen and were joined by Harrison as an additional guitarist. At this point the three of them split from the other members of the band and formed The Silver Beatles with John's friend Stuart Sutcliffe on bass. With a succession of drummers, including the reserved Pete Best, they followed their local success by serving an apprenticeship in clubs in Hamburg, Germany. There they developed their own songwriting style distilled largely from cover versions of numbers by artists including Buddy Holly and Chuck Berry, but infused the music with their own fresh and energetic style. In Hamburg they discovered a heady lifestyle of easily-available drugs, strong local beer, and the charms of German women and the band enjoyed plenty of each. They also shortened their name to The Beatles. Shortly before the band was due to return home Sutcliffe left to move in with his girlfriend, Astrid. He died soon after of a brain hemorrhage.

Back in England in 1961 their show was seen by department-store owner Brian Epstein and following a brief "chat" he became their manager.

Though he had never managed a pop group Epstein, with his tailored suits, aristocratic breeding, and excellent education was soon steering the band towards greater glory. The following year they were joined by Ringo Starr on drums and the foursome had their chart breakthrough with the single "Love Me Do." Shortly after, in early 1963, they released "Please Please Me," the first of many number one hits. This was the year that "Beatlemania" was born and with the release of "I Want to Hold Your Hand" in 1964 this phenomenon became transatlantic.

They were the first British group to break the US stranglehold on writing original material and the first US tour of the Fab Four was met by scenes of mass hysteria and adulation. Their records were bought in the millions. The highlight of the American tour was their appearance on the popular Ed Sullivan television show where The Beatles were first seen by a mass audience. Through continued recording as well as work on films such as *A Hard Day's Night* (1964), *Help!* (1965), and *Yellow Submarine* (1968) they became the musical leaders of the decade, setting a precedent for other groups to begin playing and experimenting with their own songs.

As the sixties moved on so, too, did the Beatles. The band reached new levels of maturity and the growing complexity of their musicianship, as well as the sophistication of their lyrics, saw the band recording a variety of different styles from the simple, almost nursery rhyme, "Yellow Submarine" to the biting political commentary of "Eleanor Rigby". The raw vitality of their early work gave way to intelligent parodies of earlier pop styles and social observation, which were scored with a variety of instruments. In addition to the central instruments (guitars, drums, and bass strings) brass, sitars, and the

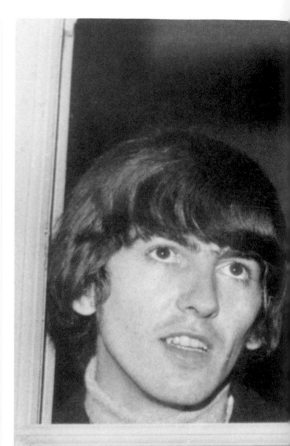

electronic sounds of studio experiments developed The Beatles' sound. Fuelled by psychedelic drugs and the band's growing interest in Eastern religion and philosophy, the brilliant albums *Rubber Soul* (1965), *Revolver* (1966), and *Sergeant Pepper's Lonely Hearts Club Band* (1967), chart the transition from pop band to full fledged leaders of the youth movement. While each album has a

distinctive character, they all manifest The Beatles' instinctive feel for melody and musical structure and are undoubtedly among the best-crafted works by any musicians of the 20th century. They made pioneering use of the modern recording studio, inspired by producer George Martin, particularly on *Sergeant Pepper's Lonely Hearts Club Band*. This album was the first pop record to be

conceived as a thematic work and is widely considered to be The Beatles masterpiece and a record which encapsulates the spirit of the revolutionary sixties. After this album, however, the band members pursued increasingly separate interests, and their final album *Let it Be* (1970) was followed by their break up which was surrounded by financial bickering. After the split they each went on to

individual success. Tragically, on December 8, 1980, John Lennon was assassinated on the street outside his New York apartment. Fans around the world mourned his loss.

The Beatles made 13 albums and three films together. Their music has influenced each succeeding generation of rock and pop groups around the world and their records continue to sell in staggering quantities.

B

Branson, Richard
1950–
British entrepreneur

With a knack for publicity the affable Branson built his empire on the youth culture of the 1970s. While still only a teenager, Branson set up a mail-order record company and soon attracted a number of big names to his own Virgin label. The launch of Virgin Atlantic airline in 1984, a £200-million stock market flotation in l987, and crossings of the Atlantic in balloons and boats, have kept the "happy hippie" millionaire in the spotlight. Recent diversification of the brand has produced: Virgin cola, available in the "Pammy" (a bottle inspired by Pamela Anderson); Virgin clothes; Virgin make-up and Virgin pensions. The Virgin business is also running part of the British rail network, with some adverse publicity. In 1998 Branson made another attempt to circumnavigate the world in a hot air balloon. It ended prematurely when his team had to ditch in the Pacific after technical problems.

Braun, Wernher Von
1912–1977
German engineer

Born in Germany, von Braun was an engineer whose area of expertise was liquid-fueled rockets. At the age of 25 he was technical director of the German experimental weapons research center at Peenemünde, on the Baltic Sea, and his design for the V2 rocket – the first ballistic missile to carry a warhead – set the pattern for future Russian and American liquid-fueled rockets. After World War II he went to the United States as technical adviser to the rocket program at the White Sands Proving Grounds in New Mexico. In 1950 he lead the Redstone missile program and continued to developed rockets for the US Army, adapting his work for the space race of the 1950s and 1960s. At NASA von Braun designed the enormous *Saturn V* launch vehicle that launched the *Apollo 11* mission to the moon in 1969.

Brezhnev, Leonid Ilich
1906–1982
Soviet politician

The last real Stalinist to hold power in the Soviet Union, Brezhnev was leader of the coup, which toppled Khruschev in 1964. General Secretary of the Communist Party of the Soviet Union (CPSU) from 1964–82, his time in office is noted as an era of both stability and stagnation in the domestic and foreign policies. Brezhnev believed that technical progress and scientific management would solve the Soviet Union's troubles. This approach initially led to positive results in the economy, as well as to progress in improving relations with the West. However, Brezhnev's initiatives ran into difficulty in both areas. The grim conservatism of his rule was best exemplified by the crushing of the "Prague Spring" in 1965. He proclaimed the right of Soviet intervention in any client state where Communism was threatened, but also signed the Helsinki Accord in 1976. He is remembered for the persecution of dissidents like Sakharov, the Afghanistan conundrum, and a legacy of widespread industrial decay.

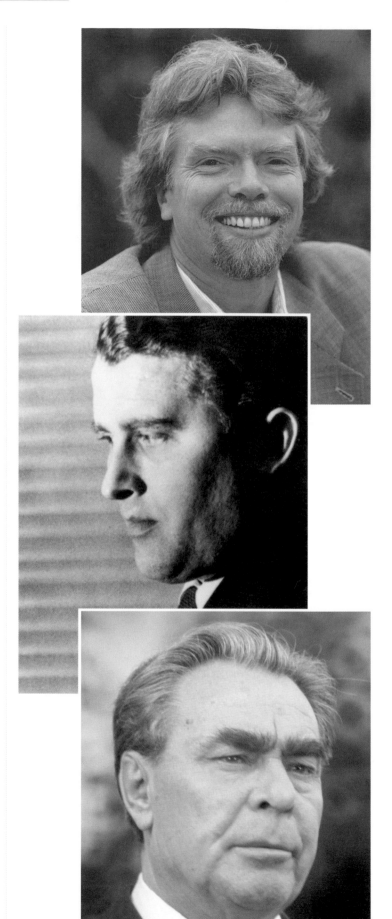

Bush, George Herbert Walker
1924–
American politician and president

Born in Milton, Massachusetts but
brought up in Greenwich,
Connecticut. Bush graduated from
Phillips Academy at Andover,
Massachusetts, in 1942 and joined
the US Navy to fight in World War II.
He was a pilot, and he survived being
shot down in the Pacific Ocean. After
the war he graduated from Yale,
majoring in economics. He moved
with his family to Texas, went in to
the oil business and in 1953 co-
founded the Zapata Petroleum
Corporation. In 1954 he was
appointed President of the Zapata
Offshore Company, specializing in
drilling equipment. He was a

millionaire by the age of 41.

Bush was elected to the House of
Representatives in 1966, but gave up
his seat after two terms to run for the
Senate. He was defeated, but despite
this was made US Ambassador to the
UN in 1971–1973, Chairman of the
Republican National Committees
1973–74 and director of the CIA
from 1976–77. After this he focused
on business interests. In 1980 he
concentrated on organizing support
for the Republican Party presidential
nomination. The Reagan-Bush ticket
defeated incumbent President Jimmy
Carter and Vice President Walter
Mondale in 1980, and they were re-
elected in a landslide in 1984.

Bush inherited the Presidency in
1988 having famously pledged to
voters in New Hampshire: "Read my

lips: no new taxes." After years of
neglect for the environment under
Reagan, Bush moved to reauthorize
the Clean Air Act in his first year in
office, establishing higher standards
for air quality and requiring cleaner
burning fuels. This reflected an
agreement between big businesses and
environmentalists that had eluded the
federal government for years. The
problems which Ronald Reagan had
found intractable – a weakening
economy, a dangerously unstable
Middle East and the failure of the
economy to respond to limited
treatment – eroded Republican
support, which not even the success
of the lightning desert campaign
against Saddam Hussein, could
reverse, and Bush was defeated in his
1992 re-election attempt.

Cagney, James
1899–1986
American actor

After working various jobs, Cagney broke into vaudeville, eventually making it to Broadway. Movies followed, and in *The Public Enemy* (1931) he lit up the screen by shoving a grapefruit into Mae Clark's face. He made a series of cheap, quick and popular tough-guy pictures. He proved the depth and sensitivity of his acting in *A Midsummer Night's Dream* (1935), playing Bottom, and in *Angels with Dirty Faces* (1938) was cast alongside Bogart. Cagney then changed direction, first to romance, then comedy, where he revealed a masterful sense of timing. His popularity was ensured when he played George M. Cuban in *Yankee Doodle Dandy* (1942). In the 1950s he tried directing, continuing to act in *Man of a Thousand Faces* (1957) and showing a deft comic touch in the hilarious *One, Two, Three* (1961). Retiring that year, Cagney received the American Film Institute's Life Achievement Award in 1974; he made a final movie, *Ragtime* in 1951.

Calder, Alexander
1898–1976
American sculptor

Originally trained in engineering, Calder studied at the Art Students' League. New York, 1923–25. The son and grandson of distinguished American sculptors, his line drawings of the circus, made in 1925, were the inspiration for his lively sculptures "drawn" with wire. These also spawned a miniature mechanized circus made in scrap materials (1926–31), with which he gave performances in his studio. Increasingly convinced that "art was too static to reflect our world of movement," from 1930 he produced mechanized abstract constructions and in 1932 invented the *mobile*. Organic shapes cut from tin were suspended on wire, producing infinitely variable, graceful compositions and, similarly, his static abstract works, or "stabiles" reveal dramatically different aspects from successive viewpoints.

Capote, Truman
1924–1984
American writer

Born in New Orleans, Louisiana, Capote's early novels, *Other Voices, Other Rooms* (1948) and *The Grass Harp* (1951) are essentially novels of the American South, although they also contain many fine surrealist and gothic moments. *Other Voices, Other Rooms*, Capote's first novel, is a tale about a southern boy's recognition of his homosexuality and was published when he was 23. *In Cold Blood* (1966) deals with a Kansas murder case – this "non-fiction novel" – proved a bestseller and was made in to a movie of the same title in 1967. His work is primarily praised for its technical virtuosity and acute observation. His other books include *A Tree of Night and Other Stories* (1949), *The Muses Are Heard* (1956), and *Breakfast at Tiffany's* (1958). He also wrote the script for the musical *House of Flowers* (1954) and had creative input to the movie *Beat the Devil* (1954).

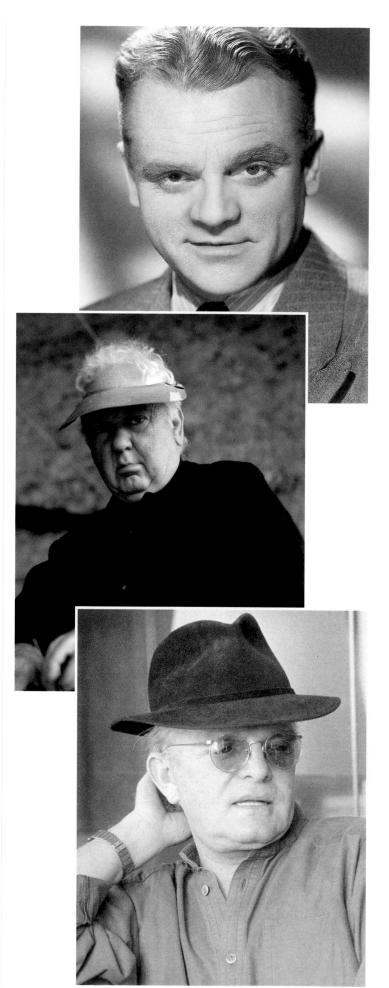

C

Capone, Al[Alphonso]
1898–1947
American gangster

Born in Naples, Italy Capone was raised in Brooklyn, New York after his parents emigrated to the United States. Punished for hitting his teacher, he left school in the seventh grade and was initiated into organized crime by then joining his first gang. He spent his early years in gangs; starting in the James Street Boys, a gang run by Johnny Torrio, and later the Five Points Gang. In a youthful fight he was slashed by a razor across the face and was nicknamed "Scarface."

After Torrio moved to Chicago, Capone helped to remove the boss, Torrio's uncle Big Jim Colosimo in

1920, to take control of the huge brothel business. Colosimo did not want to get involved with alcohol. But after taking control Torrio and Capone diversified, with a bootlegging operation in the era of prohibition and drew in tremendous amounts of money. At the age of 26, Capone succeeded, when Torrio retired in 1925, to inherit control of much of Chicago's gambling and sex industry and supplied the city with illegal drink. In 1927 he was reputed to have a personal fortune of $100 million. He increased his "territories" by dispatching rival gangs; he was famous for allegedly organizing the elimination of his competitors in violent gang wars that culminated in the St Valentine's Day massacre in 1929.

Capone was loved by the public

who saw him pictured in the company of movie stars, famous business people and political figures. However after the St Valentine's Day massacre was reported in all the newspapers, the public's opinion of gangsters changed: bootlegged alcohol was tolerated, wholesale slaughter was not. Although he was certainly a murderer and an extortioner, he was eventually tried for federal tax evasion. He was sentenced to 11 years plus fines of $80,000 in 1931. He served most of his time in Alcatraz where there were several attempts on his life.

He was released in 1939 after a nervous breakdown and spent the rest of his years in his Miami Beach mansion, apparently crippled by the last stages of syphilis.

Carlos II, King Juan
1938–
Monarch of Spain

The grandson of King Alfonso XIII, Juan Carlos was born in Rome and educated in Switzerland and Madrid. Despite the turbulence of the Spanish monarchy and the Spanish Revolution (1936–39), Juan Carlos was groomed to succeed General Francisco Franco. Declared heir to the throne in 1969, he restored the monarchy after Franco's death in 1975. He married the daughter of King Paul of Greece, Princess Sofia in 1962. He instated gradual democratic reform, with a parliamentary government and new constitution in 1978, to popular approval Juan Carlos successfully averted a right wing attempt to overthrow the government in 1981 and is determined to maintain a constitutional democracy in Spain. He is commander-in-chief of the armed forces, and while he can select a candidate for prime mister, his choice must be approved by parliament. His son Prince Felipe is the next in line to the throne.

Chanel, Coco [Gabrielle Bonheur]
1883–1971
French fashion designer

Chanel's clothes and accessories have become a lasting symbol of elegance. Her earliest patterns were revolutionary, designed to be worn without corsets; they had fewer linings, and were thus less rigid than contemporary fashions. In 1916 she began to work with jersey which proved so successful that she began to manufacture the material herself. Having introduced the twin set, designed to be worn over her wide-legged "yachting pants," she threw a succession of new fashion ideas at the world during the 1920s such as collarless cardigan jackets and quilted handbags on gold chains. She was the archetypal "garconne" in this period: slim, flat-chested with a short haircut. In the mid-1910s she concentrated her energies on manufacturing and closed her salon. In 1954, at the age of 71, she shocked and delighted the fashion world with a show of revamped prewar designs.

Chaplin, Sir Charles Spencer
1889–1977
British actor and director

Chaplin was a legendary figure in his own lifetime. Aged 35 in his first year in Hollywood, he evolved the tramp character as he went along: the funny walk, the bowler hat, the cane and moustache, the baggy pants. In 1920 *The Kid* was an enormous box office smash, and he became an international star. Having co-founded United Artists in 1919, Chaplin resisted sound as long as he could; *City Lights* (1931), and *Modern Times* (1936) are essentially silent movies. Though there are great moments in later movies, the use of sound revealed flaws, chiefly a tendency to become excessively sentimental. He was criticized for not fighting in World War I, his left-wing politics, his refusal to become an American citizen, and his alleged fondness for teenage girls. He and his family were forced to move to Switzerland during the McCarthy era, but in 1971 he returned to the United States to receive a special Academy Award.

C

Carson, Johnny
1925–
American television talk show host

Born in Corning, Iowa, and educated at the University of Nebraska, Carson taught himself magic as a teenager and first performed in public at the age of 14. After graduation he worked in radio in Omaha, Nebraska and in Los Angeles. He worked as a writer for Red Skelton and eventually got his own show (1955–56). He hosted the daytime show *Who Do You Trust?* (1957–62) in New York and got his big break in 1962, succeeding Jack Paar, to host NBC's *The Tonight Show*. Carson's easy-going, slightly ironic style increased the show's popularity, making it a staple on late-night television. It accounted for a substantial portion (17%) of NBC's profits and inspired several imitators. Carson's management of guests through the predictable chat-show formula was done with aplomb and frequent innuendo. His opening monologue, adroit style candid humor and his rapport with the audience became a well-copied model for hosts throughout the television industry. After a 30-year run he retired from the show in 1992. Carson then signed a contract with NBC that would allow him to develop and star in other television programs. In recent years, Carson has made the headlines for his large charitable donations, primarily to the Carson Memorial Cancer Center, but also to his alma mater.

C

Castro, Fidel
1926–
Cuban politician

Fidel Castro is the authoritarian ruler of Cuba and as such is the creator of the only Communist state in the New World to date.

He was born on a farm in the Mayari principality near Birán, Cuba, and as a youth, attended Catholic schools in Santiago de Cuba and Havana. He married Mirta Diaz-Balart in 1948 and in 1949 the couple had a son, Fidel Castro Diaz-Balart, who has since served in his father's government. Castro's involvement in politics started while he was studying law in Havana where he became a student agitator. As an opponent of the existing regime he was soon imprisoned under the Cuban dictator Batista after an unsuccessful uprising in 1953. He was sentenced to 15 years imprisonment but was released under an amnesty in 1955. At that time his politics had not yet embraced Communism but were anti-imperialist and nationalist. Following his release Castro fled the country and trained as a guerrilla in Mexico where he founded the 26th of July Movement with the intention of returning to Cuba to overthrow Batista. In December, 1959 Castro landed in Cuba with a small group of 81 insurgents — including the notorious "Che" Guevara. The band found a stronghold in the Sierra Maestra mountains and from there waged an effective guerrilla war with Castro proving himself as a brilliant leader and tactician as well as a shrewd politician. He brought his fight to a triumphant conclusion in January 1959 when, following an attack by the revolutionaries, Batista fled Cuba; his support from the army and the United States having collapsed.

As prime minister Castro's regime was initially marked by moderation and he welcomed democrats into his party. However, his reforms soon grew more radical and he instigated a "Marxist Leninist program" with the popular support of the Cuban people, whose living conditions he had improved. The communist revolution saw property confiscated, antagonists killed or driven into exile, and the departure of thousands of professional and middle class Cubans from the island. It soon became obvious that the elections that Castro had promised the people would never materialize.

In 1961, the United States, concerned at having a Communist regime on its doorstep, helped to organize and finance an invasion force of 1,500 Cuban exiles. The force landed on the coast of Cuba, at the Bay of Pigs in the southwest, on April 17. The invasion which was intended to fuel a counter revolution was, however, crushed. A leak had prepared Castro for the landing and his forces prevented the exiles from moving inland. By April 19, the remaining 1,200 were taken hostage and an embarrassed United States government was compelled to supply Cuba with $53 million in food and drugs to ensure their safe return. The result was a total U.S. economic embargo. Nevertheless, Castro's success consolidated his power and he publicly announced the Communist regime.

However, Castro was now isolated and turned to the Soviet Union for support. This was forthcoming and, consequently, Cuba was dependent on the USSR from this time onward, until the dissolution of the Soviet Union in 1991. Under Castro, Cuban society was braced by massive amounts of technical, military, and economic help from the Soviets who were eager to establish a dominance so close to the Americas.

In 1962 the U.S. became aware that the USSR was building launch sites for nuclear missiles on Cuba. U.S. President John F. Kennedy demanded the removal of all Soviet nuclear weapons and the two-week stalemate was a time of enormous tension, with the threat impending nuclear war. It is indicative of Castro's position with the Soviet politicians that during the crisis and negotiations he was not consulted by either the American or Soviet governments. Eventually, the Soviets yielded though with the provision that the U.S. would not interfere with Castro's regime or try again to overthrow him.

The Cuban Missile Crisis marks the end of Castro's executive power, which was now transferred to a council. Despite this, Castro has maintained his dominance and his rule over the small country has been rife with political, social, and economic mismanagement. The only improvements that were made to Cuban society are a direct result of economic support of the Soviet Union which, at its height in the 1970s, totaled an injection of $3 million per day. With Soviet supplements, Castro's government made considerable progress with healthcare and education but following the collapse of the Soviet bloc many of the new hospitals and schools that were opened have had to be closed down. The Cuban government can no longer afford to pay the doctors, nurses, and teachers needed to operate them. As Castro's close ally "Che" Guevara once said; "A lack of industry in a country is a reason for calling that country underdeveloped, and there is no doubt that Cuba fits that description."

Opinion is divided on Fidel Castro's term of power, some say that he has benefited Cuba and others that he is an autocratic tyrant who has ruined Cuba's economy. Nonetheless it can be said that Castro possesses great charisma and political skill. He remains in power to this day and commands the unquestioning respect and loyalty from his colleagues. In recent years Castro has allowed small political reforms, which recognize the free market and encourage the tourist trade but, apart from this, still vigorously maintains the communist regime which he instituted.

C

C

Chiang Kai-Shek
1887–1975
Chinese statesman

Chiang was heir of Sun Yat-Sen's revolution, but his reforms were first stalled by steady Japanese annexation of China in the 1930s, and then by the corruption of the ruling clique. Known for his strong will, nationalism, and unyielding anti-Communist stance, Chiang, a Christian was forced to unite with the communists by his own Manchurian troops who kidnapped him in 1936, and he stemmed the Japanese tide by costly tactics. World War II, when he was one of the Big Four, was his finest hour. After losing the Civil War that followed, he was unable to prevent the Communists splitting the broad coalition of the Kuomintang. The founding party of modern China was driven into the offshore bastion of Taiwan. Chiang turned Taiwan into a successful capitalist enclave with American backing and remained its President until his death.

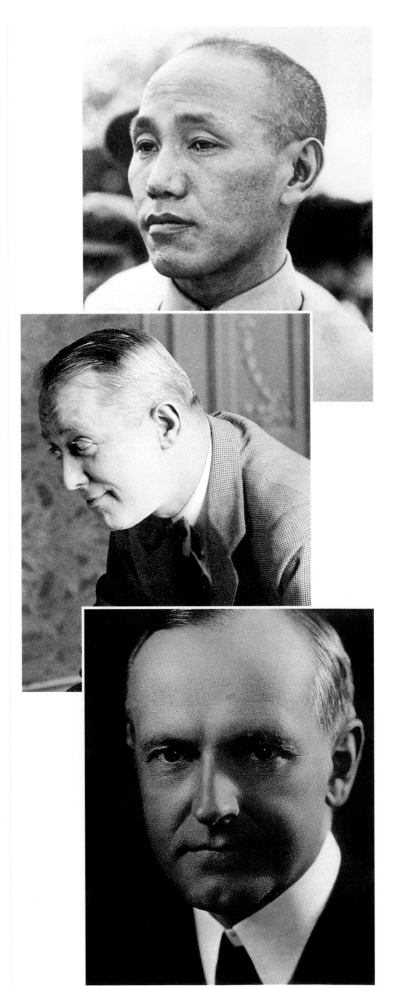

Cohan, George Michael
1878–1942
American composer

A multi-talented writer who was also an actor, director and playwright, Cohan was a composer who wrote many patriotic songs including the well known "You're a Grand Old Flag", "Give My Regards to Broadway," and "Over There." He starred in more than 20 musicals, but had started out in a vaudeville act with his family billed as The Four Cohans. He first appeared on Broadway in *The Governor's Son* (1901) and his first successful musical was *Little Johnny Jones* (1904). Other productions he was involved with include *Forty-five Minutes from Broadway* (1906), *Broadway Jones* (1912), *Hello, Broadway* (1914), and *The Song and Dance Man* (1923). He adapted other writer's works for the stage, and in 1925 wrote an autobiography *Twenty Years on Broadway*. His career was the inspiration for the movie *Yankee Doodle Dandy* (1942).

Coolidge, [John] Calvin
1872–1933
American politician and president

A New England lawyer, he was guided as President by the maxim, "more of the office desk and less of the show window." He was Governor of Massachusetts in 1919. As Vice President he succeeded to the White House on Harding's death in 1923 and for the next six years presided over a seemingly prosperous nation – for which his pragmatic but ill-founded fiscal policies took the credit. Coming from an uncomplicated background and outlook his economic philosophy was straightforward: success came to those who worked hard and were honest. His impact on the country was limited. Only six months after his retirement before the 1928 election, the Wall Street Crash ushered in the Depression.

Carter, Jimmy [James Earl]
1924–
American politician and president

Jimmy Carter was born into a small farming community in Plains, Georgia. He was the first member of his family to go to college. He spent a year at Southwestern College in 1941, followed by a year at the Georgia Institute of Technology before attending the Naval Academy Annapolis from which he graduated in 1946. He returned to peanut farming in 1953.

He entered the political fray in 1962, serving two terms in the state senate. In 1966 he ran for the Democratic nomination for Governor of Georgia and was defeated. He was bitter about the defeat, and for a while

he decided to do missionary work in some Northern states and to speak about Christianity across the South. However he stood again in 1970 and won. As Governor of Georgia (1970–74) Carter proved a strong defender of Civil Rights. His "zero-based budgeting system" ensured exact financial accountability by departmental heads.

Carter won the Democratic nomination for President in 1976, winning the campaign in the wake of Richard Nixon's disgrace and his promises to restore morality and honesty to the federal government. He branded the tax situation "a national disgrace' and fought to improve the economy. He proved to be an adept negotiator. He signed the first SALT (Strategic Arms Limitation Treaty) with

the USSR agreement and brokered the peace treaty between Israel and Egypt in 1979. During his term of office, few of the campaign promises materialized, some were abandoned, and others were not liked by congress. However the Islamic revolution in Iran created a major foreign policy problem. The storming of the American Embassy in Tehran and the capture of 53 hostages was not resolved until his last day in office. On January 20, 1981, the day of Reagan's inauguration Carter agreed to the restoration of Iranian assets in U.S. banks, which had been frozen, and agreed to U.S. non-interference in Iran's affairs.

Although defeated in the 1980 presidential race, after leaving office he continued to work for better human rights throughout the world.

C

Churchill, Sir Winston
1874–1965
British politician and international statesman

Churchill probably deserves description as the greatest Briton of the century. The epitome of the British Bulldog spirit, his spirit persuaded the nation, when it stood alone against Hitler's hordes in 1940, that victory could still be won. A man of great courage and talent, he played many roles during his eventful life — soldier, politician, statesman, journalist, painter, and devoted family man. In possession of a keen intellect, his wit and humor are legendary.

Churchill's eventful life started near Oxford where he was born at Blenheim Palace in 1874, the third son of the 7th Duke of Marlborough, Lord Randolph Churchill and his beautiful American wife Jennie Jerome. Churchill's early life was largely unhappy, his society parents had little time for their children and he particularly despised Harrow, the school where he was educated and which bored him. However, the young Winston found relief in stories of heroism and war, bravery and daring-do and he also cultivated a passion for poetry and history. Later in life he would write a definitive biography of his ancestor and national military hero, John Churchill, first Duke of Marlborough as well as other influential historical accounts.

Following graduation from the Royal Military College in 1894, Churchill was commissioned into the 4th Hussars with whom he served in Cuba, India and Sudan. The latter provided his first taste of fighting when in 1898 he participated in the Battle of Omdurman. During his military career, Churchill had occasionally written for British newspapers, who liked his style and so in 1899 he was sent by the *Morning Post* to cover the Boer War in South Africa. Here he achieved celebrity back in Britain by staging a daring escape from the Boers after he was captured.

Election to parliament fulfilled his budding political ambitions in the year 1900. Initially a member of the Conservative Party, his allegiance turned to Liberal policies and he defected to that party in 1904. The Liberals were victorious at the general election of 1905 and Churchill entered government for the first time as under secretary of state for the colonies. Despite a loathing of public speaking his ability was soon recognized and in 1908 came a promotion to his first cabinet post as president of the Board of Trade. During this successful year he also celebrated marriage to Clementine Hozier; herself a woman of formidable intellect and strong political views, she was a perfect match and sparring partner for the aspiring Churchill and the marriage was one of great affection, bringing great happiness to both.

Further promotions followed; in 1910 to the more prominent position of Home Secretary and in 1911 he was made lord of the Admiralty where he supervised the modernization of Britain's warships.

The advent of World War I began a turbulent period in a previously meteoric career. The failure of the daring Gallipoli campaign, which he planned, culminated in his dismissal from the Admiralty and he entered active service in France until offered the post of munitions minister under Lloyd George in 1917. From 1918 to 1921 he was secretary of state for war and air but in 1922 suffered further disappointment when Lloyd George's government fell from power in 1922.

Two years later, in 1924, Churchill returned to Parliament; this time as a Conservative, the party he had spurned 20 years earlier. His wry comment on the change of heart was typical of his sense of humor; "Any fool can rat, but I flatter myself that it takes a certain ingenuity to re-rat." Now occupying the office of Chancellor of the Exchequer, his term was fraught with problems. His measures failed to remedy a bad economic situation and plunged the country into further depression. During the General Strike of 1926 he referred to the strikers as "the enemy" and this *faux pas* was to dog him for years to come, with his mishandling of the economy creating a reputation which effectively lost him the 1945 election immediately after the war. He fell from office again in 1929 and it would be a further ten years until he would return — the outspoken critic of Hitler and of the appeasement policy that Prime Ministers Baldwin and Chamberlain had taken until the German invasion of Poland forced Britain to declare war. Initially, Churchill served at his old post in the Admiralty until Chamberlain resigned in 1940, in despair at Allied defeats. While Hitler invaded the Netherlands, Churchill assumed the mantle of Prime Minister and war leader. On May 14, four days after his appointment, Churchill delivered this moving and historic speech to Parliament:

"I say to the House as I said to Ministers who have joined this government, I have nothing to offer but blood, toil, tears and sweat. We have before us an ordeal of the most grievous kind. We have before us many, many months of struggle and suffering. You ask, 'what is our policy?', I say it is to wage war by land, sea and air. War with all our might and with all the strength God has given us, and to wage war against a monstrous tyranny never surpassed in the dark and lamentable catalogue of human crime. That is our policy. You ask, 'what is our aim?', I can answer in one word. It is victory. Victory at all costs – victory in spite of all terrors – victory, however long and hard the road may be, for without victory there is no survival. Let that be realized. No survival for the British Empire, no survival for all that the

British Empire has stood for, no survival for the urge, the impulse of the ages, that mankind shall move forward toward his goal. I take up my task in buoyancy and hope. I feel sure that our cause will not be suffered to fail among men. I feel entitled at this juncture, at this time, to claim the aid of all and to say, 'Come then, let us go forward together with our united strength.'"

As a tactician and diplomat he immediately proved successful. Relations with the U.S. were buoyed by Churchill's friendship with President Roosevelt and following the disaster on the beaches at Dunkirk, where the British army lost most of its equipment in retreat, America began to supply arms to the war effort. Churchill's personal influence with the American president was also a deciding factor in the U.S. entry into the conflict a year later.

Having witnessed the full horror of World War I, Churchill was resolute

that the terrible bloodshed should not be repeated and his brilliant strategy made steady incursions into the German front while preserving the lives of the troops. By 1943 the Allies had started to make gains on the European continent. Although Churchill's direction of the course of the War by this date was overruled by the strategy of American commander-in-chief Dwight Eisenhower, he was a national hero when the Allied armies bowled into Berlin, the final bastion of Hitler and the German Army.

But, 1945 was a bittersweet year. Soon after Germany's unconditional surrender Churchill was ousted from Downing Street in a landslide victory for the opposing Labour Party and though in public he accepted defeat without rancor, in reality he was deeply wounded and determined to reverse the nation's decision.

His political vigor returned Churchill to power in 1951 and though

his administration lacked the incredible show of will of the war years he served a creditable term of office. In 1953 however, shortly after being knighted by the new queen, Elizabeth II, he suffered a stroke, which diminished his famous energy, although he courageously remained in office until 1955.

In retirement Churchill turned to other pursuits including painting, writing and travel. He published the acclaimed four volume, *History of the English Speaking Peoples*, the last in a series of historical works and his artwork displayed great talent. At the grand age of 90 Churchill died on January 24, 1965 and is, to date, the only commoner to be granted a state funeral.

Churchill's influence on the 20th Century was decisive. Without his energy, vision and courage the world would, perhaps, be a very different place today.

C

Clinton, William Jefferson Blythe
1946–
American politician and president

At forty-six William Jefferson Clinton, was the youngest man to be elected President of the United States of America since John F. Kennedy, to whom he has been equated on many occasions, and who directly inspired the young Clinton to public office after shaking his hand at the Rose Garden in 1963.

He was born William Jefferson Blythe in Hope, Arkansas, on August 19, 1946, a few months after the death of his father, for whom he was named. When he was four his mother remarried, to Roger Clinton, and after the birth of his younger brother, he took the family name.

At school Bill excelled as a fine academic student and a promising musician — his mastery of the saxophone being a skill with which he would entertain audiences at public appearances during the 1992 Presidential Election campaign. After graduating from high school Clinton attended Georgetown University from 1964–1968, then Oxford University in England as a Rhodes scholar from 1968–1970, and finally Yale Law School from 1970–1973. It was here that he met Hillary Rodham.

In 1976 Clinton became Attorney General for Arkansas, his first political post, and rose to the governorship in 1978. However, he failed to win a second term and had to wait a further

four years before he was elected again to the office in which he served until 1992. During that year he was elevated to the Presidency, defeating George Bush and independent candidate Ross Perot in the election. Clinton is the first Democratic President to have won two terms since Franklin Roosevelt, and despite public scandal and calls for his impeachment, he remains popular. His party's success in winning seats from the Republicans during the mid term elections of 1998 was seen as a mandate from the nation for him to continue as President in the midst of the Lewinsky sex scandal which his

C

Clinton, Hillary Rodham
1947–
Lawyer and First Lady

Hillary Rodham, is an equally formidable woman who in 1991, while her husband was still relatively unknown, was named as one of the top 100 lawyers in the US. Staying with her husband despite the rigors of public scandal, she is a dynamic figure in her own right and has been a valued partner, particularly during the 1992 Presidential Elections when she campaigned ceaselessly on his behalf. Since moving into the White House Hillary has proved to be an effective political force rather than taking the traditionally passive role of First Lady.

Born Hillary Diane Rodham in Chicago on October 26, 1947, the daughter of a successful fabric-store owner, her early life was marked by academic flair. She graduated from Wellesley College, where she had studied political science, in 1969, and Yale Law School, with Bill, in 1973. Following graduation Hillary worked for the Children's Defense Fund as a staff attorney as well as for the House Judiciary Committee's Watergate hearings. In 1975 Hillary wed Clinton and, following his election to Governor in 1978, became the First Lady of Arkansas. She proved an able advisor to her husband as well as continuing to work in law and, in the latter field, earned a national reputation as an advocate of women's and children's rights through her various publications and court cases.

After winning the Presidency, Clinton installed Hillary as the head of the Task Force on National Health Reform in 1993 and in this position she has displayed her usual efficiency and skill. Though the victim of charges of nepotism and feminism from detractors as well as receiving criticism for her role in the Whitewater affair, she has proved equal to all obstacles and less partisan spectators view her as a model for the modern American woman.

Hillary is the mother of the Clintons' daughter, Chelsea (born 1980), and the author of *It Takes a Village* (1996).

opponents attempted to use to his detriment.

As President, Clinton has a notable record of achievement. He has created new law measures which have revived the American economy as well as reducing the national deficit, raised living standards, reformed public education, and signed the Brady Bill which makes a waiting period obligatory for gun purchases. Other acts for which he has been widely praised include the Family and Medical Leave Act which protects the jobs of those parents who have sick children to care for, a tough attitude towards crime, and the GOALS 2000 bill which has reformed national health care. He is also committed to the peaceful resolution of world conflicts and despite a tough stance towards Iraq, has been instrumental in bringing about peace talks elsewhere in the Middle East, Ireland, and has sent aid to Russia. During his second term, American prosperity has continued — a fact that has aided his cause against charges of obstruction of justice brought by Independent Council Kenneth Starr during very public revelations about Clinton's relations with Monica Lewinsky.

Cousteau, Jaques Yves
1910–1997
French conservationist, marine explorer, author, and documentary film-maker

Cousteau was on leave from the French Navy when he borrowed a pair of goggles and became hooked on underwater exploration. After World War II he was appointed head of the Underwater Research Group of the French Navy. In 1943, with Emile Gagnan, he invented the aqualung – a self-contained breathing apparatus (SCUBA) that allowed a diver to swim freely underwater. He later worked with Auguste Piccard on the first bathyscaph – a submersible capable of diving to great depths. With these devices, and his research ship Calypso, he was able to pioneer the exploration of the ocean floor. He founded the Cousteau Society – a conservation group dedicated to the preservation of the underwater world – in 1974, and became director of the Oceanographic Museum in Monaco. He is best known for his groundbreaking movies *The Silent World* (1956) and *World Without Sun* (1966): each won an Academy Award as the best documentary feature of the year.

Curie, Marie
1867–1934
Polish-French scientist

Curie graduated in physics from the Sorbonne in 1893. She decided to study the rays given off by uranium and its ore – a phenomenon recently discovered by Henri Becquerel. Working with her husband Pierre, she isolated the new elements polonium and radium in 1902. For their work on radioactivity they were jointly awarded the Nobel Prize for Physics in 1903, along with Henri Becquerel. She was awarded the Nobel Prize in Chemistry in 1911 for her discovery of polonium and radium, and became the first person ever to be awarded two Nobel Prizes. With the outbreak of World War I she instigated X–ray services in military hospitals. She eventually died of cancer, brought on by exposure to the radioactive elements with which she worked. Her notebooks are still too radioactive to handle. She was the first woman scientist to gain worldwide acclaim: the unit of radioactivity of a substance was named the curie (ci) after her.

Dalai Lama [Tenzin Gyatso]
1935–
Tibetan Buddhist leader

Aged five when he was recognized as the reincarnation of the 13th Dalai Lama, who had died in 1933, the Tibetan Buddhist has achieved universal respect in his quest for world peace. The Dalai Lama remains the most poignant symbol and victim of Chinese aggression in the 1950s and the cowardice of the international community in the face of the ruthless conquest of Tibet in 1951. He left the country after an unsuccessful rebellion in 1959 and he has lived in exile in India working ceaselessly for the liberation of Tibet. He was awarded the Nobel Peace Prize in 1989 in recognition of his continuing non-violent protest. In 1995 he came in to conflict with the Chinese authorities again over the recognition of the new Panchen Lama (the second most senior Tibetan religious authority).

Cronkite, Walter Leland Jr.
1916–
American television newscaster

While a student at the University of Texas, 1933–35, Cronkite worked for radio stations and a newspaper. He dropped out of college to become a reporter and covered the fighting in Europe during World War II for United Press International – for which he was one of the first accredited correspondents. He was among the first newsmen to take part in a raid over Germany in a B-17, and he flew with the 101st Airborne in the Netherlands. He reported at the Nuremberg War Trials after the war and served as United Press bureau chief in Moscow 1946–1948.

In 1950 Cronkite joined CBS News as the Washington correspondent. For 20 years he was the anchorman for CBS Evening News and one of the most familiar and respected personalities in American public life. His debut on the Evening News in 1962 featured an [now] historic interview with President Kennedy. He covered all but one of the presidential conventions and campaigns between 1952–1980. His style established him as a trusted figure and his reports on the 1968 Tet Offensive and Watergate scandal greatly influenced public opinion. He retired as anchorman in 1981 but remained a special corespondent and also held a position on the board of directors until 1991.

In the 1990s he continued to broadcast, hosting public affair and cultural programs well as *The Cronkite Report*, a show focusing on contemporary American problems and broadcast quarterly on The Discovery Channel. He also appeared on educational programs on the Learning Channel. He won many awards during his illustrious career, including five Emmys and the George Polk Journalism Award (1971). Since leaving CBS he has published books on international relations and current affairs and as well as his autobiography, *A Reporter's Life,* in 1996. He has also continued to give lectures and narrate documentaries.

41

D

Davis, Bette
1908–1989
American actress

In more than 50 movies during her career, Davis often played a flinty, acid-tongued woman who could speak words as though spitting nails. Her combat in the offices of Hollywood movie companies earned her a reputation too. She made her Broadway debut in *Broken Dishes*, in 1929, and by 1930 she was in Hollywood. Not a classic beauty, she was electrifying in *Of Human Bondage* (1934), and *Dangerous* (1935) won her an Academy Award for Best Actress. *Jezebel* (1938) won her a second Academy Award. Audiences liked her best when she was bright and bitchy. In the late 1940s her career slowed, but she fought back with *All About Eve* (1950); possibly her finest movie. When her career faltered again she took out advertisements announcing her availability and took work in horror pictures. After the success *Whatever Happened to Baby Jane* (1962) she continued acting, and in 1977 was the first woman to receive the American Film Institute Life Achievement Award.

Dayan, Moshe, Lieutenant-General
1915–1981
Israeli soldier and politician

Born on a kibbutz near lake Tiberias, Dayan fought with the Haganah, the Jewish militia force, during the 1930s. At the age of fourteen he joined the Haganah, the Jewish militia defending settlements against Arab attacks and later received anti-guerilla training from the British. In 1941 he participated in the British invasion of Vichy-French Syria where he was badly wounded, losing his left eye. After service in the Israeli War of Independence (1948), he was appointed Chief of Staff to the Israeli Defense Force in 1953, and led the IDF to victory in the Sinai campaign of 1956. In 1960 he entered the Knesset, serving as Minister of Defense during the stunningly successful Six-Day War (1967) and the more difficult Yom Kippur War (1973). He resigned in 1974, but was foreign minister in 1977, playing an important role in negations for the peace treaty signed with Egypt in 1979.

DiMaggio, Joe [Joseph Paul]
1914–1999
American baseball player

Performing with stoic grace, Joe DiMaggio was one of baseball's all-time greats. He played his entire 13-year career with a dynastic New York Yankees team, which made it to the World Series ten times in that span (winning nine of them). His greatest feat came in 1941 when he got at least one base hit in 56 consecutive games, a record that still stands. This streak was finally broken by the Cleveland Indians, but then "Joltin' Joe" ran off another streak of 16 games. DiMaggio finished his career with a 325 batting average and 361 home runs. He was also one of the best defensive players ever to play the centerfield position. Three times he won the American League's Most Valuable Player award, and he was elected to the Baseball Hall of Fame in 1955. After DiMaggio's retirement he stayed in the public eye by marrying Marilyn Monroe.

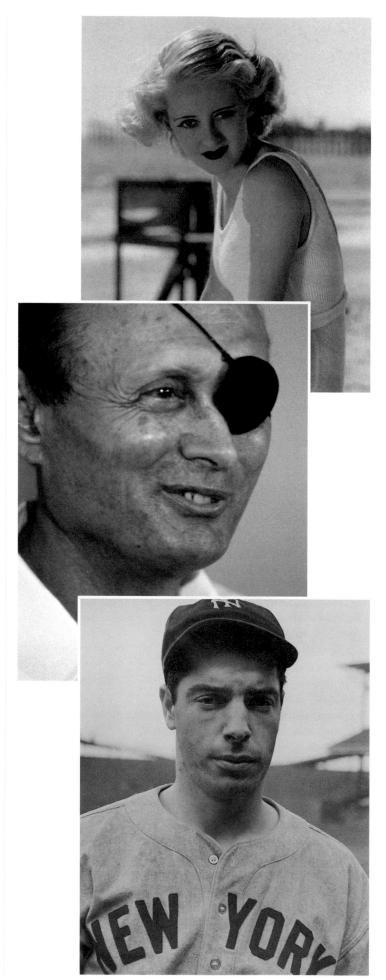

D

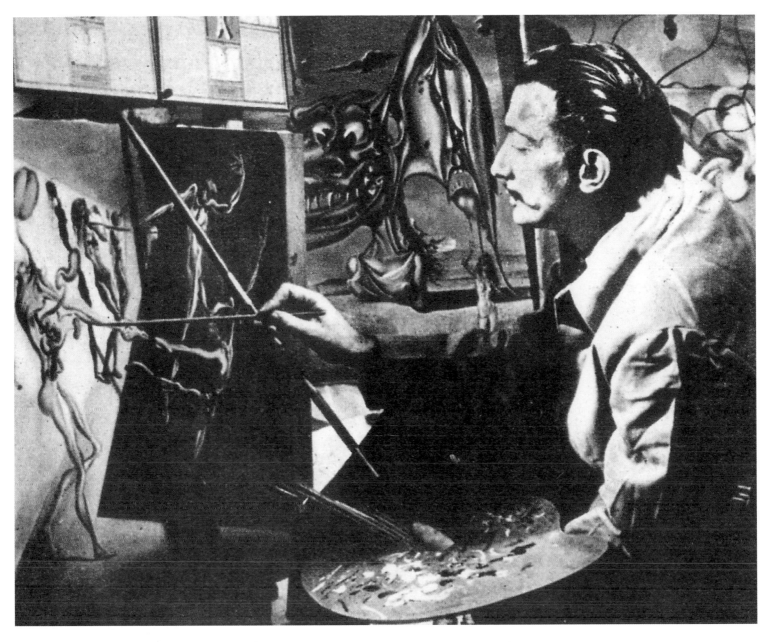

Dali, Salvador
1904–1989
Spanish painter

Dali's training at the Madrid Art School prefigures his career. Earlier suspended for inciting the students to riot, in 1926 he was expelled for "extravagant behavior." He became increasingly interested in the metaphysical painting of de Chirico and the meticulous realism of the Pre-Raphaelites. In 1929 he joined the Surrealist movement, and later collaborated with the Spanish director Luis Buñuel on the first Surrealist movies. The movies are full of images typical of Dali's paintings of the period.

After reading of Sigmund Freud's work, he developed a theory of "critical paranoia," wherein genuine delusion, as found in clinical paranoia, was cultivated, while remaining residually conscious of the deliberate suspension of reason. His paintings depicted dreams and paranoid hallucinations with an incongruously exact, photographic accuracy. Everyday objects are distorted or manipulated and presented in a dreamscape not unlike the landscape of Catalonia. The paintings highly finished, glossy surface adds to the eerieness of his world of melting watches, [*The Persistence of Memory* (1931)] giant ants, and figures from which half-open draws protrude. His paintings are characterized by meticulous detail with vibrant colors heightened by transparent glazes. He also designed and produced jewelry illustrated books and created theatrical sets and costumes. His increasingly

mannered work and his support for the Spanish dictator Franco became unacceptable to the Surrealists and in 1938 he was expelled from the group. But for the public at large, his work remained synonymous with Surrealism and he achieved international notoriety. On moving to the USA in 1940 his later paintings, often on religious themes, are more classical in style. They include *Crucifixion* (1954) and *The Sacrament of the Last Supper* (1955). Between 1940 and 1955 he devoted himself largely to self-publicity, and his paintings explore childhood memories, eroticism and other themes including his wife Gala. In 1942 he published his autobiography *The Secret Life of Salvador Dali* which was followed in 1965 by *The Diary of a Genius*.

D

Diana, Princess of Wales
1961–1997
British Royal family

Princess Diana was the most photographed person in history; a measure of her international fame and a contributing factor to her unhappiness. A glamorous socialite, who did much to promote young British fashion designers, and a tireless standard-bearer for many charities, her life was marred by a succession of excruciatingly public problems and her early death was felt by many to be doubly tragic as it seemed that she had finally overcome her private difficulties.

As the youngest daughter of the eighth Earl Spencer, she was born to a life of privilege on July 1, 1961, at Sandringham, Norfolk. Her early education took place at West Heath School at Sevenoaks in Kent where she displayed a talent for music and dancing and was an excellent pianist. In 1975, when her father succeeded to the earldom, she became Lady Diana Spencer. After leaving school Diana attended a finishing establishment in Switzerland before returning to England in 1978 and moving to London to work briefly as a nanny for an American couple. She then joined the Young England School where she became a kindergarten teacher.

On February 24, 1981, Diana's engagement to Charles, Prince of Wales, was announced and she immediately became the center of the press attention that would hound her to her death. The wedding took place at St Paul's Cathedral in London and the ceremony was watched by a worldwide audience of over 100 million television viewers. Hundreds of thousands more thronged the streets to watch the processional route from Buckingham Palace to the Cathedral.

The first of the couple's children, and heir to the throne, Prince William, was born on June 21, 1982, just over a year after the marriage. His birth was followed two years later by that of his brother, Prince Henry, or Harry as he is known to the world. To outside observers it seemed a "fairytale" marriage from the start. The couple took their young children on tours with them and were often seen dancing together at official functions.

However, over the following years it became increasingly obvious to the public that the marriage was facing difficulties. Though at first this was denied by spokespeople for the royal family, the publication of Andrew Morton's infamous *Diana: Her True Story* with its allegations of the princess suffering from bulimia and attempting suicide signalled the end of Charles and Diana's life as Britain's most celebrated couple. They separated in December 1992 and the divorce was finalized on August 28 1996. Diana was stripped of the title of "Her Royal Highness" which meant that she would never be queen, though as the mother of the heir she was granted the title Princess of Wales. During her married life Diana had been the patron of over 100 charities; following the divorce she resigned from all but a few that were of particular significance to her such as Centrepoint (a charity for the homeless), the English National Ballet, Leprosy Mission, and the National AIDS Trust. In a statement to the press she said that she wished to have "a meaningful public role with a more private life." Diana more than succeeded with the first, doing excellent work for the charities with which she was involved, notably raising awareness of HIV/AIDS issues as well as the campaign against landmines, which she brought to international attention. She also regularly visited homeless refuges in London, sometimes taking her sons with her so that they could witness the plight of those less fortunate. However, it was with children's charities that she particularly sympathized. As President of the Hospital for Sick Children, Great Ormond Street and the Royal Marsden Hospital, Diana regularly attended the bedsides of ill and disabled children and would even wear a mask and gown to watch surgeons perform on the children.

A private life was, however, something that sadly evaded the Princess. She was followed everywhere by the ubiquitous paparazzi photographers and she suffered from the publication of details about her private life in the press.

In November 1995 she made a television appearance on the BBC's Panorama news program and spoke of the pressures of her role and the difficulties in her private life and also said that she would like to earn the position of "Queen of Hearts."

On August 30, 1997, at 8:00 pm Paris time, Princess Diana was seriously injured in a car accident and died two hours after being freed from the wreckage. The car in which she was travelling with her close friend Dodi Fayed was being chased at speeds over 100 mph by photographers on motorcycles through a notoriously dangerous underpass when it crashed.

The scenes of public mourning following her death were unprecedented. Vigils were staged outside of her home at Kensington Palace and the public lined up for many hours to sign the books of condolence. On the day of her funeral millions lined the route of her coffin from St James's Palace to Westminster Abbey and it seemed that the streets of London were carpeted with flowers. After a moving ceremony, during which her brother passionately condemned the press, Princess Diana's body was taken to a small tomb on an island in a lake at her family estate. The site was specifically picked to provide the peace and privacy which was so lacking during her life.

D

D

DeBakey, Michael Ellis, Dr
1908–
Doctor

DeBakey was born and brought up in Louisiana. He graduated in medicine in 1932 from Tulane University. He stayed on to teach surgery from 1937–48, but moved to Baylor University where he was promoted to President of the Medical School in 1969.

Early in his career he was known for his work in the field of cardiovascular and heart surgery. In 1966 he successfully pioneered the use of an implanted booster pump for cardiac patients. This became known as the DeBakey device. About the size of an orange it can take over about 75% of the work done by the left ventricle. The heart continues to receive blood from the lungs, and once the patient's heart is able to function sufficiently, the pump can be removed. In later years, DeBakey has been seen as the American consultant for Russian president Boris Yeltsin during his heart bypass operation in the mid-1990s.

Deng Xiao Ping
1904–1997
Chinese statesman

A survivor of the "Long March" (1934–35), Deng endured many vicissitudes in his career. He rose to become General Secretary of the Communist Party in 1956, but fell from power during the Cultural Revolution (1966–69). He returned to favor in 1973 as Vice-Premier, but was removed by the Gang of Four shortly before Mao's death in 1976. Returning to power the following year, he supported improving relations with the U.S., viewing with suspicion the activities of the Soviet Union. Deng is infamous for quashing the student-led pro-democracy protests in Tiananmen Square with the army.

He was regarded as the elder statesman of Chinese politics, continuing to hold the reins of power in the People's Republic in the 1990s. During the mid-1990s Deng was no longer seen in public. He died from complications of Parkinson's disease in February 1997.

Doody, Howdy
1947–1976
Buffalo Bob Smith
1918–1998
TV Puppet and entertainer

Howdy Doody was first seen on NBC in 1947. The freckle-faced cowboy marionette, accompanied by "Buffalo" Bob Smith, appeared in more that 2,500 shows and their program ran for a record 13 seasons between 1947–60. The Howdy Doody Show was based on tales from Doodyville and included such memorable characters as Chief Thunderthud, Clarabell the clown, Phineas T. Bluster, Princess Summerfall Winterspring, Dilly Dally, Trapper John and Flubadub. At the beginning of each show "Buffalo" Bob Smith would ask "What time is?" and the in-studio audience (known as the Peanut Gallery) would cry out "Its Howdy Doody time!'. In 1970 "Buffalo" Bob Smith made a comeback with Howdy Doody and made hundreds more appearances over the next six years.

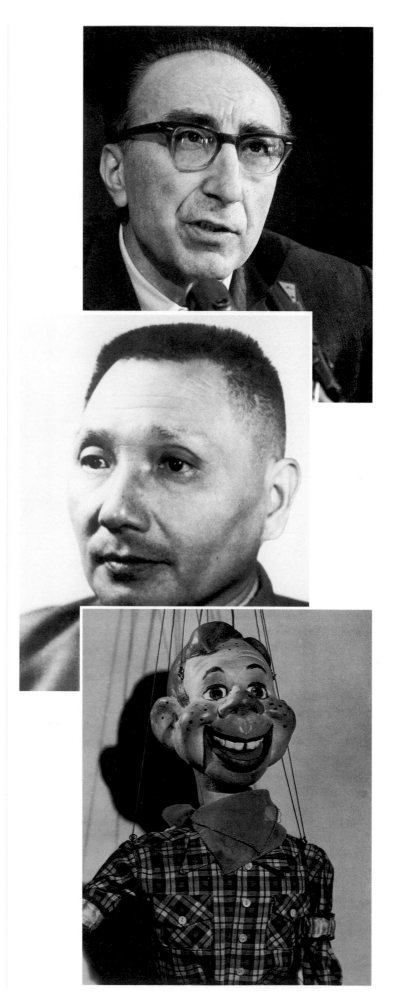

Dietrich, Marlene
1901–1992
German actress

Beautiful, aloof, sophisticated, demanding, generous and world-weary, Dietrich exercised a fascination on the world for over fifty years. Born Maria Magdalene Dietrich von Losch in Berlin, she began acting in the theater in Berlin for, among others, the famous theatrical director Max Reinhardt. She was a well-known theater actress by the 1920s, performing on stage and in silent movies. In later years, Dietrich would deny involvement in the silent era, although she appeared in at least 17 movies. Director Josef von Sternberg cast her as the sexy vamp Lola Lola in *Blue Angel* in 1930, in which she outshone the presumed star, Emil Jannings, with remarkable singing and acting. She went to Hollywood where she was an immediate success in *Morocco* (1930) and *The Devil Is a Woman* (1935). A handful of mediocre movies in the mid-1930s were rectified with *Destry Rides Again* (1939) in which she sang "What the Boys in the Back Room Will Have." Opposed to Nazism, she defied Hitler, refusing to return to Germany and instead became an American citizen in 1939. However she remained an outsider in Hollywood, intrinsically cosmopolitan with strong European ties and a pantheon of intellectuals and international celebrities as friends. During World War II she made more than 500 appearances before American troops overseas. After the war she launched a new career as a nightclub and cabaret performer, and movies such as *Stage Fright* (1950), *Witness For The Prosecution* (1958) and *Judgement at Nuremberg* (1961) kept her film career alive. She made an internationally acclaimed theater debut in New York City theater in 1967, and made a concert tour of the U.S. in 1973. In 1978 she appeared in *Just a Gigolo*. A loving retrospective of her work entitled *Marlene*, produced by Maximilian Schell, was released in 1986. Her autobiography *Ich bin, Gott sei Dank, Berlinerin* (I Am, Thank God, a Berliner; Eng. trans. *Marlene*) appeared in 1987.

D

Disney, Walt
1901–1966
American animator and film producer

A simple cartoonist, Disney turned a failing career in animation – then a modest offshoot of the movie industry – into a global business that, over 30 years after his death, continues to produce acclaimed animated films as well as traditional live-action films and also runs theme parks in California, Florida, Tokyo, and Paris. During his life he created many of the charming cartoon characters that are, today, recognized by virtually the entire population of the world.

Disney's is an archetypal American story of success through hard work and perseverance. He was born Walter Elias Disney in Chicago on December 5, 1901, and spent much of his childhood and adolescence on a Missouri farm before traveling back to Chicago at the age of 16 to study art. After a stint serving as an ambulance driver during World War I, Disney managed to find employment, in 1920 with Ub Iwerks, a trailblazing animator, under whom the young Disney produced short cartoons – called Laugh-O-Grams – for movie theaters. In 1922 however, it was obvious that this enterprise was destined for failure, and, determined to open his own cartoon studio, Disney moved to Hollywood in 1923. A partnership was formed with his brother Roy and, with Iwerks, Disney started work on the *Alice in Cartoonland* and *Oswald the Rabbit* series of shorts. He did not, however, contribute greatly to the actual animation, preferring to invent and visualize new ideas while directing others who did the cartoon work.

Success did not come quickly and the members of the company, now including Walt's wife Lillian Bounds, the actress, lived in poverty for five years. Then another character, Mortimer the Mouse, was renamed Mickey and the company made their first "talkie," *Steamboat Willie,* in 1928, with Mickey's voice supplied by Disney himself. The cartoon was a hit and, spurred on by this prosperity, new characters such as Minnie Mouse (Mickey's girlfriend), Goofy, Pluto, and Donald Duck featured in the excellent, full-color *Silly Symphony* series that also brought to the screen the memorable *Three Little Pigs* (1933) with its hit record "Who's Afraid of the Big Bad Wolf." Disney was always keen to make use of technological development and the 1932 film *Flowers and Trees* was the first ever to fully use Technicolor.

In 1937, the studio produced *Snow White and the Seven Dwarfs*, the first full-color, full-length, animated feature film. Critical praise and box office takings flowed in equal measure and Disney quickly repeated this formula with the equally lauded *Pinocchio* (1940), *Fantasia*, (1940), *Dumbo* (1941), and *Bambi* (1942).

After World War II, Disney directed the company's efforts into live-action documentary and movies. The "True-Life Adventure" series of short films, which includes the classic *The Living Desert* (1953) broke new ground in wildlife photography while films such as *Treasure Island* (1950), *Davy Crockett*, (1955), and *Kidnapped* (1960) enjoyed enormous audiences at the cinema. Animation was not forgotten either and 1950 also saw the release of another classic Disney full-length feature – *Cinderella* – which was followed in 1955 by *The Lady and the Tramp,* and *One Hundred and One Dalmatians* in 1961. The company also continued to make cartoon shorts featuring Mickey, Minnie, Goofy, and Donald until 1956.

Disney's first theme park, Disneyland, opened in Anaheim, California in 1955. The culmination of ideas that he had been toying with since the 30s when he took his own daughters to amusement parks, Disney designed it around the studio's own movies and characters. Disneyland was an instant phenomenon and has been likened to a Versailles for the 20th century. A project on a grand scale it featured all the attractions usually associated with an amusement park as well as adventure playgrounds, fantasy worlds, parades, and visions of the future. Often imitated but never equaled, there are now four around the world.

During his lifetime Disney was awarded with many Academy Awards for his short films and a special award in 1932 for the creation of Mickey Mouse. He also received an honorary degree from Harvard. During the fall of 1966, Disney, always a heavy smoker, was diagnosed as suffering from severe lung cancer during a routine examination and he died in hospital six weeks later, on December 15, after having a lung removed. To the last, he had been working on the studio's latest full-length animation, the *Jungle Book* (1967), which was also to prove the last of the postwar classics.

After his death the studio entered a slump in its fortunes. While still extremely profitable and making good quality, entertaining movies such as *Robin Hood* (1973) and the *Rescuers* (1977), critical and box office success to rival the studio's heyday was elusive, particularly after the poor reception of *The Fox and The Hound* (1981) and *The Black Cauldron* (1985). However, these fortunes reversed in the 1980s with an influx of fresh artistic talent and new technology of which Disney would have approved. A wealth of recent animated films, such as *The Little Mermaid* (1989), *Aladdin* (1992), *The Lion King* (1994), and *Hercules* (1998), have seen a second flowering of great Disney films; while *Toy Story* (1997) and *A Bug's Life* (1999) have ensured that the studio remains at the cutting edge of technology. As the progenitor of the "Disney style," Walt Disney is established as one of the greatest entertainment geniuses of the 20th century.

D

E

Einstein, Albert
1879–1955
German-Swiss-American physicist

The human understanding of physical reality was boosted beyond measure by Albert Einstein. In his lifetime he was lauded as a thinker of the highest quality and long after his death his theories continue to form the basis for modern physics and set the standard to which scientists aspire.

Born of Jewish parents in Ulm, Germany on March 14, 1879, the young Albert moved with his family to Munich while still an infant and it was here that he received his first education. As well as the normal curriculum he also had violin lessons, and showed a natural talent for music, as well as being instructed in Judaism at home. In 1888 he began to attend the Luitpold Gymnasium; starting to learn mathematics, particularly calculus, in 1891. Three years later, in 1894, the Einstein family business – the manufacture of electrical goods – failed, and while the rest of the family moved to Milan, Italy, Albert decided to remain in Munich, though he officially opted to renounce his German nationality and consequently remained stateless for some years. The following year, 1895, Einstein took and failed an examination for entrance to the Eidgenössische Technische Hochschule in Zurich to study electrical engineering and spent the next 12 months at a secondary school in Aarau in order to reach the required entrance standard. Here he benefited from excellent teaching and facilities, and pursued an interest in physics. Returning to the ETH in 1896, he was accepted and went on to qualify as a teacher of mathematics and physics.

Einstein was not successful in finding full-time employment until 1902 when he was taken on by the patent office in Bern where he worked for seven years. During this period he began to conduct his own research in the field of theoretical physics in his spare time and wrote an astonishing amount of papers for publication. This work was all the more amazing when it is considered that it was produced in isolation and without the range of scientific literature available at a university. His efforts were eventually recognized and, in 1905, a thesis on a new determination of molecular dimensions submitted to Zurich University won him a Ph.D. degree. In the same year Einstein began work examining the findings of Max Planck in the field of electromagnetic energies and also worked on a reinterpretation of classical theories of relativity which culminated in what is known as the special theory of relativity: the famous $e=mc^2$. He also completed a third paper examining statistical mechanics. Further work on these three seminal essays, known as the, "1905 Papers," resulted in the groundbreaking Special Theory of Relativity.

Einstein by now was becoming a recognized leader in scientific thought. In 1908 he was offered a lecturing position at the University of Bern following his thesis: "Consequences for the constitution of radiation following from the energy distribution law of black bodies." A year later he entered the University of Zurich as a professor of physics and was able to leave the patent office in Bern as well as the University there. The next significant step in his work and academic career came in 1911 when he became a full professor at Karl-Ferdinand University in Prague, Czechoslovakia, and also began to make tentative predictions concerning the bending effects of the sun's gravitational force on a ray of light passing close by. This represented the first step towards experimental proof of his abstract theories.

Following a further move back to Zurich in 1912 and a new phase of research aided by his friend and mathematician Marcel Grossmann, Einstein returned to Germany in 1914, accepting a research post at the Prussian Academy of Sciences. It was an attractive position which required no teaching duties and allowed him to develop his theories. By 1915 he was able to publish, to scientific acclaim, the final and definitive version, of the General Theory.

In 1919, Einstein's work was vindicated. A British expedition to observe a solar eclipse validated his earlier predictions and Einstein became internationally famous. He was awarded a Nobel prize in 1921 and traveled the world giving lectures. Other tributes were heaped on him, including the Copley Medal of the Royal Society in 1925 and the Gold Medal of the Royal Astronomical Society in 1926.

During a visit to the United States in 1932, Einstein was offered a position at the newly created Institute for Advanced Studies at Princeton. It was originally intended that he would divide his time between this position and his post in Germany. However, a month after he left Berlin, the Nazi Party came into power and Einstein would never again set foot in the country of his birth. Offers of academic positions now came from all over the world but he elected to remain in the U.S., grappling with scientific problems, and was granted citizenship in 1940.

A committed man of peace, Einstein was appalled by the actions of the Nazis. Reluctantly setting aside his pacifism, he wrote a letter to President Franklin D. Roosevelt in 1939, which recommended that the Americans develop an atomic bomb before the Germans achieved it. However, he took no part in the manufacture of the weapon himself. In 1944, he also helped raised funds

E

for the war effort by auctioning a hand written copy of the 1905 paper on special relativity and throughout the rest of his life he promoted humanitarian causes.

A great thinker, Einstein remained at the center of his field until his death, always seeking further answers and proofs. In 1952 he was asked to become the president of Israel but politely declined, preferring to continue his contributions to physics.

He was a quiet, gentle man and superb violinist, who possessed an excellent sense of humor and made the world laugh by committing a simple error when helping a young student with their math homework. At a public lecture overflowing with people who had come to see the great scientist he quipped, "I did not realize that so many Americans were interested in tensor analysis."

Albert Einstein died on April 15,

1955. His legacy is a huge and complex body of work which has fundamentally changed the way in which we view the universe and which continues to fuel scientific endeavor to this day. In his last letter, to philosopher Bertrand Russell, written one week before his death, Einstein agreed that his name should be included in a manifesto which requested that all nations dispose of nuclear weapons.

E

Eisenhower, Dwight, General
1890–1969
American soldier, politician, and president

A great military hero who pursued peace throughout his life, "Ike" remains one of the most popular of American presidents. Though some of his policies have been critcized, in particular his endorsement of Senator McCarthy's communist "witch hunt," his personal integrity and courage were unquestionable.

The third of seven sons, Dwight was born to David Jacob and Ida Elizabeth Stover Eisenhower on October 14, 1890 in Denison, Texas. His parents were poor but devout Christians and would instill into their children values of honesty and decency. Two years after his birth the family moved to Abilene, Kansas where they settled. Here Dwight was enrolled at the U.S. Military Academy at West Point and was soon recognized as an extremely promising cadet possessing leadership qualities. He was also an excellent football player until a knee injury stopped him from playing. He graduated, as second lieutenant in 1915 and was assigned to the U.S. Army in France where he served as a staff officer, his request for combat duty being denied.

On July 1, 1916 Eisenhower was married to Mamie Geneva Doud, the daughter of a wealthy family, who would bear him two sons although the first born, Doud Dwight, sadly died at only three years of age.

While serving in a number of training camps he confirmed his early promise and established a reputation for his leadership, organizational, and training abilities. Following the war he also proved an able tactician, being among the first advocates of mobile armored tanks which, at the time, were being developed.

Eisenhower held senior positions thereafter until the outbreak of World War II. When war was declared in Europe in 1939 he moved quickly through several command posts and following the Japanese attack on Pearl Harbor in 1941 was assigned to Washington DC where he served under George C. Marshall, the Army Chief of Staff. Marshall soon grew

to trust Eisenhower and in 1942 he was appointed U.S. commander in Europe and was Allied commander in North Africa and Italy, 1942–1943. As Supreme Commander of the Allied Expeditionary Force from January 1944, his excellent organizational skills again benefited him and he held together a disparate alliance of U.S., British, Canadian, and French troops, launching the Normandy landings on June 6, 1944, and leading the Allies to victory in May 1945.

Eisenhower resigned from the army in 1952 to stand as the Republican Presidential candidate with Richard Nixon as his running mate and, with the catchy slogan "I like Ike" was elected 34th President of the U.S., repeating this triumph in 1956.

As president Eisenhower was first to admit that his policies were middle of the road. As a Republican president facing a Democrat congress, this was a wise political stance and one that helped him form a stable administration, albeit one that did not demonstrate any radical reform. Although he was a conservative by nature, he was applauded for sending troops to Little Rock, Arkansas, to enforce the desegregation of schools and extended desegregation to American

forces. At the time he famously wrote, "There must be no second class citizens in this country." However, his term was marked by a lacklustre economy which caused a small but significant rise in unemployment as well as minor recessions. This dented public trust in the Republican Party but Eisenhower's popularity was so high that he avoided criticism for this sluggish performance.

Foreign affairs were dominated by the Cold War, and although his administration took a firm line against the Soviet Union, Eisenhower himself favored a more conciliatory approach. This attitude made possible the end of the Korean War in 1953, and he also refrained from interfering in the Hungarian uprising of 1956. While he negotiated from a position of military superiority, his main objective was the maintenance of world peace and he instigated programs to aid this — notably his "atoms for peace" initiative which arranged the loan of American uranium to those countries who needed it for peaceful purposes.

As a keen golfer President Eisenhower had a putting green made on the lawn of the White House and the nation was amused to learn that he had ordered the banishment of squirrels from the grounds due to the damage that they were doing to it.

Eisenhower left the White House in 1961 and retired to his farm in Gettysburg. In his last address he stressed the need for a suitable military force but also qualified this with a warning against overspending on the military, which might damage the American way of life. In conclusion he prayed for peace, "in the goodness of time."

After a long battle against recurring illness he died on March 28, 1969. His written works are, *Crusade in Europe* (1948) his memoirs of World War II, *Mandate for Change* (1963), *Waging Peace* (1965), and *At Ease: Stories I Tell to Friends* (1967).

E

Eliot, T.S. [Thomas Stearns]
1888–1965
American poet

Eliot settled in London in 1915. He taught, worked for Lloyds Bank until 1925, reviewed books, and edited the journal *The Criterion*. He became a director of Faber and Faber in 1925, nurturing a roster of younger poets. He was equally influential as a critic and literary figure, and as a poet, *Prufrock and Other Observations* (1917) was his first collection. Other volumes of poetry were succeeded by his masterpiece, *The Waste Land*, (1922), perhaps the central text of modernism. He published several critical essays throughout his career and in the 1930s a series of plays, including *Murder in the Cathedral* (1935). The major achievement of his later poetry, *The Four Quarters* (1935–42) was first published in its entirety in 1943. He was awarded the Nobel Prize and the Order of Merit in 1948.

Elizabeth II, Elizabeth Alexandra Mary
1926–
British monarch

The elder daughter of King George VI, Elizabeth II came to the throne in February 1952, after being crowned at Westminster in June 1953. She had served as a councilor of state while her father was in Italy during World War II. She married Prince Philip, Duke of Edinburgh in 1947. Her reign has seen vast changes in the power and influence of the United Kingdom on the world stage. Many territories in the British Colonies have been granted independence but remain in the Commonwealth of Nations. The Queen's primary role throughout her reign has been one of support and continuity within the Commonwealth. She has acted as a symbol of British tradition worldwide. The possessor of a vast personal fortune, she and her son Prince Charles, the Prince of Wales agreed to pay income tax on their personal income in 1992, the first time the monarch has done so.

Earhart, Amelia
1898–1937
American aviator

Considered the greatest of the American pioneer aviators, Amelia Earhart was the first woman to gain a pilot's certificate from the U.S. National Aeronautic Association in May 1923. Her greatest triumph came on May 21, 1932 when she landed in Northern Ireland at the end of the first solo Atlantic flight by a woman. The crossing from Harbor Grace, Newfoundland had taken 14 hours 54 minutes and set a world non-stop distance record for women. She was awarded honors by the French and American Governments. Again in a Lockheed Vega, she made the first solo flight by a woman from Honolulu to California on January 11–12, 1935. She and her navigator disappeared near Howland Island in the South Pacific on July 2, 1937 during an around-the-world attempt.

Fleming, Sir Alexander
1881–1955
British bacteriologist

Fleming began making progress in the study of antibacterial mechanisms after World War I. In 1928 he noted that a culture plate containing *staphylococci* bacteria had killed the bacteria around it. He identified the mold as *Penicillium notatum*, and noted that the antibacterial substance, penicillin, was effective against many other pathogenic species. In 1929 he reported that penicillin was non-toxic to animal tissue and "may be an efficient antiseptic…' against penicillin-sensitive microbes. Unable to produce a pure extract, Fleming's confidence that penicillin would one day be stabilized and purified was vindicated when in 1940 Ernst Chain and Howard Florey achieved this. Within two years the antibiotic's remarkable effects were established. This discovery revolutionized the fight against bacterial infection and Fleming received the Nobel Prize for Medicine jointly with Florey and Chain in 1945.

Fokker, Anthony Herman Gerard
1890–1939
Dutch aviation pioneer and engineer

A keen inventor, at 29 Fokker attended automobile school in Germany, where in 1910 he helped build and test two ill-fated airplanes. In 1911, with the help of Jacob Goedecker, he built a successful Spider monoplane. Fokker Aviation was founded in 1912, becoming the Fokker Aircraft Factory in 1915, supplying Germany with fighter planes in World War I. After the Armistice, Fokker re-established aircraft production in the Netherlands and went on to build factories in the United States where he became a US citizen. Fokker greatly influenced airplane development and construction, in particular the use of welded steel tubing in the fuselage. His autobiography *The Flying Dutchman* was published in 1931.

Ford, Gerald R.
1913–
American politician and president

A graduate of Yale University in Law, Ford could have taken up the chance to play professional football in 1935 instead of politics. Ford became President in 1973 after the disgrace first of Vice-President Spiro Agnew, whom he replaced, and then of his patron, President Richard Nixon. A prominent conservative, after 25 years in the House of Representatives he had earned a reputation for honesty which helped him survive the Watergate scandal. He had the misfortune to be in charge when the economy was at its weakest since World War II, crippled by high inflation and unemployment. Initially vilified for pardoning Nixon prematurely, Ford's decision to airlift thousands of Vietnamese refugees to the USA won him renewed public acclaim, although insufficient for his re-election in 1976.

Forbes, Malcolm Stevenson
1919–1990
American businessman and publisher

Born in New York City, in 1919, Forbes was raised in New
Jersey. He was educated at Princeton, and became editor and
publisher of *Forbes*, a then-floundering business magazine
founded by his father 40 years before. Circulation and
profits soared, making him a multimillionaire; he became
known for his extravagant parties and colorful hobbies, from
hot-air ballooning to collecting Fabergé eggs. He was keen to
enter politics and served on the New Jersey legislature in the
1950s, and twice ran for governor. In the 1980s he was
known as a close companion of Elizabeth Taylor. He died of
a heart attack on February 24, 1990.

Faulkner, William [Cuthbert]
1897–1962
American novelist

Faulkner's first publication was a book of poems *The Marble
Faun* (1924), and his first novel, *Soldiers Pay*, about the
return home and subsequent death of a disabled soldier,
appeared in 1926. Two further novels were written between
that and the appearance of *The Sound and the Fury* in 1929,
one of his most famous novels. Mississippi was also the
setting for the subsequent *As I Lay Dying* (1930), which
showed his comic talents to be as considerable as his tragic
vision of the decay of the American South. His popularity
was not as great as his literary reputation, and he periodically
wrote Hollywood scripts for his living. His later fiction is
very different, though he won two Pulitzer Prizes, for *A Fable*
(1954) and for *The Reivers* (1962), his last novel. He was
awarded the Nobel Prize for Literature in 1950.

Fitzgerald, F. [Francis] Scott
1896–1940
American novelist

Fitzgerald left the army in 1919 to go into advertising in
New York and then finished the semi-autobiographical novel
This Side of Paradise (1920). He married Zelda that year, and
published *Flappers and Philosophers*. The stories *Tales of the
Jazz Age* and the novel *The Beautiful and the Damned* both
appeared in 1922 as the Fitzgerald lifestyle was speeding up.
Life in privileged Great Neck, Long Island, provided the
inspiration for *The Great Gatsby* (1924), his finest novel.
More short stories, more traveling and a series of mental
illnesses for Zelda preceded and succeeded the appearance
of *Tender Is the Night* in 1934. Brief periods as a screenwriter
led to a Hollywood contract in 1937, where he worked on
The Last Tycoon. It remained unfinished at his death, from
alcoholism, for which he had been fired.

F

Dit is een foto, zoals
ik me zou wensen,
altijd zo te zijn.
Dan had ik nog wel
een kans om naar
Holywood te komen.
Anne Frank.
10 Oct. 1942

(translation)
"This is a photo as I would wish
myself to look all the time. Then
I would maybe have a chance to
come to Hollywood."
Anne Frank, 10 Oct. 1942

Frank, Anne [Annelise]
1929–45
Holocaust victim

A young Jewish German diarist who achieved fame in death. In 1933, at the beginning of Adolf Hitler's reign over Nazi Germany, Anne Frank and her family left Germany for Amsterdam. When the Netherlands were invaded by the Nazis in 1941, Anne was forced to transfer from a public to a Jewish school. Under occupation the threat of deportation to forced labor camps was too great, and she and her family were compelled to go into hiding with four other exiles on July 9, 1942. They lived in the sealed-off rooms in her father's food-products office building. Here Anne catalogued the day-to-day existence with candor, thoughtfulness and the precociousness that showed her age. Food and other supplies were secretly supplied by Gentile friends. The hiding place was discovered on August 4, 1944 by the Gestapo after a tip-off, and all those inside arrested. The family was sent to Auschwitz, and here Anne's mother died. Along with her sister, Anne was sent to the concentration camp at Bergen-Belsen, where they both died less than a year later of typhus. Her father was found in the hospital at Auschwitz when it was liberated by Russian troops and survived. Anne's Dutch diary was found in their former hiding place in Amsterdam among papers rescued by friends and given to her father. Published as *Het Achterhuis* (*The House Behind*) in 1947, it appeared (1952) in the U.S. as *Anne Frank: The Diary of a Young Girl*. Since then it has been translated into 50 languages. It was dramatized for the stage under the title *The Diary of Anne Frank* in 1956 and filmed in 1959. A new English version of the diary was published in 1995, restoring material that had been edited out earlier. In 1998 a few extra pages were also found, apparently relating to her parents and have now been included.

F

Franco, Francisco
1892–1975
Spanish statesman

A cunning politician and fascist who deserves a reputation as one of the most ruthless people in a century that has been plagued by tyrants, Franco ruled Spain with an iron fist from 1936 until his death in 1975. A quiet, sober, and religious man, it was his firm belief throughout his life that he alone had saved Spain from anarchy and that his authoritarian regime was entirely justified.

Franco was born and grew up in a small town called El Ferrol in Galicia, a north-western province of Spain where he enjoyed an uneventful childhood. His father, Nicholas, was an officer in the Spanish Navy and, following in his footsteps, Francisco was admitted into the Military Academy at Toledo in 1907. He graduated from here as a second lieutenant in 1910 and in 1912 volunteered to fight in the Moroccan War against the Riffians where he saw active combat duty as an officer and won praise and respect for his intelligence and courage. However, he made few friends, being a self-possessed man who remained aloof from his colleagues.

Franco's reputation as an excellent officer ensured that he rose swiftly through the ranks, achieving the position of major at 23 and commander of the Spanish Foreign Legion at 30. While filling this rank he further impressed his superiors by leading an attack which gained victory over the Moroccan leader Abd el-Krim and at 34 he was again promoted, becoming the youngest general in Europe.

The following years were a tense period in Spanish history and Franco's fortunes would rise and fall with successive governments. The new Spanish Republic (1931–1936) provoked many military conspiracies from which Franco carefully distanced himself but in 1934 he was applauded by conservatives and reviled by the left for his repressive actions against a miners' revolt in Asturias. The following year the

conservative government appointed him Chief of General Staff, a promotion which was politically nullified a year later in 1936 by the Popular Front government. They made him military commander of the Canary Islands, a post which was the equivalent of banishment. In the Canaries, Franco found a hotbed of military and conservative rebellion and he turned his efforts to their Nationalist cause. Soon after, on July 18, 1936, the rebellion was launched, quickly sparking the Spanish Civil War.

Franco's strategy took him to Morocco where he took command of the Spanish garrison and lead them in an invasion of southern Spain, gradually advancing on Madrid, the capital. By September, Spain's territories became split between Nationalist and Loyalist forces and, following the death of the head of the anti-Republic conspiracy, General José Sanjurjo, the Nationalists declared their own government. Franco was appointed head of state and Generalissimo of the army on October 1, 1936. In 1937 he abolished all political parties apart from the rebel Falange Party of which he became head, giving himself the title El Caudillo (The Leader).

Victory over the Loyalist forces took Franco an arduous three years — despite his absolute ruthlessness he proved a cautious tactician and his campaigns

were characterized by intelligent, cunning strategy. However, on April 1, 1939, he was triumphant and the war ended. In an act of unprecedented atrocity Franco then ordered Spain purged of Loyalist supporters and many hundreds of thousands were either executed or imprisoned.

The repercussions of the civil war would last for many years. Franco's government was riddled with corruption, Spain's economy had been destroyed, and the country was shunned by the international community. Given the terrible problems facing him, Franco wisely distanced Spain from World War II though declaring non-belligerency rather than neutrality and initially courting an alliance with Germany and Italy. Throughout the conflict he turned his support to whichever side appeared to be winning although in 1946 it was revealed that he had formed plans to enter the war on the side of the Axis powers.

In 1947, Franco transformed his dictatorship into a monarchy with himself as regent, able to choose his successor, and in the 1950s took small steps to moderate his authoritarian regime. At this time his fascism became anti-Communism and this helped to re-establish diplomatic relations with the Western powers although these were always strained.

Towards the end of his life Franco exercised his power as regent and in 1969 elected as his successor Juan Carlos, the grandson of Spain's last ruling monarch, Alfonso XIII. By 1973 his health was failing and he stepped down from his role as premier of the Spanish government though he retained the positions of head of state, commander of the armed forces, and leader of the Falange. Franco's authority was passed to Prince Juan Carlos in 1974 due to his worsening illness. The dictator died in Madrid on November 20, 1975 and within two years of his passing Spain had swept away almost every trace of his regime.

F

Ford, Henry
1863–1947
American motor manufacturer

Undoubtedly the father of mass production in the automobile world, Henry Ford's early days were involved in motor sport. He built his first car in 1901 and founded the Ford Motor Company in 1903. The famous Model T Ford, introduced in 1905, was the car that built Ford's reputation, and over 15 million were sold in an 18-year production run. This success allowed Henry Ford to buy out all his shareholders in 1919, giving himself sole control. In 1935 Ford introduced the V8 engine, a configuration that, in America at least, remains popular today. Ford was also involved with airplane construction throughout World War II. Henry Ford made the motor car affordable to a great number of people for the first time. Sons Edsel and Henry Ford II kept the company in the family after Henry's death.

Frost Robert
1874–1963
American poet

Robert Frost was the closest thing to a national poet that America possessed. Born in San Francisco, he had various jobs before moving with his family to England in 1912. His first two volumes of poetry were published there *A Boy's Will* (1913) and *North of Boston* (1914) – which contained "Mending Wall" and "The Death of a Hired Man." In 1915 he returned to the United States where he continued writing poetry with some success. The New England he celebrated with patriotic conservatism in these and following collections is one of everyday rural simplicity, self-reliance, and plain-dealing values which Frost himself popularly came to represent. Frost was awarded the Pulitzer Prize for poetry four times (1924, 1931, 1937, 1943); in 1961, he became the first poet to read a poem ("The Gift Outright") at a presidential inauguration.

Marquez, Gabriel Garcia
1928–
Colombian novelist

Gabriel Garcia Marquez is one of the foremost novelists of the 20th century. He was educated at a Jesuit college in Bogota and became a journalist at the age of 18. He came to Europe in 1954 for the newspaper *El Heraldo*, and began his career as a novelist during this period with *Leaf Storm* (1955) and *No one Writes to the Colonel* (1961). The imaginary town of Macondo – decaying, remote, surrounded by swamp – provides the setting for much of the work culminating in the immensely successful *One Hundred Years of Solitude* (1967). In 1975 Garcia Marquez published *The Autumn of the Patriarch,* a more cerebral, yet comic, exploration of myths of dictatorship. He has also published collections of short stories. He was awarded the Nobel Prize for Literature in 1992.

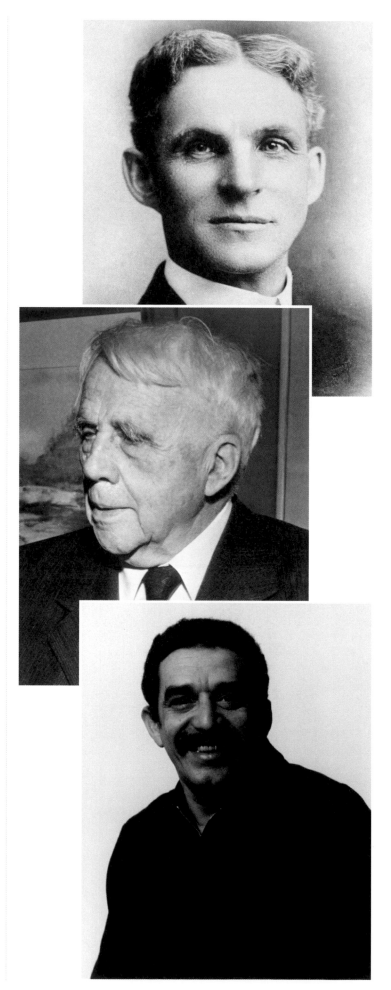

Freud, Sigmund
1856–1939
Austrian psychiatrist and psychoanalyst

Born in Freiberg, Freud and his family moved to Leipzig when he was three to escape anti-Semitic riots. Shortly afterwards they settled in Vienna, where Freud went to university. His original desire was to study Law, but he decided to change to medicine shortly before beginning his studies. Eager to study natural science, he started some research on the central nervous system in his third year. Completely absorbed in his studies, he failed to attend other courses and had to stay for an extra three years to qualify.

In 1885 he studied under Jean Chariot, who at that time was treating nervous disorders by the use of hypnotic suggestion. He greatly influenced Freud's interest in psychopathology. Freud's early interest in neurology and hypnosis led him to believe that some neurological symptoms had psychological significance. He began to study the dreams and parapraxes (slips of the tongue) of his patients, and developed the notion that much thinking takes place outside our conscious awareness, in a part of the mind which he called the unconscious.

Freud was also quick to understand that the evolving relationship between doctor and patient, which he called the transference, was an important diagnostic and therapeutic tool, in that the patient would always relate to the analyst in ways which shed light on his other important relationships. Freud encouraged the use of the couch, to enable the patient to free-associate and thereby reveal the unconscious mental processes at the root of their neurotic disturbance. This has left us with an almost universal image of what a psychiatrist's room must look like. Also associated with Freud are well known terms such as the Oedipus Complex, and the *ego*, *id*, and *superego*.

To escape Nazi persecution Freud moved to London in 1938. He is remembered as the undisputed "father of psychoanalysis," although he was never accorded full recognition in his lifetime.

G

Gates, Bill [William]
1955–
American software designer

More than any other person this century, Bill Gates has changed the way we work. His brainchild – the Windows operating system – is now an integral part of an enormous proportion of computer systems and businesses around the globe. Sales of it, and other software packages that his company, Microsoft, writes and manufactures have made him the world's wealthiest individual, with private assets totaling well over $50 billion. Currently Microsoft employs over 20,000 people in 48 countries.

Bill Gates was born on October 28, 1955. his father was an attorney and his mother a schoolteacher, University of Washington regent, and chairwoman of United Way International. A gifted child, by the time that he was 15 Bill had invented a device that regulated traffic patterns in Seattle. Interested in computers from an early age he dropped out of Harvard in 1975 in order to co-found Microsoft with his school friend Paul Allen. The company furthered his ambition of "a computer on every desktop, running Microsoft software" by developing the languages needed to operate the early microcomputers.

Collaboration with IBM led to the Microsoft Disk Operating System (MS-DOS) which dominated the early market for personal computers and ensured that Microsoft took a huge step forward. By 1983, DOS was licensed to over 100 computer vendors, making it by far the dominant operating system. In 1986, Microsoft was floated on the stock exchange and Gates became an overnight multi-millionaire.

Following the lead of Apple, whose Macintosh operating system was more user friendly than MS-DOS, in the late 1980s Gates launched the Windows operating system to great acclaim. Version 3.0, unveiled in 1990 became a major influence on the computer

market and made Microsoft the first personal computer company to achieve sales of over $1 billion in a single year. In 1992 Gates was presented with the National Medal of Technology by President George Bush. Microsoft's own programming teams were well placed to exploit Windows and allowed Microsoft to expand from being an operating systems and languages vendor to a supplier of major mainstream applications.

Consequently many of Microsoft's application programs, such as word processors and spreadsheets, are now as ubiquitous as the operating system itself.

Despite the rapid growth of the company, Gates maintains close hands-on control of the day-to-day running of Microsoft, keeping in contact with staff around the world through email. His workers are expected to work long hours and generally do so gladly for the rewards are great. The foresight and vision of their Chairman is legendary and Gates plays an active role in strategy planning and new product development. Gates' stated mission for his company is that Microsoft will continue to improve and advance software technology in order to allow more people to use computers easily and more enjoyably. It is a purpose that Microsoft rigorously maintains and

spending on research and development accounts for a large proportion of the company's annual income.

In 1995, Gates published his vision of the future of technology and society, written with Nathan Myhrvold, Microsoft's chief technology officer. *The Road Ahead* was released in 20 countries and became a number one bestseller around the world. Gates revised the book extensively in 1996 to further detail the importance of interactive networks, the internet, to human society and the second edition also became a bestseller.

Gates also nurtures an interest in other technologies and is a member of the board of the Icos Corporation, a biotechnological research company; owns shares in Darwin Molecular, and has recently founded the Corbis Corporation which has a huge archive of art and photography which is stored digitally. With Craig McCaw, pioneer of the cellular phone, he has also invested in a scheme to achieve a global two-way broadband telecommunications service by launching hundreds of satellites into low orbit. He also regularly donates large amounts to charities and has said in an interview that while he is alive he intends to give away 90% of his fortune.

He married a former employee, Melinda French Gates on January 1, 1994 and the couple have a daughter, Jennifer Katherine Gates, born in 1996. In his spare time Gates enjoys reading, golf, and plays bridge.

Despite criticism and allegations of plagiarizing the ideas of others, Gates is a clever and ruthless entrepreneur who has revolutionized the way that humans interact with technology. With Microsoft he is slowly building a global monopoly in almost every mainstream area of software and, with the company's internet browser, he is also attempting to develop dominance over cyber-space.

G

De Gaulle, Charles, General
1890–1970
French soldier, politician and president

Described as, "The most famous of Frenchmen," De Gaulle could claim to have had a vast impact on the course of his country over the century. As leader of the resistance during the German occupation of World War II he also organized France's role in the Allied victory and became an international hero. As the first President he shaped modern France and cultivated an enigmatic persona, comporting himself as an austere figure of historical greatness. A scholar and writer as well as a great political and military leader, he possessed a biting wit though he was renowned as a man who never laughed and who had no friends. He was, in fact, a devoted and benevolent family man with a great attatchment to his wife and known to his three grand children and innumerable nieces and nephews simply as "Uncle Charles."

Charles André Marie Joseph de Gaulle was born in Lille on November 22. The son of wealthy parents who fostered in him their devoutly Catholic values and patriotism, he was given a classical education before being admitted to the famed St Cyr Military Academy in 1910 where, despite his reticence, he would sometimes delight his colleagues with a brilliant renditition of the "nose speech" from *Cyrano de Bergerac* — an act that was accentuated by his own enormous nose. Graduating in the top 15 of his class he elected to serve in the 33rd regiment commanded by Marshal Henri Pétain who would become De Gaulle's mentor for the next 20 years and, after that, his deadly enemy. De Gaulle saw service in World War I as a lieutenant and was wounded three times and taken captive by the Germans. Following the war he was cited for gallantry by Pétain. On returning to France after 32 months in prison camps, during which he made no less than five attempts to escape, De Gaulle married the daughter of a biscuit manufacturer, Yvonne Vendroux,

who would become his closest companion throughout the rest of his life. The couple would have one daughter, Elizabeth, who remained sickly throughout her life and required much nursing in her youth.

Next De Gaulle served in many places around the world, notably in occupied Germany and the Middle East and also studied and lectured at the French war college, Ecole Superieure de Guerre. During the thirties he was rapidly promoted through the ranks, mostly thanks to Pétain — although the publication of his book, *The Army of the Future* (1934), promoting new ideas in modern warfare, caused controversy in military circles.

In spite of his reputation as a maverick, by the outbreak of World War II De Gaulle had achieved the rank of Brigadier General and conducted one of the few successful French campaigns against the German invasion of 1940. On June 5, of that year, he was promoted to undersecretary of war by the premier, Reynaud, who resigned straight after. Concerned that his successor, Pétain, was about to surrender, de Gaulle fled to London. Here he made an historic radio broadcast to the French nation urging the people to resistance of the Germans and a continued struggle, becoming the symbol of the resistance with his cry of "France has lost a battle, but France has not lost the war." Pétain responded by pronouncing the death sentence upon his former protege. De Gaulle however, with the support of the Allied leaders, formed a provisional government and, after the Normandy invasion of 1944, re-entered France and assumed control. He quickly organized the country and was able to aid the Allies in the final defeat of the Nazis. After resigning in January 1946 De Gaulle went into retirement and his career was considered finished.

Nevertheless, in 1958, the Algerian

War threatened to spill over into civil war in France and de Gaulle was called upon to form a government. He was granted emergency powers and total authority for a period of six months and in this time he drafted a new constitution giving a large amount of executive power to the president. This was ratified by the electorate who consequently elected him president of the Fifth Republic in December 1958. He was to serve his country in this position for a further decade until his resignation in 1969 but de Gaulle's first problem was to solve the Algerian crisis. This he managed with a minimum of bloodshed using diplomacy and use of his executive power where necessary to quell rebellion. Further acts as President would later include: bringing France into the European Common Market while cooling the French relationship with the U.S.; developing a nuclear capability in both the military and for the country's energy; and building a relationship with Communist China as well as Third World countries where France had previously established colonies.

De Gaulle's resignation in 1969 was a direct result of the student protests and strikes of 1968. His contempt for left-wing tactics lead him to mismanage the situation and a minor ballot in 1969 registered the country's dissatisfaction with him. Stepping down as president on April 28, he handed the French republic to his close colleague Georges Pompidou.

He retired to his estate in Colombey-les-deux Églises where he finished his postwar memoirs before dying on November 9, 1970. His memoirs both pre- and post-war were stamped with nobility, grandeur, and were acclaimed in France's famous literary circles. Within them de Gaulle states, "Glory gives herself only to those who have always dreamed of her."

G

G

Garbo, Greta
1905–1990
Swedish actress

Beautiful and sensitive, Garbo was the most magnetic actress in the history of the movies. Not a typical Hollywood sex symbol, when her first movie, *The Torrent,* was a huge success, she received top billing. Frequently Garbo's characters acted outside the prescribed social code and suffered for it, as in *Anna Karenina* (1935). She got more publicity than any other star simply by running away from it. She made some of her best movies during the talkie era, notably *Ninotchka* (1939), which showed her comic talents. In the early 1940s, when some of her box-office appeal had faded and a new wind of puritanism was sweeping Hollywood, she simply retired. But her legend grew stronger, and for more than 40 years after her last movie was released, she remained the most famous star in the world.

Gehrig, Lou [Henry Louis]
1903–1941
American baseball player

The great New York Yankee teams of the mid-1920s to mid-1930s featured two contrasting heroes. One was the flamboyant Babe Ruth, known for his epic home runs and robust appetite for life. The other was strong, silent Lou Gehrig, a Columbia University-educated first baseman whose entry into the record books was both dignified and unassuming. Known as "The Iron Horse," Gehrig played a then record 2130 consecutive games. Gehrig was voted the league's most valuable player (MVP) in 1927 and 1936. He had a career batting average of .340, while slamming 493 home runs, including 23 grand slams, a major league record at the time. He retired early in the 1939 season and was elected into the baseball Hall of Fame later that year. He died of amyotrophic lateral sclerosis, a rare nerve disorder that is now known as Lou Gehrig's Disease.

Getty, John Paul
1892–1976
American industrialist

The son of a wealthy oil speculator, Getty entered the business in Oklahoma in 1914. In 1930 he inherited his father's company and during the Depression used his excellent cash position to buy up oil shares at low prices. Between 1942–1961 he was president, general manager, and principal owner of the Minnehoma Financial Corp. In 1949 he obtained a 60-year oil concession in Saudi Arabia which vaulted him into the billionaire class. Married and divorced five times, Getty started acquiring an art collection in the 1930s. This formed the nucleus of the J. Paul Getty Museum in Malibu, which opened to the public in 1974. On his death he bequeathed his legendary wealth to the museum. With enormous buying power, the Getty Museum and associated research institutes played a controversial part in the international art market during the 1980s. In 1992 it was re-housed in a purpose-built building designed by Richard Meier.

G

Gandhi, Mahatma Mohandas
1869–1948
Indian politician

Gandhi opposed the might of the British Raj with the non-violent ethos of the ascetic. A London-trained lawyer, he was sent by a Bombay-based firm as a legal adviser to Durban, South Africa. Here he was appalled at the denial of civil liberties and political rights to Indian immigrants. He first used a policy of passive resistance and non-cooperation against the racism of turn-of-the-century South Africa authorities, fighting for elementary rights for Indian laborers. He had been greatly influenced by the writings and principles of both Leo Tolstoy and Henry David Thoreau. Gandhi used the term *Satyagraha* (Sanskrit for "truth and firmness") for the act of passive resistance and civil disobedience. The South African Government eventually made concessions to Gandhi's demands in 1914, including recognition of Indian marriages and abolition of the poll tax for them.

Gandhi deployed *Satyagraha* on a vast scale in India against the British, particularly in the salt march of 1930. He became a symbol of free India, revered as a saint, and given the title "Mahatma." He returned to a simple ascetic way of life, of prayer, meditation and fasting. As leader of the Congress Party he tried to keep a dialogue with the British alive, suffering periods of imprisonment when it failed. Interred by the British during World War II, he was released due to failing health. When independence was granted, in 1947, it partitioned India and created the new Muslim state of Pakistan. Riots followed and it was for urging tolerance for the Muslim minority in India that Gandhi was assassinated by a Hindu fanatic, Nathuram Godse.

Such was the effect of his death, the United Nations General Assembly set aside a period of mourning, and all countries sent condolences. Gandhi's legacy was to inspire non-violent protest elsewhere, notably in America where it was employed by the Civil Rights movement under Martin Luther King, Jr.

G

Gershwin, George [Jacob]
1898–1937
American composer

The name Gershwin is redolent of images of the roaring twenties and the Jazz Age. A playboy, man about town, and musical genius, George is arguably the first man to bring America to the arena of serious music with his "folk opera" *Porgy and Bess* as well as other serious compositions, and he was also adept at penning popular tunes, movie scores, and vaudeville shows, often in collaboration with his lyricist brother Ira. His prolific output ensures that, despite a tragically early death at 38, he left a large body of work that is of consistently superb standard and which continues to be recorded by many modern stars. His audience has never diminished; Gershwin shows are still staged, to critical acclaim, and recordings of his songs continue to sell in huge quantities. His music is a highly personal interpretation of European classical, jazz, and black styles and, while always catchy, beautiful, and melodic, it is characterized by deceivingly complex rhythm arrangements which lend a sophisticated and individual flavor to his work.

He was born George Gershovitz in New York on September 26, 1898, to Russian immigrants Morris and Rose and it was Ira, his elder brother, that was originally intended to be the musician of the family. However, at the age of nine, after listening spellbound to a friend playing the violin, he appropriated his brother's piano and soon taught himself to play by ear. At age 12 he was given lessons at which he excelled under tutor Charles Hambitzer, who brought to his young protégé the music of Debussy and Ravel. At school Gershwin was not so successful, he was a poor scholar though a natural athlete and left at 15 to pursue a career in music.

As the youngest song plugger in Tin Pan Alley, he was employed by Jerome K. Remick at $15 per week while he used his spare time to compose songs. The first of these to be published (in 1916) was called "When You Want 'Em You Can't Get 'Em" but, though Gershwin was overjoyed, the song did not enjoy any great success. Later in the same year he experienced another step in his career when a different song was used by Sigmund Romberg in a show. In 1917, Gershwin left Remick and toured the vaudeville circuit as a pianist before being hired as a songwriter by the publishing house T.B. Harms.

Gershwin's breakthrough came in 1919. His first Broadway show, *La La Lucille*, was a minor success, running for 100 performances, written in 1917, "Swanee" was heard by the famous Al Jolson and adopted for his tour. Benefiting from Jolson's fine vocal performance, it was a smash hit and sold in excess of two million records within a year of its release. Gershwin was now firmly on the path to fortune.

Over the following five years Gershwin consolidated his success, writing the music for *George White's Scandals*, the 1922 version of which included his one act opera, *Blue Monday*, his first serious piece to be performed. He was also commissioned to write a jazz piece for a concert at Aeolian Hall in New York City. The resulting work, "Rhapsody in Blue," was performed with the composer as piano soloist and won great critical acclaim. As the twenties progressed so too did Gershwin's career, spectacular musical extravaganzas flowed from his pen to be performed by the cream of American performers such as Fred Astaire, Ginger Rogers, W.C. Fields, Jeanette McDonald, Fanny Brice, Bob Hope, and many other huge stars. He greatly enjoyed the fame and became a highly celebrated and popular figure on the social scene, often to be found sitting at the piano during sophisticated *soirées* where he would entertain the enraptured guests with renditions of his own compositions.

The late twenties and early thirties saw a progression into satire and with Ira, George wrote the popular *Strike up the Band* (1927) and *Girl Crazy* (1930). The latter is one of the best examples of the brothers' work and features the classic song "I Got Rhythm". 1930 was also the year that he made his first trip to Hollywood to score the movie *Delicious* and he also tried his hand at conducting at a stadium concert of his own music. In 1932 Gershwin was awarded the first Pulitzer Prize for drama for the outstanding political satire *Of Thee I Sing* which was to be the last big success of his lifetime. His next two musicals both ran for less than 100 performances each, and what has since been recognized as his masterpiece, the opera *Porgy and Bess*, written in 1935 and based on the book by DuBose Heyward, closed after mixed reviews and only a few performances. During the next two years he concentrated on films, and scored *Shall We Dance?* for Fred Astaire and Ginger Rogers and *A Damsel in Distress,* for Astaire, Joan Fontaine, and Gracie Allen.

In 1937 after suffering from dizziness and headaches, George Gershwin slipped into a coma. Two naval destroyers were dispatched by the White House to collect Dr. Dandy, America's preeminent brain surgeon from his holiday yacht but by the time he arrived in Hollywood it was too late. Gershwin died of a brain tumor on July 11, 1937.

He was a man of huge talent and great generosity who helped other musicians with their careers. His music remains timeless.

G

G

Gleason, Jackie
1916–1987
American entertainer

After winning a talent contest at 15, Gleason embarked on a career in show business. Performing in carnivals and nightclubs in the 1930s, his talent was recognized when he appeared in *Follow the Girls* (1945), by executives at NBC who gave him the title role in *The Life of Riley* (1949–50, 1953–58). He gained in popularity with *The Jackie Gleason* show at CBS from the 1950s, where he introduced the character of Ralph Kramden, in *The Honeymooners*. Gleason won an Academy Award nomination for his role in *The Hustler* (1961) and won a Tony for his performance in the Broadway musical *Take Me Along* (1959). He was elected to the Television Hall of Fame in 1985.

Graham, Billy [William Franklin]
1918–
American evangelist

Billy Graham can claim to have personally preached the Christian gospel in more countries and to more people than anyone else in history. Ordained as a minister in 1940, he began his evangelical crusade in 1949 in Los Angeles. An eloquent preacher, he has traveled widely offering a personal invitation to be "born again." Unlike so many religious leaders who have achieved a cult following, Graham has retained integrity, devoid of scandal. He is a forceful, charismatic and eloquent preacher, and attracts thousand to his rallies. He has become world famous through the televised movies of his rallies, and through numerous articles and books including *Peace with God* (1953), *Secret of Happiness* (1955), *World Aflame* (1965), *How to Be Born Again* (1977), *A Biblical Standard for Evangelists* (1984), and *Hope for the Troubled Heart* (1991).

Graham, Martha
1894–1991
American dancer, teacher, choreographer and director

One of the founders of modern dance, Graham's American pioneer ancestry and west-coast childhood had a profound influence on her creative work. She studied and danced with Denishawn (Ted Shawn and Ruth St Denis) from 1916–23 and made her solo debut in 1926, after which she began to develop her own ideas and classroom technique. Graham's pivotal work of the early years was *Primitive Mysteries*, but the 1935 *Frontier* looked more like the Graham style to come. Her most memorable depiction was the *Bride in Appalachian Spring* (1946), but she later began to draw on Greek mythology and female protagonists for her themes: Medea (*Caves of the Heart*, 1946), Jocasta (*Night Journey*, 1947), and *Clytemnestra* (1958). Graham finally gave up dancing in 1973, and retired to head her school and company.

G

Glenn, John Herschell, Jr.
1921–
American astronaut

Glenn began his career as a pilot in the United States Marine Corps, flying 149 combat missions in World War II and the Korean War. In 1957 he was chosen as the first person to fly supersonic, non-stop across the United States, setting a record of 3 hr 22.3 min 8.4 seconds. Glenn had another first when he became the first American in orbit on February 20, 1962. He was one of seven men selected for the Project Mercury space flight training and was the oldest of the group. The Russians had succeeded in sending the first man into space: Yuri Gagarin orbited the Earth once for

108 minutes on April 12, 1961 in the *Vostok 1* spacecraft. Glenn made three revolutions of the earth; taking 4 hours 55 minutes in the Project Mercury Gemini Capsule called *Friendship 7*. His flight was significant in that he used his hand controls to demonstrate that man could pilot a spacecraft in orbit and on re-entry. He returned to Earth, landing in the Atlantic Ocean near the Bahamas and was hailed a national hero.

Glenn retired form the Marine Corps in 1965 and became a businessman and a consultant to NASA. He is much decorated, having received among other honors, the Distinguished Flying Cross five times and the Air Medal with 18 clusters. He was elected to the United States

Senate in 1974 as a Democrat for Ohio. He was an unsuccessful candidate for the Democratic presidential nomination in 1984. He has served on the Special Intelligence Committee (1997–99) and the Government Affairs Committee, the Armed Services Committee (1985–98). He announced that he would retire in 1999.

He returned to space, somewhat controversially, in October 1998, assigned to serve as payload specialist. This mission supported a variety of research payloads including deployment of the Spartan solar-observing spacecraft, the Hubble Space Telescope Orbital Systems Test Platform, and investigations on space flight and the aging process.

G&H

Grant, Cary
1904–1986
British-born American actor

Grant was one of the most famous screen personalities in the world, playing a succession of light romantic comic leads. He appeared on Broadway before Hollywood beckoned, and first starred opposite Mae West in *She Done Him Wrong* (1933). It wasn't until the late 1930s that his gifts for screwball comedy flowered on screen, beginning with *The Awful Truth* (1937). By the late 1940s Grant was the established master of roles requiring a sophisticated man-about-town. Then other leading men of his generation were turning to aging character roles, Grant was still handsome and in top form in movies such as *Charade* (1963) at the age of 59. What set him apart from other actors was his air of never taking himself too seriously. Witty and urbane off screen as well as on, he once remarked, "I play myself to perfection."

Hammarskjold, Dag
1905–1961
Swedish diplomat

Hammarskjold entered the diplomatic service in Sweden. He was initially finance specialist for the foreign office and was involved with the European Recovery Program conference of 1947. He was Sweden's deputy foreign minister in 1951, and traveled as a member of the Swedish delegation to the UN in 1952. He was elected Secretary General of the UN in 1953.

An exponent of UN intervention to preserve world peace, he traveled widely on missions of great political significance and personally persuaded Nasser to accept a force which held the Middle East peace line for a decade. He died in an air crash, probably the result of sabotage, on his way to arrange for another *cordon sanitaire*, in the Congo. He was posthumously awarded the Nobel Peace Prize in 1961.

Hawking, Stephen William
1942–
British physicist

Graduating from Oxford, Hawking obtained a doctorate at Cambridge and remained there to become a Fellow of the Royal Society and Lucasian Professor of Mathematics. His research field was Einstein's theory of relativity. He found it did not account for such concepts as black holes or the Big Bang. His subsequent work has developed both these concepts considerably. In his student days he contracted the severely disabling motor neuron disease which has confined him to a wheelchair ever since. All the complex mathematics of his work is carried out in his head. He is also a popular communicator. His book, *A Brief History of Time* (1988), has been very successful in bringing the complex concepts of cosmology and theoretical physics to a wider audience.

Goldwyn, Samuel
1882–1974
American film producer

Born in Warsaw, Goldwyn emigrated to America at the age of 13. When he arrived in the United States his surname was changed to Goldfish. He became a naturalized U.S. citizen in 1902. Goldwyn entered the movie business in 1913 when he joined a fruitful partnership with Jesse Lasky and Cecil B. De Mille, forming the Jesse L. Lasky Feature Play Company, which released its first movie, *The Squaw Man*, in 1914. A mere three years later he formed the Goldwyn Picture Corporation with Edgar and Archibald Selwyn. The following year he adopted the company name for his own. The company merger with Louis B. Mayer Productions and Metro

Pictures in 1923 to create Metro Goldwyn Mayer (MGM) but Goldwyn was forced out after arguing with his partners. He became an independent producer in 1923 and formed a particularly productive relationship with director William Wyler, who made such quality movies as *Dead End* (1937), *The Little Foxes* (1941), and *The Best Years of Our Lives* (1946). He acquired a reputation for making quality movies, and was the first producer to use known authors to write screenplays, among them Robert Sherwood, Sinclair Lewis, and Lillian Hellman. He also prided himself on the actors he employed, introducing several unknowns who went on to became stars: Ronald Colman, Danny Kaye, Lucille Ball, Eddie Cantor, Will Rogers, Susan Hayward, Gary Cooper, and David Niven. He was famous for

his "Goldwynisms," sayings such as "Include me out"; "A verbal contract isn't worth the paper its written on." He was also a great philanthropist.

Some of Goldwyn's more remarkable motion pictures are regarded as classics: *All Quiet on the Western Front* (1930), *Street Scene* (1931), *Arrowsmith* (1931), *Dodsworth* (1936), *Stella Dallas* (1937), *Dead End* (1937), *Wuthering Heights* (1939), *The Little Foxes* (1941), *Pride of the Yankees* (1942), *The Secret Life of Walter Mitty* (1947), *Guys and Dolls* (1955), and *Porgy and Bess* (1959). He won an Academy Award for best picture for *The Best Years of Our Lives* (1946). In 1946 the Academy of Motion Picture Arts and Sciences awarded him the Irving Thalberg Memorial Award and in 1957 the Jean Hersholt Humanitarian Award.

Hearst, William Randolph
1863–1951
American publisher

Hearst was a multimillionaire publisher whose enjoyment of power and lavish lifestyle inspired Orson Welles' movie *Citizen Kane*. He became editor of his father's paper, the *San Francisco Examiner*, in 1887, and increased circulation by publishing sensational and salacious stories until 1890, when it was profitable, after which he gradually acquired a chain of newspapers. Hearst's name became a byword for the power of the media to make or break careers and influence the course of world events. He unsuccessfully tried to enter politics. He had an affair with actress Marion Davies in 1917, and even started building a castle at San Simeon. By the 1930s, however, his empire on the brink of bankruptcy, Hearst was forced to sell off his assets, but was still able to leave a vast fortune, estimated at over $200 million.

Hefner, Hugh
1926–
American magazine publisher

Hefner began his career as subscription and promotion writer for *Esquire* magazine. In 1953 he created the first issue of *Playboy* in his Chicago apartment. Featuring Marilyn Monroe, on the cover it sold 51,000 copies. As editor of *Playboy* magazine Hefner turned it into one of the most popular men's magazines with a raunchy mixture of nude centerfolds and light-hearted articles by leading writers. In the 1970s, the company expanded it horizons producing *Playboy*-brand consumer products, such as cigarette lighters and apparel, and opening the *Playboy* mansion. Changing tastes led to falling sales and Hefner passed the editorship of the magazine to his daughter in 1982. Since then Playboy Enterprises has diversified. Hefner still embodies the uninhibited lifestyle, appearing in silk pajamas and expounding on the delights of viagra.

Hellman, Lillian
1905–1984
American dramatist

Hellman was a playwright whose work is remarkable for its subject matter as well as the construction and story development. Her plays include: *The Children's Hour* (1934), *The Little Foxes* (1939), *The Searching Wind* (1944), *Another Part of the Forest* (1946), *The Lark* (1955) – a story of Joan of Arc – and *Candide* (1956), based on the satire of the same name by the French writer Voltaire.

For *The Watch on the Rhine* (1941) Hellman was awarded a New York Drama Critics' Circle Award in 1941, and she received another in 1960 for *Toys in the Attic*. All of her plays have been made into movies except *Candide*. In 1970 her autobiography, *An Unfinished Woman* (1969), won the National Book Award in arts and letters.

Gorbachev, Mikhail Sergeyvich
1931–
Russian statesman

The youngest Soviet leader since Stalin succeeded Lenin, Gorbachev was a remarkable and forceful leader who changed the course of Russian history. Trained as a lawyer at Moscow State University, he joined the Communist Party in 1952. Back home in Stavropol, he rose steadily in the regional party hierarchy becoming first secretary of the regional party in 1970: he was summoned to Moscow in 1978. There he became a protégé of Yuri Andropov, whose influence secured for Gorbachev full membership in the Politburo, the party's chief policy-making body, in 1980.

General Secretary of the Communist Party from 1985, and the youngest member of the Politburo, he embarked on a radical program of reform based on two premises: *perestroika* (restructuring) and *glasnost* (openness). The Soviet people achieved greater freedom of expression than they had enjoyed for over 50 years, but *perestroika* introduced dramatic socio-economic changes, which only gradually revealed their benefits. Under the new policies a new freedom of information appeared, and some limited free-market mechanisms were set in place.

Gorbachev was well received abroad and in foreign policy agreed to major arms limitation treaties in 1987 and 1990, effectively ending the Cold War. His acquiescence to the dismantling of Communist regimes in Eastern Europe in 1989 culminated in the reunification of Germany in 1990, but at the same time he refused to countenance the breakup of the Soviet Union into its constituent republics. Facing growing criticism at home, he strengthened his personal powers as President in 1990 but in 1991 was overthrown in a hard-line coup. He survived thanks to Boris Yeltsin's resistance but to remain in power was forced to promise more rapid reforms and to disassociate himself from the now discredited Communist party. Gorbachev resigned all his offices in December 1991, announcing the official dissolution of the Soviet Union into independent republics.

Since resigning he has criticized the government's policies, particularly the rapid pace of economic reform and the policy towards former Soviet republics.

Hepburn, Katherine
1907–
American actress

Hepburn may well be the most respected actress ever to emerge from Hollywood because she has never confused her star image with her strong individualism. An instant success in *A Bill of Divorcement* (1932), several popular movies followed, including *Morning Glory* (1933) for which she won her first Academy Award. She hit her stride as a screwball comedienne in *Bringing Up Baby* with Cary Grant in 1938; *Woman of the Year* (1942) was the first of many movies with Spencer Tracy, including *State of the Union* (1948) and *Desk Set* (1957). Their final movie was *Guess Who's Coming to Dinner* (1967). With Bogart she scored a triumph with *The African Queen* (1951), and she won the Best Actress Award at Cannes for her performance as the drug-addicted mother in *Long Day's Journey into Night* (1962). Opposite Henry Fonda in *On Golden Pond* (1982) she was still a consummate performer.

Hepburn, Audrey
1929–1993
American actress

Born Edda van Heemstra Hepburn-Ruston in Brussels, she remained with her mother in the Netherlands throughout World War II . As a result of the Nazi occupation she suffered many health problems associated with malnutrition. She later worked as a model and began her acting career in 1951. She starred in many classic movies, her delicate waif-like look epitomizing the 1950s' ideal heroine. She starred in many movies, including *War and Peace* (1956), *The Unforgiven* (1960), *Charade* (1963), and *My Fair Lady* (1964). She was awarded an Academy Award for best actress for her role in *Roman Holiday* and was nominated for her roles in *Sabrina* (1954), *The Nun's Story* (1959), *Breakfast at Tiffany's*, and *Wait Until Dark* (1967). From 1988 Hepburn worked as a special ambassador for UNICEF.

Hillary, Sir Edmund Percival
1919–
New Zealand mountaineer

Hillary learned to climb in the New Zealand Alps, but in the early 1950s graduated to climbing in the central Himalayas. In 1953 he joined a British expedition led by Colonel John Hunt, which aimed to conquer Mount Everest. On the morning of May 29, Hillary and the Sherpa Tensing Norgay (1914–1986) traversed the last ridge and became the first men to climb the world's highest mountain. He was knighted for his achievement later that year. His next adventure was to the Antarctic. Under the leadership of Vivian E. Fuchs, he was the New Zealand party leader for a trans-Antarctic expedition sponsored by the Commonwealth of Nations. They crossed Antarctic by tractor reaching the South Pole on January 4, 1958 becoming the first people to cross since Robert Scott in 1912. Hillary's autobiography is titled, *Nothing Ventured, Nothing Won* (1975).

Guevara, Che [Ernesto]
1928–1967
Argentine revolutionary

From a middle-class Argentine family in Rosario, Argentina, Guevara was the eldest of five children. He originally trained as a doctor, qualifying in 1953. As a result of his travels through Latin America in his vacations in the 1950s, he became convinced that violent revolution was the way for the masses to overcome their poverty and inequality.

After qualifying, he went to Guatemala, where Jacobo Arbenz was attempting to bring about a social revolution. However, in a coup supported by the CIA in 1954, Arbenz was overthrown. Guevara was convinced that the United States

would attempt to overthrow any leftist regime. Traveling to Mexico he met Fidel Castro, who was a political exile from Cuba at the time. He fought with Castro in Cuba from 1956 against the dictator Fulgencio Batista. When Castro came to power Guevara served as minister of industry in his government (1961–65) and helped guide him to the pro-Communist path. Guevara wrote about the two years with Castro in *Pasajes de la guerra revolucionaria* (1963; trans. *Reminiscences of the Cuban Revolutionary War,* 1968).

Guevara became famous in the West for his many attacks against the United States' foreign policy and his outspoken objections to imperialism and neo-colonialism. Throughout the 1960s Guevara's writings reflected not

only his own views but Cuba's policies, as can be seen in *El socialismo y el hombre en Cuba* (1965; trans. *Man and Socialism in Cuba,* 1967) – an examination of Cuba's brand of Communism – and the influential, *guerra de guerrillas* (1960; trans. *Guerrilla Warfare,* 1961).

He disappeared for a period for two years during the mid-1960s, joining with other guerillas to fight in the civil war in the Congo. In 1966 his efforts to train guerrillas in Bolivia was thwarted when he was captured by the Bolivian army, shot near Vallegrande on October 9, 1967. A strong opponent of the influence of the United States in the Third World, Guevara became a legendary figure and a model for radical students the world over.

H

Hemingway, Ernest
1899–1961
American novelist

America's most celebrated and prolific writer, Hemingway was a novelist, journalist, poet, and adventurer. Awarded both the Pulitzer Prize and the Nobel Peace Prize, his deceptively simple prose explores many themes, including the moral decay of America and the despair of war which placed him as leader of a group of authors which includes F. Scott Fitzgerald, John Dos Passos, and Hart Crane who were labeled the "lost generation." His work was based on his own extraordinary experiences and has become a landmark in modern American literature.

Ernest Miller Hemingway was born in Oak Park, Illinois, on July 21, 1899, to Clarence and Grace Hemingway — the second of their six children. As a child he enjoyed idyllic summers with his family at Walloon Lake near Petoskey; a setting which he would later describe as an "earthly paradise," where he spent his time hunting and fishing with his father. Graduating high school in 1917, Hemingway decided to pursue a career in journalism rather than going on to college and joined the *Kansas City Star* as a rookie reporter. At that time, World War I was raging in Europe though Hemingway was unable to join the battle due to his poor eyesight. Instead, he volunteered as a Red Cross ambulance driver and was posted to Italy.

He was badly wounded by shrapnel on July 8, 1918, on the Italian front at Fossalta di Piave, and while recovering had an affair with a nurse, Agnes von Kurowsky. These experiences were later to surface in one of his most famous novels, *A Farewell to Arms* (1929), which narrates the story of a wounded ambulance driver on the Italian front and his passion for the British nurse Catherine Barkley. Hemingway's affair with Agnes proved

shortlived and painful, and following his recuperation he returned to the U.S. in January 1919.

Keen to resume his work in journalism he found a job writing features for the *Toronto Star* almost immediately. In 1920 he was employed as editor of a trade journal in Chicago and while there he met Hadley Richardson, who became his wife in the fall of 1921. Lead by Hemingway's desire to be in Europe, the couple moved to Paris in December of the same year and for the next year and a half the writer traveled extensively around the continent working for the *Toronto Star* as a foreign correspondent covering, in particular, the Greco-Turkish War. While in Paris, Hemingway met Robert McAlmon who published his first serious work; a slim volume called *Three Stories and Ten Poems*. There followed a short move back to Toronto where their first son, John, was born but Hemingway was smitten with Europe and, determined to make his mark as a serious writer, he resigned from the *Star* and the family returned to Paris in early 1924.

His second volume, *In Our Time* (1924), was also published in Paris though not to any great success. However, in 1925 he added a further 14 short stories to the existing

vignettes and the book was taken by New York publisher Boni & Liveright. Hemingway's prose had begun to develop a typically pithy style and the combination of romanticism and stark realism which would characterize his work. The following year two works were published – *The Torrents of Spring* and *The Sun Always Rises* – both of which were praised by critics and bought by the public in increasing amounts. The second of them, drawing on Hemingway's experiences in France and Spain, cemented the author's position as foremost writer of the "lost generation." In 1927 he divorced Hadley and married Pauline Pfieffer with whom he would have a second son, Gregory.

With his reputation firmly set, the next three decades would see Hemingway produce a torrent of superb literature as well as war correspondence from both the Spanish Civil War and World War II, notably participating in the liberation of Paris in 1944. Other novels to be produced include the classics *A Farewell to Arms* (1929), *To Have and Have Not* (1937), *For Whom the Bell Tolls* (1940), *Across the River and into the Trees* (1950), and *The Old Man and the Sea* (1952). In addition to this he also published several volumes of short stories, collaborated on the political film *The Spanish Earth*, and wrote a non-fiction work on bullfighting, *Death in the Afternoon* (1932).

His work as a journalist and his personal wanderlust took Hemingway around the world. He lived for 12 years in Florida but during that time was often to be found dude ranching in Wyoming, fishing off Cuba, or traveling around Europe. From 1933 to 1934 he went on safari through Kenya and Tanzania, returning home to write the non-fiction *Green Hills of Africa* (1935) and two short stories set in Africa. He also purchased an

H

estate in Cuba, La Finca Vigia, reported from China with his third wife, Martha Gellhorn, and, following American entry into World War II, he armed his own cabin cruiser, *Pilar*, and searched the seas of the Caribbean for German submarines for two years. In addition to this he married his fourth wife, Mary Welsh, in 1946.

At the end of his second African safari (1953–54), Hemingway was involved in two airplane crashes which prevented him from collecting his Nobel Peace Prize.

In 1960, Hemingway was hospitalized, suffering from high blood pressure, liver disease, diabetes and the depression that had dogged him for years. On July 2, 1961, in Ketchum, Idaho, he committed suicide by shooting himself with a shotgun. He left behind a large amount of material which would continue to be published for years to come, including the brilliant, *A Moveable Feast* (1964) and *The Garden of Eden* (1986).

His was a life of unparalleled adventure; his words captured the flavors of his age, expressed the thoughts and feelings of a generation, and touched many lives.

H

Himmler, Heinrich
1900–1945
German politician

Himmler joined the Nazi party in 1925 and between
1926–1930 was the director of propaganda. He was
promoted to head of the *Schutzstaffel* (SS) in 1929 and in
1934 was in control of the Gestapo. As Hitler's top
policeman, Himmler crushed Rhom's *Sturmabteiling* or
Brownshirts, turning his SS into the instrument of enforcing
the *Führer*'s will, as well as a model of Aryan racial
"superiority." He put into practice the politico-eugenic
theories he had formulated then on a European scale, with
horrifying results. Himmler exercised overall control of the
concentration camps and the "Final Solution", of which he
told his staff: "it is a page of glory in our history, which will
never be written." He was minister of the interior in 1943,
and later director of home front operations, and commander
of the German forces operating within German borders.
Himmler committed suicide by swallowing poison on
capture by the British in 1945.

Hirohito, Emperor
1901–1989
Japanese monarch

Hirohito was educated in Japan, but was the first Japanese
prince to leave his native land. He acted as regent during his
father's illness, and became emperor in 1926. Having
allowed a militaristic party to dominate the government, he
was drawn into a war with China (1937–45) and an alliance
with the Axis powers, leading to involvement in World War II.
In 1945, Hirohito broadcast an unconditional surrender of
Japan in a search for peace. In co-operation with the Allied
forces, Japan was converted to a democratic nation. Having
publicly renounced his divinity, he signed a new constitution
in 1947, creating a constitutional monarchy that limited his
role to a largely ceremonial function. He avoided prosecution
in the War Crimes trial of 1946–48. He was a keen marine
biologist and was recognized for his studies in this field.

Hoffman, Dustin
1937–
American actor

Although short and unremarkable in looks, talent and brains
have made Hoffman a superstar, bold in his choice of roles
and willing to take chances. He was chosen by Mike Nichols
to play a young man floundering in a cynical world in *The
Graduate* (1967)and went on to prove he wasn't a flash in
the pan with *Midnight Cowboy* (1969). Essentially a character
actor, he went on to choose challenging, rather than
charismatic roles in his movies. In *Little Big Man* (1970) he
aged on screen from adolescence to over 100 years old.
Deftly playing a father who learns to nurture his son in
Kramer vs. Kramer (1979), he at last earned a much-deserved
Academy Award for Best Actor. Then came his sensitive,
subtle performance as a man pretending to be a woman in
Tootsie (1982). Hoffman won his second Best Actor Academy
Award for *Rain Man* (1988).

Hitchcock, Sir Alfred
1899–1980
British film director

Although he trained as an engineer, Hitchcock began his film career working in silent movies, designing the card titles, and working as a scriptwriter before directing in the 1920s. He made the first important British "talkie," *Blackmail* (1929). After a series of movies in the 1930s, such as *The Thirty-Nine Steps* (1935) and *The Lady Vanishes* (1935), he became facinated with psychological thrillers. David O. Selznick managed to persuade Hitchcock, when he was discontented with England's low budgets and lack of technical facilities, to go to Hollywood. His first Hollywood success was *Rebecca* in 1940, adapted from a novel by British writer Daphne du Maurier which won an Academy Award for Best Picture.

His prestige increased during his most creative period in the 1950s when he made some of his most profound and suspenseful movies. These included *Strangers on a Train* (1951), *Rear Window* (1954), *Vertigo* (1958), *North by Northwest* (1959), and *Psycho* (1960). Many of his movies had implausible stories: classic plot lines involved murder or espionage, mistaken identities and an accused innocent trying to clear their name. He was regarded as not only as a master entertainer, but also as a major artist whose sensibilities were acutely attuned to the modern age of anxiety and paranoia. He used new techniques in film editing that were copied the world over in order to manipulate his audience's emotions. Unusual camera angles, acutely placed sound effects, and the feeling everything was there for a reason aided the overall impression.

He was always careful to retain full creative control of all his movies, which impressed the new wave French directors of the 1960s and 1970s such as Jean-Luc Godard and François Truffaut. He is also famous for appearing discreetly and obliquely in all of his movies. In the 1950s and 1960s he introduced and sometimes directed several television series. He received the Irving Thalberg Award from the Academy of Motion Picture Arts and Sciences and in 1979 he received the American Film Institute's Life Achievement Award. In 1980 Queen Elizabeth II of Great Britain knighted him.

H

Hitler, Adolf
1889–1945
Austrian-born German politician

Certainly the most hated and vilified figure of the century, Adolf Hitler single-handedly plunged the world into World War II and is responsible for the deaths of millions. A megalomaniac who formed a totalitarian regime based on principles of Aryan superiority and racism, his drive for power lead to German empiricism and the genocide of countless Jews, who were tortured and killed on his orders in the notorious Nazi concentration camps. His crimes against humanity surpass the imagination and the repercussions of his evil regime have lingered throughout the remainder of the century.

He was born in the Austrian town of Braunau am Inn on April 20, 1889, to Alois and Klara Hitler. His father was a stern and unforgiving man and Adolf idolized his mother; her death in 1907 had a deep impact on him. As a student he was totally incompetent, a fact which lead him to attempt a career as an artist though he was devoid of any talent. Rejected by the Academy of Fine Arts in Vienna, he spent six years in the city where, impoverished, alienated, and hopeless, he found a scapegoat for his plight in the different races of the colorful city. In particular he singled out the Jews as a danger to the "Aryan race" and became obsessed with racial purification.

In 1913 Hitler moved to Munich, avoiding conscription into the Austrian army. However, at the outbreak of World War I he joined the German army, serving in the Bavarian Sixteenth Regiment, and soon found himself relishing army life, embracing the comradeship that he had been previously lacking. Awarded the Iron Cross, First Class for bravery he particularly enjoyed the warrior's glory that the medal conferred. The German defeat in 1918 was a terrible blow to his patriotic enthusiasm, and, once

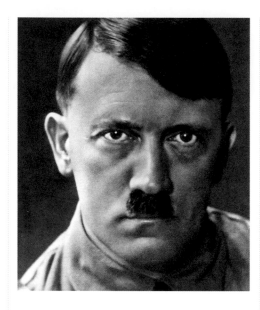

again, he found a scapegoat in the Jews who, he believed, had undermined the war effort.

Post-war Germany, the Weimar Republic, was highly unstable — reparations caused an economic depression and Communists attempted revolution. In response Hitler determined to enter politics. In 1919 he joined a small faction in Munich and transformed it into his own National Socialist Workers' Party within a year. As a leader Hitler had a forum to air his opinions and became adept at delivering vociferous speeches condemning the "enemies" of Germany. In 1923 an overconfident Hitler lead his party in the Munich Putsch, a failed attempt to bring down what he believed to be a government made up of Jews and Marxists. He was imprisoned at Landsberg for his part in the action and before being released, after serving only nine months of a five year sentence, had written *Mein Kampf* (My Struggle). The book was a political diatribe against the perceived enemies of Germany — Jews, Marxists, liberals, decadent capitalists — and crystalized the Nazi philosophy of Aryan purity and elitism as well as calling for

expansion into Europe and Russia.

Quickly re-establishing himself in his party, Hitler's rise in power was slow but indefatigable. By 1925 he had consolidated his position and formed an elite force of trusted lieutenants such as Hermann Goering, Heinrich Himmler, and Joseph Goebbels. By 1930 his was the second largest party in the Reichstag and had its own paramilitary wing — the *Sturmabteilung* (or Brownshirts). In January 1933, he was given the position of Chancellor and two months later the Reichstag passed the Enabling Act which delivered to Hitler four years of unopposed dictatorial power.

Hitler came to power legitimately as an answer to the rise of Communism and to the great slump in Germany but he soon assumed tyrannical powers, disbanding all political parties but his own. When the president, Hindenburg, died in 1934, Hitler also assumed his powers and functions.

The triumph of his will was in creating a Greater Reich, as outlined in *Mein Kampf*, and Hitler named himself the *Führer* (supreme leader). Though enjoying popular support due to Germany's swift economic recovery Hitler reigned with an iron fist; Himmler was charged with creating the SS (*Schutzstaffel*, or Blackshirts) and this powerful force terrorized even the slightest threat to the *Führer*'s power. Abuse of the Jews became more and more systematic; concentration camps were set up by the SS and Gestapo, and in 1935 laws were passed which deprived Jews of their citizenship.

In 1936, in accordance with the dictates that had been laid out in *Mein Kampf*, Germany began to re-arm in contravention of the Versailles treaty. Hitler's objective was a single united Germany which would invade and colonize Eastern Europe. Proceeding cautiously at first, Hitler soon realized that the rest of Europe was prepared to appease him rather than go to war and his plans continued apace.

With his morale boosted in 1939 by the easy annexing of Austria and the unopposed invasion of Czechoslovakia, Hitler ordered the attack of Poland. Poland's integrity was assured by Britain and France and both now declared war on Germany. World War II had begun.

The German campaign was initially highly successful; France soon fell to German armies and the Axis Alliance with fascist Italy meant that these two powers extended control over most of mainland Europe, Scandinavia, and Northern Africa. During the German *Blitzkrieg* campaigns of 1939–40 Hitler was hailed as a great military leader and until the Battle of Britain in late 1940 he had not tasted a single defeat. Within the growing German empire Hitler quickly instituted the "New Order" a regime of terror reinforced by the concentration camps and also set about the "Final Solution," the systematic liquidation of European Jews.

In June 1941, Hitler made his first major error by invading his ideological enemy and previous ally, Russia. In the same year, the United States entered the war against his Japanes allies, an eventuality that Hitler had hardly considered and he was forced to declare war. His single-minded pursuit of his other foe, the Jews, diverted the war effort and lost Germany some of her finest scientific talent, including nuclear physicists.

The German General Staff, who had had their misgivings about the war quelled by the lightning conquest of France, almost invariably deferred to Hitler in the strategy for the Eastern Front. This led to the disaster of Stalingrad. Failure of the Officers' Bomb Plot in July 1, 1944 tightened Hitler's grip on command and he eventually became totally isolated, physically and mentally.

Adolf Hitler committed suicide in his bunker as the Red Army broke into Berlin. The war he had started sounded the death knell of the British Empire, but ironically helped create another: the Communist empire in Eastern Europe.

Holliday, Billie
1915–1959
American jazz singer

The first and arguably the greatest female jazz singer, Holliday possessed unique timing and the ability to turn even a hackneyed lyric into an emotional experience. Born Eleanora Fagan, she had a disrupted childhood and was entertaining in Harlem clubs in her early teens She made her first record with Benny Goodman, and had a sensational success with her stage debut in 1935. Early records included "They Can't Take That Away From Me" with Count Basie (1937) and "Any Old Time" with Artie Shaw (1938), while "Lover Man" (1944) is perhaps her most famous. By the time she toured Europe in 1954 and appeared at the first Newport Jazz Festival, her voice had coarsened and her range narrowed; she died from a kidney infection after years of alcohol and drug abuse. Jazz fans and fellow singers recognized her greatness instantly, but she did not attract a wide public during her lifetime.

Hoover, Herbert Clark
1874–1964
American politician and president

Hoover rose from being a day laborer in a California mine, to mining engineering to become the 31st President of the United States. He achieved world fame with his World War I Commission for Relief in Belgium, which sent five million tons of food and clothing to German-occupied Flanders. In 1917 he was made the U.S. Food Administrator with sweeping powers which were extended eventually to a famished Europe. After the Armistice, Hoover started a European Children's Fund, giving free meals to eight million children, and supervised relief in the Great Russian Famine. He was Harding's Secretary of Commerce and in 1929 succeeded him in the presidency. He was overwhelmed by the Wall Street crash and was defeated by Roosevelt in 1932.

Hope, Bob
1903–
American actor and entertainer

Born Leslie Towne Hope in England, he arrived in Cleveland, Ohio, when he was four years old. He first appeared on Broadway in *The Sidewalks of New York* (1927). Between 1928–32 he worked as a stand-up comic, eventually, winning national attention as a radio comedian. In 1939 he starred in *The Cat and the Canary* with Paulette Goddard, and his popularity became firmly established when he teamed up with Bing Crosby and Dorothy Lamour in a series of "Road" pictures: *The Road to Singapore* (1940), *Road to Zanzibar* (1941), *Road to Utopia* (1946), *Road to Rio* (1947), and *Road to Bali* (1953). He appeared in more than 60 movies. He entertained American troops throughout World War II, the Korean War, the Vietnam War, and the Gulf War. Hope's many television and cabaret appearances, as well as his concerts to entertain the troops, have ensured lasting popularity.

Hoffa, Jimmy Riddle
1913–1975
American union Leader

Hoffa was born in Brazil, Indiana, his father, a coal miner, died when he was seven. He began work at the age of 17 as a warehouseman for the Kroger Company and had his first brush with unions when he organized a strike there. In 1933 he was the Teamster agent in Detroit for Teamster Local 299. By the 1940s he had formed and headed the Michigan Conference of Teamsters. Moving up through the hierarchy, he was vice president of the Teamsters Union in 1952 and international president by 1957. He was renowned as a hard and effective bargainer, somewhat intimidating to

politicians. After organizing the centralization of the administration and bargaining of the Teamsters in the international office, he negotiated a countrywide agreement with trucking companies in 1964, the first such national contract. Such energetic leadership increased the membership of the Teamsters to more than two million, and helped make it the biggest union in the United States.

Throughout his high profile career there were rumors of links with organized crime and Hoffa was subjected to many governmental investigations. He was jailed in 1967 for 13 years for jury tampering, pension fund fraud, and conspiracy. He was offered a deal by Richard Nixon, after lengthy negotiations:

early release on the condition that he resign his office and refrain from any union activities until 1980. He tried to fight the restrictions in court but was unsuccessful. He also allegedly tried to undermine his successor at the Teamsters. His continued efforts to re-establish his position in the union may have contributed to his disappearance in 1975.

Hoffa was last seen at a suburban restaurant in Bloomfield Hills, Michigan, where he had evidently arranged to meet Anthony Provenzano, a Teamster boss and reputed Mafia figure, and Anthony Giacalone, a Detroit mobster. Neither man would admit to having seen Hoffa that day. Hoffa was declared legally dead in 1983.

Horowitz, Vladimir
1904–1989
Russian-American pianist

Making his debut in 1921, Horowitz began his concert career at the relatively late age of 20 but was quick to make an impact on London six years later, with a sensational performance of Rachmaninov's D minor concerto. In the United States, the power, finesse, and tonal mastery of his playing caused a sensation. His career was interrupted by three years of illness, beginning in 1936, from which he recovered and resumed his former position and prestige. He won many awards for his artistry, including the Royal Philharmonic Society Gold Medal (1972). He made a well-publicized comeback tour of the Soviet Union in the 1980s, performing there for the first time in 61 years.

Hubble, Edwin Powell
1889–1953
American astronomer

Hubble, for whom NASA's space telescope is named, was actually a law student who turned to astronomy. Early in his career (1914–17) he was associated with Yerkes Observatory at the University of Chicago. He joined Mount Wilson Observatory in California where he worked with the newly opened 100 inch (250 cm) reflector and, in the 1920s, made two of the most significant discoveries in astronomy. First he proved that so-called "spiral nebulae" were actually separate galaxies beyond the Milky Way. Then, in 1929, he announced his shattering conclusion that the universe is expanding like a balloon being inflated. The galaxies are moving apart at speeds that increase with distance; this is known as Hubble's Law and is the foundation of modern cosmology. After 1948 Hubble supervised research at the 200 inch (508 cm) telescope at Paloma Observatory.

Hussein, Saddam
1937–
Iraqi politician

Saddam Hussein emerged as a key figure after the Ba'athist coup of 1968 and became Iraqi President in 1979. It wasn't until his move to the capital in 1955 that he took an interest in politics and joined the Arab nationalist movement. After studying law in Cairo, he returned to a successful career in the Ba'athist party. He played a major role in domestic politics, negotiating an agreement with separatist Kurdish leaders giving them autonomy. This later collapsed, leading to brutal fighting. He was also involved with nationalizing the country's oil industry, Iraq's main source of wealth. He consolidated his dictatorship with a war against the Ayatollah Khomeini's fundamentalist Iran. This eight-year struggle was followed by the invasion of Kuwait in 1990 and the American-led United Nation's counter-attack to liberate it. A dangerous maverick in Middle East politics, especially since surviving the Gulf War, he continues to have the upper hand in the psychological war that has followed, particularly over dismantling his chemical arsenal.

H

Hoover, J. Edgar
1895–1972
American lawyer and FBI director

For over 50 years from 1924 until his death, Hoover was synonymous with the FBI (Federal Bureau of Investigation). He initially studied law and was admitted to the bar in 1917, joining the staff of the United States Department of Justice in the same year. First serving as a file reviewer, he was appointed assistant to the Attorney General two years later. He was steadily promoted, rising to be the head of the Bureau of Investigations of the Department of Justice in 1924. This division became the Federal Bureau of Investigations in 1934, and J. Edgar Hoover was named its director. He remained there for 48 years, serving under every president from Coolidge to Nixon.

Hoover instituted many techniques and procedures that were effective in the apprehension of criminals. Hoover is to be credited with organizing the FBI to be a proficient and professional department. He set up a fingerprint file, which once established, developed into the world's largest scientific crime detection laboratory.

His national security policing concentrated on making the FBI the most efficient law-enforcement administration ever. From the gangsters of prohibition, to the Communist subversives of the 1950s to the Civil Rights protesters of the 1960s, Hoover's officers surveyed every aspect of national security. During World War II, Hoover's officers worked in counter-espionage and anti-sabotage. They were highly successful in preventing German and Japanese agents from interfering with the Allies war effort. However, while investigating almost every radical group he maintained a hands-off policy toward the Mafia, who were able to operate without hindrance.

In later years, Hoover's reign over the FBI was criticized, and he was accused of exceeding his legal jurisdiction. He remained a controversial figure, but his contribution to modern police investigative methods was a lasting legacy. His writings include *Persons in Hiding* (1938), *Masters of Deceit* (1958), *A Study of Communism* (1962), and *Crime in the United States* (1965).

H

Hughes, Howard
1905–1976
American entrepreneur, millionaire

A pioneering aviator, movie-maker, and businessman, Hughes was the richest man in America of his time and also the strangest.

His father, Howard, known as "Big Howard," was owner of Hughes Tool Company and inventor of a successful oil drilling bit which had made him a small fortune. "Little Howard" was born on Christmas Eve, 1905 and experienced a disconcerting childhood, attending no less than seven schools and graduating from none of them. As a boy he would spend hours on end in a workshop that his father had presented Howard when he was six. Here he explored his fascination with mechanical objects, building his own radio at the age of 11, and at 13, having been refused one by his father, his own motorcycle. After a disappointing and short career at Harvard, Howard won a bet with his father and, against the wishes of his family, chose flying lessons as his prize; thus starting a passion for aviation.

In the fall of 1923 Hughes' mother died to be followed a little over a year later by his father. Hughes was now 17 and the owner of 75% of Hughes Tools. Under the conditions of his father's will he was to be granted control of the company at 21: Howard appealed against this in court and won. At 18 the young man now had an annual income of approximately $2 million. Aware that he did not possess the skills necessary for running the business, Hughes appointed accountant Noah Dietrich as manager. Dietrich's interview lasted a week, during which he accompanied Hughes on a rail ride across America. Not once during the trip was the business mentioned but at the end of it Hughes announced

that Dietrich was hired. He would go on to manage Hughes Tool Company for 30 years.

In 1925 Hughes agreed to help finance a film project in Hollywood provided that he was allowed unlimited access to the set. His first movie, *Swell Hogan*, was a flop but Hughes, with typical dedication, learned everything he could of the business of making movies. On one memorable night he was found dismantling a projector to see how it worked and by the morning had rebuilt it to perfect working order. Enthralled by show business Hughes, then in his early twenties, bought controlling shares in a chain of theaters and a company developing color film. During the next two years he worked with director Lewis Milestone to make three acclaimed movies, the last of which, *Two Arabian Knights*, won the 1927 Academy Award for Best Comedy.

By 1932 Hughes was bored of the film industry and, though he continued to pursue financial interests in the business, he turned to his former enthusiasm for flying for new excitement. Consequently, he took a job with American Airlines as a baggage handler and co-pilot for the wage of $250 per week under the name of Charles Howard. Leaving after a few weeks he next bought a seaplane and helped customize it to his own specifications before spending 18 months flying it across America with mechanic and co-pilot Glen Odekirk. He was growing increasingly eccentric, landing on a whim and disappearing for days on end before returning to Odekirk to resume the flight.

There followed a passion for racing his aircraft and Hughes spent two years working closely beside

Odekirk and engineer Dick Palmer developing his own plane, the H-1. After toiling ceaselessly, sometimes around the clock, the aircraft was finished in 1935 and Hughes insisted that its maiden flight would be registered for the record books with himself at the controls. It easily shattered the existing air speed record and Hughes became a national celebrity overnight.

The next landmark in Hughes' life came when he purchased a majority shareholding in the small and ailing company of TWA. With an injection of his cash and a plan to provide the world's first transatlantic passenger flights, the company would become

H

one of the most successful of its time — pouring huge profits into Hughes coffers. In the late 1950s, however, the company placed Hughes in an extremely unusual position. Keen to become self-controlling, TWA sued Hughes for his shares: as chairman he was effectively financing a lawsuit against himself. The company won and Hughes received payment of $750,000,000 for his share of the business, becoming the richest man in the world and America's first billionaire in one transaction.

The latter part of Hughes life remains shrouded by mystery and the little that is known portrays him sinking into drug addiction and increasing insanity. His refusal to pay taxes saw him disappear into a reclusive world where he surrounded himself with Mormons as well as his trusted advisor, ex-FBI agent Robert Maheu, whose job it was to keep him ahead of the law and away from the public. He refused to use the telephone and insisted that any item that he handled be covered with a Kleenex towel. In 1966 Maheu moved Hughes to the penthouse suite at the Desert Inn in Las Vegas. After six months the management asked him to leave. Hughes responded by buying the hotel. He then bought several more casinos including the Silver Slipper because its lights shone through his window and annoyed him.

Howard Hughes was an extremely complex individual – a talented and inventive engineer, organizer, playboy, businessman, a brave aviator, and eccentric – who always finished what he set out to do, no matter what the cost. He was married twice but his attempts to totally control his two wives soon brought divorce, and he also had a passion for beautiful men. Hughes created some lasting achievements such as the films *The Front Page* (1931) and *Scarface* (1932) but, sadly, will be remembered mostly for his insanity. He died on board an airplane on April 5, 1976, and left no legally valid will.

Huston, John
1906–1987
American film director

Huston tried his hand at a number of professions before settling on a career in the movies. A maverick movie-maker he was noted for his association with Humphrey Bogart on *The Maltese Falcon* (1941), *The Treasure of the Sierra Madre* (1948) and *The African Queen* (1952), and for some of the screen's most intelligent literary adaptations, such as *Moby Dick* (1956), and *The Dead* (1987). Huston was intrigued by characters who pursue their dreams to the point of obsession: even when they fail. He is impressed by the grandeur of their aspirations. His direction helped win Oscars not only for himself (*Sierra Madre*) but his family: Walter Huston (*Sierra Madre*) and his daughter Anjelica (*Prizzi's Honor*). He was awarded the Legion of Merit and was promoted to the rank of major for making three documentaries for the United States Army during World War II.

Jobs, Steve
1955–
American home computers designer

Famed for his vision, Jobs dropped out of college in 1972 to design video games for Atari. But when he and Steve Wozniak teamed up in Jobs' parents' garage to build the Apple II, he became the marketing man, and was responsible for purchasing. He has a reputation for being driven and it was this nature which led to the success of the Apple Macintosh. In the 1980s he sold his shares at a low price in order to set up NeXT Inc., making powerful and stylish home computers, however they subsequently concentrated on making software. In 1986, he acquired the computer division of Lucas Films, which include Pixar Animation Studios, producers of the highly successful groundbreaking *Toy Story* in 1985. Jobs has again been instrumental in the revival of Apple computers where he has been working since 1997.

Jordan, Michael
1963–
American basketball player

Regarded by many as the greatest player ever, Michael Jordan has had an exceptional basketball career. He started with the Chicago Bulls in 1984 and was named Rookie of the Year. He led the NBA in scoring for seven consecutive seasons (1987–1993). He headed the team, the Chicago Bulls, which won its first NBA championship title in 1991, and won again in 1992, 1993, 1996, and 1997. Jordan was also a member of the United States Olympic basketball team that captured the gold medal at the 1992 Olympics and the 1996 Olympics.

Jordan announced his retirement in 1994, but after a year playing baseball for the Birmingham Barons (an affiliate of the Chicago White Sox) he returned to basketball. He is the only player to have received the league MVP four times.

Jackson, Michael
1958–
American pop singer

Jackson joined his brothers' band at the age of 5. His dancing ability as well as his singing made him the natural leader of the group. After eight years with the Jackson Five the young Michael had limited success with his first two solo efforts. The next two albums missed the top forty altogether and it wasn't until the 1979 album *Off the Wall* that he found his feet. *Thriller* (1982) made No. 1 on both sides of the Atlantic, earning an unprecedented eight Grammy awards and showed he had made the transition from precocious teenager to mature recording artist

once and for all.

The Jacksons reformed for a tour in 1984 to promote their album *Victory*. In 1985 along with Lionel Richie, Jackson co-wrote "We are the World" a song performed by over 40 musicians. The profits from audio and video sales went to alleviate world hunger.

The 1987 album *Bad* enjoyed similar success, and he was soon established as one of the most successful entertainers ever, grossing over $100 million in 1990 alone.

His next album, *Dangerous* (1991), and the single "Remember the Time" (1991) were also bestsellers. In 1995 the double album *HIStory* was released after a period of unflattering publicity worldwide. Half of the album is a

compilation of the most successful songs from *Thriller*, *Bad*, and *Dangerous*, while the other half is a collection of original compositions. In 1996 Jackson won a Grammy Award for the music video "Scream" (1995), which he created with his sister Janet. That same year he and Lisa Marie Presley, daughter of the late rock singer Elvis Presley, whom he had wed in 1994, divorced after 18 months of marriage. In 1996, he married for the second time to Deborah Rowe, an assistant to his dermatologist. They have two children, Prince Michael Jackson Jr. (b.1997) and Paris Michael Katherine (b.1998). Jackson's autobiography, *Moonwalk*, was published in 1988.

John Paul II
1920–
Polish Pontiff

For almost 2,000 years the popes have wielded power and influence that makes the fleeting reigns of monarchs, ministers, and tyrants seem insignificant in comparison. John Paul II is the latest Pope in a dynasty which can trace its roots directly back to St Peter, Christ's appointed vicar. As such he holds sway over the Catholic people of the globe — a population of billions — and commands respect from believer and non-believer alike. A man of charisma, piety, and energy, John Paul II has traveled more than any Pope before in his mission to spread the word of God and strengthen the church for the coming millennium.

He was born Karol Wojtyla on May 18, 1920, in Wadowice, near Krakow, in a Polish state that was to enjoy just a few more years of liberty before it was carved up by the Nazis and the Russians at the beginning of World War II. As a young man he suffered two grievous blows — first the death of his mother, then the death of Edmund, his brother, who was struck down with scarlet fever, contracted from a patient he was trying to save in a hospital where he worked as a doctor. They were profound events that were to draw Karol closer to God and then the priesthood.

Karol was a popular boy at school, good at soccer and other sports; he also had a natural charm that endeared him to young women. After school he became a student in Polish literature at the Jagiellonian University of Krakow, where he displayed a keen ability in foreign languages and continued to pursue his love of outdoor sports. When the Germans invaded, however, they targeted intellectuals, and the university professors were arrested, forcing the college to close. Karol became a chemical worker and a laborer in a

limestone quarry, continuing his studies in secret with a friend and a teacher who had evaded arrest.

In 1942, he vanished, following his father's death. While relatives surmised that he had been rounded up by Germans for shipment to a slave labor camp, in actuality he had been taken to the house of the archbishop of Krakow with four other clandestine students to continue his

studies in safety. It was while he was under the cleric's tutelage that he decided once and for all on a career in the priesthood.

He was nearly eliminated by the Nazis in August 1944, when the Germans made a sweep of Krakow to prevent young men and intellectuals from rising up as the Red Army was banging on the gates of the city. Karol survived by hiding in the basement of an apartment that the Nazis, in their haste, didn't search.

With the war over and the university reopened, he continued his studies. He actively studied for the priesthood as well, receiving ordination on November 1, 1946, the Feast of All Saints. On the next day, he celebrated his first mass.

The lure of the Eternal City was a powerful one for the young priest. He decided to resume his studies at the Angelicum University in Rome where he received a doctorate in ethics. Further degrees in philosophy followed at Lubelin University in Krakow where, in 1964, he was appointed archbishop. In 1967 he achieved election to the College of Cardinals thanks to the patronage of Paul VI. He was then 47 and the second-youngest living cardinal. Before he even achieved this dignified post he made himself an authority in the church on matters ranging from birth control (to which he was, and remains, steadfastly opposed) to the education of Africans in missionary schools. He had become so influential by the mid-1960s that it was his treatise on contraception that persuaded the pope in 1968 to issue his *Humanae Vitae* encyclical, in which he reinforced the papacy's ban on all methods of artificial birth control.

The conclave that was to elect him came with the death of John Paul I in 1978. When the two-day conclave was over, 99 out of 108 cardinals gave

J

their vote to Karol Wojtyla. He accepted and took the name John Paul II.

It soon became obvious that the new Pope would not be content to be a simple figurehead. His targets were the regimes of Eastern Europe, and it was arguably his return to Poland that set in motion events that would lead to the collapse of the Iron Curtain countries. He landed there in June 1979, despite the attempts of Breznhev, the Soviet leader, to persuade the Polish Communists to cancel his visit, and delivered an address that would sweep away decades of church policy, stating: "Christ cannot be excluded from human history in any part of the globe, from any latitude or longitude of the earth. Excluding Christ from human history is a sin against humanity."

In the first 100 days of his pontificate, John Paul II honed his vision for the church. He exhorted priests not to water down the mission of the church; he championed celibacy before marriage and fidelity in it; he lambasted abortion and praised mothers who refused to have them even when their own lives were at risk; he instructed American bishops to keep a close eye on church discipline and stood firmly against women priests, despite hopes that he would be susceptible to the idea. The Pope began to move with the speed of an international celebrity and executive rather than an elderly religious cleric. He was carried in a "pope-mobile" so that people could see him, organized mass rallies, photo opportunities, kissed babies, and induced hysteria wherever he went.

However, on May 13, 1981 disaster nearly struck when a fanatic, Mehmet Ali Agca, fired several shots — two of which hit the Pope as he drove around St Peter's Square. John Paul II was wounded in his right elbow, the stomach, and the index finger of his left hand. Fortune was smiling on the Holy Father: doctors discovered that one bullet had missed his central aorta by a fraction of an inch. He later visited his would-be killer in a Roman prison, comforting him as he dropped to his knees and begged forgiveness.

Now an old man who has undergone an operation for a cancerous tumor, a man who looks tired at public meetings, Pope John Paul II — *Time*'s 1995, Man of the Year and an international best-selling author with his book *Crossing the Threshold of Hope* — has no intention of giving up. He wants to lift the "Bamboo Curtain" on Chinese Catholics and he is set against President Clinton, who supports abortion and birth control rights in America. The Pope's message is as loud and clear as it ever was as he leads a church more united, stronger, and better equipped than it ever has been in the history of the papacy.

J

Joyce, James
1882–1941
Irish writer and poet

Although his output was comparatively small, his experimental writing made Joyce one of the major figures of literary modernism; no one has had more influence on the development of the modern novel. On return from Paris he met Nora Barnacle, with whom he lived from 1904 and married in 1931; they left for Trieste where he taught English and subsequently moved to Zurich in 1915. *Chamber Music* (1907), a collection of poems, was his first published work, followed by *The Dubliners* in 1914. The autobiographical *A Portrait of the Artist as a Young Man* appeared in 1916. His one play, *Exiles* (1918), was never a success. His greatest novel, *Ulysses* (1922), was banned for obscenity but hailed as a masterpiece. *Finnegan's Wake*, his last and most difficult work, written in spite of terrible eye infections, was published complete in 1939.

Jackson, Jesse Louis
1941–
American religious and political leader

During his time at college Jackson committed himself to the Civil Rights movement, and soon became associated with Martin Luther King Jr. He graduated from Chicago Theological College in 1966 and worked for Operation Breadbasket, whose aim was to encourage business to employ more black workers and end discriminatory practices. Later he formed PUSH, which was a more radical organization with a similar aim. Always known for his eloquent speeches, he was a well-known Civil Rights activist by the 1980s. In 1984 he was a candidate for the Democratic presidential nomination and he ran for the nomination again in 1988. Jackson is an excellent negotiator, and has used his skills to secure the release of high-profile American hostages, most memorably in Kuwait during the Gulf War (1990) and during the Kosova Crisis of 1999.

Kissinger, Henry
1923–
American politician

Born in Germany, Kissinger became a U.S. citizen five years after arriving with his parents in 1938. He served in the U.S. Army between 1943–46. He taught at Harvard in the department of government in 1954, and served as occasional foreign policy advisor to Presidents throughout the 1950s and 60s. In 1969 he became Assistant for National Security affairs for President Nixon. Kissinger's years as U.S. Secretary of State (1973–77) saw diplomatic relations resumed with China, the end of the Vietnam War, and the start of the SALT (Strategic Arms Limitation) agreements with Russia. His peripatetic diplomacy, the Pax Americana, was less effective, however, in pacifying the Middle East after the 1973 war, and his "pre-emptive" strike against Cambodia in 1975 has been widely blamed for leading to the Khmer Rouge coup and resulting holocaust. In 1973 he receive the Nobel Peace prize for negotiating an end to Vietnam War.

Jung, Carl Gustav
1875–1961
Swiss psychologist

Jung had a wide background in life sciences, and started his work on word association at university. He believed that a patient's responses to stimulus words revealed "complexes," a term which has since become universal. This work brought him international recognition, and led to some collaboration with Freud. With the publication of *Psychology of the Unconscious* (1912; trans. 1916), however he separated from Freud over the issue of infantile sexuality. Jung emphasized the importance of the quality of parent-child relationships and the effect of parental disorder on children. In 1921 he produced a major work, *Psychological Types* (trans. 1923),

where he dealt with the relationship between the conscious and unconscious and proposed the now well-known personality types, extrovert and introvert. He argued that, in addition to the "personal unconscious," there was a "collective unconscious," the latter relating to racial experiences and collective beliefs, built up over generations. Jung theorized that by understanding how the personal unconscious is linked to the collective unconscious a patient could achieve a state of individualism of wholeness of self. He developed his theories, drawing on a wide knowledge of mythology, history, and travels to diverse cultures, stressing the importance of religion and symbolism. His psychotherapeutic studies were particularly successful on middle-aged or elderly patients, who felt that they

had lost meaning to their lives. Many had lost religious belief.

His influence was considerable, and led to the development of the school of Analytical Psychology. He was one of the first psychiatrists to attempt a psychological understanding of schizophrenia. He wrote extensively on his subject, especially on analytical methods and the relationship between psychology and religious belief. In later years he was professor of psychology at the Federal Polytechnical University in Zurich (1933–41) and professor of medical psychology at the University of Basel (1943). Jung believed that Germany held a special place in the Europe, and the rise of the Nazis was a significant event to him. He was branded (wrongly) a Nazi sympathizer after he delivered some hotly contested opinions.

K

Kennedy, John Fitzgerald
1917–1963
American politician and president

The world mourned when John F. Kennedy was shot dead by an assassin. A charismatic, charming, and articulate man, he was a president beloved by the people who elected him and greatly admired around the world.

John Kennedy was born in Brookline, Massachusetts on May 29, 1917. Descended from Irish Catholics, who had crossed the Atlantic in the previous century, his father, Joseph Kennedy, was a respected and skillful businessman who became a multi-millionaire, head of the Securities and Exchange Commission, and ambassador to Great Britain under Franklin Roosevelt.

John's educational career was exceptional, culminating in the publication of his Harvard honors thesis on British foreign policies of the 1930s, called *Why England Slept*, in 1940 — the same year of his graduation. Soon after, in 1941, Kennedy joined the U.S. Navy and during World War II was assigned the command of the PT109, a boat which was sunk by the Japanese in 1943. Kennedy showed genuine heroism during the event and saved several of his crew. However, due to malaria and a back injury he was discharged in 1945.

Kennedy's career in politics began the following year when he was elected to the House of Representatives. A popular congressman, he supported social legislation that aided his working class constituents and advocated the firm anti-Communist foreign policy that would characterize his career.

In 1952 he was elected to the Senate and a year later married Jacqueline Bouvier. As a senator his term was somewhat lackluster, partly because recurring back problems prevented him from taking his seat throughout much of 1954 and 1955. During his illness however, Kennedy compiled the biographies of a number of American political heroes. The resulting book, *Profiles in Courage* (1956), won him a Pulitzer Prize for biography in 1957.

After an unsuccessful attempt to be nominated as the Democratic Vice-President in 1956, Kennedy raised his ambitions to the White House and with the financial backing of his family created a well organized campaign that won him the nomination in the first ballot. Realizing that as a northern Roman Catholic his popularity would be weak in the south he wisely chose Senator Lyndon Johnson of Texas as his running mate and built a highly effective election campaign based on tough defense, health, housing, Civil Rights, and a dynamic economic plan.

In 1961 Kennedy was elected the youngest ever president and the first Roman Catholic to occupy the White House. Nevertheless, it was by a very small majority and many of his domestic policies would be stopped by Congress. As president he immediately acted on his antipathy to Communism and ordered the Bay of Pigs invasion of Cuba in April 1961. The resulting rout by Castro's forces was an embarrassment to the new president and to regain popular support he pushed forward the ideals of the American space program with its aim of putting a man on the moon by the end of the decade. Kennedy's anti-Communist policies also caused tension at meetings with Soviet premier Nikita Khrushchev in the same year and resulted in the construction of the Berlin Wall. The American president used this as an excuse to appropriate increased funds from Congress for defense.

The Cuban Missile Crisis of 1962 brought to a head the East-West Cold War conflict. Finding that the Soviets were building and stocking nuclear missile launch pads in Communist Cuba, Kennedy ordered a naval and air blockade of the island. For a period of two weeks relations between the U.S. and the Soviet Union were strained to breaking point before the Soviets eventually backed down in exchange for an American promise that it would not interfere with Cuba. Possibly as a result of this, 1963 saw the two powers sign a treaty banning the atmospheric testing of nuclear weapons.

Nevertheless, Kennedy remained as emphatic as ever in his attempts to stop the spread of Communism, supplying financial and military aid to South Vietnam throughout 1963.

By the end of 1963 the presidential campaign of 1964 was looming, and Kennedy traveled to Dallas to promote the Democrat cause. While driving in a motorcade on November 22 he was shot in the head and died soon after. The killer was named as Lee Harvey Oswald and no motive could be found for the shooting. Conspiracy theories have since multiplied though little evidence can be found to support any.

Kennedy Onassis, Jacqueline Bouvier
1929–1994
American first lady

Jackie Bouvier was born in Southampton, New York, on July 28, 1929. A gifted student, she was educated at Vassar College, the Sorbonne in Paris, and Washington University. After graduating she took a job as a reporter and photographer before marrying John Kennedy in 1953. Their first child was sadly stillborn and another died during infancy but two children, Caroline (1957–) and John (1960–) survived.

As first lady, Jackie was often uncomfortable with the demands of her role and her partnership with her husband was often strained due to his relationships with other women. However, she proved equal to the task and became a sophisticated fashion setter and a patron of the arts.

At Kennedy's funeral she impressed the nation with her courage and stoicism and for many years she was an international celebrity, representing the acme of style and class. In 1968 she caused a furor by marrying again, to Greek shipping magnate Aristotle Onassis, but her role as a fashion icon was unaffected.

Following the death of her second husband she surprised the nation yet again by returning to work, despite having a considerable personal fortune, and until her death in 1994 was employed as an editor in the book publishing houses of New York City.

K

Khomeini, Ruhollah [Rohollah Hendi],
1900–1989
Iranian politician and theologian

Khomeini confined himself to teaching theology in Qom until the modernizing policies instituted by the Shah of Iran led him to take an increasingly radical political stance. He was particularly vocal against the "White" revolution that introduced many western ideas such as equal rights for women and secular (non-religious) education in 1960. He became the focal point for unrest and in 1964 was banished to Iraq. In 1978 he was declared *persona non grata* and took refuge in France from where he unleashed a propaganda campaign that in 1979 brought down the Shah. The Ayatollah's theocracy became a byword for doctrinaire extremism and the many thousands who died in his prisons were matched by the losses in the long war he waged with Iraq.

Khrushchev, Nikita
1894–1971
Soviet politician

As Soviet Prime Minister (1958–64) Khrushchev dismantled the Stalinist system which he had survived by becoming clown prince to the tyrant. But similar clowning, as at the United Nations, did not delude foreign statesmen about his propensity for dangerous brinkmanship. His adventurism twice threatened war: in Hungary in 1956, and more seriously in the Cuban missile crisis in 1962. He was the first publicly to confirm the Stalinist Terror and along with Bulganin he became the embodiment of the new thaw of peaceful co-existence. Khrushchev was also instrumental in encouraging the Soviet space program, which saw the launch of Sputnik I in 1957, as well as building up an arsenal of nuclear weapons. Rivals toppled him in 1964 after his attempts to reorganize the party, the state structure, and, to radically increase agricultural production.

Keller, Helen Adam
1880–1968
American author

Keller was left deaf and blind after a childhood infection. No method was found to educate her until she was seven, when a teacher from the Perkins Institute for the Blind — Anne Mansfield Sullivan (later Macy) — devised a method of teaching her to read and write. Using Braille, she was able to write using a special typewriter. She learned to speak in 1890 after a month of lessons, and in 1904 she graduated from Radcliffe College with honors.

Throughout her life she worked tirelessly to raise funds for the American Foundation for the Blind. She went on lecture tours worldwide across Europe, Africa, Japan, and Australia. Keller was a socialist and pacifist, but after World War II she visited veterans in American hospitals. She wrote about her life in several books.

K

King, Billie-Jean
1943–
American tennis player

As a young girl in California, Billie-Jean King worked at odd jobs to save for her first tennis racket; she went on to become one of the top players in the history of the women's game. In 1961 with partner Karen Hantz she won the Wimbledon doubles — the youngest team to win at that time. In 1962, aged 18, she defeated the leading women's player of the day, Margaret Smith Court, at Wimbledon. Throughout her long career she won 12 Grand Slam singles titles, including three in 1972, and she won a record 20 Wimbledon championships, including six in singles play, ten in doubles play and four in the mixed doubles. She turned professional in 1968 and in 1971 she became the first woman tennis player to make $100,000 in a year. King's other major victories during her career included the singles title at the 1968 Australian championships (later the Australian Open) and at the 1972 French Open.

An advocate of equality in women's sports, she famously secured a victory over former men's star Bobby Riggs in an exhibition match, heralded as a "Battle of the Sexes," in 1973. The match recorded the largest television audience and largest prize money at the time. She helped found the Women's Tennis Association, and the Women's Sports Foundation, an organization dedicated to enhancing women's sporting experience. She campaigned relentlessly for a separate women's tour and obtained financial backing for it from several high profile sponsors. In 1974 she and husband Larry King started World Team Tennis, but after financial problems it folded in 1978. She revived it again on a smaller scale in 1981.

After retiring from playing she worked as a player-coach for the Philadelphia Freedoms, the first women to coach professional male athletes. She has also worked as a commentator, and in 1996 was coach to the United States team at the Olympic Games in Atlanta.

K

King, Martin Luther, Jr.
1929–1968
American Civil Rights leader

Martin Luther King Jr. was a towering symbol of moral leadership and social change. He devoted his life to the fight for equality for all oppressed groups — the poor, disadvantaged, and, particularly, the African American population of America. A student of the teachings of Mahatma Gandhi, his tactics of non-violent civil disobedience and public displays of dissatisfaction through rallies and mass marches were highly effective, and forced changes to the constitution of the United States.

He was born in Atlanta, Georgia, on January 15, 1929, to the Reverend Michael (later Martin) and his wife Alberta Williams King. The second of three children, he grew up in a devout and politically active family who embraced the church as a means to social change for African Americans. He studied at Morehouse College and came under the influence of the college president, Benjamin Mays, and other members of the Christian activism group whose politics of radical change made King determined to become a minister in order to serve society. He received a bachelor's degree in sociology from Morehouse in 1948, went on to Crozer Theological College, and finally studied at Boston University where he gained a doctorate in philosophy in 1955. It was here that he met Coretta Scott. The couple married in 1953 and the following year King rejected various offers of academic employment and accepted his first pastorate at the Dexter Avenue Baptist Church in Montgomery.

Within a year of his arrival a local Civil Rights activist, Rosa Parks, flouted segregation laws on public transport. She sparked a year-long boycott of the bus service by local African Americans which was organized and lead by King. Despite his house being bombed and charges being brought of conspiracy to interfere with the company's operation, Montgomery's public transport was eventually desegregated in 1956 and the success of the action brought the pastor into the national limelight as a leader for the Civil Rights movement. King immediately started an energetic campaign, traveling the country, speaking publicly of the injustice of inequality, and working on a book, *Stride Towards Freedom* (1958).

Seeking to build on the momentum of the Montgomery campaign, he joined with other black ministers to found the Southern Christian Leadership Conference (SCLC) of which he was voted president. He also continued to travel tirelessly, promoting the SCLC agenda of black voting-rights. Keen to increase his understanding of Gandhi's peaceful insurgence, King next toured India in 1959. At the end of that year he moved back to Atlanta to be closer to the SCLC headquarters and became co-pastor of the Ebenezer Baptist Church with his father.

Though his public profile as a black spokesperson increased, King was initially careful not to initiate mass protest. But in 1960 a wave of student protest escalated black assertion. King was sympathetic to the Student Nonviolent Coordinating Committee (SNCC), speaking at their founding meeting and joining a sit-in. The two organizations, the SNCC and SCLC, though occasionally in conflict, would assist each other in organizing some of the historic mass rallies which took place in the following few years. The most memorable of these would be the huge March on Washington on August 28, 1963, where King made his momentous "I Have a Dream" speech. Soon after, in January 1964, he was elected the first African-American Man of the Year by *Time* magazine. During the same year he was awarded the Nobel Peace Prize.

The protests culminated in a major success for King and his supporters in the passing of the Civil Rights Act of 1964. King was jubilant but determined to go on fighting inequality.

Despite the celebrity and adulation that he attracted, King's leadership of the Civil Rights movement was constantly threatened during its later stages; notably by Malcom X who condoned violent self-defense and, rather than King's peaceful integration, promoted the notion of Black Nationalism. Malcolm X's message attracted many followers among African Americans in the northern cities and King was hard pressed to maintain control over the movement to a sufficient degree that it would not impede the passage of the 1965 Voting Rights Act.

Other forces were also gathering to impede his progress. The director of the FBI, J. Edgar Hoover, stepped up his program to curtail King's efforts fearing an escalation of the already intensifying white counter-protest which was bringing violence to the streets of urban areas. King's criticism of American action in Vietnam and the drain on anti-poverty finances that it caused also initiated a depletion of support from white liberals. Nevertheless, King stuck to his principles and spent the early part of 1968 making plans for another huge march on Washington to demand an "Economic Bill of Rights" which would end all forms of discrimination.

Responding to his conscience, however, King stopped his organizational work and flew to Memphis to join a strike by the city's sanitation workers. There, on April 4, 1968, he was shot dead by James Earl Ray. Martin Luther King's death was seen as a plot to undermine the cause and immediately sparked riots in black communities around America — many are still convinced that Ray was a part of a larger conspiracy.

In 1983, January 15, King's birthday was designated a public holiday. He remains one of the most admired and revered men of the 20th century and his mark on society is indelible.

K

Kelly, Gene
1912–1996
American actor, dancer, choreographer, and film director

His mother taught Kelly in her Pittsburgh dance school before he entered Pittsburgh University, where he directed the annual graduation "Cap and Gown" shows. In 1939 he went to New York and appeared in musicals, but his big break came in 1949 in *Pal Joey,* which was almost immediately recreated for the screen in Hollywood. He subsequently appeared in and co-directed such popular film musicals as *On the Town* (1949) and *Singin' in the Rain* (1952). The most ambitious of his dance productions were for *An American in Paris* (1952) and *Invitation to the Dance* (1956). Less well known, however, is his ballet *Pas de Deux* (1960) for the Paris Opera Ballet, set to music by George Gershwin. Throughout his career, Kelly received several honors.

Lawrence, T.E. [Thomas Edward]
1888–1935
British soldier and author

"Lawrence of Arabia" was an outstanding scholar, and the research for his thesis *Crusader Castles* (1936) enabled him to travel to the Middle East. On the outbreak of World War I he was assigned to military intelligence in Egypt, his empathy and understanding of the Arab world making him the ideal candidate. In 1916 Lawrence became adviser to Prince Faisal in Arabia, assisting in his revolt against the Arabs' Turkish rulers and protecting the British advance into Syria. At the peace conference, at the end of the war, Lawrence became disillusioned by the great powers' lack of interest in giving a just settlement to the Arabs. In 1922 Lawrence joined the RAF in an effort to live anonymously. Soon after his retirement in 1935, he was killed in a motorcylce accident. Lawrence was also a writer, his most famous work being the autobiographical, *The Seven Pillars of Wisdom* (1926).

Lindbergh, Charles, Brigadier General
1902–1974
American engineer and pilot

Tall and handsome, Lindbergh learnt to fly in 1922. He became a celebrity overnight after making the first non-stop solo flight from New York to Paris, crossing the North Atlantic on May 20–21, 1927, and winning a $25,000 prize offered by Franco-American philanthropist Raymond B. Orteig. Arriving in Paris in the *Spirit of St. Louis,* he was greeted as a hero. As an advisor to US Airlines, he flew surveys with his wife over the North Pacific, North Atlantic, and Arctic for air routes and landing fields. The kidnap and murder of their son and their subsequent press hounding led to their move to England in 1935. He returned to America in 1939, and campaigned for American neutrality in World War II but later helped improve warplanes. He flew combat missions across the Pacific and in Europe for the United States Air Force. Post-war, he worked with PanAm and the USAF ballistic missiles program.

L

Lenin, Vladimir Ilyich
1870–1924
Russian statesman

A revolutionary and founder of the
Bolshevik party, Lenin was upheld for
over 65 years as the founder of the
Soviet Union. Having studied
Marxism at the University of St
Petersburg, his involvement with
revolutionary politics earned him three
years' exile in Siberia from 1897. He
moved to Switzerland in 1900. In
1901 he changed his name from V. I.
Ulyanov to V. I. Lenin to confuse
police, after his elder brother had been
hanged for planning to assassinate
Tsar Alexander III. He became leader
of the Bolsheviks in 1903, but
remained in exile abroad until 1917

except for a brief return to Russia
during the abortive revolution of 1905.
Lenin was opposed to World War I
when it broke out in 1914, declaring
that it was forcing workers to fight
against each other for the benefit of
the bourgeois. After the deposition of
the Tsar Nicholas II, Lenin returned
to Russia with German connivance in
March 1917 in a "sealed train" and
won power in the October Revolution
that year. During the Civil War
(1918–21) he commanded the
Bolsheviks and fought off foreign
intervention as well as the White army.
Successful in establishing Bolshevik
power, he founded the Comintern in
1919 to spread the revolution, and
also instituted the New Economic
Policy in 1921, which permitted

limited free enterprise. A shrewd
political operator, Lenin devoted his
life to the furtherance of Marxism, his
writings and action, making a
significant contribution to the
ideology. Lenin did not successfully
espouse any solutions to overcome the
problem of how to build a workers'
state in a peasant society. Historians
differ in their opinion of him. Some
believed there is continuity between
his ideas and those of Stalin, while
others emphasize the pluralistic New
Economic Policy he endorsed in the
last years of his life. What is certain is
that Lenin was the principal
revolutionary leader of twentieth-
century Europe, whose visionary
realism led the Bolsheviks to seize and
maintain power.

Luce, Henry Robinson
1898–1967
American publisher

Luce was famous for founding *Time,* the first weekly
magazine, which he launched with Briton Hadden in March
1923. He focused on critical analysis of American business
and industry. Its circulation rose steadily until by 1960 it was
selling 2.5 million copies per issue. In 1930 Hadden and
Luce launched *Fortune* magazine, followed by *Life* in 1936,
and *Sports Illustrated* in 1954. *Life* ceased to be a weekly
publication because of rising costs in 1972, and was revived
as a monthly magazine in 1978. Luce continued as editor-in-
chief of his magazines until 1964. His publishing empire
extended to movies, radio, and television, including such
well-known series as *The March of Time* and Time-Life
Books. In the 1930s he caused a sensation when he divorced
his wife and married the playwright Clare Boothe Brokaw.

MacArthur, Douglas, General
1880–1964
American soldier

In 1937 MacArthur retired from the US Army.
Commissioned from West Point in 1903, he had served in
the Philippines (1903–06), at Vera Cruz (1914), had
commanded a division in France (1918), served as
Superintendent of West Point (1919–22) and as U.S. Army
Chief of Staff (1930–35), and attained the rank of General.
An intelligent and gifted strategist, MacArthur was recalled
to duty as commander of US forces in the Far East in July
1941. Evacuated from the Philippines on President
Roosevelt's orders in May 1942, he returned as Supreme
Allied Commander, Southwest Pacific, in early 1945. He
accepted the Japanese surrender in September 1945. In
1950, when the North Koreans invaded the South, he
became commander of United Nations' forces. A year later,
he was sacked by President Truman for criticizing U.S./U.N.
policy.

Madonna [Madonna Louise Veronica Ciccone]
1958–
American pop singer

Madonna's debut album of 1983 produced three successful
singles and brought her instant success in the US, aided by
coverage on MTV. Video exposure brought her sexually
provocative image to the fore. In 1985 she entered the record
books with eight top ten hits, and *True Blue* (1986), *Like a
Prayer* (1989) and *Bedtime Stories* (1994) established her as a
leading female artist. Her 1998 release was the meditative
Ray of Light, which has been lauded as the best album of her
career so far. Cited by sections of the feminist community as
a positive role model for women, she is also the arch foe of
America's moral right, with her outrageous stage antics. She
appeared in the film version of the musical *Evita* in 1996
that was accorded mixed reviews. On October 14, 1996, she
gave birth to a daughter, Lourdes.

M

Malcolm X
1925–1965
American political activist

After serving a seven-year term of imprisonment for "hoodlum activities," Malcolm X discovered Islam. His father was a Baptist minister and outspoken follower of Marcus Garvey, a black Nationalist leader of the 1920s. After Malcolm's father was murdered by the Klu Klux Klan, his mother suffered a nervous breakdown, and he along with his siblings were taken into care by the welfare department. Malcolm was sent to a foster home and then reform school. He later moved from Michigan to Boston, Mass. to live with his sister, and tried various jobs before becoming

involved with criminal activity. He was sent to prison for burglary, and while there read the teachings of Elijah Muhammed, who advocated racial separation.

On his release from jail, in 1952, he erased his original name in the manner of Nation of Islam followers who regard family names as a symbol of white slaveholders. In the 1960s Malcolm X preached Black Power to congregations in search of new identity within a racist society. He was one of the most prominent and eloquent members of the Nation of Islam. He helped found many new mosques and was instrumental in increasing the membership. For a period he was assigned to Mosque Number Seven in

Harlem, New York. He was outspoken against the Civil Rights movement and believed the use of violence was justified for self-protection. He was seen as fanatical by the Civil Rights activists and, after describing the assassination of President Kennedy as a "case of chickens coming home to roost," he was suspended from the Nation of Islam. He broke away from the group to form the Organization of Afro-American Unity (OAAU) in 1964. In the same year, when he returned from a pilgrimage to Mecca, he advocated racial solidarity renouncing previous teachings that all whites are evil. While addressing an OAAU rally in 1965 he was assassinated, allegedly by rival black Muslims.

M

M

Mandela, Nelson
1918–
South African political leader

Mandela's long crusade for equality in South Africa has inspired millions around the world. Public outrage at his life sentence for protesting against segregation in his homeland focused efforts to end the dominant white regime and gained him support from around the globe. His dedication to the campaign eventually culminated in his release and historic election as South Africa's first black president.

Nelson Rolihlahla Mandela was born on July 18, 1918, in a small village in the Transkei region of South Africa where his father was a councillor to Acting Paramount Chief of Thembuland. He grew up listening to tales of valor from the tribal history told by the elders at the Chief's court and early in life he became determined to make his own contribution to his peoples' struggle for freedom. Following the best education that the local missionary school could provide, Mandela was sent to the secondary school at Healdtown and then the University College of Fort Hare. His political concerns surfaced for the first time here and he was suspended for his involvement in a student protest boycott. Determined to finish his education, he traveled to Johannesburg where he managed to complete his Bachelor of Arts degree by correspondence. Following graduation Mandela began studying law. His aim was to provide legal representation for the black population who at the time had no recourse to the law at all. In 1942 he also took the first step on his political journey by joining the African National Congress (ANC), a group dedicated to the destruction of the apartheid system which maintained rigid racial segregation in South Africa.

The ANC was initially a small group lead by the young Anton Lembede. During the 1940s however, Mandela and some 60 compatriots worked tirelessly to transform it into a political movement which would give a voice to the millions of blacks who were uneducated, oppressed, and ruthlessly exploited by the minority of white landowning class. Their ultimate goal was to completely dismantle the apartheid system, redistribute the land, and provide education and representation for every member of the black population. Mandela's dedication impressed senior members of the ANC and he swiftly ascended through the ranks. At first he espoused peaceful protest and the non-violent weapons of strike, boycott, civil disobedience, and non-cooperation. In 1952 he was arrested for his part in the "Campaign for the Defiance of Unjust Laws," but the court was forced to release him as he had consistently encouraged his followers to adopt peaceful forms of protest. However, he was prohibited from further action for a period of six months. Mandela used the time to establish the country's first black law practice and at the end of 1952 he was elected as deputy president of the ANC.

Despite being hounded by the authorities, Mandela continued to work for peaceful liberation throughout the 1950s — through his legal practice and the ANC. He played a key role in popular resistance to the Western Areas removal and also helped introduce Bantu Education. In 1955 the Congress of the People adopted the Freedom Charter, which stated the dissatisfaction and the demands of the black people, and Mandela traveled extensively to summon support for its aims. White concern about his activities was mounting however, and the late 1950s saw a concerted effort to thwart both Mandela and his campaign.

In 1961 South Africa was rapidly moving towards becoming a republic. Mandela warned the government that failure to include the black population in the new constitution would result in widespread strike actions. They responded with military force and Mandela was forced to go into hiding. As a last resort, he and the leaders of the ANC formed the *Umkhonto we Sizwe* — an armed wing of the ANC — and Mandela was appointed as their commander. While returning from a diplomatic trip abroad Mandela was arrested in 1962 and sentenced to five years imprisonment for inciting strike action. While serving this term he was charged with sabotage and his sentence was lengthened to life.

During the next 27 years he became a symbol of black South Africa's struggle for equality, and the world's most famous political prisoner. Change in South Africa during his incarceration was a slow process but during the 1980s colored people, though not blacks, were finally given the vote. This proved a stepping stone, and fueled by growing condemnation around the world, which included economic sanctions from many western governements, President F.W. De Klerk began remodeling South African society to eradicate the inherent racism of apartheid. In 1990 De Klerk ordered Mandela's release — that year they shared the Nobel Peace Prize which Mandela accepted on behalf of all those people who had worked towards the goal of peace and equality. He particularly thanked the people of Norway, who had long backed the fight against apartheid while the rest of the world stood by. In the first free elections to be held in the country, Nelson Mandela was voted into power by a huge majority on May 10, 1994. Mandela's triumph has been marred by violence between rival factions of the Zulu Inkatha movement and the ANC, yet South Africa is slowly moving towards peace and prosperity under his guiding hand.

M

Mao Tse-Tung
1893–1976
Chinese statesman

Founder of the Chinese Communist Party and, with Marx and Lenin, one of the shaping forces of Marxist Communism. Chairman Mao, by destroying Nationalist power, achieved the unification of China and is responsible for the largest social revolution of all history.

A peasant's son, Mao was born on December 26, 1893, in the Hunan province where he grew up working in the fields. He learned the art of argument early in life as there was much antagonism between himself and his father, throughout which Mao's mother was a constant source of care and support. During his formative years China was a politically turbulent country, and as a student in the provincial capital Mao was aware of the new trends and social currents that were filtering through the country after the Qing Dynasty was overthrown by the Nationalist, Sun Yat-Sen.

In 1918 Mao traveled to the international capital Beijing to work as a library assistant at the university and tried to extend his education on the meager income which this employment supplied. Here he became contemptuous of the mainly bourgeois classes that could afford the education that the university offered and found sympathy with politically radical figures. Many of these would later on be appointed to positions of power within the Chinese Communist Party.

Mao married for the first time in 1920. His wife, Yang Kaihui, the daughter of one of his more radical teachers, would be executed by the Chinese Nationalists ten years later. In the year following his wedding, Mao helped to found the Chinese Communist Party (CCP) in Shanghai and took on the role of leader of the Hunan province. The party quickly moved to form an alliance with the republican Nationalist party — Kuomintang — and the following years were devoted to the organization of the CCP in his province and planting the seeds of revolution in the peasant labor force.

In 1927, the Kuomintang leader Sun Yat-Sen died and was succeeded by Chiang Kai-Shek, who immediately renounced the alliance with the Communists. With Chiang Kai-Shek actively purging all Communist influence, Mao fled to the mountains of south China. Here he established a base and an army to defend it. His election as Chairman of the first All-China Congress of Soviets in December 1931 coincided with the Manchuria Incident and the beginning of Japanese aggression against China. Mao, who had turned his home province into a Red enclave, called for a common front with the Kuomintang against the Japanese, but Chiang Kai-shek, obsessed with destroying the Communists, instead forced them into the 6,000-mile long march to northern Shansi. Mao set up a new base in Yenan.

However, the opposing factions of Kuomintang and CCP were driven to put aside their differences when the Japanese invaded in 1937. Mao's stature and the popularity of the CCP rose steadily during the conflict; his essays "On Contradiction" and "On Practice," both published in 1937, as well as "On New Democracy" (1940) established him as an important military and Marxist thinker and he was lauded as a defender of the country.

The alliance of convenience with Chiang did not survive the war and Mao steadily drove the Nationalists off the mainland during the Civil War of 1946–49. China was now completely under the control of the Communists, lead by Mao Tse-tung, and in 1949 was declared as the People's Republic of China.

The theories worked out when he was a guerilla in Shansi did not survive the realities of transforming the economy of China. Mao's response was The Great Leap Forward of 1958, an attempt to increase industrial production by molding China's vast population into rural "people's communes." Incompetent organization and resistance from the people however, resulted in a massive decrease in crops, general starvation, and the loss of millions of lives. Consequently Mao lost his position as head of state.

Determined to reverse his fortunes Mao continued to provoke action by the people and struggled to win public support against his successor, Liu Shaoqi. "The Cultural Revolution," of 1966, in which Mao revived the old revolutionary spirit by destroying bureaucracy and culture, also made him the subject of hysterical adulation.

With the military and the backing of millions of followers to whom his *Little Red Book* of sayings and buttons printed with a picture of the leader were distributed, Mao became the center of a widespread personality cult which swept him back into power.

He remained as the head of state until his death on September 6, 1976. During his lifetime Mao fundamentally changed the face of Chinese society, and became a powerful and highly controversial figure on the world stage. Mao's actions and policies have had a deep impact on the structure of the rest of the world — though his economic leadership can be seen to have failed, his ideas and theories are influential throughout the Third World to this day and remain deeply ingrained in Chinese society.

M

Mantle, Mickey Charles
1931–1995
American baseball player

The long New York Yankees dynasty (26 pennants in 39 seasons from 1927–64) saw its last true superstar in Mickey Mantle. Mantle slugged 536 home runs, which earned him a place on the all-time list for switch hitters Mantle replaced Joe DiMaggio in 1956 as center fielder for the New York Yankees. A Hall of Fame Center fielder, Mantle won three MVP awards and swatted a record 18 World Series homers. He achieved all this despite a condition that caused bone inflammation in his left leg and continual injuries to his leg muscles and knees.
In 1967, in an effort to spare his legs, Mantle became a first baseman. He retired before the 1969 season and was elected to the Baseball Hall of Fame in 1974. Mantle is shown on the near right.

Marshall, Thurgood
1908–1993
American Supreme Court judge

The first black justice on the Supreme Court of the United States, Marshall had a long and varied career. He came from a long line of pioneering ancestors: his grandfather was a slave who joined the army during the Civil War (1861–65); his mother was one of the first women to graduate from Columbia's Teacher's College in New York. Marshall graduated from Lincoln University in 1930 and went on to graduate first in his class from the Howard University of Law in 1933. From 1939 to 1961, he served as director and chief counsel for the NAACP Legal Defense and Education Fund. There he helped form a strategy to fight racial segregation. He was instrumental in creating precedents in law which laid the groundwork for the Civil Rights movement. While at the Supreme Court he was at first part of the liberal majority, but later became the only dissenting voice against an increasingly Conservative court.

Matisse, Henri
1869–1954
French painter

Matisse began to paint in 1890, working through a variety of influences, before developing a personal style in which naturalistic color was suppressed in favor of apparently arbitrary hues. His aim was to "transpose feelings into color," and he attempted to enhance its emotive force by distortions of form. His style reached a high point of expressive abstraction in *La Dance* and *La Musique* (1909–10). From 1914 he returned to a more naturalistic style. Working mainly on the themes of Mediterranean Interiors, Odalisques, and still-life, he made free use of textile patterns as a subsidiary decorative element. He had been making sculpture since 1900 and he also produced theater designs, illustrated books, and murals. From 1948 arthritis forced him to work in colored cut-paper and these simple, bright compositions are a fitting testimony to perhaps the greatest master of color in the 20th century.

Mailer, Norman
1923–
American writer

Raised in Brooklyn and educated at Harvard and later at the Sorbonne in Paris, Mailer served in the Pacific with the U.S. Navy, an experience which provided the raw material for *The Naked and the Dead* (1948), one of the best books to emerge from World War II. This was both a critical and a financial success. His writing frequently explores the unconscious urges that can drive behavior, with sex and violence playing major roles that express a strong liberal philosophy and bitterness towards the world.

Mailer wrote fairly continuously in the 1950s and 60s, producing some critical disappointments: *Barbary Shore* (1951) and *The Deer Park* (1955). His reputation was revived by *The White Negro* (1957) and *Advertisements for Myself* (1959). He explored the place of violence in modern American life in the two novels *An American Dream* (1965), *Why Are We in Vietnam?* (1967) and *The Executioner's Song* (1979), based on the life of convicted murderer Gary Gilmore. Perhaps his most ambitious work was *Ancient Evenings* (1983), about which critical opinion is divided. A polemical writer who utilizes many different styles, including a hybrid genre of faction, he has won two Pulitzer Prizes (*The Armies of the Night*, 1968, and *The Executioner's Song*). In 1969 he ran, unsuccessfully, for mayor of New York City. He remains a controversial figure: one of modern America's most colorful, exasperating and exhilarating writers who constantly challenges critics and readers alike.

His other work includes: *Tough Guys Don't Dance* (1984), a detective story that was made into a motion picture in 1987; *Harlot's Ghost* (1991), a lengthy novel about the Central Intelligence Agency (CIA); *Oswald's Tale* (1995), about Lee Harvey Oswald, the accused assassin of United States president John F. Kennedy; and *Portrait of Picasso as a Young Man: An Interpretative Biography* (1995). Mailer's novel *The Gospel According to the Son* (1997) aims to relate the life of Jesus Christ from the first person perspective of Jesus himself. Mailer has also written, directed, and appeared in a number of movies.

M

Mead, Margaret
1901–1978
American anthropologist

The work of Dr. Margaret Mead gave the field of anthropology a popular appeal that it had never experienced before. Her studies of the gender roles and courtship rituals among indigenous peoples was groundbreaking and she became a highly influential figure in American society during her lifetime; pronouncing opinions on such diverse subjects as child psychology, feminism, oceanic ethnology, and cross-cultural communications. Sometimes criticized for a lack of objectivity, her views on the formation of society persuaded many and were deeply influential in the evolution of American culture.

From early childhood she was taught to be open-minded and to observe those around her. She was born on December 16, 1901, to parents who were forward thinkers. Both were teachers and her mother had been a suffragette. Margaret was encouraged to play with children from every racial and economic background; an unusual attitude in the early part of the century and one that gave Margaret a sense of difference that she would later claim to have taken great pride in.

Her educational career lead eventually to Barnard College in New York City, where Mead studied anthropology under the academically renowned Franz Boas. She graduated in 1923 and married Luther Cressman soon after taking a place at Columbia University to continue her studies. Research for the course took Mead to the South Pacific for a nine-month stay in 1925 and here she observed adolescents in order to assess biological and cultural influences on behavior. The dissertation that she subsequently wrote, *Coming of Age in Samoa* (1928), contrasted the Samoan adolescents with those of the US and was subsequently published. It brought Mead instant notoriety and controversy but many were swayed by her conclusions. During the journey home she also met Reo Fortune who later became her second husband.

Further field trips — to the island of Manus, off the coast of New Guinea in the late 1920s and the Indonesian island of Bali (with her third husband Gregory Bateson) in 1936 — resulted in books that further enhanced her reputation as one of America's foremost anthropologists. *Growing Up in New Guinea* (1930) and *Sex and Temperament in Three Primitive Societies* (1935) broadened her observations of cultural formation and *Balinese Character: A Photographic Analysis* (1941) introduced the extensive use of photography as an anthropological tool.

Academic and popular success followed. From 1948 to 1950 she held the post of Director of Research in Contemporary Cultures at Columbia University; in 1954 she became adjunct Professor of Anthropology at the same university. In 1969 she was appointed full professor and head of the social science department in the Liberal Arts College of Fordham University at Lincoln Center in New York. During this time she also spoke publicly about modern social issues such as birth control, abortion laws, the generation gap, and environment issues as well as serving on domestic government and international commissions. She was also an ardent feminist though highly critical of the women's movement, which she found flawed due to its condemnation of men. Her own view of society called for absolute equality rather than the raising of one group over another, and she repeatedly called for a complete revision of gender relations. Mead's particular interest though was the family and the problems facing young people in a swiftly changing society — this was an area of study that she returned to many times throughout her career.

Determined to have a child of her own with Bateson, Mead suffered several miscarriages before finally bearing a daughter, Mary Catherine Bateson, in 1939. During Mary's very early childhood her mother was friendly with a young pediatrician, Dr. Benjamin Spock, and agreed to follow his novel ideas on child-rearing herself. His book, *The Commonsense Book of Baby and Child Care* (1946), later revolutionized the way in which American parents raised their children.

Mead continued to write throughout her life and published many works which have become fundamental anthropological texts. Notable among them are: *And Keep Your Powder Dry: An Anthropologist Looks at America* (1942), which compares American culture to seven others; *Male and Female* (1949); *Soviet Attitudes Toward Authority* (1951); *New Lives for Old* (1956); *Culture and Commitment: A Study of the Generation Gap* (1970); and her memoirs, *Blackberry Winter* (1972). In addition to her books, for 17 years she also co-authored a monthly column in *Redbook* which tackled the social problems of women. A reappraisal of her work during the 1980s has cast doubt on many of her methods and conclusions but a host of admirers continue to support her work.

In 1926 Mead had taken a job as an assistant curator of ethnology at the American Museum of Natural History in New York. It was an association with the museum that would continue throughout her life, culminating with her being awarded the honorary title of Curator Emeritus in 1969. Following her death from cancer on November 15, 1978, the Museum initiated the Annual Margaret Mead Festival of Anthropological Films.

However, perhaps the honor that held the most significance for her, was being named Mother of the Year, in 1969, by *Time* magazine.

Mayer, Louis B. [Burt]
1885–1957
American film executive

A ruthless, quick-tempered businessman, Mayer combined an astute financial sense with an intuitive feeling for public taste. In his early career he was a film distributor and theater manager. He moved to Los Angeles in 1916 and founded his own film production company, Louis B. Mayer Productions. After various mergers, he was Vice-President and General Manager of MGM from 1924 until 1951, and the most powerful magnate in 1930s and 1940s Hollywood. "With more stars than there are in the heavens," MGM produced wholesome escapist entertainment that reflected Mayer's tastes and moral convictions. Some of his most outstanding successes were *The Big Parade* (1925), *Ben Hur* (1926), *Grand Hotel* (1932), *Dinner at Eight* (1933), and the *Andy Hardy* series, all of which were family orientated, patriotic, and uplifting.

McCarthy, Joseph
1908–1957
American politician

A practicing lawyer before serving in the U.S. Marine Corps during World War II, McCarthy attained the rank of captain while serving in the Pacific. He stood for the Senate as a Republican in 1946. He used his witch-hunt against "Reds under the bed" to advance his career in the 1950s. His system was to proclaim the "guilt" of his victims, usually by innuendo, and create an atmosphere of paranoia inside, and outside the infamous House of Representatives Committee on Un-American Activities. Celebrities in the science and showbusiness fields were seen denouncing their friends as Communists on camera. The bubble, which had been kept inflated by the moral cowardice of his senatorial colleagues finally burst at the televised trial hearings in 1954, and McCarthy was discredited. However he was cleared of all charges despite being censured by the Senate for the methods he used.

Messerschmitt, Willy
1898–1978
German aircraft engineer

Designer of gliders from 1921, Messerschmitt founded Messerschmitt Flugzeugbau in Bamberg 1925. He began to design monoplanes in an age when biplanes were still common. Trials showed the monoplane had a speed advantage. In 1928 he became a manager of BFW and then, in 1933, a director. With the rise of the Nazi Party he turned to designing military aircraft. The Bf109 fighter set a world speed record of 379 mph (610 km/h) in 1939. The Luftwaffe took about 35,000 Bf109s. He also designed the Me163 Komet, a rocket-powered plane, and the precursor of the Me262, the first jet fighter put in production.

Arrested by the Allies in 1945, Messerschmitt spent three years behind bars. On the lifting of the ban on German aircraft manufacture in 1963 he returned from Spain. He joined forces with others to form the Messerschmitt-Bölkow-Blohm group which produces satellites, missiles, and airplanes.

M

Meir, Golda [Goldie Mabovitch]
1898–1978
Israeli politician

Goldie Mabovitch and her family emigrated from Russia to the United States to escape a Cossack pogrom. She met Ben-Gurion in Milwaukee and started working for the Zionist cause at 15. With her husband, Morris Myerson, she emigrated to Palestine in 1921 where they joined a kibbutz. Throughout the 1930s and 40s she served in various organizations in Palestine, Europe, and the U.S. and in 1940 took over the political department of Histadrut, the labor federation. During the war she proved to be an eloquent and forceful speaker for the Zionist cause. The political campaign for

a Jewish national state benefited by $50 million from her fundraising in the United States. In 1946 when the head of the political department of the Jewish Agency, Moshe Sharett, was arrested by the British, she temporarily replaced him. She worked tirelessly for the release of him and many other comrades and the Jewish refugees who had broken immigration laws by settling in Palestine. When Sharett took up diplomatic service, she officially settled to his former position.

She was a signatory of the Proclamation of the Independence of the State of Israel in 1948 and she was appointed Ambassador to the Soviet Union and then Labor Minister in 1949. She implemented large building programs for roads and housing and

supported unrestricted immigration of Jews to Israel. She changed her name to Golda Meir on appointment to Foreign Minister in 1956.

At this time Israel began a policy of helping African states in order to enhance diplomatic relations among uncommitted nations. She was Secretary General of the Mapai party and of the United Israel Labor Party from 1966–68. Meir became Prime Minister on Eshkol's sudden death, a post she held between 1969–74. She was attempting to negotiate a diplomatic peace settlement in the Middle East when the fourth Arab-Israeli war broke. Blamed for delaying mobilization in the 1973 Yom Kippur War, for which Israel was poorly prepared, Meir resigned. In 1974 she wrote the best-selling, *My Life*.

De Mille, Cecil B.
1881–1959
American film director

De Mille's name is synonymous with sex, sadism, sanctimoniousness, and spectacle. Sometimes known as the "founder of Hollywood" after the success of *The Squaw Man* in 1914 he is probably best remembered for epic productions such as *Samson and Delilah* (1949) and *The Ten Commandments* (1956) which were huge successes. Between 1900–13 he worked in theater-acting, managing, and writing (in partnership with his brother William). In Hollywood he made 70 movies, each of which he directed and produced. He produced three unsuccessful movies at MGM, but in 1931 he returned to Paramount Studios where he began his production of big-budget epics. He received an Academy Award in 1949 for: "37 years of brilliant showmanship." In 1952 he received the Thalberg Award, and 1952's, *The Greatest Show on Earth* won the Academy Award for Best Picture.

Miller, Arthur
1915–
American playwright

Born in New York, Miller came to prominence in 1947 with *All My Sons,* a strong drama, followed in 1949 by the far more impressive *Death of a Salesman,* for which he won a Pulitzer Prize. *The Crucible* (1953), which won a 1953 Tony Award, uses the Salem witch trials of 1692 as a powerful parable for McCarthyism; Miller himself later refused to name names to the House of Representatives Committee on Un-American Activities, which was investigating the spread of Communism in 1956. He was convicted of contempt, a decision later overturned. Fame came too, from his 1956 marriage to Marilyn Monroe to which *After the Fall* (1964), alludes. They were divorced in 1960. Most of his work is concerned with the responsibility of each individual to other members of a society and is simply and colloquially written.

Miller, [Alton] Glenn
1904–1944
American bandleader

Raised in a middle-class home in Iowa, Glenn Miller started his musical career as a passable trombonist working with famous American bands before deciding to form his own band in 1937. Initially unsuccessful, the band received almost constant airplay during a stint at the Meadowbrook Ballroom in New Jersey and the Glen Island Casino in New York in 1939 and became the world's most famous big band. Playing such immortal numbers as "Moonlight Serenade," "In the Mood," and "Tuxedo Junction," Glenn Miller brought his distinctive swing sound before a global audience during World War II when he joined the US Army. Miller died when the plane carrying him to France after D-Day crashed in heavy fog over the English Channel.

Ho Chi Minh [Nguyem That Thankh]
1890–1969
Vietnamese statesman

"Uncle" Ho's was the second successful postwar revolution in the Orient, but unlike Mao he was a sophisticated, cosmopolitan figure who only returned to his country in 1945. His early life was wretched, but he was able to attend a school and became apprenticed at a technical institute in Saigon. He worked as a seaman between 1911–14, and having visited many ports ended up in London between 1915–17.

He spent the years 1917–23 in Paris, helping to found the French Communist Party and, by proxy, its Indo-Chinese equivalent. In 1919 he addressed a petition to the world powers at the Versailles conference, demanding equal rights for subjects under French Colonial rule in Indochina. He did not achieve a response however. He took part in training courses in Moscow at the end of 1923, and was later to turn up in China, under an assumed name. He was forced to leave upon a military crackdown on Communist activities but returned in 1930 to form the Indo-Chinese Communist Party.

He spent the next few years as an arbitrator between factions that allowed some revolutionary action. After brutal repression by the French, Ho was condemned in absentia to death as a revolutionary.

In 1938 he formed the Vict Minh and led the fight against the Japanese in Vietnam. He declared himself First President of the Democratic Republic of Vietnam (1946–54). Its army, the Viet-Minh, swept the French from Indochina in 1954 after eight years of bloody conflict, and established a people's republic in the north of which he became President (1954–69). The regime eventually became repressive and totalitarian, agricultural reforms were not successful. His last eight years were spent in the increasingly bloody struggle to unify Vietnam, as the Americans poured in troops and aid to shore up the rival Saigon regime. He did not live to see his dream turn sour in a destitute, albeit united Vietnam.

M

Monroe, Marilyn
1926–1962
American actress

Nearly 40 years after her death, Monroe remains the quintessential sex symbol of the 20th Century, and each year adds a fresh crop of books to the already huge collection of works devoted to her. A natural beauty who was transformed from a fresh-faced young model to an ethereal siren, Marilyn's life was punctuated by melancholy, insecurity, and neurosis. Her natural talent for acting was constantly overlooked by Hollywood; while aspiring to star in the classics she was usually typecast as a dizzy blonde in lightweight comedy roles.

Born on June 1, 1926, in Los Angeles, California and registered as Norma Jeane Mortenson, there was some confusion as to who her father was and she later used the name Baker. Her childhood was heartbreakingly sad. Given away by her mother, Gladys Monroe Baker, Norma spent her first seven years with foster parents before Gladys reclaimed her. Soon after, Grace McKee, a friend of Norma's mother declared Gladys insane and had her committed to a psychiatric hospital. For the remainder of her childhood years Norma was shunted from family friends to orphanages and was abused on at least two occasions.

In 1942, at the age of 16, she married James Dougherty. Her husband joined the merchant marines soon after and Norma went to work in an aircraft factory. She was spotted there by a photographer and after a short, but successful, modeling career she divorced Dougherty and decided to try and become an actress in Hollywood. Signed by 20th Century Fox in 1946, Norma Jean changed her name to Marilyn Monroe and had her first role in *Scudda-Hoo! Scudda-Hay!* the same year. Her single line was "Hi Rad!" Fox dropped her a year later and her contract was picked up by Columbia, though they did not use her.

An affair with Johnny Hyde, executive vice-president of the William Morris Agency, brought an upturn in Marilyn's career. Johnny used his influence to gain her small parts in the Marx Brothers' Movie, *Love Happy* (1950), as well as *The Asphalt Jungle* (1950), and *All About Eve* (1950). Fox signed her to a new contract on improved terms and she continued to appear in a number of movies, which brought her increased public attention. By 1951 Marilyn's fan mail numbered over 2,000 letters per week and in 1952 the studio assigned her the lead female roles in *Don't Bother To Knock* and *Monkey Business*. It was about this time that the press found that she had featured in a nude calendar years before. Marilyn turned the potentially disastrous story into a publicity scoop, frankly admitting that she had been down on her luck and had needed the money. When asked if she had had anything on at all, she famously retorted, "Yes of course — I had the radio on." The calendar became a collector's item and Marilyn's career was boosted. In 1952 she also began an affair with the baseball hero Joe DiMaggio.

Her next big movie was *Gentlemen Prefer Blondes* (1953) in which she costarred with Jane Russell. The performance won her the best actress award from *Photoplay* magazine and she and Russell were invited to add their hand and footprints to the collection at Grauman's Chinese Theater. Marilyn was being offered bigger roles now in better films; 1953 also saw her take the *femme fatale* lead in *Niagara* and she also made *How To Marry a Millionaire* with Lauren Bacall and Betty Grable.

In 1954 she married DiMaggio. They were a golden couple — America's greatest sporting hero and brightest actress. After a honeymoon in Japan, Marilyn flew to Korea where she entertained troops at a large outdoor concert. She would later describe these moments as her happiest times.

Back in Hollywood she began work on *The Seven Year Itch* (1955). Frequently late on set, it was obvious that her short marriage was in difficulties. Joe and Marilyn divorced soon after — their marriage had lasted for only nine months. However *The Seven Year Itch* was the biggest box office hit of the year. Following the divorce Marilyn moved to New York where she enrolled in the acting studio run by Lee Strasberg. About the same time she began a relationship with playwright Arthur Miller which culminated with their marriage in 1956.

The following few years saw Marilyn produce some of her best acting. She was beautifully vulnerable and ethereal in *Bus Stop* (1956), satirized herself perfectly in *Some Like It Hot* (1959), and superb in *The Misfits* (1961). The latter was written especially for her by Miller and she co-starred with Clark Gable, who she had fantasized was her father as a child. It was to be her last role however. Divorced from Miller in 1961, she had been secretly committed to psychiatric hospitals on a few occasions in the previous years. With a growing dependence on drugs, her reputation as difficult to work with had spiraled. Marilyn was erratic at best and quite often eccentric. There were also rumors of affairs with President John F. Kennedy to whom she famously sang "Happy Birthday," at a concert in New York and his brother Robert.

In 1962, she began work on, *Something's Got to Give,* but was fired by Fox soon after. She had rarely shown up on set. Ironically, the footage that survives shows Marilyn at her incandescent best. Marilyn Monroe was found dead of an overdose in her bed on August 4, 1962. There was no suicide note and theories persist that she was murdered. In all probability though, her death was accidental. She was due to remarry Joe DiMaggio, who had been a constant support in her last months, just a few days later.

M

Moore, Sir Henry
1898–1986
British sculptor

For 40 years Moore was considered Britain's greatest living artist. After war service he attended Leeds School of Art and the Royal College of Art, London (1919–23). He taught at the Royal College (1925–32) and Chelsea School of Art (1932–39). Early on Moore rejected classical precepts of beauty and proportion, preferring to charge his work with expressive variety and formal vigor. These were qualities he found in ancient Meso-American and Middle-Eastern, as well as in the work of Italian quattrocento painters such as Masaccio. Throughout his work truth to the material, so that its inherent physical qualities were always a major part of the finished work, was apparent. Most of his work was inspired by natural forms: the female figure and mother and child were much-explored subjects.

Morrison, Toni
1931–
American novelist

Toni Morrison is arguably the foremost black woman writer working in the United States today, and a major influence on the development of the American novel. Her fiction has an extraordinary epic range and is rich in allegory. It is often placed within a tradition that includes Hawthorne, Melville, and Faulkner. It draws on a number of forms, from oral narratives and African folk-tales, to the syncopated rhythms of improvised jazz. It attempts to excavate the forgotten and silenced histories of black culture and experience, and celebrates the energies discovered, while exploring the cost. Her most recent novels are undoubtedly the finest: *Beloved* (1987) set in the last days of slavery; *Jazz* (1992) is a formally daring narrative, using musical improvisation as a model to capture the experience of life in Harlem after the World War I. In addition to her Pulitzer Prize, Toni Morrison was awarded the Nobel Prize for Literature in 1993.

Mother Theresa, [Agnes Gonxa Bojaxhiu]
1910–1997
Albanian nun

Undoubtedly one of the most heroic characters of the century, this tiny nun gained universal respect for her work among the poor in Calcutta. After personal experience of the horrific living conditions in Calcutta as a teaching member of the Sisters of Loretto, she was granted permission to found her own order, the Missionaries of Charity, in 1948. The order was designed specifically to offer practical aid to the dying and destitute of the city. The work of these Sisters has now spread internationally. Despite her age, and increasing health problems, she remained highly active building hospitals, schools, orphanages, and leper colonies. When photographed with world leaders she continually provided a poignant reminder of the inadequacy of the Northern Hemisphere's response to the third-world crisis. She was awarded the Nobel Peace Prize in 1979.

M

Moses, Edwin
1955–
American athlete

A natural athlete, Moses had originally planned a career as a physician. He was a successful high school track athlete and hurdler but it was an academic scholarship that sent him to Morehouse College. He continued to participate in athletics as a student, honing his skills and technique. He graduated with a degree in Physics in 1978, and moved to California to train while working as an engineer. He took part in the Olympic trials shortly after graduating, and set an American record of 48.2 seconds for the 400 meter hurdles. Moses went on to take part in the Montreal Olympics, winning the gold medal with a world record time of 47.64 sec. He was to break this record three more times in his career, achieving 47.02 sec in 1983.

He began a phenomenal dominance of world class hurdling in 1977 with success at the World Games in Dusseldorf, West Germany. He won his next 122 competitions, and remained unbeaten until taking part in an event in Madrid in 1987. He won the James E. Sullivan Award as best U.S. amateur athlete in 1984. Like many other athletes Moses boycotted the 1980 Olympics in Moscow, and did not take part in the competition. However he reappeared at the 1984 Los Angeles Games, taking the gold medal once more and went out with the bronze medal at the Seoul Olympics in 1988.

Moses is known as an exceptional athlete, who specialized in a demanding event and set a record for dominance of an event. Frequently a spokesman for track and field athletes, Moses used his prominence to demand better treatment and more prize money for competitors.

Mitchell, Margaret
1900–1949
American author

Mitchell is the author of just one novel. That novel, *Gone With the Wind*, is, however, the single best-selling work of fiction in history, and, after the Bible, the most widely read book in the world.

Born in Atlanta, Georgia, on November 8, 1900, Mitchell's father, Eugene Muse Mitchell, was a prominent lawyer, president of the Atlanta Historical Society, and also served on the board of trustees for the Carnegie Library. An avid reader himself, he encouraged his children to take an interest in literature. Her mother, Maybelle, was an extremely strong personality. A fiery and militant suffragette, she was the president of the local branch of the movement and also quick to punish her children with a hairbrush at the slightest disobedience. Maybelle often chaired meetings at the family home at which her political passion usually lead to shouted denunciations of the injustices of society. Her young daughter would sit and observe from the top of the stairs.

As a child, Margaret grew up listening to tales of the Civil War from her family and their friends. At an early age she suffered a bad injury while watching her older brother riding his new pony, an unnoticed fire in the basement of the house caught her dress alight, badly burning her legs.

Bedridden while she healed, her maternal grandmother entertained Margaret with stories of her own childhood during the war years. It was a topic that would be discussed often in the household over the following years. Given the family interest in history, and their Southern pride, many afternoons would be lost in recollection, all of which Margaret's agile young mind absorbed.

Her schooling confirmed that Margaret was a bright girl and following graduation she enrolled at Smith College in 1918 to study medicine. Sadly, however, her mother died just a year later and Margaret was obliged to return home to manage the household for her brother and father. Three years later, in 1922, she began a career as a journalist, writing articles and an advice column under the name Peggy Mitchell for the *Atlanta Journal*. Misfortune struck again: a string of injuries the last of which was to her ankle, made it difficult to work and she was forced to resign.

Her husband, John Robert Marsh, was a constant support; striving to keep his wife cheerful and entertained while she was immobile. Aware of the love of books that she had inherited from her father, he often visited the library on her behalf and would return loaded down with novels. Convinced of her talent he bought her the gift of a typewriter in 1926 and ordered her to write one of her own. When she asked what she should write about, Marsh told her to write about something that she knew. Drawing on her childhood experiences she decided to make her subject the Civil War from the Confederate point of view. For the next three years Margaret filled their small apartment with paper and history books, working on the floor, bed, table — anywhere that there was space. However, she was never satisfied with her own work and only John was allowed to read the rapidly growing novel.

Gone With the Wind was finished in 1929 but it was not until 1935 that the novel found an audience. A friend who worked in publishing had informed a superior that Mitchell had a story and, intrigued, he visited her apartment. At first Mitchell denied that the book existed but, spurred on

by her friend, she eventually followed the editor down the road and presented him with the manuscript, telling him to leave quickly before she relented. It was quickly printed as a 1,000-page book and, in an astonishingly short space of time, *Gone With the Wind* broke sales records worldwide. Following a

massive wave of acclaim Margaret Mitchell was presented the Pulitzer Prize in 1937.

In 1939, the romantic tale of Scarlett O'Hara and Rhett Butler set against a background of civil strife was made into an epic feature film. Starring Clark Gable and Vivien Leigh, the movie also was a huge success and became perhaps the most famous film ever made.

Besides the unpublished novella *Ropa Carmagin* it was to be Mitchell's first and only work. On August 16, 1949, she was hit by a speeding car and killed. The popularity of *Gone With the Wind* however did not diminish over the following decades and in the 1980s Mitchell's estate authorized the publication of a sequel. *Scarlett*, by Alexandra Ripley, continues the story of Rhett Butler and Scarlett O'Hara — it became an international number one bestseller overnight, a reminder of the widespread appeal of the original novel.

Murdoch, Rupert
1931–
Australian media magnate

Born in Melbourne, Murdoch started out with *The News* in Adelaide and soon built up a publishing empire in Australia. He moved to Britain where he bought *The Sun, The News of the World, The Times,* and, *Today,* thus dominating the British press. He has been controversial, both for the down-market style of sex, crime, and sport he has brought to his papers, and for his anti-trade union policies, notably at *The News* during the international strikes of the early 1980s. Around this time, Murdoch expanded his activities into the United States, taking American citizenship in 1985, before acquiring, *The New York Post, The Chicago Sun,* and the influential, *TV Guide.* He also has substantial television interests in Australia and the United States and founded the Sky (now British Sky Broadcasting) satellite channel.

Mussolini, Benito
1883–1945
Italian statesman

Mussolini's fascism grew from his early socialism, a circle from which he had been expelled for advocating Italy's entry into World War I. He used the ideas of the post-revolutionary Gabriele D'Annunzio, particularly those concerning a revival of ancient Roman glories, linked to passionate nationalism. His lust for glory proved his downfall for it linked him inexorably with Hitler. His "March on Rome" in 1922 led the King to appoint him Prime Minister, a role which soon became dictatorial. But his office was always at the disposal of Vittorio Emmanuele, who dismissed him when the war turned against the Axis. He introduced economic and social reforms, re-claiming marshland in the Romagna and re-distributing it for settlement, but they were at the cost of political freedom. He was executed by partisans.

Nabokov, Vladimir Vladimirovich
1899–1977
Russian-American novelist, poet, and critic,

Nabokov's wealthy Russian family fled to the West in 1919. He graduated from the University of Cambridge in 1922 and on moving to Berlin started to write for a living, under a pseudonym. He wrote in both Russian and English, and his best works feature stylish, intricate literary effects. He arrived in the United States in 1940, taking citizenship in 1945. He is best known for the novel *Lolita* (1955) which caused a sensation on publication. Most of his early work was translated from the Russian in the 1960s and 70s. Nabokov moved countries again in 1959, to Switzerland where he led a reclusive life. His work includes: *Invitation to a Beheading* (1938); *King, Queen, Knave* (1928); *Mary* (1926); *Glory* (1933); *Pale Fire* (1962); *Speak, Memory* (1966); *Ada* (1969); *A Russian Beauty and Other Stories* (1973); *Strong Opinions* (1973).

Nijinsky, Vaslav Fomich
1888–1950
Ukrainian dancer and choreographer

From 1898 to 1907, Nijinsky was a student at the Imperial Ballet School in St Petersburg and later danced at the Marvinsky Theater, both in works of the old repertory and in the early works of Fokine. In 1908 he met Serge Diaghilev who became his mentor and creator of the Nijinsky legend.

A much-publicized scandal over the inadequacy of his costume in *Giselie* in 1911 led to Nijinsky's dismissal from the Marvinsky Theater and he left Russia, joining Diaghilev's independent Ballets Russes as "premier danseur." Almost all of his famous roles were created for him: *Scheherezade* (1910), *Spectre de la Rose, Carnaval, Petrushka, Le Dieu Bleu,* and *Daphnis et Chloe.* He frequently partnered Tamara Karsavina.

An incredible technician, Nijinsky's greatest quality however was his interpretive genius, able to transform himself from the comic Harlequin in *Carnaval* to the tragic puppet figure of Petrushka. He devised his own new style of choreography, inspired by Greek friezes, and his first ballet *L'Apres-midi d'un faune* was a *succes de scandale* because of his erotic gestures as the Faune. His greatest achievement was the choreography for *Sacre du printemps,* which outraged audiences who fought with supporting intellectuals on the first-night performance.

On the Ballets Russes American tour in 1913, Nijinsky married the Hungarian dancer Romola de Pulszky. The jealous Diaghilev dismissed him from the company, but was instrumental in securing his release from Hungary during World War I, whcn hc was interned. For the Ballets Russes' second American tour in 1916, Nijinsky took over as Artistic Director. His last ballet, *Till Eylenspiegel* had been conceived while interned and he was now ill and demonstrating unpredictable behavior. Nijinsky's paranoia grew worse, and he gave his last performance with Diaghilev's company in Buenos Aires in 1917. He returned to Switzerland where, after a dance recital in 1919 in St Moritz, he was pronounced insane and spent most of the next 20 years in sanatoria. Once again interned in Budapest during World War II, the Nijinskys escaped to Austria in 1945 and moved to England in 1947. He died in London in 1950, his illness cutting short not only a memorable dancing career, but also an important choreographic talent.

Namath Joe
1943–
American football player

As quarterback at the University of Alabama Namath was spotted and signed to the New York Jets of the American Football League in 1965 for a record contract — the highest paying ever at the time. In the media run-up to the 1969 Super Bowl, Namath publicly declared that the Jets would win, defeating the Baltimore Colts who were the pundits' preferred team. They were successful; Namath was named the game's most valuable player and awarded the S. Rae Hickok award as the professional athlete of the year.

For the 1977–78 season, Namath played with the Los Angeles Rams before taking retirement. After retiring he revived his on-off career as an entertainer and actor, begun in 1969, earning the nickname "Broadway Joe." Namath was elected to the Pro Football Hall of Fame in 1985.

Nasser, Gamal Abdel
1918–1970
Egyptian statesman

Nasser not only revolutionized Egypt but he was also a standard bearer for Arab and African nationalism. He was behind the Free Officers' Movement which deposed King Farouk in 1952. He made Egypt a one-party state, introduced radical land reform, ensured British withdrawal from the Nile Valley and nationalized the Suez Canal in 1956. Following the humiliation of the British at Suez his stock rose greatly in the Third World and he formed close links with the USSR. He became President of the United Arab Republic (with Syria) in 1958, a union that split in 1961. He brought about a war with Yemen in 1962–67 and the disastrous war with Israel in 1967 when he occupied the Sinai Peninsula and closed the Tiran Strait to shipping. However, Nasser is remembered as the man who rescued Egypt from Western influence, and who restored Arab dignity.

Nicholas II, Tsar
1868–1918
Russian Emperor

In 1894, on the death of his father of Alexander III, Nicholas inherited a vast, unruly empire, riven by political and social discontents, requiring a ruthless autocratic ruler to control it. Nicholas could not provide the strength or political acumen to hold his realm together. Resentment boiled over into revolution in 1905, during the Russo-Japanese War. Although Nicholas was prepared to order his troops to suppress the uprising, he also accepted the creation of an elected *duma* (parliament) but refused to allow it any power. Simultaneously, he lost the support of the aristocracy when his wife, Alexandra, came under the influence of Rasputin. By 1917, in the midst of war, revolution broke out again. In March, faced with implacable and almost universal opposition, Nicholas abdicated; in July 1918 he and his entire family were executed by the Bolsheviks at Ekaterinburg.

Nixon, Richard Milhous
1913–1994
American politician and president

Graduating in law in 1937, Nixon initially worked in the Office of Emergency Management, before joining the US Navy. He spent most of World War II in the Pacific Navy where he served as an aviation ground officer and left in 1946 with the rank of lieutenant commander.

Nixon rose to fame during the late 1940s as a member of the House of Representatives Committee on Un-American Activities. The trial of Alger Hiss gave Nixon a reputation as a die-hard anti-Communist and he was re-elected in 1948. He was appointed Vice-President by Eisenhower in 1956,

but his own first presidential bid was defeated by Kennedy in 1960.

During his time as Vice President he visited the USSR and famously took part in the "kitchen debate" — a discussion of relative merits of the United States and Communist systems — with Khrushchev. He revived his political career in the late 1960s, winning the Republican nomination in 1968, and the election itself, which was one of the closest in the nation's history. His term of office was overshadowed by the Vietnam problem, Nixon advocating "peace with honor" — a gradual withdrawal of American troops from the region. His conservative domestic and economic policies boosted US trade, and Nixon was elected for a second term in 1972

in a landslide victory.

His tenure was short-lived after he was implicated in the "Watergate Scandal." Nixon was found to have links with seven men found guilty of breaking into the Democratic Party headquarters during his election campaign. Taped transcripts of White House conversations convinced Congress that Nixon was lying about his involvement and they voted to impeach him. They accused Nixon of obstructing justice, abusing presidential power, and refusing to obey subpoenas by the House.

On August 9, 1974, Nixon resigned without admitting any guilt. In later years Nixon salvaged his reputation and was often called upon to discuss the Cold War and China.

Nicklaus, Jack William
1940–
American golfer

The "Golden Bear" has won 20 major championships, seven more than any other man in history. That total includes six titles at the Masters and five at the PGA. Nicklaus grew up in Ohio, where he was a golfing prodigy shooting 51 over nine holes in his first round, played at the age of 10. When he was 13 he shot a 69, and went on to an amateur career winning all but one of his 30 matches before turning pro in 1961. His first professional win came in a dramatic playoff against Arnold Palmer in the 1962 US Open. He was named the PGA's player of the year five times (1967, 1972, 1973, 1975, 1976), and won the PGA's Golfer of the Century award in 1988. He was successful at the Senior Open in 1991 and 1993. He has designed several highly-regarded golf courses.

Nureyev, Rudolf
1938–1993
Russia dancer and director

Nureyev's dance career began with studies of folk dancing before his first ballet lessons with local teachers at his home in Ufa. In 1955 he auditioned for and was accepted by both the Bolshoi Ballet School and the Kirov Ballet School. He chose the Kirov, and despite his late start, under his teacher Aleksandr Pushkin, Nureyev was to graduate with distinction, and joined the Kirov Ballet in 1958. Outstanding success followed his first visit to Paris in 1961, but he was ordered back to the USSR. Fearing official disapproval might end his career, he sought and was granted asylum in France. His Covent Garden debut in 1962 began the historic partnership with Margot Fonteyn. Admired for his interpretation of classic heroes, he also showed his versatility in the comedy ballet *La Fille mal gardee*. Later he became Director of the Paris Opera Ballet.

O'Neill, Eugene Gladstone
1888–1953
American dramatist

O'Neill had an unsettled early life, traveling with his family in the theatre world. The period 1907–13 was traumatic; steeped in alcohol and an attempted suicide. After a period in a sanatorium recovering from typhus he started to write plays. Between 1916–20 he was involved with the Playwright's Theatre and his contributions to their productions made their reputation. His first full-length play, *Beyond the Horizon,* was produced on Broadway in 1920. It won the first of four Pulitzer prizes in drama – others were for *Anna Christie, Strange Interlude,* and *Long Day's Journey into Night.* His reputation grew over the next 20 years as he produced wonderful pays such as *Desire Under the Elms, Mourning Becomes Electra,* and *The Iceman Cometh.* By his inspiration to other serious dramatists, O'Neill set the pace for the blossoming of the Broadway theatre.

Nehru, Jawaharlal
1889–1964
Indian Statesman

Having qualified as a lawyer in England, Nehru tried to earn a living a in his native India but he had little enthusiasm for his career. He had a lively interest in Indian politics, and like many of his generation was an instinctive nationalist. Nehru had been involved with the Congress Party since the Massacre at Amritsar in 1919. In 1921 prominent leaders of the party were outlawed in some provinces, and Nehru was among those sent to prison. Over the period of the fight for independence, Nehru was to spend a total of nine years in jail: he regarded these as normal interludes in a life of abnormal political activity.

During a period when he was General Secretary of the Congress Party, he began to take an interest in Marxism, especially after a tour to Europe and the USSR in 1926–27. Nehru was elected Congress President in 1929, at which time he presided over the Lahore discussions that resulted in the declaration of complete independence for India as its political goal. Mahatma Gandhi was still the driving force behind the move to independence, and it was not until 1942 that he recognized Nehru as his political heir.

During the 1930s several attempts were made to advance India to self-governance. British intransigence led to Gandhi's civil disobedience movements during which time both he and Nehru were jailed. World

War II saw some conflict between Gandhi and Nehru but throughout the war they still worked towards an independent state. It was not granted until 1947. Lord Wavell, negotiating on behalf of the British tried to bring the Muslim league and Congress party together and failed leading to the partition of India and creation of Pakistan.

As President of the Indian National Congress Nehru supervised the handing over of power and became the new dominion's first Prime Minister Nehru, subsequently built a reputation, as the political guru of the non-aligned countries when India became a republic. The dynasty he founded with his daughter Indira Gandhi seemingly perished with the assassination of her son, Rajiv Gandhi in 1991.

Orwell, George [Eric Arthur Blair]
1903–1950
British writer

Born in Bengal, India, and educated in England, Orwell's first job was with the Indian Imperial Police in Burma. He left in 1927 to escape imperialism, and started an initially unsuccessful writing career. A commission from Gollancz produced *The Road to Wigan Pier* (1937), and later the Spanish Civil war prompted *Homage to Catalonia* (1938). His first novel, *Burmese Days* (1934), uses much of his experience in Burma. It started a pattern of fiction based on emotionally isolated and sensitive characters in difficult environments. During World War II he worked for the BBC in India, and in 1943 was Literary Editor of *The Tribune*. More social commentator than novelist his works include: *Down and Out in Paris and London* (1933), *Coming Up for Air* (1939), *Animal Farm* (1944), and *Nineteen Eighty-Four* (1949).

Owens, Jesse [James Cleveland]
1913–1980
American track and field star

Jesse Owens was an African-American who proved to be the dominant athlete of the Olympics held in Berlin in 1936. He sprinted to victories in the 100 and 200 meter dashes and also helped the U.S. 400 meter relay team blaze to a world record, but his most dramatic victory came in the long jump, where Owens was pitted against Luz Long, a German who seemed to embody Adolf Hitler's claim of Aryan racial supremacy. Owens nearly failed to qualify for the finals, fouling and then jumping short on his first two attempts. Getting some advice from Long, Owens adjusted his approach and sailed into the finals, where he won with an Olympic record. Long and Owens became fast friends and maintained an active correspondence until the former's death in World War II. Owens' performance made him one of the most celebrated athletes in US history.

Pankhurst, Emmeline
1857–1928
British suffragette

After the death of her husband in 1898, Pankhurst (née Goulden) devoted herself to gaining the vote for women in Britain. In 1903 she and her daughters Christabel, Sylvia, and Adela founded the Women's Social and Political Union (WSPU). Known as "suffragettes," they and their followers adopted extreme measures to gain publicity. Many were arrested, put on trial, and imprisoned. Although other women were alienated by such actions, Emmeline Pankhurst did succeed in bringing the issue of female suffrage to the fore. During World War I Pankhurst diverted the energy of the women's movement to the war effort, encouraging women to enter male-dominated occupations. By 1917 she reformed the WSPU as the Women's Party, fielding 16 candidates for the 1918 election. None was elected, but in that year women over the age of 30 gained the vote; 10 years later they achieved full suffrage.

O'Keeffe, Georgia
1887–1986
American painter

O'Keeffe was born in Sun Prairie, Wisconsin and went to the Art Institute of Chicago and the Arts Students' League of New York. She supported herself through her studies by doing some commercial art and between 1913 and 1916 she taught art in schools and colleges in Texas and other Southern States.

In 1915 O'Keeffe broke with her academic training to experiment with abstraction, deriving images from an intense, direct study of nature and emphasizing the formal qualities she discerned in organic things. In 1919

the photographer Alfred Stieglitz showed interest in her abstract drawings and exhibited her work at "291," his gallery in New York City. They became close friends and married in 1924. Her work continued to be exhibited and promoted by him until his death in 1946.

During the 1920s she produced works based on magnified botanical subjects, particularly flowers, as in *Black Iris III* (1926). From 1929 she found inspiration in the majestic terrain of New Mexico, where she moved in 1949, and also became fascinated by the forms of bones. The stark, monumental *Cow's Skull: Red, White, and Blue* (1931), is among the first isolated studies, while later works

placed skulls or pelvic bones in a desert setting, where they float surreally in perspectiveless space. She is famous for the purity and lucidity of her work, where items are dealt with representationally, boldly patterned, clearly colored and starkly linear. The precision and austerity of her work can be linked with artists Charles Sheeler and Charles Demuth, but O'Keeffe's abstraction was all her own. Most of her work was produced in the 1920s to 1940s but she continued to paint until the 1980s. In later life, she became inspired by airplane flights and added sky and clouds, to her paintings, as seen from the air. A strikingly original artist, O'Keeffe was a pioneer of modernism in the U.S.

Olivier, Laurence, Baron Olivier of Brighton
1907–1989
British actor and director

Olivier's reputation as a virtuoso thespian is unparalleled; during his lifetime he brought to both stage and screen an extraordinary intensity and his interpretations of many Shakesperian plays are regarded as definitive. Distinguished, handsome, and gifted, his most outstanding work was probably on stage. An electrifying performer, Olivier was also a champion of the theater and his work to promote culture was rewarded in 1970 when he became the first member of the acting profession to be raised to a life peerage by Queen Elizabeth II.

His life began in Dorking, Surrey, in south-east England, where he was born on May 22, 1907. The young boy was a precocious child, a quick learner, and, from an early age, a keen actor. There was no doubt as to which profession he would choose and he trained at Central School of Speech Training and Dramatic Art in London during the early 1920s before making his stage debut in 1926 as a member of the Birmingham Repertory Company. Although Olivier's early performances did not go unnoticed, he did not achieve overnight fame and it was not until 1930 that he had his breakthrough in a performance of Noel Coward's *Private Lives* which dazzled critics. Although Olivier made his first screen appearance in the 1930 film *Too Many Crooks*, he initially concentrated on building a classical reputation; working almost exclusively in the theater and to ever-mounting acclaim. A particularly memorable performance was in Shakespeare's *Romeo and Juliet* (1935) where he shared the stage with John Gielgud. His portrayal of the Danish prince in *Hamlet* is also reported to have been stunning. To prepare for the role

Olivier researched Freudian psychology and his tortured performance was astonishing.

In 1939 he was offered the role of Heathcliff in an adaptation of *Wuthering Heights*. Olivier's good looks and skilful acting in the film catapulted him to international stardom overnight and many more offers flooded in. In 1940 he made a further two films — *Rebecca* and *Pride and Prejudice* in which he captured the hearts of women around the world by playing the romantic lead roles. This year also saw him divorce his first wife, Jill Esmond. A second marriage, to the beautiful Vivien Leigh, followed soon after and throughout the 1940s they were Hollywood's golden couple, starring in many films and plays together.

Returning to England in 1944 after war service, Olivier was appointed co-director of the Old Vic. Feeling himself to be in his natural element the following years produced some of his best performances in a variety of roles, many of which were filmed. The first of these was *Henry V* which was released in 1945. Olivier received an Academy Award for his performance in the lead role and it is widely believed that it has not been surpassed by any actor since. *Hamlet*, in 1948 won Olivier Academy Awards for Best Actor and Best Picture and was followed by *Richard III* (1955), and *Othello* (1965). During this period Olivier also continued to work in the theater in many of Shakespeare's most famous roles and, in 1947, he was knighted — becoming Sir Laurence Olivier.

At the end of the 1950s Olivier sought fresh challenges in his career and began to take on fewer classical parts. His range as an actor was

phenomenal and he soon found new success with his dark portrayal of the decrepit vaudevillian Archie Rice in John Osborne's *The Entertainer* which he filmed in 1960 after a popular run in the theater. In 1962 he was appointed as the director of the newly formed National Theatre Company appearing in such varied plays as Shakespeare's *The Merchant of Venice*, August Strindberg's *Dance of Death*, and Anton Chekhov's *Three Sisters*.

While his professional life continued to be outstanding, Olivier's personal affairs were often fraught. Amid rumors of a homosexual relationship with comedian Danny Kaye, he was divorced from Leigh in 1960 but married again in 1961, to British actress Joan Plowright. By the mid-1970s Olivier was in his sixties and his famous athleticism was diminished by a series of illnesses. He resigned from the National Theatre and retired from the stage in 1973 but continued to work in film and television throughout the remainder of his life. His performances won applause and, more Oscar nominations for films such as *Sleuth* (1972), *The Marathon Man* (1976), and *The Boys from Brazil* (1978). His many television appearances included Eugene O'Neill's, *Long Day's Journey Into Night* (1973), *Love Among the Ruins* (1975), and, *Brideshead Revisited,* (1982) which won him an Emmy.

Laurence Olivier died on July 11, 1989. His last years were spent writing his memoirs, *Confessions of an Actor* (1982), and another book, *On Acting* (1986). In a life that was distinguished by awards his final tribute was to be buried in Westminster Abbey, only four other actors before him had been so honored.

P

Pavlova, Anna [Anne Matveyevna]
1881–1931
Russian dancer

Having resolved to become a dancer as a young girl, Pavlova entered the St Petersburg Theatre School. Two years before her graduation, she danced on the Maryinsky stage in the Pas des Almées in *La Fille du Pharaon*. Her superb graduation performance of 1899 brought her to the attention of the critics. In 1903 she danced the role of Giselle and the Fairy Variations in the Prologue of *Sleeping Beauty*, before achieving the role of Aurora in 1908. Having danced 18 leading roles on the Maryinsky stage, in 1907 Fokine created for her the role of Cygne (the Dying Swan) which became her most famous solo. She toured abroad with the Russian Imperial Ballet in 1908, and settled at the Ivy House in London in 1912, her home for the rest of her life. Fragments of her dancing the Dying Swan were filmed in Hollywood by Douglas Fairbanks in 1924–25. Never strong, Pavlova died of pneumonia at the relatively young age of 49.

Peron Eva [María Eva Duarte]
1919–1952
Argentine politician

Eva Duarte began an acting career at the age of 15, singing in nightclubs and trying to work her way to stardom. She was a successful radio soap actor in 1944 when she met Juan Peron. She became his second wife in 1945. Peron was a charismatic leader of the fascist party, the Peronista, which overthrew President Castillo in 1943. In 1946 he was elected president, and Eva began to take an active role in politics. Eva Peron rapidly became the second most influential person in Argentina. The people affectionately called her "Evita," and it was she who rallied the support of the ordinary workers *descamisados* ("shirtless ones") for her husband's party. Reviled by her opponents, Evita sought the Vice Presidency in 1951 but was blocked by the military. She died from cancer in 1952.

Piaf, Edith
1915–1963
French cabaret singer

Born Edith Gassion, she was a street singer at age 15 and was nicknamed *piaf*, or "sparrow". She worked in her father's troupe initially, but later in cafes where in 1935 she was noticed by a cabaret owner. By the mid-1940s she was the most popular singer in France, with her husky, melancholy voice, tough songs and soul-baring delivery. "La Vie en Rose," became an international standard as did, "Non, Je ne Regrette Rien," but her most characteristic material did not translate well. She received encouragement from Maurice Chevalier, and worked in movies, operetta and comedy. In 1958 her memoirs, *Au bal de la chance* (trans. *To the Dance of Chance*), were published.

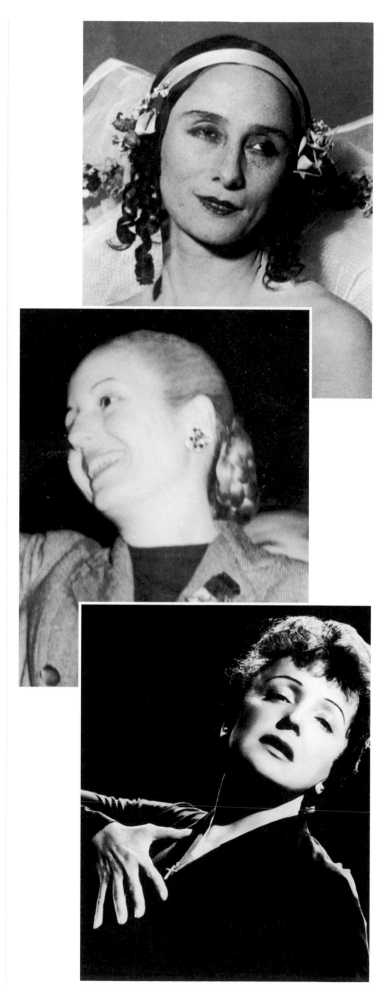

P

Patton, George, General
1885–1945
American soldier

Patton graduated from the U.S. Military Academy in 1910. He came from a family with a long tradition of military service. He was a keen student of the American Civil War, especially interested in the strategy of the great cavalry leaders. He was commissioned into the U.S. Army as a second lieutenant after his graduation. On General John Joseph Pershing's expedition to Mexico in 1917, he served as his aide-de-camp. In France in World War I Patton established and ran the tank training school. He led the 1st U.S. Tank Brigade in 1918 and

became a firm believer in armored mechanized warfare.

In November 1942 he led the armored forces that took Morocco, and went to take Tunisia in May 1943. In July 1943 he commanded U.S. forces in Sicily, although his reputation was marred when he slapped a battle-shocked soldier, for which he publicly apologized later. A flamboyant general, in March 1944 he assumed command of the U.S. Third Army, taking it to Normandy in August. Thereafter, he advanced across the Seine and into Alsace-Lorraine before crossing the Rhine and sweeping through southern Germany into Czechoslovakia. In December 1944 his forces played a

crucially strategic role in the Battle of the Bulge. He was a controversial figure throughout World War II, known to be uncompromising and outspoken with an aggressive combat strategy that ignored classic military rules. Nevertheless he had tremendous support from the ranks who referred to him as, "Old Blood and Guts." Patton served as military governor of Bavaria after the war. However his lenient policy towards the former enemy led to constant criticism and he was relieved of the post. He died in a jeep accident in late 1945 shortly after being named head of the Fifteenth Army. His memoirs, *War As I Knew It,* was published posthumously in 1947.

P

Picasso, Pablo
1881–1973
Spanish painter

Undoubtedly one of the greatest geniuses of the modern era, Picasso's work in a variety of different mediums has had the largest influence on the world of art of any single artist in the 20th century.

Born in Malaga, Spain on October 25, 1881, his natural talent was evident from a very early age. Fortunately Pablo's father, Jose Ruiz, a professor of art, soon recognized his son's natural ability and the young boy was encouraged and nurtured by both parents. At the tender age of 14 he was an artistic prodigy and completed the month-long entrance to the Academy of Fine Arts in Barcelona in a single day. Adopting his mother's maiden name as more exotic than the common Ruiz, Picasso was instructed there and, later, at the renowned Academy of San Fernando in Madrid.

His early work displays a keen awareness and understanding of the avant-garde movement which was pushing the boundaries of art at the turn-of-the-century. The most notable of his early influences were Henri de Toulouse-Lautrec and Paul Cézanne. In 1900 Picasso returned to Barcelona, at that time a hive of intellectual and artistic activity, and became well known at the famous cabaret Els Quatre Gats.

The suicide of a friend in Paris sparked Picasso's "blue period" which lasted from 1901 until 1904. During this time he made many studies of the poor and despairing from a predominately blue palette — a color which, for Picasso, symbolized the mental anguish and loneliness that he experienced. In 1904, he took permanent residence in the French capital and entered what became known as his "rose period." The colors of his painting took on a lighter hue and he became fascinated with depicting the scenes that he found in the lives of traveling circus performers. In the following years his work showed more maturity and independence of existing styles.

In Paris he painted *Les Demoiselles d'Avignon*, in 1907. This piece is seen as having enormous significance in both Picasso's development as an artist and that of art in general. Together with Georges Braque, he was experimenting with the ideas that would soon be formalized as Cubism. Using the medium of sculpture as well as paint, the two artists brought Cézanne's reduction of nature to basic forms a new simplicity. Influenced by the sharp definition of African and Iberian sculpture, their work demonstrated three dimensions on flat surfaces by the manipulation of planes. From 1911 to 1913 Picasso and Braque worked closely with this new model of art and developed it further, introducing novel materials such as chair caning to the paintings.

The 1920s brought a prolific period of artistic exploration for Picasso. While other artists worked to formalize his and Braque's cubist ideas, Picasso moved on. Though frequently returning to the earlier style, he also worked in the Classical mode and took an interest in early Surrealism. His admirers were many and he enjoyed work in the theater where he designed many sets. Always seeking originality, he became a pioneer of working sculpture in wrought iron from 1929 to 1931, and in the early 1930s turned his hand to graphic illustration.

His most widely recognized work of art was produced in 1937. Outraged by an air attack, during the Spanish Civil War, on the ancient Basque capital of Guernica, Picasso painted the harrowing *Guernica*. The painting, in white, black, and gray is a fierce condemnation of war. Symbolic images — the dying horse, the minotaur, and a hand clutching a broken sword — are fused with representations such as a woman screaming as she holds a dead baby. The chaos and fear of the scene is tangible and *Guernica* is pre-eminent among Picasso's most powerful pieces.

Following World War II which was spent in occupied Paris, Picasso moved to the South of France where he established a home and workshop. His work, which had become quite bleak during the war years, found a fresh vitality and began to express a dreamlike quality. During the next two and a half decades he remained prolific, working in lithography, paint, ceramics, and sculpture right up until his death. In the later stages of his career he was responsible for forging a complete re-evaluation of the field of lithography. His printmaking turned what was considered a mundane manufacturing task into an art form. In turn, this would later influence Andy Warhol to experiment with his own printing techniques to great effect.

In total Picasso's artistic career lasted over 75 years. A man of great energy, vision, and innovation, he created thousands of works of art during his lifetime. From early on Picasso believed that the meaning of life was to be found in art rather than nature, and, if his reasoning is followed, Picasso's art has completely changed our vision of the world and humanity's place in it. It has certainly had a profound effect on high culture. Pablo Picasso was a truly great artist and an affectionate family man who was always more at ease with children rather than adults. He died on April 8, 1973, in Mougins, France at the age of 91.

P

P

Pius XII, Pope
1876–1958
Italian Pontiff

Eugenio Pacelli came from an aristocratic family: his father was dean of the college of Vatican lawyers. He was ordained in 1899, departing from family tradition. He served in various posts, as Professor of Canonical Law at the Pontifical Institutes of the Apollinaire, and of Ecclesiastical Diplomacy at the Academy of the Noble Ecclesiastics in Rome. After 1904, he was involved with the new codification of canon law in (issued in 1917). Appointed archbishop of Sardes in 1917 and Apostolic Nuncio to Bavaria, he attempted a papal mediation to conclude World War I on behalf of Benedict XV. His work in Germany and other countries after 1920 gave him a reputation as an able diplomat. Elected Pope in 1939, political circumstances forced him to adopt a studied neutrality during World War II, and he has since been criticized for his failure to condemn Nazi atrocities and anti-Semitism.

Pound, Ezra
1885–1972
American poet

Born in Idaho and educated in Pennsylvania, Pound left for Europe in 1908, and published *A Lume Spento (trans. With Tapers Quenched)*, his first of many collections of poems, in Venice. In London, he taught and published more poetry and a volume of critical essays, *The Spirit of Romance* (1910). A founder of the Imagist movement, he gradually moved away in search of greater poetic freedom. The first three of his major projects, the *Cantos,* appeared in 1917, and he continued to work on them, meanwhile publishing *A Draft of XVI Cantos* in 1926. His politico-economic theorizing led him to anti-Semitism and won the admiration of Mussolini. He was returned to the U.S. in 1945, and held in an insane asylum until 1958, when he returned to Italy. The last part of the *Cantos* was published in 1970.

Porter, Cole
1891–1964
American songwriter

Cole Porter began writing songs as a law student while at Yale and Harvard Universities. He completed his first professional score for the musical revue, *See America First,* in 1916. In 1917 he joined the French Foreign Legion, later transfering to the French Army. He returned to America after the war. He came to live at the center of a social whirl, unhindered by snobberies attached to race or background, and hid his homosexuality behind his marriage to the socialite Linda Lee Thomas. His brilliantly written songs, for which he unusually wrote both words and music, include "Let's Do It," "Night and Day," and "Anything Goes." There were many others from 27 shows and revues such as *Kiss Me Kate* and *Rosalie*.

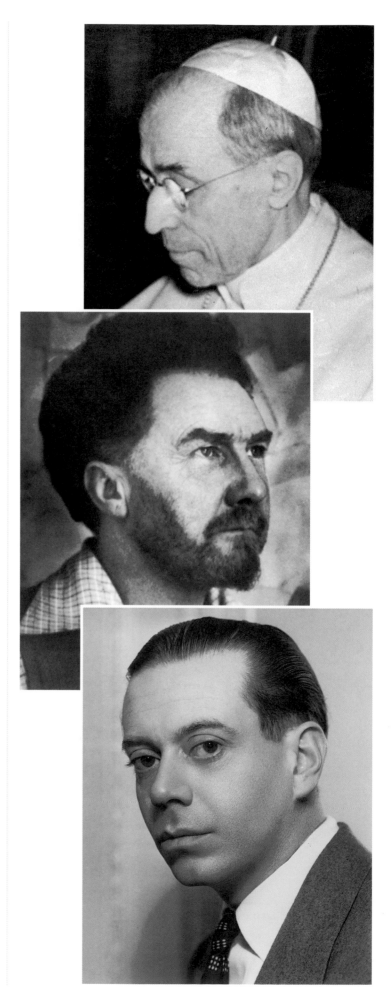

P

Pot, Pol
1928–1998
Cambodian politician

At the time that Pol Pot was growing up, Cambodia was a Buddhist kingdom under French control. His birth name was Saloth Sar, which he changed twice, once in Paris during the early 1950s to Khmer Da'em (meaning original Cambodian) and then by the mid-1970s he became known as Pol Pot. In the late 1940s, Pol Pot traveled to Paris, France. While taking a course in radio electricity, he linked up with the French Communist party.

Returning to Cambodia in 1953 after failing his courses in Paris, Pol Pot became involved in the movement for liberation from French colonial rule. He joined the Cambodian and Vietnamese Communists. Later that year Cambodia acquired its independence. Pol Pot was promoted through the ranks of the Worker's Party of Kampuchea (later the CPK – Communist Party of Kampuchea). By 1963 he was Secretary General. During 1967–75 the CPK (later renamed Khmer Rouge) became a popular guerrilla force. During this time Pol Pot ordered that a thousand Vietnamese-trained comrades be silently murdered. By 1978 half the members of the party's Central Committee, which had rarely met, had also been dispatched.

Determined that Cambodia should not be reliant on its neighbors, Pol Pot asserted that the country should return to pre-Buddhist days. He wanted to return to an agriculture-based economy. Having defeated the American-backed Phnom-Penh regime with his Khmer Rouge forces in 1975, he was able to impose his crazed, bloodthirsty brand of Marxism unchecked until the Vietnamese invaded and ousted him. During his reign of terror, 1.7 million people died from starvation and brutality. Cambodia was cut off from the world: arms were purchased from China in exchange for rice and endangered wildlife; religion was suppressed; neighboring countries attacked. After defeat in 1979, Pol Pot fled with his army to the Thai border. By 1996 his campaign to retake power had faltered. In 1997 rumors that Pol Pot had been taken hostage by the Khmer Rouge started to circulate and filmed evidence that he had died was released in 1998.

P

Presley, Elvis
1935–1977
American rock and pop singer

Presley was the prototype teen idol of the rock 'n'roll explosion of the 1950s, a potent combination of rebellion and sex which inspired so many great performers. In turn he popularized black music, his style originating from the blues and gospel music of the deep south. From the earliest days of his career, Elvis's attitude, looks, and talent made him the hero of the young world-wide. His fame and notoriety reached such magnitude that by the early 1970s he could arrive unannounced at the White House wearing his trademark satins and be assured of an immediate audience with the president.

Born in Tupelo, Mississipi on January 8, 1935, Elvis grew up in poverty, a fiercely overprotective mother sheltering him while his father served a brief prison sentence. As a young child he expressed interest in music, joining the local church to sing gospel and, at the age of ten, he won a prize for singing with a rendition of *Old Shep* — a song he would later record.

Soon after his father was released from prison, the family moved to a one-room apartment in Memphis where Elvis attended a vastly overcrowded new school. Eager to be noticed he experimented with his image, dying his dark blond hair black, wearing loud clothes and growing the side burns which would become his trademark.

In 1953, with encouragement from his teacher, he participated in a school production, easily stealing the show with several songs, including his favorite, *Old Shep*. An electrifying performance was met with enthusiastic applause, feeding Elvis's growing confidence. However, it seemed inconceivable that he could make a career of his passion and when he graduated in 1953 it was with the intent to become an electrican.

Events took an exciting turn in 1954 when Elvis noticed an advertisement at Sun Studios offering to make cheap recordings. With his mother's birthday approaching, combining his talent with the desire to present her with a thoughtful gift seemed like a good idea and he approached the studio to record *That's All Right Mamma*, written by black artist Arthur Crudup. The $4 that he handed over would change his life. Presley's unique style and powerful performance was instantly recognised by producer Sam Phillips as having enormous potential. Phillips was soon proved right and the first day that the song was broadcast on air it proved a Memphis sensation, immediately receiving 7,000 orders.

Following this initial success Elvis toured with a backing band, the Blue Moon Boys, and quickly developed a sound that could not be classified by existing terms of standard country and western or rhythm and blues. The enormous impact of the band in the Southern States and the publicity that they attracted with their frenetic playing and screaming audiences attracted the attention of promoter Colonel Tom Parker in 1955. By November of that year Parker had successfully negotiated the purchase of Presley's contract by RCA Victor and with his aggressive management style he began to engineer Presley's rise to international stardom. In 1956 *Heartbreak Hotel* was released, an instant hit, it remained at number one in the U.S. for an incredible eight weeks. It was followed by *Hound Dog, Don't Be Cruel, Love Me Tender,* and *All Shook Up*: their success confirming Presley's position at the top of America's music industry. Parker, quick to spot potential revenue, explored every consumerist angle, ensuring that merchandise was quickly produced to appease the 400,000 teenagers that joined the Elvis Presley Fan Club within six months of his first single. Presley's overnight fame soon resulted in TV appearances which captivated the nation's youth and outraged their parents. These were soon followed by film deals, including the successful *Love Me Tender* and *Jailhouse Rock*. In total he would appear in 33 movies of variable quality.

In March 1958 Elvis joined the military service, and was posted to Germany soon after the death of his mother. It was here that he met Priscilla Beaulieu in 1959 and conducted a secret relationship with her, given that she was a mere 14-years old and he was 25. In 1960 he finished his service and was welcomed home by screaming fans. Two years later he was living with Priscilla though the couple would not marry until 1967, soon before the birth of their daughter Lisa Marie. In the 1960s Elvis lost ground to the UK invasion led by the Beatles and the Rolling Stones, but in 1969 he made a successful effort to re-enter the limelight.

His marriage inevitably broke down due to neglect and Priscilla became involved with her karate instructor, leaving Presley in February 1972, before divorcing him in 1973. After the break-up, Elvis gradually became a recluse with a growing dependency on drugs and food.

The years of gorging, excessive drug use, and hectic touring finally caught up with him, resulting in a twisted colon, glaucoma, and respiratory trouble. The prescribed drugs that he took elevated to class-A narcotics stronger than heroin and he also developed a morbid interest in death, to the point where he watched a friend being embalmed.

On May 29, 1977, he walked offstage during a concert in Baltimore due to health problems. In August, the same year, he was found dead.

During the last 20 months of his life Presley had been prescribed 12,000 amphetamines, sedatives, and other narcotics. He left behind phenomenal record and memorabilia sales as a reminder of his status as rock's most potent phenomenon ever and his home, Graceland, is now a place of pilgrimage for millions of fans worldwide.

P

Potter, Beatrix
1866–1943
British author

An only child of wealthy parents, Beatrix Potter was privately educated and had a solitary childhood. However, holidays in Scotland and the English Lake District inspired her love of animals. Beatrix Potter started off trying to publish her botanical drawings and notes but was unsuccessful. Having written *The Tale of Peter Rabbit* for a sick child, she decided to publish it privately. It was well received and later her work was published commercially by Frederick Warne & Co. She went on to create several more animal characters in many whimsical tales and also prepared the illustrations for them. Her books include: *The Tailor of Gloucester* (1903), *The Tale of Squirrel Nutkin* (1903), and *The Tale of Benjamin Bunny* (1904). When not writing she lived on her farm with her husband, a solicitor, and bred Herdwick sheep.

Rasputin, Grigori Yefimovich
1871–1916
Russian monk and charlatan

Rasputin was undoubtedly one of the key factors contributing to the fall of the last Tsar of Russia, Nicholas II. He rose to influence in 1907 through his miraculous ability as a *starets*, or holy man, to relieve the pain of the Tsarvitch Alexis' hemophilia, succeeding where the best surgeons had failed. This gave him an entree to court which he exploited greedily in a scandalous life of debauchery, arousing the jealousy of the aristocracy and dragging the image of royal family and court down further. Rumors of his orgies scandalized Russia. The Tsarina Alexandra was completely under his hypnotic spell and, as she guided the Tsar, Rasputin's political influence soon grew. Key political and military personnel were chosen or dropped according to his whim. He was assassinated by a group of monarchists led by Prince Felix Yusupov.

Robeson, Paul
1898–1976
American actor

Robeson's most famous role was that of Joe, the slave in *Show Boat* (1936), leaving audiences thunderstruck with his singing of *Ol' Man River*. The public delighted in the vibrancy of his base baritone and he became a popular concert artist. His first appearances on Broadway in 1924 had been in Eugene O'Neill's *All God's Chillun Got Wings* and *The Emperor Jones*. Other stage roles were made in *Black Boy* (1926) and *Porgy* (1928). In the late 1940s he stunned theater audiences with his portrayal of Shakespeare's *Othello*, after which his career fell apart due to his espousal of communist causes. He was an outspoken advocate of the Soviet Union. In the 1950s he refused to sign a loyalty oath and his US passport was revoked for a time. He was an active civil rights campaigner as well.

R

Rachmaninov, Sergei
1873–1943
Russian composer and pianist

Like many brilliant musicians, Rachmaninov began studying the piano at an early age. In 1985 he was accepted at the Moscow Conservatory. There he studied with piano teachers including many famous names: the stringent disciplinarian Nikolay Zverov; eminent Russian composers Anton Arensky and Sergey Taneyev and his most important musical mentor, Peter Ilich Tchaikovsky. Rachmaninov's cousin, Aleksandr Siloti, gave him the heritage of his own teacher, Hungarian pianist and composer Franz Liszt.

Many think of Rachmaninov as the composer of the ever-popular second piano concerto or of the *Rhapsody on a Theme of Paganini*. However few realize that he was also the composer of the most exquisite songs and, although not as popular as his piano concertos, they give a valuable insight into the more intimate side of his character. Sadly these songs are not performed as often as they deserve.

His first work to establish him as a composer was his opera *Aleko* (1893). Written in the same year was *Trio Elégiaque*, in memory of Tchaikovsky. Due to a poor reception for his Symphony No. 1 in D Minor (1897) he did not compose for three years. Instead he concentrated on conducting and working as a pianist. Between 1900–17 he produced many exceptional pieces: Piano Concerto No. 2 in C Minor (1900); Symphony No. 2 in E Minor (1906); the symphonic poem *The Isle of the Dead* (1909); the *Liturgy of St. John Chrysostom* (1910); *The Bells* (1913), based on a poem by American writer Edgar Allan Poe; *All-Night Vigil* (1915).

In 1917 to escape the turmoil in Russia, Rachmaninov moved to the United States where he continued to compose. It has also become apparent from recordings that Rachmaninov was an exceptional pianist of virtuosic quality and probably one of the finest pianists the 20th century will ever see. His compositions are considered the last major expression of the romantic era.

Runyon, Alfred Damon
1880–1946
American journalist

For many years, starting in 1918, Runyon was a journalist whose column was syndicated for the Hearst newspapers. Previously he had reported on the war in Mexico between 1912 and 1916 and in Europe during World War I. His writing after the wars was mostly about the gangster underworld, which he had a tendency to romanticize. He also wrote about Broadway characters, and was noted for his use of slang and metaphor. An expressive short story writer, his collections include *Guys and Dolls* (1931), *Take It Easy* (1938), and *In Our Town* (1946). *Guys and Dolls* was later produced as the highly popular musical on Broadway in 1950, then made into a hit movie, and revived again on Broadway in the 1990s.

Rockefeller, John D.
1839–1937
American industrialist and philanthropist

Brought up by religious parents to be painstaking and unscrupulous, John D. Rockefeller was well equipped to succeed. Still in his 20s, he helped to establish an oil refinery in the backwoods of Ohio, which, in 1870 became Standard Oil. He realized that he would do better without competition, and when bullying failed he set up interlocking directorships to control other refineries and virtually monopolized the American market. (By 1878 he had control of 90% of the market.)

Eventually the Supreme Court invoked anti-trust laws, but well before then Rockefeller had relinquished close control of his empire and spent most of his time organizing great philanthropic projects through his Rockefeller Foundation. At its peak Rockefeller's personal fortune was estimated as being $1 billion.

Rockwell, Norman
1894–1978
American painter and illustrator

Rockwell achieved enormous popularity in the U.S. through the illustration work he executed in oils, particularly his *Saturday Evening Post* covers (1916–63). His humorous, sentimental evocations of small-town life and edifying, patriotic images embodied what many wished to imagine as the spirit of America. His work was also seen in, *Ladies' Home Journal, Boy Scout Calendar,* and *Look.* His favorite subjects were everyday events, and he frequently used his neighbors as models. His attention to detail and realistic painting are almost photographic in quality. Throughout his career he designed many posters, the *Four Freedoms* being his most famous. Based on the principles announced by the president, Franklin D. Roosevelt in 1941 and incorporated into the Atlantic Charter, reproductions of them are still popular.

R

Rodin, (François) Auguste René
1840–1917
French sculptor

The son of a police official, Rodin failed to be accepted in the Ecole des Beaux-Arts and so studied art at a free school for artisans and in the galleries of the Louvre. He spent many years in semi-apprenticeship, working for other sculptors, notably Ernest Carrier-Belleuse. During this time he worked together with the Belgian artist on architectural sculpture for the Bourse in Brussels. After a visit to Italy in 1875, Rodin was heavily influenced by the work of Michelangelo and Donatello, especially the treatment of movement and muscle action.

Rodin sometimes distorted the anatomy of his subjects in order that they might produce a more truthful representation of the inner states of his subject. His works, produced in bronze and marble, used the appearance of the surface, and extreme delicacy of form to convey more than beauty. In 1877 he exhibited *The Age of Bronze* at the Salon. Its extreme realism confounded viewers who accused Rodin of using plaster casts from living models to achieve the finished result. Between 1858 and 1875 Rodin produced several important sculptures including *Man with the Broken Nose*. His ability to represent the human form and express a wealth of hidden meaning is exemplified by the nude statue of *St. John the Baptist* exhibited in 1880.

His most famous popular sculptures — *The Kiss*, *The Thinker*, *Adam*, and *Eve* — were all studies for a commission for the Musée des Arts Décoratifs in Paris. The commission, a bronze door, was to have represented the Gates of Hell, inspired by scenes from Dante's, *Inferno*. Although not completed, the separate components are acclaimed as individual masterpieces. In 1886 Rodin finished a monumental bronze sculpture of, *The Burghers of Calais*, which is an exquisite representation of the historical figures. Although linked by touch and condemned to death, each man clearly displays individuality, in his reaction to his circumstances.

Rodin was also a portrait artist, painting many famous Frenchmen, including Honoré de Balzac, Victor Hugo, and Jules Bastien-Lepage, as well as producing busts of artists, Jules Dalou, Carrier-Belleuse, and Pierre Puvis de Chavannes.

R

Roosevelt, Theodore
1858–1919
American statesman and president

Perhaps the most popular President in American history, Roosevelt's reforming policies helped to form the progressive tone that has characterized the remainder of the century in the U.S.. "Teddy" was a complex character. An early environmentalist he was also a big-game hunter. A military man, he was awarded the Nobel Peace Prize for helping to end the Russo-Japanese War. He was also a writer and historian of merit, as well as being a man of great wit and colorful personality. Public affection for him was so great that, "Teddy Bears," were named after him.

Born in New York City on October 27, 1858, into a patrician Dutch family, he was a sickly youth. His father instilled into him the virtues of self-discipline, mental courage, and a firm morality. Consequently Theodore became a keen sportsman in an effort to overcome his physical weakness as well as a dedicated student. After graduating from Harvard in 1880, Roosevelt married Alice Lee and entered the political arena. He was elected in 1882 and served three consecutive one-year terms in the New York Assembly where he supported legislation which benefited working people. During the 1880s he also began studying and writing his extensive texts on American history. Published works during the decade included, *The Naval War of 1812* (1882), *Essays on Practical Politics* (1888), and the first two of the four-volume series, *The Winning of the West* (1889-96). From 1884 to 1886, after the death of both his mother and wife, Roosevelt, a devastated man, moved to Dakota where he lived as a cowboy. He married again within three years, however, this time to Edith Kermit Carow.

Returning to New York in 1886 his bid to become mayor ended in failure.

However, three years later he was appointed as a U.S. Civil Service commissioner in Washington D.C. and his political career began in earnest. In 1895 he attained the position of President of the New York Police Board. With a habit of grabbing headlines, Roosevelt gained a national reputation in this post. His reward was the job of Assistant Navy Secretary, to which President McKinley appointed him in 1897. A year later Roosevelt resigned.

War had erupted with Spain and, in typical idiosyncratic style, Roosevelt felt determined to aid his country. Organizing a privately raised regiment of cavalry, named the "Rough Riders," with himself at the head, Roosevelt lead a charge up Kettle Hill which made him a national hero.

His return to New York after the American victory was triumphant and he easily won the governorship in 1889. However, his colleagues were so outraged by his reforms that they resolved to, "kick him upstairs" and Roosevelt was shunted into the job of Vice-President. On September 14, 1901, President McKinley succumbed to an assassin's bullet and Roosevelt moved into the White House as the 26th President.

Due to fears within his own party that his reformist zeal would spell disaster for the Republicans, Roosevelt initially assured them that he would maintain caution and follow McKinley's policies. A steadily rising popularity increased his confidence and Roosevelt began to stamp his own personality onto the office. He moved against the big money interests, indicting 30 corporations for breaking the anti-trust laws, created the Department of Commerce and Labor, and brought in the Pure Food and Drugs Act. Roosevelt also assisted Chief Forester

Gifford Pinchot in creating vast expanses of national parkland, attempting to initiate a culture of conservationism in American society. In foreign policy his motto was, "speak softly and carry a big stick." In 1903 he successfully concluded negotiations with the new state of Panama to cede a Canal Zone for the construction of the waterway, which he traveled to oversee in 1904.

Elected President again in that year, he continued with his program of

progressive reform. The Monroe Doctrine, which Roosevelt proposed, proclaimed the U.S. as guardian of the Western Hemisphere and served the President's imperialist intentions of expanding American influence around the world. He was awarded the Nobel Peace Prize in 1906, and, after an eventful presidency, retired in 1909.

On his return from a grand tour and safari around Africa in 1910 he found that his successor, William H. Taft was presiding over a hopelessly divided Republican Party. A number of disputes drew Roosevelt back into politics and in 1912 he ran for president again, this time as an independent candidate. During the campaign, Roosevelt was shot in an attempted assassination. Seeing that the wound to his chest was non-fatal Roosevelt conversed with the startled gunman before proceeding on his tour. Nevertheless, he was defeated by Woodrow Wilson and returned to a life of study and writing, producing his autobiography in 1913. His last hope of a return to politics was dashed in 1916 when the Republicans nominated Charles Evans Hughes as their candidate.

Three years later, Theodore Roosevelt died at his Oyster Bay home on January 6, 1919. He was a humane man whose office was conspicuous for its concern with beneficial works. Roosevelt lead his country from a position of staunch morality and genuine concern and his passing was deeply mourned by the nation.

R

Roddenberry, Gene
1921–1991
American television producer

Gene Roddenberry worked as a pilot and police officer
before becoming a writer. He started developing a science
fiction TV series in the mid-1960s. The result, *Star Trek,* was
set in the 23rd century. It ran from 1966–69. It told of the
adventures of a starship crew as they boldly went, "where no
one had ever gone before." From the outset, Roddenberry, as
executive producer, carefully guided the storylines to show
human frailty. It was widely syndicated and built up a loyal
base of fans.

Star Trek: The Motion Picture was released in 1979, but he
had little active involvement with the other movies (released
in 1982, 1984, 1986, 1989 and 1991). He was actively
involved with the creation of the follow-up series *Star Trek:
The Next Generation* (1987–94). Other spin-offs include *Star
Trek: Deep Space Nine* (started 1993), and *Star Trek: Voyager*
(started 1995) and many books.

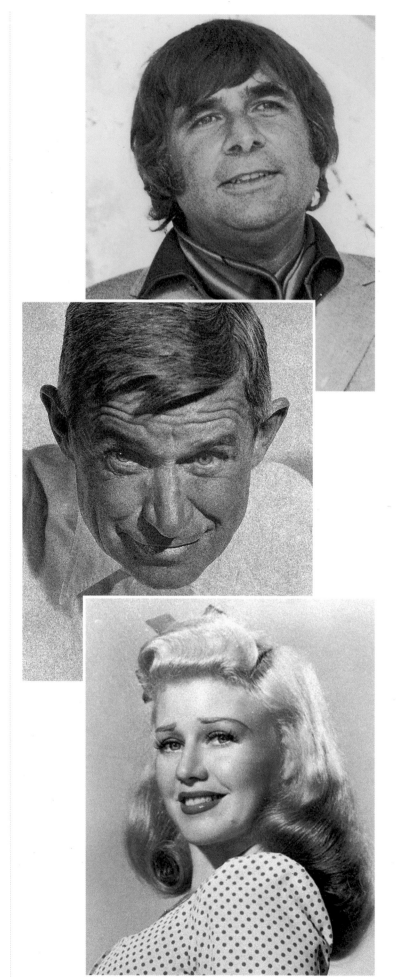

Rogers, Wil
1879–1935
American humorist

A comic of the vaudeville school, Rogers had his career
curtailed by a flying accident in 1935. He made his debut in
1905 and later developed a routine of humorous monologues
and rope tricks. He achieved huge popularity. Around 1914
he could be found in *Ziegfeld Follies* in New York City. He
had a successful movie career beginning in 1918, appearing
in more than 60 movies, and found a new audience with the
advent of sound. Rogers also wrote a series of syndicated
articles for newspapers in which he belittled great figures of
the day and discharged his unique philosophy of life. He also
produced some books, which include *The Cowboy Philosopher
on Prohibition* (1919), *Illiterate Digest* (1924), and *Will Rogers'
Political Follies* (1929).

Rogers, Ginger
1911–1995
American actress

Rogers started on the stage at 14, touring with a vaudeville
troupe until 1929. She started her movie career while still on
Broadway, in the movie *Top Speed*, and in 1931 she was in
Hollywood in minor parts. However she was swept into
movie immortality in the arms of Fred Astaire. Their 1930s
musicals were some of the best Hollywood ever made. In
Flying Down to Rio (1933) they stole the show: their obvious
chemistry on screen encouraged RKO to pair them in other
movies: *Top Hat* (1935), *Swing Time* (1936), and *Follow The
Fleet* (1936). Rogers made other movies during the years
with Astaire, and afterwards tackled various roles, winning
an Academy Award for *Kitty Foyle* (1940). In the 1950s and
1960s she pulled in the crowds on Broadway and on the
London stage played the lead in, among others, *Hello Dolly!*
and *Mame*.

R

Robinson, Jackie [Jack Roosevelt]
1919–1972
American baseball player

In 1941 Robinson left college to join the U.S. Army. He graduated from Officers' Candidate School a second lieutenant, into what was then a segregated army. Arrested when he refused a driver's order to move to the back of a bus, Robinson was acquitted at a court-martial. He was honorably discharged in 1944 with the rank of first lieutenant.

One of the most important moments in 20th century sports came in 1947 when Jackie Robinson debuted with the Brooklyn Dodgers, breaking the color barrier and paving the way for generations of African Americans to play Major League baseball. Branch Rickey, president of the Dodgers, had signed Robinson — a former four-sport star at UCLA — to a minor league contract for the 1946 season. Robinson had played that year at Montreal (AAA), enduring some vicious racism, but still leading the league in hitting with a .349 average. The next year he came up to the Dodgers amid much fanfare and controversy. Some of his opponents on the field tried to spike him, and in St Louis he was not allowed to stay in the team hotel. Robinson remained stoic, and played brilliantly, winning Rookie of the Year Honors. Two years later he was voted the league's Most Valuable Player. Over a 10-year career Robinson hit .311. He retired from the game in 1956 rather than be traded to another club. He was inducted into the Baseball Hall of Fame in 1962, the first African American man to receive the honor.

Had he been given the opportunity he would have liked to have moved into team management, but no club was forthcoming with an offer. Instead he promoted African-American business enterprises in Harlem, New York, promoted Civil Rights and was a businessman. From 1964–1968 he was Special Advisor for Civil Rights to Governor Nelson Rockefeller. He collaborated with Alfred Duckett on a book of his life, *I Never Had It Made* (1972). His self-composed epitaph on his grave reads: "A life is not important except in the impact it has on other lives."

R

Reagan, Ronald
1911–
American politician and president

Reagan's place in history is the subject of continuing controversy. After a successful career as a Hollywood movie actor he moved into politics, and, at the age of 69, was the oldest man ever sworn in as President. While fostering economic renewal, at the end of his administration, America — traditionally the world's biggest creditor — owed $400 billion. Balancing this, his negotiations with Soviet premier, Mikhail Gorbachev, were instrumental in bringing an end to the Cold War.

The child of John and Nelle Reagan, Ronald was born on February 6, 1911, in Tampico, Illinois. His parents were committed Democrats and instilled their, "New Deal" politics into their son. A promising sportsman and enthusiastic actor, Reagan completed his education at Eureka College where he studied economics and sociology. Following graduation he was keen to start work in the entertainment industry and soon landed a job as a sportscaster. In 1937, he was successfully screen-tested by Warner Brothers.

His acting career spanned the next two decades, during which Reagan made 53 films of variable quality. His first appearance was in, *Love is On the Air* (1937), and his best performances were in, *Brother Rat* (1938), *Dark Victory* (1939), and *King's Row* (1941). Elected as president of the Screen Actor's Guild, he became heavily involved in the McCarthy-inspired Communist purges of the movie industry, and his loyalty shifted from the Democrats to the Republican Party. After the dissolution of his first marriage, to actress Jane Wyman, he married another actress, Nancy Davis, in 1952. He moved into television in the 1950s, and later presented the popular favorite, "Death Valley Days" from 1962 to 1965.

By the beginning of the 1960s, Reagan's involvement in politics was burgeoning. A respected conservative public orator, he began to win the political respect that had eluded him as an actor. In 1966, he managed a landslide victory in California and became governor of the state. Reagan's opposition to tax increases enhanced his popularity and he went on to win a further term. By the time he left the office eight years later, California's budget was extremely healthy and Reagan was widely regarded as having performed excellently.

Six years later he was nominated as the Republican candidate for the 1980 Presidential election. With George Bush as his capable running mate and a television manner honed over many years in the media, Reagan cast off doubts about his advanced age and presented himself as a moderate but effective choice. Promising economic stability, increased spending on the military, and a less intrusive government, he easily defeated Carter and was inaugurated as America's 40th President on January 20, 1981. Only 69 days later he was shot by a would-be assassin and narrowly escaped with his life. Despite fears for his health he returned to office after making a rapid recovery with his reputation strengthened by the ordeal.

His first measures as President were aimed at stimulating economic growth: cutting taxes in addition to legislation which curbed government control over business regulation were intended to entice investment. In reality, the national deficit quickly mounted. His administration had the appearance of succeeding but the hidden cost soared into the trillions of dollars. The "Reagan Revolution" ground to a halt and, by 1982, unemployment reached levels unseen for 40 years. Foreign policy also faced difficulties. American peacekeeping forces in the Lebanon were suffering substantial casualties and arms control negotiations with the Soviets stalled. However, in 1983 the economy firmed and gradual decreases in unemployment levels boosted Reagan's appeal in time for his announcement that he would run for a second term at the beginning of 1984.

As ever, a master of the media, Reagan exuded optimism during the campaign. Though it seemed unclear what his policies were, apart from the re-stated promise that taxes would not be raised, he won a resounding and unexpected victory.

Reagan's second term was equally fraught with problems. The Iran-Contra scandal found members of his administration to have been involved in underhand activities such as the covert sale of arms to Iran and the siphoning of funds to the Contras. Reagan denied all knowledge of the dealings and his competency was subsequently called into question. In public the president seemed increasingly decrepit, notably bumbling during a conference with Mikhail Gorbachev and referring to Britain's Princess Diana as Princess David. However, despite consistent avocation of his "Star Wars" program, Reagan eventually managed to reach some agreement with the Soviet leader. An agreement to limit some nuclear weapons was signed and Reagan made an historic visit to Moscow in 1988. Perhaps Reagan's most critical act as President was to pursue policies that enabled Gorbachev to dismantle the old Communist regime.

Later that year Bush succeeded him as President. He also inherited a massive national deficit and spiraling recession. But, Reagan's popularity was higher than ever when he left office. Since his retirement political historians have continued to argue over the value of his term. In 1994, a statement was made informing the world that Ronald Reagan had been diagnosed as suffering from Alzheimer's Disease.

R

R

Rodgers and Hammerstein
American musical creators

The collaborative career of Richard Rodgers as composer and Oscar Hammerstein II as lyricist and librettist spanned 16 years. Together, they became the most influential and successful theater writers in history, creating a new form of theater – the musical drama – a form that has been emulated by many composers since. Their shows, which blend musical comedy and operetta, continue to enjoy massive popularity and are still successful on stage as well as having been made into classic films. Their impressive array of awards numbers 34 Tony Awards, 15 Academy Awards, two Pulitzer Prizes, two Grammy Awards, and an Emmy Award. *Time* Magazine and CBS News, in 1998, placed them among the top 20 most important artists and entertainers of the 20th century. Early in 1999, a postage stamp was released in the U.S. in their honor.

Richard Rodgers
1902–1979

Richard Rodgers was born to William and Mamie Rodgers on June 28, 1902, in New York, New York. From an early age he learned to appreciate and love music as both of his parents enjoyed operetta. At the age of six they took him to see, "Pied Piper," an experience that was to shape his destiny. From the moment that the curtain was raised, the young boy was transfixed by the glamor of the stage. As he grew up it was obvious that Richard was a prodigiously talented musician — at 17 he was composing musicals with Lorenz Hart while studying music at Columbia University. Their prolific collaboration, which lasted from the 1920s into the 1940s, produced more than 40 shows and film scores that were successful around the world including, *On Your Toes* (1936), *My Funny Valentine* (1937), *Pal Joey* (1940), and, *Bewitched* (1940). Their work broke the mold of the Tin Pan

Alley musical, evolving Rodgers' ideas for musical plays which had a libretto.

Hart died in 1943, at which time Rodgers went into partnership with Oscar Hammerstein II — a partnership that was to remain exclusive until the latter's death. Both were at the height of their artistic powers, and the shows that they created together were masterpieces.

After Hammerstein's death, Rodgers continued to write, taking over his colleague's duty as lyricist to produce hit musicals including, *No Strings* (1962), and, with lyricist Stephen Sondheim, *Do I Hear A Waltz?* (1965). Richard Rodgers died on December 30, 1979, soon after the opening of his last Broadway musical. In 1990, he was commemorated with the renaming of Broadway's 46th Street Theater, which became The Richard Rodgers Theater.

Oscar Hammerstein II
1895–1960

Hammerstein was born into a theatrical family on July 12, 1895, also in New York, New York His father was the manager of the Victoria Theater, while his grandfather, the first Oscar, built theaters and produced shows at the Manhattan Opera House. His uncle, Arthur, was also a successful Broadway producer.

Hammerstein attended Columbia University from 1912 to 1916, studying law, but left before completing his course to take a job as assistant stage manager at his uncle's theater. Determined to achieve success, he wrote constantly and among his first works were several pieces for varsity shows that were penned with Richard Rodgers, who was an undergraduate at Columbia, and Lorenzo Hart. His first stage play, *The Light* (1920), which his uncle produced, was a failure, lasting

only four performances. Nevertheless, Hammerstein persevered, writing lyrics and librettos, usually in collaboration with Otto Harbach. In 1923, he was vindicated when *Wildflower* opened to general acclaim. The musical, which he had written with Harbach, Vincent Youmans, and Herbert Stothart, proved to be the first of many similar successes and for the next two decades, the heyday of Broadway musicals, Hammerstein penned typically witty and sophisticated musicals with some of the greatest musical talents of the time including the masterpiece, *Show Boat* (1927), with Jerome Kern, *Song of the Flame* (1929), with George Gershwin, and the highly acclaimed, *Carmen Jones*, a reworking of Bizet's opera, *Carmen*, which opened in 1943, shortly before Hammerstein joined forces with Richard Rodgers.

Oscar Hammerstein II died on August 23, 1960. The last song that he wrote was "Edelweiss," for, *The Sound of Music* (1959). In 1996, over 100 years after his birth, no less than three of his musicals were playing on Broadway.

Rodgers and Hammerstein Musicals:

1943 —	Oklahoma!
1945 —	Carousel
1947 —	Allegro
1949 —	South Pacific
1951 —	The King and I
1953 —	Me and Juliet
1955 —	Pipe Dream
1959 —	The Sound of Music

R

R

The Rolling Stones
British pop group

Jagger, Mick (1943–)
Jones, Brian (1942–1969)
Richards, Keith (1943–)
Stewart, Ian (1938–1985)
Taylor, Mick (1949–)
Watts, Charlie (1941–)
Wood, Ronnie (1947–)
Wyman, Bill (1936–)

Epitomizing the sex, drugs, and rock' n' roll lifestyle, and courting scandal with their wild behavior throughout the 1960s and 70s, the "Stones" attitude has been emulated by countless other rock groups. Perhaps the most enduring band of the century, they have produced some of the most instantly recognizable tracks in rock history. At its best, their music is a testament to the songwriting genius of Richards and Jagger. Fusing the former's elegantly spare guitar work with Jagger's twisted lyrics and tortured vocals, the Rolling Stones' music often has a dark and restrained grandeur, which is unmistakable.

Mick Jagger and Keith Richards were childhood friends. However, while attending different schools they did not see each other for many years. They met again, years later, on the platform at a local railway station where Jagger noticed that Richards was carrying a bag of rare import albums from the US. The pair fell into discussing their mutual love of blues music and, as a result, formed a band in 1963. They were joined by Charlie Watts (drums), the mercurial and gifted Brian Jones (guitar), and Bill Wyman (bass). The latter was older than the rest of the band but his access to better quality equipment assured his place. An additional member was Ian Stewart who played piano. Not fitting the image of a Rolling Stone, Stewart was never listed as an "official" member though he played an important role in the development of their music; writing, recording, and playing with the band right up until his death in 1985.

The Rolling Stones were first spotted by the aggressive young promoter Andrew Oldham, who carefully nurtured their bad boy image through the early years. Originally the band played covers of classic rhythm and blues tracks and it was Oldham who locked Richards and Jagger in a room together, refusing to let them out until they had written a recordable song. The result was, "Satisfaction." Released in 1965, it was a statement of rebellion that caught the British mood of the time. In the same year Wyman, Jones, and Jagger were each fined £5 for urinating against the wall of a gas station. This brush with the law confirmed their position as rebels and throughout the rest of the decade they were pitched in the media as the antithesis of the clean-cut Beatles.

Massively successful within a very short space of time, the band took advantage of the Beatles' door-opening tour of the US and enjoyed immense popularity. Their concerts were the scenes of mass hysteria at which the music was overwhelmed by screaming teenagers. Through the flower power movement of the late 1960s, their occasionally lukewarm efforts were balanced by some fine albums, including, *High Tide and Green Grass* (1966), *Between the Buttons* (1967), and *Let It Bleed* (1969).

The end of that decade marked a difficult time for the band. Drug busts and conflicts with the authorities sapped their creativity and in a notorious incident a fan was killed in the crowd by a Hell's Angel at a concert in Altamont, California. An increasingly drug-addled Jones was sacked from the group and found dead in a swimming pool soon after.

However, the Stones emerged from the destruction triumphant with the release of the classic single "Jumpin' Jack Flash" and started the new decade with two superb albums — *Sticky Fingers* (1971) and *Exile on Main Street* (1972) — with Jones'

replacement Mick Taylor on guitar. In 1971, they also founded their own record company, Rolling Stones Records, with its famous tongue poking out of a pair of lips trademark. Nevertheless Richards' involvement with drugs and Jagger's elevation to the jet-set left them directionless for much of the remainder of the 1970s with the exception of the best-selling album,

Some Girls (1978). This album saw them joined by ex-Faces guitarist Ronnie Wood following the departure of Taylor.

The 1980s were wilderness years for the band — their excessive concerts hid a somewhat tired mediocrity and Jagger and Richards both pursued solo projects while constantly fueding. In 1989 however, the two patched up their differences

to record, *Steel Wheels*, hailed as their best work for a decade. They followed it with massive world tours and found a form again which demonstrated that, at their best, they are still one of the finest live acts around.

Wyman amicably retired in 1992 shortly before the Rolling Stones started work on the Grammy-winning, *Voodoo Lounge* album (1994). Widely respected for their

musicianship and energy, they have now been inducted into the Rock Hall of Fame and continue to play around the world. As Jagger once said at a press conference in the 1960s, "Yeah, I'll be doing this when I'm old, as long as I'm still getting my rocks off." At the time of going to press the band are nearing the end of another lengthy world tour promoting their *Bridges to Babylon* album.

R

Roosevelt, Franklin Delano
1882–1945
American statesman and president

The only man to have served more than two terms as President of the United States, Franklin D. Roosevelt was responsible for leading America out of the Great Depression and into World War II.

He was born to a wealthy, socially active family at Hyde Park, New York on January 30, 1882. As a youth his education was supplied by his parents and a succession of private tutors and Franklin became fond of solitary pursuits such as collecting stamps and birds. However, though somewhat introverted, he was a bright and friendly boy, an able athlete, and he also enjoyed frequent trips to Europe with his family.

His education later continued at the prestigious Groton Preparatory School in Massachusetts and then Harvard where he received a degree in history after only three years' study. Next he attended New York's Columbia University where he impressed again, passing his bar examination in 1907. While here he fell in love with a distant cousin, Eleanor Roosevelt, and married her in 1905. The bride was given away by her uncle, President Theodore Roosevelt. From university, Franklin went on to join a law firm in New York City where he was employed for three years before making the decision to enter politics.

As a Democrat, he was first elected to the New York State Senate in 1912, a considerable achievement in a traditionally Republican district. In 1913 Woodrow Wilson appointed Roosevelt as Assistant Secretary of the Navy, a post which he held for seven years and in which he displayed his usual zeal and efficiency. As a result his reputation increased steadily and in 1920 he was nominated as the Democratic candidate for Vice President. However, Democratic policies found little popular support and Roosevelt returned to private life.

The following year while on vacation Roosevelt contracted poliomyelitis, a devastating disease which left him without the use of his legs. Eleanor's help and encouragement during his recovery was fundamental to him returning to his political career in 1924.

Elected Governor of New York in 1928, Roosevelt's progressive and dynamic style soon made him popular. In particular his measures to protect the state from the ravages of the economic depression that was beginning to grip the U.S. were widely applauded and added weight to his burgeoning reputation. Roosevelt was unsurprisingly reelected in 1930 and in 1932 was nominated as the Democratic Party presidential candidate. After a strenuous campaign, Roosevelt defeated Hoover in November 1932 by a massive seven million votes and entered the White House.

His first task as President was to combat the depression that was now devastating the country. His response to the crisis was the "New Deal," a legislative package that provided relief, recovery, and reform. Its success saved many Americans from starvation, boosted stock market confidence, and began the slow reversal of America's fortunes. It also helped Roosevelt win a landslide victory in the 1936 election and a further two terms in 1940 and 1944.

During the war years Roosevelt's foresight and personal control as Commander in Chief of the U.S. Armed Forces proved decisive. Though the U.S. was initially neutral, the president's hostility to Hitler's regime lead to a steady supply of American weapons to Britain and the USSR. Roosevelt was eager to participate in the war despite the mixed feelings of the population: following the Japanese attack on Pearl Harbor, in December 1941, and the declaration of war against America by the Axis powers four days later, he was quick to make an impact. Working closely with Winston Churchill, the British Prime Minister, the two men personally planned Allied tactics and, in spite of his failing health, Roosevelt's intervention helped turn the tide of the war in favor of the Allies.

However, the constant pressure of the conflict eventually took its toll. On April 12, 1945, he suffered a massive stroke at his holiday home in Warm Springs, Georgia. Two and a half hours later Franklin D. Roosevelt died — just one day short of complete military victory in Europe.

His term of office was remarkable in many ways, primarily because his brilliant actions during the Great Depression can be said to have saved the entire capitalist system and paved the way for an era of American prosperity. He also helped fashion the Democrat Party into the liberal reformist movement that it is today, appealing to the laboring classes and minority voters. Roosevelt's presidency has become a landmark in U.S. history.

Roosevelt, Anna Eleanor
1884–1962
First Lady

Eleanor Roosevelt's contributions to American society are manifold. An energetic and tireless worker for social causes and a radical reformer, her work for the underprivileged was exemplary and she was a staunch campaigner for the rights of racial minorities and women.

Born in New York City on October 11, 1884, Eleanor was raised by her maternal grandmother following the premature deaths of both parents. An intensely unhappy childhood made her shy girl and it was not until she

attended the Allenswood finishing school in England that she began to develop a strong personality. Here she was nurtured by the headmistress, Marie Souvestre, who encouraged Eleanor to become a popular school leader, and she returned to America to make her social debut altogether more confident. However, she soon tired of the social scene and instead found voluntary work among the poor of New York.

She married Franklin D. Roosevelt, a distant cousin, on March 17, 1905, and over the next 11 years the couple had six children, only five of whom survived. Never comfortable merely filling the expected role of hostess while her husband forged a political career, Eleanor involved herself with the Red Cross during World War I and, following the war, the League of Women Voters.

After Roosevelt's election as President she became a powerful voice on behalf of a wide range of social causes, particularly through her daily newspaper column "My Day" and her own radio show, both of which she used as a platform to air her strong political views.

Eleanor outlived her husband by almost 20 years and during that time as a U.S. delegate to the United Nations, she was instrumental in drafting the U.N. Declaration of Human Rights. She was also socially active right up to her death and always at the heart of her large family. A prolific writer, her many books include, *This I Remember* (1949) and, *The Autobiography of Eleanor Roosevelt* (1961). Eleanor Roosevelt died on November 7, 1962, and is buried next to her husband in the rose garden at Hyde Park in New York.

R&S

Ruth, Babe [George Herman]
1895–1948
American baseball player

Babe Ruth is easily responsible for the popularity of the game of baseball. In 1920, his first season with the New York Yankees, Ruth slugged 54 homers. As the centerpiece of the Yankees' "Murderer's Row" in 1927, he hit 60 home runs, a single-season record surpassed eventually by Roger Mans in 1961. All told, Ruth scored 714 homers, a figure finally eclipsed (by Henry Aaron) in 1974. Ruth began his career as a pitcher with the Boston Red Sox in 1914. He helped pitch Boston to three World Series, then was made an outfielder so that his hitting talent could be used everyday. After the 1919 season the Sox traded Ruth to the Yankees and the Yanks went on to become the sport's greatest dynasty. One notable anecdote about his career relates to the incident in which he apparently predicted completely accurately when and where he would hit a home run in the 1932 World Series.

Salk, Jonas Edward
1914–1995
American microbiologist

Salk achieved his medical degree in 1939 and was appointed assistant to the professor of epidemiology at the University of Michigan. In 1947, he was created the head of the virus research laboratory at the University of Pittsburgh. Later he was Research Professor of Bacteriology (1949–54), Professor of Preventative Medicine (1954–56), and Professor for Experimental Medicine (1957–63). Working on an anti-influenza vaccine lead Salk and his colleagues to develop the first safe and effective live vaccine against poliomyelitis in 1952. Previous attempts had failed causing several deaths and cases of paralysis. Salk used Enders' virus culture method and took extra precautions to ensure that he produced a safe vaccine. Despite many objections from other researchers, mass clinical trials showed it to be 80–90% effective. His courage and persistence paid off: between 1956 and 1958, 200 million injections were administered without a single case of vaccine-produced paralysis.

Sandburg, Carl
1878–1967
American poet

Sandburg was a journalist, writing editorials for the *Chicago Daily News* when his use of colloquialism and free verse in, *Chicago Poems* (1916) caused critical controversy. Between 1918–33 he wrote several other volumes of poetry including, *Corn Huskers* (1918), *Smoke and Steel* (1920), and *Good Morning, America* (1928). All are typical of his expression of faith in the common person and optimistic hope for America.

His interest in idiom is evident in the ballad compilation, *The American Songbag* (1927). His prose works include a life of Abraham Lincoln and the family chronicle, *Remembrance Rock* (1948). He is perhaps most respected for his six-volume work of the life of Abraham Lincoln. Sandburg's interpretation is a considered exploration of all the available material on the subject. Sandburg won the Pulitzer Prize for *Complete Poems* in 1951.

S

Sadat, Anwar
1918–1981
Egyptian politician

Sadat was chosen for a military career and he joined Nasser in plotting against the British-led monarchy. During World War II he was jailed twice — once in 1942, but he later escaped — for making contacts with Germans. Sadat was also later tried, and acquitted, on charges of plotting to murder a pro-British politician in 1946. In 1950 he joined the Free Officers' Organization and took part in the armed coup against the Egyptian monarchy in 1952. During Nasser's presidency, Sadat held various offices.

He became Vice President of

Egypt in 1969 and succeeded to the Presidency on Nasser's death in 1970.

On the domestic front, Sadat tried to introduce a policy of decentralization and a relaxing of the political structure. However, it is for foreign affairs that he is best known. He tried to reclaim the Sinai Peninsula by attacking the Israelis during the Yom Kippur holiday in 1973. However, having asserted his own charismatic leadership, and having turned from his predecessor's pro-Communist and Arab Nationalist path, he opened the way to a peace treaty with Israel. Sadat broke ranks with the Arab bloc to sign the first peace treaty with Israel in Jerusalem in 1977. The Camp David Accords followed and, along with the Israeli

Premier Menachem Begin, he shared the 1979 Nobel Prize for Peace.

Sadat's popularity and standing among Arab nations had soared after the Yom Kippur War, being the first leader to retake land from Israel. However he later defied Islamic sentiment to suppress Islamic fundamentalism. Sadat's popularity rose in the West, after the signing of the peace treaty, but back in Egypt there was a lot of internal opposition and deepening economic problems. In 1981 he arrested hundreds of Muslim fundamentalists and political opponents and, as a direct result of this, in October he was assassinated while reviewing a military parade commemorating the Arab-Israeli war of October 1973.

S

Sinatra, Frank
1915–1998
American singer and actor

The "Chairman of the Board," "Ol' Blue Eyes," or simply "The Voice," Sinatra was the object of hysterical adulation 20 years before the Beatles hit the American market. His distinctive, flowing vocal technique was held as masterful by critics and his interpretation of songs was definitive. His career in both film and music spanned half the century and, since his death, he remains a cultural icon around the world.

Francis Albert Sinatra was born to Italian immigrants Dolly and Anthony on December 12, 1915, in Hoboken, New Jersey. His childhood years were, by all accounts, happy and he had the love and support of both of his parents, although it is reported that his mother would often dress her baby son in girls' clothes, as she had wanted a daughter. Frank's father wanted his son to become a boxer, but the young man had other ideas. As a student he was far more interested in organizing the glee club and singing in bands than he was in sport or academic study and, at the age of 15, Sinatra dropped out of school and went to work. His first job was unloading trucks for the local newspaper, but a performance by Bing Crosby in Jersey City so impressed the young Sinatra that he decided to become a singer too.

His first singing jobs were working local dances and parties and earned him just $3 a night. However, after winning a small talent competition he was asked to join a band and spent the next six months on the road with the Hoboken Four. Sinatra was indefatigable in his pursuit of his chosen career and after returning from the tour he waited on tables in a roadhouse where he also sang. At the same time he made 18 New York radio programs a week for free in the hope of gaining attention. Sinatra's dedication paid off. A radio broadcast direct from the roadhouse was heard by the bandleader Harry James and he was quickly signed up. With the James band Sinatra recorded, "All or Nothing At All," which soon became his first hit.

In 1940 Sinatra met Tommy Dorsey, who had traveled to watch Sinatra perform. Dorsey liked what he heard and asked him to join his own band. Sinatra accepted and over the next two years made over 80 recordings with Dorsey's orchestra including, "I'll Never Smile Again," "Let's Get Away From It All," and "This Love of Mine." Nevertheless, Sinatra was intent on becoming a solo artist like his idol Crosby, and in 1942 he struck out on his own. His concerts soon became scenes of hysteria as teenage girls, "bobbysoxers," flocked to see him perform and swooned in their thousands at the skinny young singer.

Within a year of leaving Dorsey's band, Sinatra had his first solo hit, "Night and Day." He had also become a regular fixture on national radio, and starred in the movie, *High And Higher* (1943). Over the next decade Sinatra's success was dizzying. More films were made including, *Anchors Aweigh* (1945), *On The Town* (1949), and the excellent 1945 short, *The House That I Live In* which won him an Academy Award and also produced the massive hit "Nancy With the Laughing Face." By the end of the 1940s though, a stormy marriage to Ava Gardner preluded a disastrous slide in Sinatra's popularity and many considered his career over.

Showing the same determination of the early days in the roadhouse, Sinatra fought to land the role of Maggio in the film, *From Here to Eternity* (1953). The film won him another Academy Award as Best Supporting Actor and Sinatra was back on top. Over the next seven years he released 13 brilliant albums with his arranger Nelson Riddle — all of which went into the top five. Movies included, *Guys and Dolls* (1955), *High Society* (1956) in which he starred with his hero Bing Crosby, and the harrowing, *The Man With the Golden Arm* (1956), in which he portrayed a heroin addict. The latter film saw him nominated for yet another Oscar.

In addition to this, Sinatra's popularity on stage was phenomenal and he traveled the world performing to enraptured audiences. Singing songs that have become modern classics such as, "It Was a Very Good Year," "Strangers in the Night," "My Way," and, "New York, New York," his powerful but subtle style placed him far above most of his contemporaries and he continued to win many new fans.

Sinatra tried retiring in 1971 but soon became bored and within two years was back on stage and in the movies. His place in the upper echelons of celebrity was now assured, and throughout the remainder of his life he continued to successfully record, act, and sing around the globe. His voice never failed him and even in his 80s he could overwhelm the vocals of many of the famous guests who shared a stage with him.

Frank Sinatra died on May 14, 1998. Though he had always fostered a "tough" image as a member of the "rat pack" who were notorious for their high living, he was a generous man who donated millions to charity, particularly those involved with the welfare of children. He won many awards during his lifetime for his humanitarian efforts, his acting skills, and his superb singing. Among them was a Legend Award which he received at the 1994 Grammy Awards. It was a fitting tribute to a man whose talent was so great.

Sanger, Margaret
1883–1966
American birth-control pioneer

Leader of the birth-control movement, Sanger braved arrest to further her cause. She toured the world teaching birth control and authored many books including the classic, *What Every Girl Should Know* (1916). Originally trained as a nurse, her work in a poor area of New York showed her that there was a need for information regarding contraception and she decided to abandon nursing. In 1914, she was indicted for attacking the Comstok Laws. Jailed for public nuisance in 1916 she served 30 days in the Queen's County Penitentiary, where she enlightened inmates about contraception. Winning her appeal after her release paved the way for physicians to give birth control advice in New York City. She published the *Birth Control Review* (1921–28) and founded the American Birth Control League. She received the American Women's Award in 1931.

Schweitzer, Albert
1875–1965
German missionary

Having devoted the first 30 years of his life to scholarship and music, Schweitzer spent the rest in service to humanity. Ordained in 1900, Schweitzer was a respected theologian, producing works on, *The Quest of the Historical Jesus* and, *The Mysticism of Paul the Apostle*. He qualified as a doctor in 1913, and set up a missionary station at Lambaréné, in French Equatorial Africa (now Gabon), building a hospital to combat leprosy and sleeping sickness. For the period 1917–18 Schweitzer, a German national, was interned in France. He occupied his time writing, *The Decay and the Restoration of Civilization* and, *Civilization and Ethics* (both 1923). Apart from periodic fund-raising trips to Europe, he remained in Africa, demonstrating by example his "reverence for life." He received the Nobel Peace Prize in 1952.

Simpson, O.J. (Orenthal James)
1947–
Football player and celebrity

Simpson's success as a running back in college led to his selection as an All-American in 1967 and 1968. He won the Heisman Trophy as the best college football player in 1968. He spent most of his professional football career playing for the Buffalo Bills, although he was traded to the 49ers in 1978, one year before his retirement. He is considered one of the most talented running backs in the National Football League history. He worked as a TV commentator, and appeared in cameo acting roles after his retirement. He came to worldwide attention in 1994 as the defendant in the trial for the murder of his former wife, Nicole Brown Simpson, and her friend Ronald Goodman. Simpson was acquitted of all charges but in a civil trial in 1997 was found responsible for their deaths.

S

Solzenhitsyn, Alexander
1918–
Russian novelist

Born in Kislovodsk in the Caucasus and educated at the University of Rostov, Solzenhitsyn was the son of a Cossack and a teacher. He fought in the Red Army during World War II achieving the rank of captain of the artillery, but was arrested for criticizing Stalin and sent to a labor camp in 1945. For eight years he taught mathematics and wrote. Released in 1953, he spent three more years in exile before being rehabilitated in 1956. He subsequently became a teacher and started to write more seriously.

As the process of de-Stalinisation started, there was a loosening of censorship on cultural expression. *One Day in the Life of Ivan Denisovich* (1962) is his stark account of life in the labor camp. The book was a sensation both at home and abroad for being a direct and authoritative account. Two short stories appeared in book form as *We Never Make Mistakes,* (1963), and *For the Good of the Cause* (1964). *Cancer Ward* (1968) and *The First Circle* (1969) were published abroad, and in 1969 he was expelled from the Writers' Union for denouncing official censorship that suppressed some of his writings. He was awarded the Nobel Prize for Literature in 1970. Publication of the first volume of *The Gulag Archipelago,* an exposé of the Soviet prison system, prompted his deportation in 1974 to West Germany, and he emigratcd to the United States where his reputation has perhaps been inflated by his dissident status. He produced two works of non-fiction there, *The Oak and the Calf,* which depicted literary life in the Soviet Union, and *The Mortal Danger,* which analyzed what he perceived to be the dangers of American misconceptions about Russia. In the 1980s, with the introduction of *glasnost,* Solzhenitsyn's work enjoyed a revival and was again available in Russia. Charges of treason were dropped in 1991, and he returned triumphant in May 1994. In 1995 he published *Invisible Allies,* a tribute to those who had helped him smuggle his writings out of the Soviet Union.

S

Spielberg, Steven
1947–
American film director

Spielberg is the most commercially successful film director of the 20th century. His work ranges from the evocation of childhood wonder and fantasy of *Close Encounters of the Third Kind* (1977) and *E.T. — the Extra-Terrestrial* (1982) to serious adaptations from literature such as, *The Color Purple* (1985) and *Schindler's List* (1993). It has been said that whatever genre Spielberg works in, he always manages to amaze and delight. He is also an impressive businessman; with his own production studio, Amblin, a major stake in DreamWorks SKG, the first Hollywood movie studio to be formed in 75 years, as well as several other media businesses. His annual income was in excess of $280 million for 1997 alone.

Born in Cincinatti, Ohio, on December 15, 1947, his father was a respected electrical engineer and his mother an acclaimed concert pianist. As a boy, Steven was fascinated by film, and as young as 13 he won a contest with a 40-minute film, *Escape From Nowhere*. By the age of 16 he made a profit at the local cinema with his second production *Firelight*, the film that inspired *Close Encounters*.

Despite these awards and a satisfactory attendance at the California State University, where he studied English, Spielberg was not accepted as a student at any of California's film schools.

Instead, film legend has it, he used more subversive methods to get into the film business. It is alleged that while on a guided tour of Universal Studios Spielberg managed to slip away from the rest of the party and find a disused janitor's closet. After some cleaning, this became his office and he would walk past the security guards, dressed in a suit, each morning.

His first project was a 24-minute film called *Amblin*, about a pair of hitchhikers. A budget of $15,000 was raised from a friend and Spielberg turned it into a piece that received much critical acclaim and several awards. Universal responded by signing him for seven years and putting him to work in the Television Division, where he directed many shows including the first episode of "Columbo" and a TV movie called *Duel* that was highly praised and released in cinemas outside America.

In 1974, his first feature was released *Sugarland Express*; like *Amblin*, it won great critical praise including the Best Screenplay Award at the 1974 Cannes Film Festival. His commercial breakthrough came in 1975 when, *Jaws* was released. A blockbuster success at the box office, it was nominated for Best Picture at the 1976 Academy Awards and picked up three Oscars that night — for editing, sound, and original score. Spielberg's career subsequently took off, and in quick succession he has directed some of the best known movies ever; including *Close Encounters*, *ET*, the *Indiana Jones* trilogy (1981, 1984, and 1989*), Back to the Future* (1986), *Who Framed Roger Rabbit* (1988), *Jurassic Park* (1993). He also proved that he could approach more serious film making with, *The Color Purple, Empire of the Sun* (1988), *Schindler's List, Amistad* and most recently *Saving Private Ryan* (1998). Of the top ten largest grossing films of all time, four are directed by Spielberg. And *Jaws* was also named by the American Film Institute as one of the best 100 movies ever made as were several of his other films.

In interviews, Spielberg has consistently said that his films are based on childhood fears and wonders that he has never grown out of. His personal life has also assured him the constant companionship of children from whom he takes inspiration — he has three children of his own, from two marriages, as well as an adopted son and a stepdaughter from his second marriage to Kate Capshaw.

Amblin, Spielberg's production company named after his first professional film, was formed in 1982. He owns 100% of the company and, as its first feature was *ET*, it was immediately successful. Twelve years

later, in 1994, he joined media and music industry moguls Jeffery Katzenberg and David Geffen to form the DreamWorks SKG company. DreamWorks SKG includes the biggest and most technologically advanced of Hollywood's studios, which now produces live action and animated feature films, television shows, computer games, and music. Spielberg has also invested heavily in the internet business "idealab!," and owns half of a restaurant chain, Dive!

Critical reviews of Spielberg's work have been mixed, yet it is acknowledged that all of them are technically brilliant and well produced — particularly the special effects. It can perhaps be said that Spielberg has ushered in the age of the Hollywood blockbuster, an era of slick, glossy film made specifically to appeal to mass audiences.

S

Steinbeck, John
1902–1968
American novelist

John Steinbeck was born in California and used the lives of rural workers in his home state to provide the material for his early work. His characters are often simple and remain heroic although defeated by their struggle in life. First achieving success with *Tortilla Flat* (1935), his following novels *In Dubious Battle* (1936) and *Of Mice and Men* (1937) are more explicitly concerned with migrants' conditions. His greatest work, *The Grapes of Wrath* (1939), is an epic. The original and authentic tale is also seen as a document of social protest, and is now an American classic. Other books include: *The Moon Is Down* (1942), *Cannery Row* (1945), *The Wayward Bus* (1947), *East of Eden* (1952), *The Winter of Our Discontent* (1961), and *America and Americans* (1966). He won the Nobel Prize for Literature in 1962.

Stewart, James
1908–1997
American actor

This leading actor with his inimitable slow drawl and gangly walk played honest heroes for more than 50 years. Stewart's sincerity and slightly embarrassed air caught on with the public in *You Can't Take It With You* (1938), *Mr Smith Goes to Washington* (1939), and *The Philadelphia Story* (1940), which brought him an Academy Award. He moved smoothly into a variety of roles after the war with a wonderful performance in the classic *It's a Wonderful Life* (1946), and the gentle *Harvey* (1950). He also played detectives, western heroes, and the lead in Hitchcock blockbusters such as *Rear Window* (1954) and *Vertigo* (1958). He served as a pilot in World War II, attaining the rank of Brigadier General in the USAF. He received a special Academy Award in 1985 as well as the Medal of Freedom. His book *Jimmy Stewart and His Poems* became a bestseller in 1989.

Sullivan [Jo]Anne
1866–1936
American teacher

Anne Sullivan graduated from the Perkins Institute for the Blind in 1886. Partially blind herself, she was hired as a private tutor for Helen Keller, then a blind and deaf six year old. With infinite patience and imagination Sullivan began to enable Keller, who had not had any education, to communicate with the world using a manual alphabet. As Keller, a gifted and intelligent woman, gained in notoriety, so did Sullivan, who accompanied her to Radcliffe College. There Sullivan read for Keller and "translated" the lectures in to Keller's hand. Keller graduated in 1904. In 1905 Sullivan married the literary critic who had been helping Helen Keller with her autobiography. John Albert Macy and Anne Sullivan separated in 1913, and Sullivan then traveled with Keller on her lecture tours world-wide.

S

Stalin, Josef [Josef Vissarionovich Dzhugashvili]
1879–1953
Russian statesman

As a child, Stalin won a scholarship to the T'bilisi Theological Seminary in the Georgian capital in 1894. However, exposure to the radical ideas of many of the other students and the reading of illegal literature (such as the works of Karl Marx) caused him to leave the seminary and become a revolutionary. Stalin spread Marxist propaganda while employed as an accountant, and in 1902 organized a workers' demonstration. He was arrested by the Imperial Police and sentenced to exile in Siberia. However, by 1904 he had escaped and was back in Georgia.

A failed priest and bank robber, Stalin was successful as a propagandist for Bolshevism in his native Caucasus, and in raising funds at gunpoint. Lenin dubbed him "the wonderful Georgian," and co-opted him onto the party's Central Committee. As a political commissar he helped his future chief of the armed forces, Voroshilov, defend Tsaritsyn (later Stalingrad, now Volgograd) against the White Army. In 1922 Lenin appointed him Secretary of the Central Committee of the Party, the key post he held for the next 30 years. Lenin soon regretted the promotion and in his pre-deathbed "Testament" specifically warned the other old Bolsheviks against him. Stalin brought trumped-up charges against them at the Moscow Show Trials of 1936 and

had them shot. He had already caused over a million deaths by collectivizing the farms, against the Old Comrades' advice. He went on to purge the Army, leaving it almost fatally weakened to resist Hitler's 1941 invasion. A combination of the strong industrial infrastructure produced by successive five-year plans and the talent of generals like Zhukov threw the Nazis back to Berlin and annexed their Eastern empire. The Yalta Peace Conference (1945) confirmed his conquests, which were held by extending his secret police terror and slave-labor system. Paranoia affected his judgment; he miscalculated over the Korean War and the Berlin Airlift and died in 1953, as he was about to arrest more plotters against him. His memory still has an uncomfortable resonance in his demolished empire.

S

Spock, Benjamin (McLane)
1903–1998
American pediatrician

One of the most esteemed doctors of the 20th century, Spock overthrew an entire regime of childraising philosophy, rejecting authoritarian rules in favor of a more intuitive and child-centered approach. His book, *Baby and Child Care*, has been translated into 42 languages and has sold more than 50 million copies around the world. In addition to this he was a noted political activist, jailed for speaking out about the Vietnam War.

Benjamin McLane Spock was born in New Haven, Conneticut on May 2, 1903. He graduated from Columbia University's College of Physicians and Surgeons in 1929; while a student he also rowed for the gold-medal U.S. crew team in the 1924 Olympics. After leaving university Spock served residences in New York City hospitals and began a six-year course at the New York Psychoanalytic Institute. This made him the first person to have undertaken professional training in both the areas of pediatrics and psychology. Towards the end of the 1930s the energetic young doctor opened a private practice and was also a popular teacher of pediatrics at Cornell University's Medical College, again in New York City. During this time he also contributed to many magazines on the subject of child care. From 1943 to 1945 he served as a psychiatrist in the U.S. Navy and began to condense his studies and beliefs in his specialist field. The result was the book that would become so famous and which was first published, under the original title of *The Commonsense Book of Baby and Child Care*, in 1946.

Before Spock, parents were expected to follow an arbitrary set of rules about when to feed children and when to put them to bed; parents were warned not to spoil their children by feeding them on demand or responding to their crying. His book encouraged maternal tenderness and gave parents

the confidence to listen to their children and to answer their needs more instinctively. He taught that each child should be treated as an individual, so that its innate character could be allowed to develop. Critics have complained that Spock was "the father of permissiveness" and was responsible for a generation of spoiled, undisciplined children. The doctor later conceded that he had indeed, erred too much on the side of flexibility. More recent editions of the book have evolved slightly and it now urges parents to set standards and provide discipline where necessary. It was an instant success, however, and edition after edition sold out. With his academic career now assured, Spock went on to prominent teaching jobs at the medical schools of the Universities of Minnesota, Pittsburgh, and finally the Western Reserve University where he settled from 1955 to 1967. He maintained his reputation as America's foremost expert in childcare, however, and wrote extensively for magazines and newspapers as well as producing further books.

In 1962 Spock's humane attitude led him to enter politics for the first

time. He was appalled at President John F. Kennedy's announcement that the U.S. would test nuclear weapons and immediately joined the National Committee for a Sane Nuclear Policy (SANE). The organization swiftly capitalized on acquiring such an illustrious new member and the doctor appeared on national television in an advertisement which warned of the effects of radiation in a baby's milk. Spock also spoke publicly against the Vietnam War and, after supporting Lyndon Johnson, was outraged at the escalation of the conflict under his administration.

In protest, he joined a 1967 march on the Pentagon as well as supporting other peaceful anti-war activities. In 1968 he was tried and convicted to two years' imprisonment for inciting draft evasion, though the sentence was quashed on appeal. This brought him further blame for supposedly producing a nation of spineless young men. His next book, entitled *Decent and Indecent* (1970), detailed his pacifist ideals and two years later Spock ran for government at the head of his own People's Party. Receiving only 1% of the vote, he ran a second time in 1976 as the party's vice-presidential candidate at the age of 73. But again the People's Party failed to make any great impact.

Spock, always a dynamic man, continued to speak out as a liberal pacifist until he was in his 80s and in 1989 he was arrested at a protest against Trident nuclear testing. He published his memoirs *Spock on Spock*, in the same year but soon after his health deteriorated. His battle against illness was long and underlined another social problem — care for the elderly. Despite the earnings from his books, his wife had to make a public appeal to pay for the medical care that the doctor required. The cost was estimated at $16,000 per month. He died on March 15, 1998.

S&T

Stein, Gertrude
1874–1946
American writer

Gertrude Stein originally planned to become a psychologist. However, by 1903 she was settled in Paris where her home and collections of modern art became a focus for the avant-garde. Stein was instrumental in bringing modern art to a wider audience, through her salon and writings. She named her life-long companion, Alice B. Toklas, as the author of her popular *Memoir Autobiography of Alice B. Toklas* (1933). Apart from her essays and collection of poetry, *Tender Buttons* (1914), she wrote experimental prose noted for its non-representational form. Her masterpiece and most accessible work is *Three Lives* (1909). Stein's innovative style was frequently misunderstood. She explained some of her theories in a collection of talks she delivered while on tour — *Lectures in America* (1935).

Taft, William Howard
1857–1930
American politician and president

Taft held not only America's highest executive office, as 27th President of the United States (1909–13), but also, later, the top legal post, as Chief Justice. Appointed Solicitor General in 1890, he moved in 1900 to the newly conquered Philippines where he became the first Governor, pacifying the Church over its confiscated lands with a payment of $7 million. As Secretary of War from 1904 he supervised the construction of the Panama Canal, and in 1908 succeeded Roosevelt as President. Roosevelt expected Taft to continue his reforms, but Taft was more conservative. His special excise tax on corporations passed as the 16th Amendment. Theodore Roosevelt stood against him in 1912 and split the vote, as a result of which Taft ran third. Taft became Chief Justice of the Supreme Court in 1921–30.

Taylor, Elizabeth
1932–
British-born American actress

Groomed by her mother to be an actress, Taylor was just 12 when she starred in *National Velvet* (1942), and she matured quickly, playing romantic roles well beyond her years, such as Amy in *Little Women* (1949). She began taking her acting seriously in 1951 with *A Place in the Sun,* co-starring Montgomery Clift and Shelley Winters, and was soon a top box-office superstar and one of the best-publicized women in the world. While her private life and many marriages fueled public interest, she won an Academy Award for *Butterfield 8* (1960), and another for *Who's Afraid of Virginia Woolf?* She has emerged as a magnificent character and now works tirelessly for charities. She received a lifetime achievement award from the American Film Institutes in 1993.

Truman, Harry S.
1884–1972
American politican and president

Truman was unable to go to college because of his family's financial circumstances, and he was unable to enter the army because of his shortsightedness. So, he began work, first as a timekeeper and later as a bookkeeper. In 1906 he returned home to help his mother run the family farm and continued for the next ten years. When America entered World War I, he signed up in the U.S. Army, and helped with recruitment. After the war, Truman became a Democrat and entered local politics, eventually becoming a county judge. He began a highly successful four-year term as presiding judge in 1926, completely reforming the operation of local infrastructure, and was re-elected for another term. With a strong record behind him, Truman was able to get elected to the Senate in 1935. In Washington he continued his fight against corruption, and despite involvement in the Prendergast Scandal, was re-elected for a second term. The re-election was not forecast, and on his return to the senate his colleagues welcomed him back with a standing ovation.

Truman's tough, courageous response to the challenges posed by the dawn of the nuclear era turned him from Roosevelt's understudy into one of the great presidents. He gave the order to drop the A-bombs; promulgated the Truman Doctrine, giving aid to countries fighting Communism; provided economic means to the same end with the Marshall Plan; faced down Stalin over the Berlin blockade; was godfather to NATO and committed the U.S. to the Korean War. Less successful in domestic politics, he failed to get his "Fair Deal" reforms through Congress, which in 1947 passed the Taft-Hartley Act, curbing workers' rights, over his veto. Lurid spy cases like those of Hiss and the Rosenbergs, and public fears of both Communist subversion (culminating in the McCarthyite trials) and about the Soviet nuclear threat, undermined Truman's resolve. He declined to run for re-election in 1952 and retired to be a revered Democratic elder statesman. His years in office are recorded in his memoirs *Year of Decisions* (1955) and *Years of Trial and Hope, 1946–1952* (1956), and his account of life in retirement in *Mr. Citizen*.

T

Temple, Shirley
1928–
American actress

Curly-headed Shirley Temple became a Hollywood star at the age of six. She made 19 movies for Fox between 1934 and 1937, usually appearing as an orphan who found a new family, or the child of a single parent who found a new mate for them. Her ability to tap dance and sing and, appealing lisp propelled her to celebrity status. In 1934, a year in which she starred in four movies, she received a special Academy Award for her outstanding contribution to film. Her movies were immensely popular. She made several successful movies as a teenager, but retired in 1949. As an adult (now Shirley Temple Black) she has had a distinguished career in politics and diplomacy serving as U.S. ambassador to Ghana (1974–76), and to Czechoslovakia (1989–1992).

Trotsky, Leon
1879–1940
Russian politician

A leader of the Russian Revolution, Trotsky was the most powerful man after Lenin in the Soviet Union. Using his talents as an orator and writer, Trotsky helped organize the October Revolution in 1917, and when the Bolsheviks took control became Commissar for Foreign Affairs. He established the Red Army as an effective force during the civil war (1918–21), but his influence declined after Lenin's death in 1924. A ruthless, energetic man, Trotsky was not a political infighter and was distrusted by Stalin who sent him into exile and denounced him as a traitor. He was expelled from the USSR in 1929 and later tried to form an anti-Stalin opposition from his base in Mexico, articulating theories which have inspired a romantic brand of workers' socialism ever since. He was murdered by a Stalinist agent.

Trump, Donald.
1946–
American real estate developer

Trump came to the public's attention when at the age of 28, he built a convention center on the site of the derelict Penn Central Railroad yards in New York City. Later he put together a mega-deal to renovate the Commodore Hotel into the Grand Hyatt Hotel (1980). He became known as an acute businessman and controversial builder. In the late 1980s, Trump was seemingly at his peak: he had a billion dollar empire, owned an airline (Trump Shuttle), a football team (the New Jersey Generals), and numerous casinos. He wrote *The Art of the Deal* (1987) about his career to that date. The changing global economy forced Trump to restructure his debt burden in 1990 when facing bankruptcy, and he had to relinquish some parts of his business.

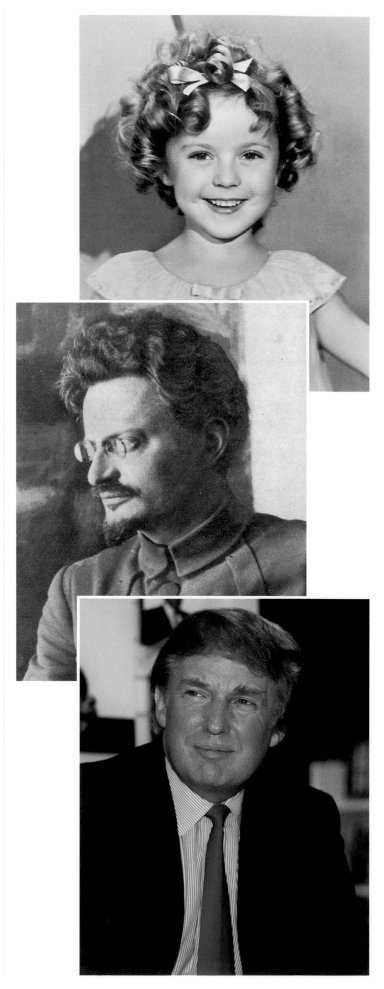

T

Thatcher, Margaret, Hilda, Baroness
1925–
British politician and prime minister

Thatcher gained a degree in Chemistry at Oxford and between 1947–51 worked as a research chemist. In 1951 she married Dennis Thatcher, a prosperous businessman. She studied for the bar, and from 1953 she worked as a tax lawyer. Thatcher first stood for parliament in 1950, and although she increased the Conservative vote by 50%, was not elected. She entered parliament in 1959. Appointed Education Secretary by Heath in 1970, she supplanted him as party leader in 1975 and won the 1979 general election for the Conservatives. She advocated a reduction in state controls and encouragement to private enterprise. The 1980s saw the consolidation of fiscal caution, privatization of industry and social programs (including healthcare, school management and housing), and self-help policies, that came to be known as Thatcherism. Combative in foreign affairs, her decisive handling of the 1982 Falklands Campaign undoubtedly contributed to the landslide election victory of 1983. The second term of office nearly came to an abrupt end when an IRA bomb came close to wiping out the entire Cabinet at the Conservative Party conference in Brighton in 1984. Thatcher was relentless in her pursuit of the trade unions, considerably reducing their power, particularly after the year-long miners' strike (1984–1985). Unemployment troubled her administration but the economy boomed until 1987. Elected for a third term in 1987, she became the longest-serving Prime Minister this century and the only one of the 20th century to serve three consecutive terms. Despite being a respected world leader, disaffection with policies such as health cuts, the poll tax, and her hostility to Europe seemed to undermine Thatcher's standing in both the country and within the ranks of the Conservative Party. In November 1990, after party-splitting elections, she was replaced by John Major as leader and Prime Minister. She has kept active since, creating The Margaret Thatcher Foundation and making lecture tours worldwide.

T

Twain, Mark (Samuel Langhorne Clemens) 1835–1910
American writer

Philosopher, humorist, writer, lecturer, traveler — Mark Twain was America's foremost man of letters at the beginning of the century, and also the best loved. His lectures frequently reduced the audience to such laughter that they were too weak to move from their chairs, and, though his life was tarnished by the tragedy of early deaths in the family, he never lost the gentle humor and stoicism that are so apparent in his many works. His own adventures rival those of any of his stories, and his work has been an enduring influence on literature throughout the remainder of the century.

Born in Florida on November 30, 1835, Samuel Clemens' family moved, while he was a young boy, to the Mississippi river town of Hannibal, which would have such an influence on his writing of the Tom Sawyer stories. His education was of the most basic and came to an abrupt end when his father died in 1847 and the family was hard pressed to avoid crisis. Young Samuel, at the age of 12, joined a printing company as an apprentice for room and board, and learned his trade until his brother, Orion, bought the *Hannibal Journal*, a small newspaper, in 1850. Run by the two brothers, with a third — Henry — joining as an apprentice, Sam had his first experience of writing for print; usually when his older brother was absent and much to his dismay when he returned. Samuel enjoyed writing short burlesques about local people and though they helped sell the paper, Orion did not approve.

The small town became too limiting for Samuel and in 1853, while still only 17, he began traveling, going to New York for a World's Fair and then Washington,

before returning South after an absence of over a year to work with his brother once more. In 1857, he decided to become a South American adventurer and set off for New Orleans on a riverboat to find a ship that would take him further south. Instead, he was smitten by the huge riverboats plying the 1,200 miles of the Mississippi and spontaneously decided to become a pilot — an incredibly difficult profession that demands an intimate knowledge of every inch of those 1,200 miles. Nevertheless, Samuel achieved his goal within 18 months and was soon known as one of the best pilots on the river. It is from here that he took the name "Mark Twain," this being regularly shouted across the decks when soundings found a depth of two fathoms.

With the advent of war, Samuel spent a miserable two weeks in the rain as a Confederate volunteer before resigning and heading for Nebraska with his brother — a story that was later told in *Roughing It* (1872). He then became a miner, looking for gold, but was singularly unsuccessful. Luckily the owner of a local paper to which Sam had been sending contributions, the *Virginia City Enterprise*, recognized his talent and offered him the job of editor. Sam had to walk 130 miles to Carson City to take him up on the offer.

Making his own regular contributions to the paper under the name Mark Twain, he soon found local success but was forced to leave town in a hurry after becoming involved in a duel. Although the argument ended amicably enough, dueling was illegal under Nevada law. Though still contributing to the paper, as well as several others, he

returned to mining until the fuss died down. At Angel's Camp he heard the story of a trained frog, while swapping yarns around the stove, and made a few notes. The story, which he called "The Celebrated Jumping Frog of Calaveras County" (1865) became Twain's first major success after it was published in New York's *Saturday Press*, and was taken up by many other publications around the world. The story caused a furor and Twain became known as the "Wild Humorist of the Pacific Slope."

Financial reward came in 1867 when Twain was commissioned to sail on one of the first Mediterranean cruises and contribute regular letters to the *Alta-California* newspaper in California. The *Quaker City* voyaged for five months, during which time Twain duly sent his observations back to the paper. He returned to find that he was famous and publishers were clamoring for a collected work of the letters. He completed the volume, called *The Innocents Abroad*, in 1868 with the editorial help of a friend's sister, Olivia Langdon, who he married in 1870. The book was a huge success, selling nearly 100,000 copies in the first three years and being reprinted many times.

The couple settled in Buffalo, New York, but their early married life was blighted almost immediately. Their first son, Langdon Clemens, was born sickly, and died in 1872, the year that Twain's second book, *Roughing It,* was published.

After traveling to England and Scotland, where he was besieged by admirers, Twain and his wife and new baby, Susy, returned to the US and a new home. The house in Hartford was at the center of a circle of writers and artists including Charles Dudley

T

Warner, with whom Twain collaborated on his next work *The Gilded Age* (1873). Twain was by this time a rich man but a series of bad investments and get-rich-quick schemes were beginning to strain his finances. Eventually he would be declared bankrupt, owing $100,000, in 1894, although a world tour giving lectures paid this debt and recouped his fortune.

Meanwhile, he wrote many new books. Works such as *The Adventures of Tom Sawyer* (1875), *The Prince and the Pauper* (1882), *The Adventures of*

Huckleberry Finn (1884, and arguably his masterpiece), and *A Connecticut Yankee in King Arthur's Court* (1889) were enormously successful all over the world. Honors were also heaped upon him, including an honorary doctorate from Oxford University, which Twain regarded as the highest of achievements for a poor printer with no education.

Success was, however, tempered with tragedy. Susy died in 1894, while Twain was in England, and Olivia passed away in 1904. Twain's writings subsequently became more

pessimistic in his later career. His own death came in 1910, soon after a second daughter, Jean, died. Right up until the end of his life he was a kindly and generous man who enjoyed the company of children, and he is remembered as a writer whose work revolutionized American literature. His travel writing has been emulated many times but never equaled, and his fiction, including the great Huckleberry Finn and Tom Sawyer stories are classics that continue to delight each new generation.

Valentino, Rudolph
1895–1926
Italian-born American actor

Valentino was the leading man of the 1920s, typecast as a
Latin lover. His animal magnetism, flashing dark eyes,
elegant clothes, and aura of mystery and wickedness made
him a great idol and sex symbol of the silent-movie era.
Contacts and luck brought him the lead in *The Four
Horsemen of the Apocalypse* (1921), a record-breaking smash
hit. *The Sheik* (1921) made women swoon and started an
Arabian fad in interior decorating. He also starred in *Camille*
(1921*)*, *Blood and Sand* (1922), *The Young Rajah* (1922),
Monsieur Beaucaire (1924), *A Sainted Devil* (1924), *The Eagle*
(1925), and *The Son of the Sheik* (1926). In 1926 he was
rushed to hospital with a perforated ulcer. When it was
reported that he had died, his fans became hysterical: his
funeral was a national event at which rioting broke out.

Van Allen, James Alfred
1914–
American physicist

Van Allen was educated at the University of Iowa where he
became professor in 1951. In World War II he worked with
the U.S. Navy and developed radio-proximity fuses. His
subsequent experience in rocketry with discarded V2 rockets
and with balloon-mounted equipment helped him to develop
miniaturized instruments and study the upper atmosphere.
His detectors in the first successful American satellite,
Explorer 1, discovered the Van Allen Belts — the doughnut-
shaped regions of radiation produced by solar particles
trapped in the upper atmosphere by the Earth's magnetic
field. They are a hazard to astronauts and to satellite
instruments.

Wallenberg, Raoul
1912–1947
Swedish diplomat and politician

Wallenberg was a diffident member of a wealthy banking
family. He was sent to work as the foreign representative
of a European company. When Hungarian Jews were
threatened by Eichmannn's mass deportations to Auschwitz,
Wallenberg was sent to Hungary as a diplomat and made it
his mission to rescue as many people as possible. Ignoring
Nazi threats, he persuaded the Hungarian authorities to let
him issue four times the number of protective Swedish
passports authorized and may have saved up to 10,000 lives.
Arrested by the Soviets in 1945, he disappeared without
trace. After Swedish inquiries, Soviet authorities produced a
document claiming he had died of a heart attack in 1947,
but ex-prisoners reported he was alive in the 1950s, and
maybe into the 1970s.

Valera, Eamon De
1882–1975
American-born Irish politician

De Valera was born in America but educated in Dublin. He was a teacher of mathematics in Ireland before becoming a supporter of the Irish language revival and an activist for Irish Independence. He joined the Irish Volunteers in 1913 and took part in the Easter Rising in 1916. He was the last commander to surrender: only his American citizenship saved him from execution. Sentenced to life imprisonment he was released in a general amnesty of 1917. Later that year he was elected President of the Sinn Fein.

Following further imprisonment on the charges of suspicion of rebellion and escape, he traveled to the U.S. to rally support for the cause of Irish Republicanism and campaigned against the Anglo-Irish Treaty of 1921. He raised $5 million in support of the revolutionary cause and was elected president of the Irish republican government in exile. In 1922 when the Dáil Éireann (Irish Parliament) ratified a treaty with Great Britain that de Valera thought was a degrading settlement (it excluded Northern Ireland and imposed an oath of allegiance to the British), he resigned his position. His opposition put him in prison once again for 11 months. In 1926 he founded the Fianna Fail Party,

which he led to victory. Also in 1932 De Valera was president of the executive council of the Irish Free State, or Éire, and upon creation of a new constitution in 1937 was elected the new premier, eventually severing links with Britain. Also in 1932 de Valera was president of the League of Nations council, and in 1938 president of the assembly.

His political and economic policies were characterized consistently by nationalism and isolationism. He successfully negotiated a policy of neutrality for Ireland through World War II; thus bringing about a temporary prosperity. From 1959 he served two terms as President of the Irish Republic, retiring from public life in 1973.

Warren, Earl
1981–1974
American Supreme Court Judge

Warren was in public office continuously for 50 years. He was district attorney of Alameda County (1925–39), Attorney General of California (1939–43), and a Republican governor of the state for three terms (1943–53). In 1953 Eisenhower nominated him for Chief Justice of the Supreme Court, a position he held until retirement in 1969. Warren reigned over the Supreme Court at a time when there were changes in constitutional law in the areas of race relations, criminal procedure, and legislative appointment. In 1953 he passed a landmark ruling that separate education for children according to race was unconstitutional, and in 1966 ruled that a man must be read his rights before questioning by police. In 1963 he was chairman of the commission that investigated the assassination of President Kennedy.

Watson, James
1928–
American biochemist

In 1950 Watson received a Ph.D. from the University of Indiana, and in 1955 went on to join the faculty of Harvard. In the years 1951–53 Watson worked at the Cavendish Laboratory at Cambridge University. Using research carried out by Maurice Wilkins, Watson and British biophysicist Francis Crick deciphered the complex structure of the building block of life — DNA (deoxyribonucleic acid). Additional confirmation for the molecule's from was produced by American biochemist Arthur Kornberg. In 1962 Watson and Crick received the Nobel Prize in Physiology or medicine. In 1968 Watson published *The Double Helix* which retold the story of the discovery. Between 1988 and 1992, Watson helped direct the Human Genome Project, at the National Institute of Health.

Wayne, John
1907–1979
American actor

Although his most fervent admirers would agree that the only part "Duke" could play was himself, to millions he personified rugged masculinity. Wayne shot to stardom in the movie *Stagecoach* (1939), changing the image of the western from a kids' entertainment to a vehicle for a real story. He was continually cast until the mid-1970s, usually portraying cowboys. His most successful non-western was *The Quiet Man* (1952), about an Irish-American boxer who returns to the old country. Stricken with lung cancer in 1964, after a serious operation he went back to making movies, including *True Grit* (1969), for which he received an Oscar. Although he never really recovered his health, he continued to make pictures. Wayne was posthumously awarded the Congressional Medal of Honor, the highest decoration of the United States.

Walësa, Lech
1943–
Polish politician

A labor union activist, Walësa was trained in a state technical college, and began working as an electrician in 1967 at the Lenin Shipyard. Having participated in strikes in 1970 and again in 1976, Walësa was dismissed for his role in organizing anti-government protests. Between 1976 and 1980, he was only sporadically employed, spending most of the time in labor-organizing activities. It was during the August 1980 work stoppages that he came to international recognition. Walësa and other union officials had been fired from the shipyard: other workers were protesting this, and increasing food prices. A stand-off

between workers and management led to stalemate. In September 1980 the *Solidarnösc* (the Solidarity trade federation) was formed, with the full backing of the Roman Catholic Church. "Solidarity" quickly became a successful opposition to the military-backed Polish Communist Government. By the middle of 1981 it boasted 10 million members. The government officially recognized the union in October and Walësa was careful to control the degree of antagonism. However, the government, sensing trouble and supported by the Soviet government, imposed martial law in December 1981, and imprisoned the leaders.

Although released, Walësa remained under surveillance. He was awarded the Nobel Peace Prize in 1983. Thereafter

Solidarity, although an underground movement, grew in power, impeding President Jaruzelski's efforts at reform. Forced to negotiate with the union, the government legalized the movement in 1989 and allowed it to take part in a general election. A coalition government headed by Solidarity was voted to power. In December 1990 Walësa was elected President, but as a result of his confrontational style and his refusal to reform the abortion laws, he was not re-elected in 1995. Since then he has worked in opposition. The period 1990–95 was turbulent in Polish politics: there were five different governments, and Walësa dismissed two of them. His pledges to eliminate unemployment and create a market economy did not seem to make it to fruition.

Warhol, Andy
1930–1987
American painter and film maker

Warhol was the most internationally known Pop artist of the 1960s. His multiple images of dollar bills, Campbell's soup cans, Coca-Cola bottles, and Marilyn Monroe epitomized an era overwhelmed by consumer madness, the mass media, and exaggerated star cults, of which he was one. Obsessed by the idea of mass-production, he called his studio The Factory, and adopted silkscreen printing, which eliminated any trace of the artist's hand, as his medium. His work neither projects nor demands emotion, and images such as *Electric Chair* (1965) are a subtle comment on the emotional bankruptcy of a society numbed by media bombardment.

He was born Andrew Warhola on August 6, 1928, in Pittsburgh, Pennsylvania. A prodigious talent at an early age, he studied at the Carnegie Institute of Technology, Pittsburgh from 1945 to 1949 and moved to New York in 1950 where he began working as a commercial artist. Developing an excellent reputation over the decade, he became the most sought after commercial artist in the city and was known for his experimentation. Towards the end of the 1950s he used a silkscreen technique for the first time to produce images of comic book superheroes for a department store window display. Further use of this process created representations taken from advertisements and newspaper photos of public personalities. The technique itself involved transferring a photographic image to the canvas using the silkscreen, creating an image which could be reproduced indefinitely. Inks would then be added to the canvas, giving each repetition a slight individuality. In retrospect these innovations can be seen as the founding moments of the Pop Art movement which gained in significance as the 1960s progressed.

At the start of the new decade Warhol's attention turned to direct

representations of consumer products, most famously the Campbell's soup can. Derided as simply pandering to consumerism by many critics in his own country, Warhol's work was lauded in Europe, Australia, and Japan. Now a celebrity, he cultivated a complex public personality. Aware of the need to maintain a media profile he grabbed headlines with quotable phrases such as, "In the future everyone will be famous for 15 minutes," yet remained elusive.

The late sixties saw Warhol move into film, producing a series of pieces including *Sleep* (1963), *Empire* (1964), and *The Chelsea Girls* (1966). In these, Warhol portrayed an intentionally seedy sexuality coupled with themes of time, boredom, and repetition. He also began to work with a rock group called the Velvet Underground whose tortured songs of drugs, perversity, and boredom perfectly captured his own ethos of the time. Led by Lou Reed, the Velvet Underground's most distinctive sounds were Reed's monotone voice and John Cale's viola, on which the bridge was filed down to give a dissonant tone. Warhol introduced the group to German actress Nico, whose smoky voice mirrored Reed's and they recorded their first album together under the aegis of the artist who toured extensively with them.

In 1968, Warhol was shot three times in the chest by Valerie Solanis who had worked in some of Warhol's films. He was taken to hospital and pronounced dead soon after. However, following a heart massage he was revived. Returning to The Factory the next year, he founded a magazine, *Interview* which took advantage of Warhol's extensive contacts in the worlds of fashion and art and pandered to his great love of gossip. In 1975 he published his personal manifesto, *The Philosophy of Andy Warhol: From A to B and Back Again* (1975), which was followed ten years later by *America* (1985). The later stages of his career were marked by a more somber approach than he had previously taken. However, the sale of mass-produced screen prints of Mao Tse Tung made him a fortune in the mid-1970s.

Perhaps his greatest creation was his own personality. Always enigmatic, Warhol contrived to be at the heart of society and culture yet remained personally aloof and elusive. Much given to gossip, he would talk on the telephone for hours on end with friends who ranged from the most famous celebrities to unknown transsexual performers. Warhol committed himself to the pursuit of the obscure and surreal and loved the seediness of New York life. One of his favorite haunts was Studio 54, the permissive nightclub frequented by the jet-set.

Andy Warhol died on February 22, 1987, after a routine operation. During his last years he had continued to produce work of a consistent quality though he never managed to match the heady days of experimentation at The Factory during the 1960s and 1970s. Warhol was an enormously influential artist whose legacy to the 20th century is in forging a new form of art which dealt directly with the cultural impact of the postmodern era. To commemorate his life and work the Andy Warhol Museum was opened in Pittsburgh in 1994.

Welles, Orson
1915–1985
American actor and director

A child prodigy, Oscar winner, and a genius, Orson Welles was a man of many talents. An iconoclast, he detested the Hollywood establishment and remained a steadfastly independent moviemaker throughout his life. Indeed, his classic *Citizen Kane* was made virtually single-handed. Despite the great success of this masterpiece, Welles was forever looking for more money to back his latest brainchild, and wandered the world, acting in various productions, some great, some negligible, in order to earn the necessary money to finance his intensely personal movies. Initially successful on radio due to a deep, rich voice that belied his tender years, Welles's other achievement was a production of H. G. Wells's *War of the Worlds* that was so convincing that it caused panic throughout America.

Born George Orson Welles on May 6, 1915, in Kenosha, Wisconsin, his father, Richard Welles, was an inventor and his mother the renowned concert pianist and beauty, Beatrice Ives. Their son's prodigious talent was obvious from an early age — the young Orson wrote poetry, studied music, memorized Shakespeare, and published cartoons before reaching the age of ten. However, his childhood was less than carefree. His parents separated when he was six, and two years later his mother died.

Beatrice's death heralded the start of a bitter custody battle between his father and Dr. Maurice Bernstin, a close friend of Beatrice's who recognized Orson's artistic abilities and was determined to nurture them. The two men finally reached a compromise, and Orson was sent to attend the Todd School for Boys in Woodstock, Illinois, a progressive school that encouraged his dramatic abilities as well as continuing his normal education. During vacations, Orson accompanied his father on a series of trips around the world that fostered his interest in travel and created a close bond between father and son. However, tragedy struck a second time in 1930, when Richard Welles died.

A year later Orson traveled to Ireland where he intended to paint the scenery but instead found himself auditioning for Gate Theatre in Dublin. After shamelessly lying during the audition — telling the director that he was a well-known star of New York's   Theater Guild — he was hired and went on to appear in seven Gate productions, including his professional debut in *Jew Suss*.

Over the next decade Welles reputation and confidence gradually increased as he worked tirelessly in myriad productions for both the theater and radio including the notorious *War of the Worlds* show in 1936. In 1941, he made his first film. *Citizen Kane* was based upon the life of media tycoon William Hearst and from its first showing made a huge impact in the film world — the critics adored it and it also did well at the box office. Welles directed, wrote, and starred in the movie and was awarded an Oscar for writing as well as being nominated for Academy Awards for directing and acting. Flushed with success from such acclaim, he quickly scored two more hits with *The Magnificent Ambersons* (1942) and *Jane Eyre* (1943). In 1943, after divorcing his first wife, he married the celebrated Hollywood actress Rita Hayworth.

When the U.S. entered the war in Europe, Welles was refused entry into the services as he was in less than perfect health: instead he went on tour with his Mercury Wonder Show and produced well-received radio shows such as *Hello, Americans*, *The Orson Welles Show*, and *Suspense*. He also campaigned for the re-election of President Roosevelt.

After the war, Welles's life became increasingly difficult. However, his films were still touched by genius and *The Lady From Shanghai* (1948), *The Third Man* (1949), *Othello* (1952, winner at the Cannes Film Festival), *A Touch of Evil* (1958), and *Chimes at Midnight* (1966) are among his best works. His passion for these projects was unquestionable and he went to great lengths to raise the financial backing, starring in countless film, TV, radio, and stage productions.

After the failure of an adaptation of Jules Verne's *Around the World in 80 Days* with music and lyrics by Cole Porter, which left him with huge debt to the IRS, Welles spent much of his life in Europe where he worked alongside luminaries such as Laurence Olivier on the stage in London as well as continuing to make his own films and appear in those of others.

In 1971, Welles was awarded a special Oscar at the Academy Awards and in 1975 a Lifetime Achievement Award from the American Film Institute. He died of heart failure on October 10, 1985, and was working, both in Europe and the U.S. right up until the end. On the day of his death he had recorded an interview for the Merv Griffin Show.

Windsor, Edward, Duke of
1894-1972
British royalty

Prince Charles and Princess Diana were not the first British royals to cause a sensation. When Edward VIII abdicated the British throne to pursue a romance with Wallis Simpson, an American divorcée, it caused a public furor of phenomenal proportions. To date, he is the only British monarch to resign of his own free will.

He was born Edward Albert Christian George Andrew Patrick David Windsor to Queen Victoria's eldest son, later King George V, and his wife Queen Mary on the June 23, 1894, at home as is traditional for British royalty, at White Lodge, Richmond Park. As a boy he was known as David to his family and friends and was educated at home by a tutor until he joined the naval cadets at 13, attending the Royal Navy College at Osborne before going up to Magdalen College, Oxford. At the age of 16 he was named Prince of Wales on his birthday and was duly invested a year later at Caernarvon Castle.

When World War I broke out in 1914, Edward joined the Grenadier Guards and insisted on serving some time on the front lines although, as heir to the throne, great efforts were made to preserve his safety; such valor and force of personality were typical of the young man and assured his public popularity. This was further enhanced when Edward toured Great Britain during the Depression, making compassionate public speeches that won the support of the British populace. Such was his concern for the people that he fought to instigate policies that would ease unemployment.

He was, however, a private man and enjoyed gardening at his country home, the 18th century Fort Belvoir, where he would also enjoy the company of a small group of close friends. It was here that he was introduced to Mrs Wallis Simpson for the first time. He was entranced by the sophisticated American socialite and cultivated a friendship with her, falling passionately in love with her as time passed.

In 1936, Edward's father, George V, died, and Edward, his eldest son, acceded the throne. Plans were immediately made for a lavish coronation for the popular king but, privately, Edward was planning to marry Mrs Simpson who, though separated, was still married. With characteristic determination he told the Royal family and Prime Minister Stanley Baldwin of his intention and was met with disapproval on all sides. The story was released to the press and became public on December 2, 1936, although the press in the U.S. and on the continent had been carrying sensational reports of an affair for several months. Public response was immediate and emphatic; the king must abdicate.

He resigned on December 10, and broadcast a radio statement the following evening, stating, "… you must believe me when I tell you, I have found it impossible to carry on the heavy burden of responsibility and to discharge the duties of King as I would wish to do without the help and support of the woman I love." Edward immediately left the country, leaving his brother to become King George VI. One of the new king's first acts was to name Edward Duke of Windsor on December 12.

A few months later Wallis Simpson's divorce was completed and the couple married in France on June 3, 1937. They moved to Paris where they continued to live in considerable style until the outbreak of World War II, at which time the Duke was offered the post of Governor of the Bahamas by Winston Churchill, a post that he accepted. The move to England lasted only as long as the war and after victory celebrations the couple moved back to Paris.

Edward returned to England only twice: following the death of his brother George VI, in 1952, and that of his mother, Queen Mary, in 1953.

Edward, Duke of Windsor died on May 28, 1972, and his body was returned to England to be buried in the grounds of Windsor Castle.

Windsor, Wallis [Bessie] Duchess of
1896-1986
American socialite

Born to Teackle and Alice Montague Warfield on June 19, 1896 at Blue Ridge Summit, Pennsylvania, Bessie Wallis Warfield was a bright girl from an early age. Before her marriage to the Duke of Windsor she was married twice. First to Earl Spencer (his name rather than a title) in 1916, (divorced 1927), and then to Ernest Simpson in Chelsea, London in 1928 (divorced 1937). She met Edward, then Prince of Wales in 1932 and their attraction was immediate, and the relationship with her second husband already strained.

Following her marriage to Edward in 1937, she indulged her love of fashion and entertaining at their Paris home and also in the United States, amassing a collection of fine jewelry. Her autobiography, *The Heart Has Its Reasons*, was published in 1956.

The Duchess of Windsor died on April 24, 1986, at the age of 90, and her body was laid to rest beside Edward's in the grounds of Windsor Castle.

West, Mae
1892–1980
American actress

West, of the half-mast eyelids, come-hither voice, and no-nonsense seductiveness, was a living American institution. Her aggressive sexuality and comic genius established her as the archetypal sex symbol, splendidly vulgar, mocking, overdressed, and endearing. Arriving in Hollywood in 1932 after theater success, she appeared with George Raft in *Night After Night* and began breaking box-office records. Lines like "Come up and see me" passed into common usage. She made Cary Grant a star with *She Done Him Wrong* (1933) and vied with W.C. Fields in *My Little Chickadee* (1939), but by then American puritanism was on the upswing and censorship ended her movie career. She returned to the stage, appearing in *Catherine Was Great* (1944), and later had some success with a glamorous nightclub act. Her autobiography, *Goodness Had Nothing To Do With It* was published in 1959.

Wilder, Billy
1906–1999
American film director

A Viennese-born writer-director, Wilder emigrated to Hollywood and became a director to protect his own scripts. He made some of Hollywood's most acerbic movies, including the film-noir *Double Indemnity* (1944), *The Lost Weekend* (1945), and *Sunset Boulevard* (1950). Wilder's most famous movie is probably his classic comedy, *Some Like it Hot* (1959). He had a particularly rewarding association with the actor Jack Lemmon, with whom he made seven movies, including *The Apartment* (1960) and *Avanti!* (1972). Renowned as one of the wittiest men in Hollywood, Wilder made some of the most entertaining, intelligent, and meticulously constructed movies of the sound era. He retired to his art collection in the 1980s, and received a Lifetime Achievement Award from the America Film Institute in 1986 and the Irving Thalberg Award in 1987.

Williams, Tennessee
1911–1983
American playwright

After an unhappy childhood in St Louis, this outstanding dramatist struggled to establish himself, first achieving success with his 12th play, *The Glass Menagerie* (1944). This was followed by *A Streetcar Named Desire* (1947), an exploration of Southern sexual tension and familial violence marked by the themes of emotional alienation and perversity that characterize his work, which is generally expressionist in style. It was his first Pulitzer Prize winning drama and was later filmed. Pulitzer Prize-winning *Cat on a Hot Tin Roof* (1955), a Freudian family drama, hints at the latent theme of homosexual anguish that preoccupies many of his most famous plays. Although he wrote many other plays, he was unable to repeat his early success. In his *Memoirs* (1975), he recounts his own personal problems with drugs, alcohol, and discovery of his homosexuality.

The Wright Brothers

American pioneer aircraft engineers and pilots

Wright, Orville
1871–1948
Wright, Wilbur
1867–1912

As young boys the Wright brothers often created simple mechanical toys. In 1888 they built a printing press and, with Wilbur as editor, started to publish a local newspaper *The Dayton, Ohio, West Side News*. In 1892, while still publishing, they opened a bicycle repair shop, and sometime later were designing and building their own.

Throughout their lives they continued with engineering research. Inspired by the writings of two engineers, German Otto Lilienthal and American Octave Chanute, they experimented with gliders. They investigated aeronautical data with their own glider, and went on to test the effects of air pressure on wing surfaces. The result of the knowledge gained from a ten-month research program testing wing airfoils on rigs and in a simple wind tunnel, was that they proved that planes could be best balanced by pilots rather than by engineering devices, and this concept was covered by their patent. In 1903, the brothers designed and built a propeller and put it together with a machine and a 12-horsepower engine. The most famous names in aviation, on December 17, 1903 the Wright brothers' *Flyer* made the first piloted (by Orville), powered, sustained, and controlled air flight. So great was their lead that they demonstrated a 24-mile flight in 1905 before anyone else had even flown. The site of this first flight is commemorated by the Wright Brothers National Memorial. Incredibly, the brothers then gave up flying until 1908, but in 1909 built the first military airplane for the United States Army. They produced a plane that could fly for 10 minutes at a speed of 40 mph (64 km/h). In 1910 Orville established several record when he flew for 62 minutes at an average altitude of 120 ft (36.6 m). The Wright Exhibition Team was set up to perform at airshows and the pilots trained by Orville, who was an international celebrity by then. The brothers toured Europe receiving honors along the way, and more when they returned. Wilbur died from typhoid in 1912, and in 1915 Orville sold the Wright Aeronautical Company. He later worked as an engineering consultant.

W

Winfrey, Oprah Gail
1954–
American television talk show host and entertainment executive

Oprah is one of the most highly paid and regarded women in the world as the star and producer of her own "The Oprah Winfrey Show," a television talk show which has brought her enormous popularity in the United States as well as the rest of the Western world. Motivated by a genuine compassion, following her own experiences of childhood abuse, and gifted with undoubted talent, great energy, and a formidable intellect, she is the first African-American to own her own studio: she joined Mary Pickford and Lucille Ball, as one of only three women ever to have done so. An Academy Award-nominated actress, Oprah has also won praise for her film roles, including her portrayal of Sofia in Steven Spielberg's adaptation of Alice Walker's *The Color Purple*, most recently, she starred in the critically acclaimed screen version of Toni Morrison's Pulitzer Prize winning *Beloved*.

She was born on a farm in Kosciusko, Mississippi, and reared by her grandmother who fostered learning in her grandchild from an early age. Oprah could read and recite passages from the Bible and poetry from the age of three, and amazed audiences around the local churches by quoting the sermons of James Weldon Johnson at the age of four. Her early literacy led to a voracious appetite for books and an excellent command of language.

However, this excellent start in life was followed by several years of trauma and mistreatment. Oprah moved, at age six, to live with her mother, and from this age until she was 13 she was the victim of sexual abuse. Eventually she ran away from home but was turned away from a juvenile detention center and, instead, was sent to live with her father, a rigid disciplinarian, in Nashville. Here she finally found some stability; though strict, her father forced his daughter to expect the best from herself and demanded that she read a book and produce a report about it each week.

After five years with her father, Oprah eventually found employment as a broadcaster at WVOL radio in Nashville from where she moved after two years to her first television job, as an anchorwoman and reporter for WTVF-TV, also in Nashville. At this time Oprah also attended Tennessee State University, where she majored in Speech Communications and Performing Arts. In 1976, Oprah moved to Baltimore to begin a job that would launch her career as a talk show host. She started as an anchor on WJZ-TV's news program but after two years found that she had a natural aptitude for drawing the best from guests when she became the co-host of the station's "People Are Talking" show.

Oprah's big break came in 1984 when she moved again, this time to Chicago, where she took over as the host of the local talk show "AM Chicago" and transformed the declining production into a hit show within a year. As the viewing figures soared, the show's format was lengthened to an hour per day and the name was changed to "The Oprah Winfrey Show." A year later, in 1986, Oprah's career was boosted again as the show was syndicated nationally. A year after that "The Oprah Winfrey Show" was recognized as the most popular national talk show and was showered with Emmy awards. In 1988, Oprah also received the prestigious "Broadcaster of the Year" award from the International Radio and Television Society, becoming only the fifth woman, and the youngest person, ever to have been so honored. During this phenomenal wave of success, Oprah also found time to appear in *The Color Purple*, making an extremely impressive movie debut and earning an Academy Award nomination. Her next movie appearance was in the adaptation of Richard Wright's *Native Son*, and again Oprah received excellent critical reviews.

In 1986, Oprah also formed HARPO Productions, which acquired "The Oprah Winfrey Show" two years later. As well as making quality films and television productions that reflected Oprah's own concerns, she now had total control over the format and content of her own talk show. The program became undoubtedly the most popular of its kind in the world; global viewing figures for Oprah's famous interview with Michael Jackson reached a dizzying 90 million — making it one of the ten most watched television programs ever. And, of course, she continued to address contentious issues and the emotional problems of members of the public with characteristic warmth, intelligence, and humor.

Oprah has also spearheaded a widely lauded campaign to raise public awareness of child abuse, becoming an extremely passionate spokesperson for the rights of children. This crusade has led Oprah into the world of politics — she was instrumental in President Clinton's signing of a bill, in 1993, which gave child carers the right to check the criminal record of any prospective employee.

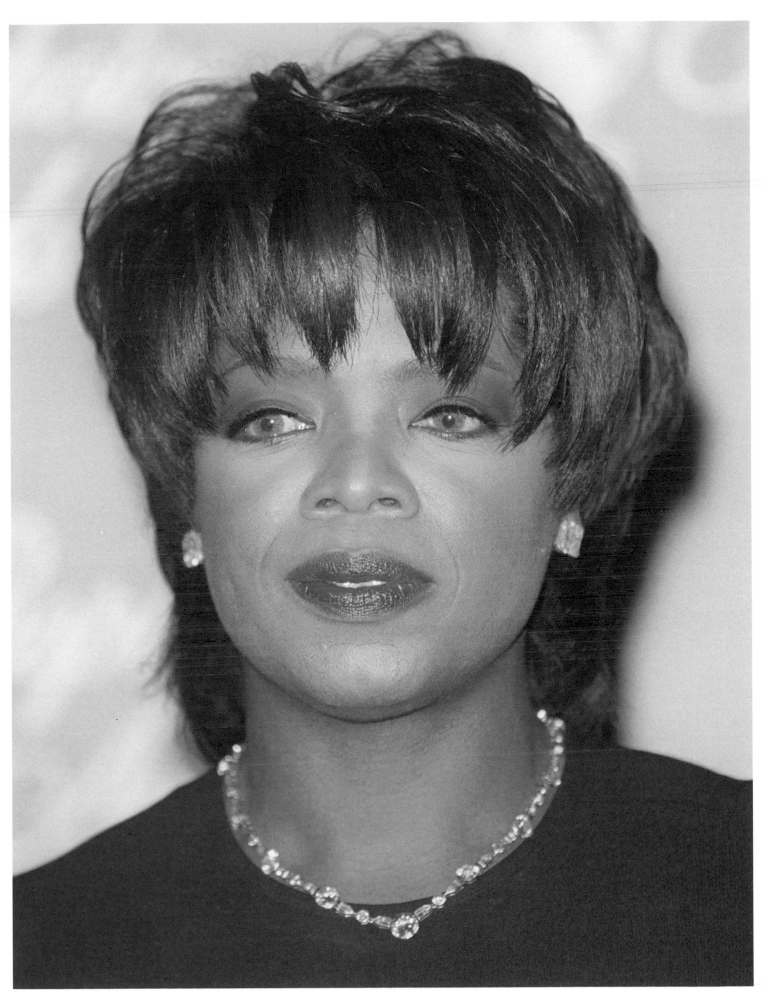

Wilson, Woodrow
1856–1924
American politician and president

Wilson's crusade to establish world peace after World War I was dismissed as utopian by the Allies at the Paris Peace Conference and by his fellow countrymen. Elected 28th President of the USA in 1913, Wilson was pushing through a reform program, when he was faced with the European war. Wilson maintained American neutrality until 1917. He tried to become the supreme arbiter at the end of the war, with his Fourteen Points, "designed to make the world safe for democracy." He was ignored by Europeans making their own territorial deals, and failed to rally support in for the League of Nations in the Senate. He wanted to turn the 1920 election into "a solemn referendum" on the Versailles Treaty but ill health forced him to retire. He was awarded the Nobel Peace Prize in 1919.

Woolf, Virginia
1882–1941
British author

In 1905, after her father's (Sir Leslie Stephen) death, Virginia, her sister Vanessa, and their brothers established a house in Bloomsbury. This became a gathering venue for the so-called Bloomsbury Group which included some of the most forward thinking and influential writers of the day. Virginia married Leonard Woolf in 1912, and together in 1917 they founded the Hogarth Press. Along with other friends, Virginia's aim was to explore the scope of a novel, and to make it more than just story telling. *Mrs Dalloway* (1925), *To the Lighthouse* (1927) and *Orlando: A biography* (1928) are some of her most famous books. Woolf also worked as a critic and had substantial influence. However, she also suffered bouts of depression and in 1941 she committed suicide by drowning.

Wyeth, N.C. [Newell Convers]
1883–1945
American painter

As a student in 1899, Wyeth studied at the Mechanic Arts School, and then spent short periods at the Normal Arts School in Boston. Between 1902–11 he was at the Howard Pyle School of Art in Wilmington, Delaware. He developed a career as a painter, muralist, and illustrator. Preferring to use oils, he produced detailed illustrations for periodicals, books and posters. Books illustrated by him included: *Treasure Island* by Robert Louis Stevenson, *Last of the Mohicans* by James Fenimore Cooper, and *Robinson Crusoe* by Daniel Defoe. Through his painting one can see his love of country life. He frequently spent winters in Chadds Ford, Pa., and summers in Port Clyde, Maine. Tragically he and his grandson were killed in a railroad accident near his home in Chadds Ford. His son Andrew Wyeth is also a painter.

W & Y

Yeats, W.B. [William Butler]
1865–1939
Irish poet

The finest poet Ireland has ever produced and one of the great figures of 20th-century literature, Yeats was born in Dublin and educated in London and Dublin, where his interest in the paranormal and mysticism developed alongside his nationalism. He abandoned his original choice of art for literature, and began to publish and edit poetry and write verse drama in the forefront of the Celtic movement. During this time he wrote *The Wanderings of Oisin* (1889), *The Lake Isle of Innisfree* (1893), in a style he believed characteristic of the ancient Celts, *The Celtic Twilight* (1893), and *The Secret Rose* (1897), which deal with Irish legends. Returning to Dublin in 1896, he became acquainted with Lady Gregory, a nationalist playwright. The founding of an Irish National Theater was one of his achievements in association with Lady Gregory and others. It went through different formulations, until becoming the Abbey Theatre opening in 1904 with three plays, two by Yeats including the propaganda piece *Cathleen ni Hoolihan* (1902). His prolific writings included essays, plays, and poetry, notably *The Wild Swans at Coole* in 1917. Eventually he abandoned his hopelessly unrequited passion for the revolutionary Maude Gonne and married Georgie Hyde-Lees, whose automatic writing helped provide him with the mystical symbolic system of *A Vision*. Published in 1925, it informed the poetry of his later years including the collections *Michael Robartes and the Dancer* (1921), which contained the celebrated "Easter 1916" and "The Second Coming," *The Tower* (1928), and *The Winding Stair*. The work of the period 1922–28 is often regarded as his most eloquent as he deepened and perfected his complex styles.

Yeats also wrote several short plays based on Celtic hero Cuchulain, combined as *Four Plays for Dancers* (1921). They were strongly influenced by the No drama of the Japanese court, from which he borrowed the use of masks, a chorus, and dance. Designed for intimate audiences, these plays brought poetry back to the theater, and were rich in mysticism, steeped with hidden meaning. He received the Nobel Prize for Literature in 1923.

Wright, Frank Lloyd
1869–1959
American architect

Frank Lloyd Wright was a pioneer in the modern style. He is considered one of the most innovative and influential figures in modern architecture and interior furnishings. Wright's long career of over 70 years encompassed modern technological developments in both building materials and techniques, and he was one of the first architects to explore and exploit the new opportunities that these exciting developments made possible.

Frank Lloyd Wright was born to William Carey Wright and his second wife, Anna Lloyd Jones, on June 8, 1867, in Richland Center, Wisconsin. Frank was his mother's favorite and she drilled into him her Unitarian values of faith in the family and a general liberal philosophy towards life.

Despite his mother's intensive educational ideas and prompting, Wright failed to graduate high school and in 1885 became apprenticed to the only builder in Madison, Allan D. Conover. Conover was also Dean of Engineering at the University of Wisconsin and he allowed his young apprentice to attend classes in the department of engineering. Here Wright received the only strict training, of any sort, that he was to receive — in draftsmanship. However, at the same time he was also receiving practical building experience in the office and by working part-time on a construction project at the university. The two years of classes that he attended before dropping out show that the young Frank Lloyd Wright had a remarkable ability in draftsmanship.

After leaving university, Wright moved to Chicago. Devastated in 1871 by a great fire, it was only now recovering and being fully rebuilt. Architects and designers from all over America, especially the Eastern seaboard, were arriving to take up the golden architectural opportunity this presented. After a brief apprenticeship to Joseph Silsbee, whose "safe" architecture soon bored him, Wright moved on to work for the firm of Adler & Sullivan.

The progressive style of Adler & Sullivan was much more to Wright's taste. One of the partners of this company, the American architect Louis Sullivan, had a profound influence on Wright and his epigram, "form follows function," came also to be at the heart of Wright's work. Wright quickly settled into the firm and, in 1889, signed a five-year contract. By this time he was given the majority of the domestic commissions that came to the firm while the principals worked on their larger, public commissions. In 1892, Wright gained recognition with one of his domestic commissions, the Charnley House: furthermore his own house at Oak Park became greatly admired. Now, clients, many of them wealthy suburban businessmen and Oak Park neighbors, started coming to him personally to design and build their homes.

These "bootlegged houses," as Wright called them, soon revealed an independent talent quite distinct from that of Sullivan. Such work also proved a great financial boon as Wright's five children were cripplingly expensive to feed and clothe. Inevitably Sullivan found out about the "bootlegged" projects and was not impressed. They parted company after a furious row and were not reconciled for 20 years. Together with several other young architects, Frank set up his own practice in Steinway Hall, Chicago. In 1894, Wright wrote *The Architect and the Machine*, the first of many papers and writings in which he would expound his theories. In his radically original designs as well as in his prolific writings he championed the virtues of what he termed "organic architecture," a building style based on natural forms.

By 1900 he was into his "Prairie House" period in which he built 33 houses in roughly ten years. By 1908 he had originated most of the principles that are today the fundamental concepts of modern architecture. During the 20 years that followed he became one of the best-known and, because of a tempestuous personal life, one of the most notorious architects in the United States. Wright spent much of his life embroiled in controversy: from the quarrels within his own family between his parents, the emotional conflicts he brought upon himself by abandoning Catherine, his first wife and mother of his six children, for a married woman, Mamah Cheney. His noisy pacifism during World War II brought him many new enemies, not to mention his anti-establishment stance towards fellow architects, planning regulations, and bureaucracy and society in general. Always arrogant and obdurate, Frank Lloyd Wright, while able to make enemies with ease, also made strong friendships and inspired tremendous loyalty from his followers.

Two editions of a folio of his work brought out by the Berlin publisher Wasmuth in 1910–11, during his year of self-imposed exile in Europe, along with a parallel exhibition that traveled throughout Europe, boosted Wright's fame in European architectural circles and influenced such key figures in contemporary architecture as Ludwig Mies van der Rohe and Le Corbusier.

Upon his return to America, and with his reputation assured on both sides of the Atlantic, Wright established Taliesin (near Spring Green, Wisconsin), the home and school that he built for himself and his followers. Wright established a

studio-workshop for apprentices who assisted him on his projects and also founded the Taliesin Fellowship to support such efforts. He embarked on a career of ever-widening achievements and began to reinforce the philosophical underpinnings of his innovative "organic" building style with its bold claim that the structural principles found in natural forms should guide modern American architecture.

Frank Lloyd Wright's winter home for the Taliesin Fellowship was Taliesin West, a complex of buildings which included a theater, music pavilion, and sun cottage, and which offered a new challenge in building materials. He first started work on the site in 1938 with apprentices from Taliesin North, and every winter for the next 22 years he and his students would continue the work of revising and enlarging the complex. Wright returned to Taliesin West in 1959 after the taxing Guggenheim Museum project had taken its toll on his health. Now aged 91, Wright was operated on in Phoenix to remove an intestinal obstruction, and despite his frailty, he appeared to come through the operation successfully. Five days later, on April 9, 1959, Wright died. Frank Lloyd Wright left behind a rich heritage of completed buildings of almost uniform splendor. He was essentially an idiosyncratic architect whose influence was immense but whose pupils were few.

ACADEMY AWARDS

Best Actor		
1927–1928	Emil Jannings, *The Way of All Flesh*	
1928–1929	Warner Baxter, *In Old Arizona*	
1929–1930	George Arliss, *Disraeli*	
1930–1931	Lionel Barrymore, *A Free Soul*	
1931–1932	Wallace Beery, *The Champ;* Fredric March, *Dr. Jekyll and Mr. Hyde*	
1932–1933	Charles Laughton, *The Private Life of Henry VIII*	
1934	Clark Gable, *It Happened One Night*	
1935	Victor McLaglen, *The Informer*	
1936	Paul Muni, *The Story of Louis Pasteur*	
1937	Spencer Tracy, *Captains Courageous*	
1938	Spencer Tracy, *Boys Town*	
1939	Robert Donat, *Goodbye, Mr. Chips*	
1940	James Stewart, *The Philadelphia Story*	
1941	Gary Cooper, *Sergeant York*	
1942	James Cagney, *Yankee Doodle Dandy*	
1943	Paul Lukas, *Watch on the Rhine*	
1944	Bing Crosby, *Going My Way*	
1945	Ray Milland, *The Lost Weekend*	
1946	Fredric March, *The Best Years of Our Lives*	
1947	Ronald Colman, *A Double Life*	
1948	Sir Laurence Olivier, *Hamlet*	
1949	Broderick Crawford, *All the King's Men*	
1950	José Ferrer, *Cyrano de Bergerac*	
1951	Humphrey Bogart, *The African Queen*	
1952	Gary Cooper, *High Noon*	
1954	Marlon Brando, *On the Waterfront*	
1955	Ernest Borgnine, *Marty*	
1956	Yul Brynner, *The King and I*	
1957	Sir Alec Guinness, *The Bridge on the River Kwai*	
1958	David Niven, *Separate Tables*	
1959	Charlton Heston, *Ben–Hur*	
1960	Burt Lancaster, *Elmer Gantry*	
1961	Maximilian Schell, *Judgment at Nuremberg*	
1962	Gregory Peck, *To Kill a Mockingbird*	
1963	Sidney Poitier, *Lilies of the Field*	
1964	Rex Harrison, *My Fair Lady*	
1965	Lee Marvin, *Cat Ballou*	
1966	Paul Scofield, *A Man for All Seasons*	
1967	Rod Steiger, *In the Heat of the Night*	
1968	Cliff Robertson, *Charly*	
1969	John Wayne, *True Grit*	
1970	George C. Scott, *Patton*	
1953	William Holden, *Stalag 17*	
1971	Gene Hackman, *The French Connection*	
1972	Marlon Brando, *The Godfather*	
1973	Jack Lemmon, *Save the Tiger*	
1974	Art Carney, *Harry and Tonto*	
1975	Jack Nicholson, *One Flew Over the Cuckoo's Nest*	
1976	Peter Finch, *Network*	
1977	Richard Dreyfuss, *The Goodbye Girl*	
1978	Jon Voight, *Coming Home*	
1979	Dustin Hoffman, *Kramer vs. Kramer*	
1980	Robert De Niro, *Raging Bull*	
1981	Henry Fonda, *On Golden Pond*	
1982	Ben Kingsley, *Gandhi*	
1983	Robert Duvall, *Tender Mercies*	
1984	F. Murray Abraham, *Amadeus*	
1985	William Hurt, *Kiss of the Spider Woman*	
1986	Paul Newman, *The Color of Money*	
1987	Michael Douglas, *Wall Street*	
1988	Dustin Hoffman, *Rain Man*	
1989	Daniel Day–Lewis, *My Left Foot*	
1990	Jeremy Irons, *Reversal of Fortune*	
1991	Anthony Hopkins, *The Silence of the Lambs*	
1992	Al Pacino, *Scent of a Woman*	
1993	Tom Hanks, *Philadelphia*	
1994	Tom Hanks, *Forrest Gump*	
1995	Nicolas Cage, *Leaving Las Vegas*	
1996	Geoffrey Rush, *Shine*	
1997	Jack Nicholson, *As Good as it Gets*	
1998	Roberto Benigni, *Life is Beautiful*	

ACADEMY AWARDS

Best Actress

1927–1928	Janet Gaynor, *Seventh Heaven; Street Angel; Sunrise*	1967	Katharine Hepburn, *Guess Who's Coming to Dinner*
1928–1929	Mary Pickford, *Coquette*	1968	Katharine Hepburn, *The Lion in Winter;*
1929–1930	Norma Shearer, *The Divorcee*		Barbra Streisand, *Funny Girl*
1930–1931	Marie Dressler, *Min and Bill*	1960	Elizabeth Taylor, *Butterfield 8*
1931–1932	Helen Hayes, *The Sin of Madelon Claudet*	1969	Dame Maggie Smith, *The Prime of Miss Jean Brodie*
1932–1933	Katharine Hepburn, *Morning Glory*	1970	Glenda Jackson, *Women in Love*
1934	Claudette Colbert, *It Happened One Night*	1971	Jane Fonda, *Klute*
1935	Bette Davis, *Dangerous*	1972	Liza Minnelli, *Cabaret*
1936	Luise Rainer, *The Great Ziegfeld*	1973	Glenda Jackson, *A Touch of Class*
1937	Luise Rainer, *The Good Earth*	1974	Ellen Burstyn, *Alice Doesn't Live Here Anymore*
1938	Bette Davis, *Jezebel*	1975	Louise Fletcher, *One Flew Over the Cuckoo's Nest*
1939	Vivien Leigh, *Gone With the Wind*		
1940	Ginger Rogers, *Kitty Foyle*	1976	Faye Dunaway, *Network*
1941	Joan Fontaine, *Suspicion*	1977	Diane Keaton, *Annie Hall*
1942	Greer Garson, *Mrs. Miniver*	1978	Jane Fonda, *Coming Home*
1943	Jennifer Jones, *The Song of Bernadette*	1979	Sally Field, *Norma Rae*
1944	Ingrid Bergman, *Gaslight*	1980	Sissy Spacek, *Coal Miner's Daughter*
1945	Joan Crawford, *Mildred Pierce*	1981	Katharine Hepburn, *On Golden Pond*
1946	Olivia De Havilland, *To Each His Own*	1982	Meryl Streep, *Sophie's Choice*
1947	Loretta Young, *The Farmer's Daughter*	1983	Shirley MacLaine, *Terms of Endearment*
1948	Jane Wyman, *Johnny Belinda*	1984	Sally Field, *Places in the Heart*
1949	Olivia De Havilland, *The Heiress*	1985	Geraldine Page, *The Trip to Bountiful*
1950	Judy Holliday, *Born Yesterday*	1986	Marlee Matlin, *Children of a Lesser God*
1951	Vivien Leigh, *A Streetcar Named Desire*	1987	Cher, *Moonstruck*
1952	Shirley Booth, *Come Back, Little Sheba*	1988	Jodie Foster, *The Accused*
1953	Audrey Hepburn, *Roman Holiday*	1989	Jessica Tandy, *Driving Miss Daisy*
1954	Grace Kelly, *The Country Girl*	1990	Kathy Bates, *Misery*
1955	Anna Magnani, *The Rose Tattoo*	1991	Jodie Foster, *The Silence of the Lambs*
1956	Ingrid Bergman, *Anastasia*	1992	Emma Thompson, *Howards End*
1957	Joanne Woodward, *The Three Faces of Eve*	1993	Holly Hunter, *The Piano*
1958	Susan Hayward, *I Want to Live!*	1994	Jessica Lange, *Blue Sky*
1959	Simone Signoret, *Room at the Top*	1995	Susan Sarandon, *Dead Man Walking*
1961	Sophia Loren, *Two Women*	1996	Frances McDormand, *Fargo*
1962	Anne Bancroft, *The Miracle Worker*	1997	Helen Hunt, *As Good As it Gets*
1963	Patricia Neal, *Hud*	1998	Gwyneth Paltrow, *Shakespeare in Love*
1964	Julie Andrews, *Mary Poppins*		
1965	Julie Christie, *Darling*		
1966	Elizabeth Taylor, *Who's Afraid of Virginia Woolf?*		

ACADEMY AWARDS

Best Director

1927–1928	Frank Borzage, *Seventh Heaven*	1962	Sir David Lean, *Lawrence of Arabia*
1928–1929	Frank Lloyd, *The Divine Lady*	1963	Tony Richardson, *Tom Jones*
1929–1930	Lewis Milestone,	1964	George Cukor, *My Fair Lady*
	All Quiet on the Western Front	1965	Robert Wise, *The Sound of Music*
1930–1931	Norman Taurog, *Skippy*	1966	Fred Zinnemann, *A Man for All Seasons*
1931–1932	Frank Borzage, *Bad Girl*	1967	Mike Nichols, *The Graduate*
1932–1933	Frank Lloyd, *Cavalcade*	1968	Sir Carol Reed, *Oliver!*
1934	Frank Capra, *It Happened One Night*	1969	John Schlesinger, *Midnight Cowboy*
1935	John Ford, *The Informer*	1970	Franklin J. Schaffner, *Patton*
1936	Frank Capra, *Mr. Deeds Goes to Town*	1971	Peter Bogdanovich, *The Last Picture Show*
1937	Leo McCarey, *The Awful Truth*	1972	Bob Fosse, *Cabaret*
1938	Frank Capra, *You Can't Take It With You*	1973	George Roy Hill, *The Sting*
1939	Victor Fleming, *Gone With the Wind*	1974	Francis Ford Coppola,
1940	John Ford, *The Grapes of Wrath*		*The Godfather, Part II*
1941	John Ford, *How Green Was My Valley*	1975	Milos Forman, *One Flew Over the*
1942	William Wyler, *Mrs. Miniver*		*Cuckoo's Nest*
1943	Michael Curtiz, *Casablanca*	1976	John G. Avildsen, *Rocky*
1944	Leo McCarey, *Going My Way*	1977	Woody Allen, *Annie Hall*
1945	Billy Wilder, *The Lost Weekend*	1978	Michael Cimino, *The Deer Hunter*
1946	William Wyler, *The Best Years of Our Lives*	1979	Robert Benton, *Kramer vs. Kramer*
1947	Elia Kazan, *Gentleman's Agreement*	1980	Robert Redford, *Ordinary People*
1948	John Huston,	1981	Warren Beatty, *Reds*
	The Treasure of the Sierra Madre	1982	Richard Attenborough, *Gandhi*
1949	Joseph L. Mankiewicz,	1983	James L. Brooks, *Terms of Endearment*
	A Letter to Three Wives	1984	Milos Forman, *Amadeus*
1950	Joseph L. Mankiewicz, *All About Eve*	1985	Sydney Pollack, *Out of Africa*
1951	George Stevens, *A Place in the Sun*	1986	Oliver Stone, *Platoon*
1952	John Ford, *The Quiet Man*	1987	Bernardo Bertolucci, *The Last Emperor*
1953	Fred Zinnemann, *From Here to Eternity*	1988	Barry Levinson, *Rain Man*
1954	Elia Kazan, *On the Waterfront*	1989	Oliver Stone, *Born on the Fourth of July*
1955	Delbert Mann, *Marty*	1990	Kevin Costner, *Dances With Wolves*
1956	George Stevens, *Giant*	1991	Jonathan Demme, *The Silence of the Lambs*
1957	Sir David Lean, *The Bridge on the*	1992	Clint Eastwood, *Unforgiven*
	River Kwai	1993	Steven Spielberg, *Schindler's List*
1958	Vincente Minnelli, *Gigi*	1994	Robert Zemeckis, *Forrest Gump*
1959	William Wyler, *Ben–Hur*	1995	Mel Gibson, *Braveheart*
1960	Billy Wilder, *The Apartment*	1996	Anthony Minghella, *The English Patient*
1961	Robert Wise, Jerome Robbins, *West*	1997	James Cameron, *Titanic*
	Side Story	1998	Steven Speilberg, *Saving Private Ryan*

ACADEMY AWARDS

Best Picture

1927–1928	*Wings*	1964	*My Fair Lady*
1928–1929	*Broadway Melody*	1965	*The Sound of Music*
1929–1930	*All Quiet on the Western Front*	1966	*A Man for All Seasons*
1930–1931	*Cimarron*	1967	*In the Heat of the Night*
1931–1932	*Grand Hotel*	1968	*Oliver!*
1932–1933	*Cavalcade*	1969	*Midnight Cowboy*
1934	*It Happened One Night*	1970	*Patton*
1935	*Mutiny on the Bounty*	1971	*The French Connection*
1936	*The Great Ziegfeld*	1972	*The Godfather*
1937	*Life of Emile Zola*	1973	*The Sting*
1938	*You Can't Take It With You*	1974	*The Godfather, Part II*
1939	*Gone With the Wind*	1975	*One Flew Over the Cuckoo's Nest*
1940	*Rebecca*	1976	*Rocky*
1941	*How Green Was My Valley*	1977	*Annie Hall*
1942	*Mrs. Miniver*	1978	*The Deer Hunter*
1943	*Casablanca*	1979	*Kramer vs. Kramer*
1944	*Going My Way*	1980	*Ordinary People*
1945	*The Lost Weekend*	1981	*Chariots of Fire*
1946	*The Best Years of Our Lives*	1982	*Gandhi*
1947	*Gentleman's Agreement*	1983	*Terms of Endearment*
1948	*Hamlet*	1984	*Amadeus*
1949	*All the King's Men*	1985	*Out of Africa*
1950	*All About Eve*	1986	*Platoon*
1951	*An American in Paris*	1987	*The Last Emperor*
1952	*The Greatest Show on Earth*	1988	*Rain Man*
1953	*From Here to Eternity*	1989	*Driving Miss Daisy*
1954	*On the Waterfront*	1990	*Dances With Wolves*
1955	*Marty*	1991	*The Silence of the Lambs*
1956	*Around the World in 80 Days*	1992	*Unforgiven*
1957	*The Bridge on the River Kwai*	1993	*Schindler's List*
1958	*Gigi*	1994	*Forrest Gump*
1959	*Ben–Hur*	1995	*Braveheart*
1960	*The Apartment*	1996	*The English Patient*
1961	*West Side Story*	1997	*Titanic*
1962	*Lawrence of Arabia*	1998	*Shakespeare in Love*
1963	*Tom Jones*		

AMERICAN PRESIDENTS

1789–1797	George Washington	1885–1889	Grover Cleveland
1797–1801	John Adams	1889–1893	Benjamin Harrison
1801–1809	Thomas Jefferson	1893–1897	Grover Cleveland
1809–1817	James Madison	1897–1901	William McKinley
1817–1825	James Monroe	1901–1909	Theodore Roosevelt
1825–1829	John Quincy Adams	1909–1913	William Howard Taft
1829–1837	Andrew Jackson	1913–1921	Woodrow Wilson
1837–1841	Martin Van Buren	1921–1923	Warren Gamaliel Harding
1841	William Henry Harrison	1923–1929	Calvin Coolidge
1841–1845	John Tyler	1929–1933	Herbert Clark Hoover
1845–1849	James Knox Polk	1933–1945	Franklin Delano Roosevelt
1849–1850	Zachary Taylor	1945–1953	Harry S. Truman
1850–1853	Millard Fillmore	1953–1961	Dwight David Eisenhower
1853–1857	Franklin Pierce	1961–1963	John Fitzgerald Kennedy
1857–1861	James Buchanan	1963–1969	Lyndon Baines Johnson
1861–1865	Abraham Lincoln	1969–1974	Richard Milhous Nixon
1865–1869	Andrew Johnson	1974–1977	Gerald Rudolph Ford
1869–1877	Ulysses Simpson Grant	1977–1981	James Earl Carter, Jr.
1877–1881	Rutherford Birchard Hayes	1981–1989	Ronald Wilson Reagan
1881	James Abram Garfield	1989–1993	George Herbert Walker Bush
1881–1885	Chester Alan Arthur	1993–	William Jefferson Blythe Clinton

AMERICAN VICE-PRESIDENTS

1789-1797	John Adams	1893-1897	Adlai E. Stevenson
1797-1801	Thomas Jefferson	1897-1899	Garret A. Hobart
1801-1805	Aaron Burr	1901	Theodore. Roosevelt
1805-1809	George Clinton	1905-1909	Charles W. Fairbanks
1809-1812	George Clinton	1909-1912	James S. Sherman
1813-1814	Elbridge Gerry	1913-1921	Thomas R. Marshall
1817-1825	Daniel D. Tompkins	1921-1923	Calvin Coolidge
1825-1829	John C. Calhoun	1925-1929	Charles G. Dawes
1829-1832	John C. Calhoun	1929-1933	Charles. Curtisr
1833-1837	Martin Van Buren	1933-1941	John N. Garnert
1837-1841	Richard M. Johnson	1941-1945	Henry A. Wallace
1841	John Tyler	1945	Harry S. Truman
1845-1849	George M. Dallas	1949-1953	Alben W. Barkley
1849-1850	Millard Fillmore	1953-1961	Richard M. Nixon
1853	William R. D. King	1961-1963	Lyndon B. Johnson
1857-1861	John C. Breckinridge	1965-1969	Hubert H. Humphrey
1861-1865	Hannibal Hamlin	1969-1973	Spiro T. Agnew
1865	Andrew Johnson	1973-1974	Gerald R. Ford
1869-1873	Schuyler Colfax	1974-1977	Nelson A. Rockefeller
1873-1875	Henry Wilson	1977-1981	Walter F. Mondale
1877-1881	William A. Wheeler	1981-1989	George H. W. Bush
1881	Chester A. Arthur	1989-1993	J. Danforth (Dan) Quayle
1885	Thomas A. Hendricks	1993	Albert Gore, Jr.
1889-1893	Levi P. Morton		

GRAMMYS

Album of the Year

1958	Henry Mancini	*The Music From Peter Gunn*
1959	Frank Sinatra	*Come Dance With Me*
1960	Bob Newhart	*Button Down Mind*
1961	Judy Garland	*Judy at Carnegie Hall*
1962	Vaughn Meader	*The First Family*
1963	Barbra Streisand	*The Barbra Streisand Album*
1964	Stan Getz, Astrud Gilberto	*Getz/Gilberto*
1965	Frank Sinatra	*September of My Years*
1966	Frank Sinatra	*A Man and His Music*
1967	The Beatles	*Sgt. Pepper's Lonely Hearts Club Band*
1968	Glen Campbell	*By the Time I Get to Phoenix*
1969	Blood, Sweat and Tears	*Blood, Sweat and Tears*
1970	Simon & Garfunkel	*Bridge Over Troubled Water*
1971	Carole King	*Tapestry*
1972	George Harrison and friends	*The Concert for Bangladesh*
1973	Stevie Wonder	*Inner Visions*
1974	Stevie Wonder	*Fulfillingness' First Finale*
1975	Paul Simon	*Still Crazy After All These Years*
1976	Stevie Wonder	*Songs in the Key of Life*
1977	Fleetwood Mac	*Rumours*
1978	Bee Gees	*Saturday Night Fever* (Soundtrack)
1979	Billy Joel	*52nd Street*
1980	Christopher Cross	*Christopher Cross*
1981	John Lennon & Yoko Ono	*Double Fantasy*
1982	Toto	*Toto IV*
1983	Michael Jackson	*Thriller*
1984	Lionel Richie	*Can't Slow Down*
1985	Phil Collins	*No Jacket Required*
1986	Paul Simon	*Graceland*
1987	U2	*The Joshua Tree*
1988	George Michael	*Faith*
1989	Bonnie Raitt	*Nick of Time*
1990	Quincy Jones	*Back on the Block*
1991	Natalie Cole	*Unforgettable*
1992	Eric Clapton	*Unplugged*
1993	Whitney Houston	*The Bodyguard* (Soundtrack)
1994	Tony Bennett	*MTV Unplugged*
1995	Alanis Morissette	*Jagged Little Pill*
1996	Celine Dion	*Falling Into You*
1997	Bob Dylan	*Time Out of Mind*
1998	Lauryn Hill	*The Miseducation of Lauryn Hill*

GRAMMYS

Record of the Year

1958	Domenico Modugno	Nel Blu Dipinto Di Blu (Volare)
1959	Bobby Darin	Mack the Knife
1960	Percy Faith	Theme From a Summer Place
1961	Henry Mancini	Moon River
1962	Tony Bennett	I Left My Heart in San Francisco
1963	Henry Mancini	The Days of Wine and Roses
1964	Stan Getz, Astrud Gilberto	The Girl From Ipanema
1965	Herb Alpert	A Taste of Honey
1966	Frank Sinatra	Strangers in the Night
1967	5th Dimension	Up, Up and Away
1968	Simon & Garfunkel	Mrs. Robinson
1969	5th Dimension	Aquarius/Let the Sunshine In
1970	Simon & Garfunkel	Bridge Over Troubled Water
1971	Carole King	It's Too Late
1972	Roberta Flack	The First Time Ever I Saw Your Face
1973	Roberta Flack	Killing Me Softly With His Song
1974	Olivia Newton-John	I Honestly Love You
1975	Captain & Tennille	Love Will Keep Us Together
1976	George Benson	This Masquerade
1977	Eagles	Hotel California
1978	Billy Joel	Just the Way You Are
1979	The Doobie Brothers	What a Fool Believes
1980	Christopher Cross	Sailing
1981	Kim Carnes	Bette Davis Eyes
1982	Toto	Rosanna
1983	Michael Jackson	Beat It
1984	Tina Turner	What's Love Got to Do With It
1985	USA for Africa	We Are the World
1986	Steve Winwood	Higher Love
1987	Paul Simon	Graceland
1988	Bobby McFerrin	Don't Worry, Be Happy
1989	Bette Midler	Wind Beneath My Wings
1990	Phil Collins	Another Day in Paradise
1991	Natalie Cole	Unforgettable
1992	Eric Clapton	Tears in Heaven
1993	Whitney Houston	I Will Always Love You
1994	Sheryl Crow	All I Wanna Do
1995	Seal	Kiss From a Rose
1996	Eric Clapton	Change the World
1997	Shawn Colvin	Sunny Came Home
1998	Celine Dion	My Heart Will Go On

GRAMMYS

Song of the Year
Songwriter(s) Award

1958	Domenico Modugno	Nel Blu Dipinto Di Blu (Volare)
1959	Jimmy Driftwood	The Battle of New Orleans
1960	Ernest Gold	Theme From Exodus
1961	Henry Mancini, Johnny Mercer	Moon River
1962	Leslie Bricusse, Anthony Newley	What Kind of Fool Am I?
1963	Johnny Mercer & Henry Mancini	The Days of Wine and Roses
1964	Jerry Herman	Hello, Dolly!
1965	Paul Francis Webber, Johnny Mandel	The Shadow of Your Smile (Theme from *The Sandpiper*)
1966	John Lennon and Paul McCartney	Michelle
1967	Jimmy Webb	Up, Up and Away
1968	Bobby Russell	Little Green Apples
1969	Joe South	Games People Play
1970	Paul Simon	Bridge Over Troubled Water
1971	Carole King	You've Got a Friend
1972	Ewan MacColl	The First Time Ever I Saw Your Face
1973	Norman Gimbel, Charles Fox	Killing Me Softly With His Song
1974	Marilyn and Alan Bergman, Marvin Hamlisch	The Way We Were
1975	Stephen Sondheim	Send in the Clowns
1976	Bruce Johnson	I Write the Songs
1977	Barbra Streisand, Paul Williams and Joe Brooks	Evergreen You Light Up My Life
1978	Billy Joel	Just the Way You Are
1979	Michael McDonald, Kenny Loggins	What a Fool Believes
1980	Christopher Cross	Sailing
1981	Donna Weiss, Jackie DeShannon	Bette Davis Eyes
1982	Johnny Christopher, Mark James, Wayne Thompson	Always on My Mind
1983	Sting	Every Breath You Take
1984	Graham Lyle, Terry Britten	What's Love Got to Do With It
1985	Michael Jackson, Lionel Richie	We Are the World
1986	Burt Bacharach, Carol Bayer Sager	That's What Friends Are For
1987	James Horner, Barry Mann, Cynthia Weil	Somewhere Out There
1988	Bobby McFerrin	Don't Worry, Be Happy
1989	Larry Henley, Jeff Silbar	Wind Beneath My Wings
1990	Julie Gold	From a Distance
1991	Irving Gordon	Unforgettable
1992	Eric Clapton, Will Jennings	Tears in Heaven
1993	Alan Menken, Tim Rice	A Whole New World (*Aladdin*'s Theme)
1994	Bruce Springsteen	Streets of Philadelphia
1995	Seal	Kiss From a Rose
1996	Gordon Kennedy, Wayne Kirkpatrick and Tommy Sims	Change the World
1997	Shawn Colvin, James Leventhal	Sunny Came Home
1998	James Horner & Will Jennings	My Heart Will Go On

NOBEL PRIZES

Physics

1901 Wilhelm Conrad Röntgen in recognition of the extraordinary services he rendered by the discovery of the rays subsequently named after him.

1902 The prize was awarded jointly to: Hendrik Antoon Lorentz and Pieter Zeeman in recognition of the extraordinary service they rendered by their researches into the influence of magnetism upon radiation phenomena.

1903 The prize was divided, one half being awarded to: Antoine Henri Becquerel in recognition of the extraordinary services he rendered by his discovery of spontaneous radioactivity; the other half jointly to: Pierre Curie and Marie Curie, née Sklodowska in recognition of the extraordinary services they rendered by their joint researches on the radiation phenomena discovered by Professor Henri Becquerel.

1904 Lord John William Strutt Rayleigh for his investigations of the densities of the most important gases and for his discovery of argon in connection with these studies.

1905 Philipp Eduard Anton Lenard for his work on cathode rays.

1906 Sir Joseph John Thomson in recognition of the great merits of his theoretical and experimental investigations on the conduction of electricity by gases.

1907 Albert Abraham Michelson for his optical precision instruments and the spectroscopic and metrological investigations carried out with their aid.

1908 Gabriel Lippmann for his method of reproducing colors photographically based on the phenomenon of interference.

1909 The prize was awarded jointly to: Guglielmo Marconi and Carl Ferdinand Braun and in recognition of their contributions to the development of wireless telegraphy.

1910 Johannes Diderik van der Waals for his work on the equation of state for gases and liquids.

1911 Wilhelm Wien for his discoveries regarding the laws governing the radiation of heat.

1912 Niles Gustaf Dalén for his invention of automatic regulators for use in conjunction with gas accumulators for illuminating lighthouses and buoys.

1913 Heike Kamerlingh-Onnes for his investigations on the properties of matter at low temperatures which led, inter alia to the production of liquid helium.

1914 Max von Laue for his discovery of the diffraction of X-rays by crystals.

1915 The prize was awarded jointly to: Sir William Henry Bragg and Sir William Lawrence for their services in the analysis of crystal structure by means of X-rays.

1916 The prize money for 1916 was allocated to the Special Fund of this prize section.

1917 Chalres Glover Barkla for his discovery of the characteristic Röntgen radiation of the elements.

1918 Max Karl Ernst Ludwig Planck in recognition of the services he rendered to the advancement of Physics by his discovery of energy quanta.

1919 Johannes Stark for his discovery of the Doppler effect in canal rays and the splitting of spectral lines in electric fields.

1920 Charles Edouard Guillaume in recognition of the service he rendered to precision measurements in physics by his discovery of anomalies in nickel steel alloys.

1921 Albert Einstein for his discovery of the laws governing the impact of an electron upon an atom.

1922 Niels Bohr for his services in the investigation of the structure of atoms and of the radiation emanating from them.

1923 Robert Andrews Millikan for his work on the elementary charge of electricity and on the photoelectric effect.

1924 Karl Manne Georg Siegbahn for his discoveries and researchin the field of X-ray spectroscopy.

1925 The prize was awarded jointly to: James Franck and Gustav Hertz for their discovery of the laws governing the impact of an electron upon an atom.

1926 Jena-Baptists Perrin for his work on the discontinuous structure of matter, and especially for his discovery of sedimentation equilibrium.

1927 The prize was divided equally between: Arthur Holly Compton for his discovery of the effect named after him, Charles Thomson Rees Wilson for his method of making the paths of electrically charged particles visible by condensation of vapor.

1928 Sir Owen Willand Richardson for his work on the thermionic phenomenon and especially for the discovery of the law named after him.

1929 Prince Louis-Victor de Brogliefor his discovery of the wave nature of electrons.

1930 Sir Chandrasekhara Venkata Raman for his work on the scattering of light and for the discovery of the effect named after him.

1931 The prize money was allocated to the Main Fund (1/3) and to the Special Fund (2/3) of this prize section.

1932 Werner Heisenberg for the creation of quantum mechanics, the application of which has, inter alia, led to the discovery of the allotropic forms of hydrogen.

NOBEL PRIZES

1933 The prize was awarded jointly to Erwin Shrödinger and Paul Adrien Maurice for the discovery of new productive forms of atomic theory.

1934 The prize money was allocated to the Main Fund (1/3) and to the Special Fund (2/3) of this prize section.

1935 Sir James Chadwick for the discovery of the neutron.

1936 The prize was divided equally between: Victor Franz Hess for his discovery of cosmic radiation, Carl David Anderson for his discovery of the positron.

1937 The prize was awarded jointly to: Clinton Joseph Davisson and Sir Geroge Paget Thomson for their experimental discovery of the diffraction of electrons by crystals.

1938 Enrico Fermi for his demonstrations of the existence of new radioactive elements produced by neutron irradiation, and for his related discovery of nuclear reactions brought about by slow neutrons.

1939 Ernest Orlando Lawrence for the invention and development of the cyclotron and for results obtained with it, especially with regard to artificial radioactive elements.

1940-1942 The prize money was allocated to the Main Fund (1/3) and to the Special Fund (2/3) of this prize section.

1943 Otto Stern for his contribution to the development of the molecular ray method and his discovery of the magnetic moment of the proton.

1944 Isidor Isaac Rabi for his resonance method for recording the magnetic properties of atomic nuclei.

1945 Wolfgan Pauli for the discovery of the Exclusion Principle, also called the Pauli Principle.

1946 Percy Williams Birdgman for the invention of an apparatus to produce extremely high pressures, and for the discoveries he made therewith in the field of high pressure physics.

1947 Sir Edward Victor Appleton for his investigations of the physics of the upper atmosphere especially for the discovery of the so-called Appleton layer.

1948 Lord Patrick Maynard Stuart Blackett for his development of the Wilson cloud chamber method, and his discoveries therewith in the fields of nuclear physics and cosmic radiation.

1949 Hideki Yukawa for his prediction of the existence of mesons on the basis of theoretical work on nuclear forces.

1950 Cecil Frank Powell for his development of the photographic method of studying nuclear processes and his discoveries regarding mesons made with this method.

1951 The prize was awarded jointly to: Sir John Douglas Cockcroft and Ernest Thomas Sinton Walton for their pioneer work on the transmutation of atomic nuclei by artificially accelerated atomic particles.

1952 The prize was awarded jointly to: Felix Bloch and Edward Mills Purcell for their development of new methods for nuclear magnetic precision measurements and discoveries in connection therewith.

1953 Frits (Frederik) Zernike for his demonstration of the phase contrast method, especially for his invention of the phase contrast microscope.

1954 The prize was divided equally between: Max Born for his fundamental research in quantum mechanics, especially for his statistical interpretation of the wave function and Walther Bothe for the coincidence method and his discoveries made therewith.

1955 The prize was divided equally between: Willis Eugene Lamb for his discoveries concerning the fine structure of the hydrogen spectrum and Polykarp Kusch for his precision determination of the magnetic moment of the electron.

1956 The prize was awarded jointly, one third each, to: William Shockley,

Marie Curie

John Bardeen and Walter Houser Brattain for their researches on semiconductors and their discovery of the transistor effect.

1957 The prize was awarded jointly to: Chen Ning Yang and Tsung-Dao Lee for their penetrating investigation of the so-called parity laws which has led to important discoveries regarding the elementary particles.

1958 The prize was awarded jointly to: Pavel Alekseyevich Cherenkov, Il'ja Mikhailovich Frank and Igor Yevgenyevich Tamm for the discovery and the interpretation of the Cherenkov effect.

1959 The prize was awarded jointly to: Emilio Gino Sergè and Owen Chamberlain for their discovery of the antiproton.

1960 Donald A. Glaser for the invention of the bubble chamber.

1961 The prize was divided equally between: Robert Hofstadter for his pioneering studies of electron scattering in atomic nuclei and for his thereby achieved discoveries concerning the structure of the nucleons and Rudolf Ludwig Mössbauer for his researches concerning the resonance absorption of gamma radiation and his discovery in this connection of the effect which bears his name.

1962 Lev Davidovich Landau for his

pioneering theories for condensed matter, especially liquid helium.

1963 The prize was divided, one half being awarded to: Eugene P. Wigner for his contributions to the theory of the atomic nucleus and the elementary particles, particularly through the discovery and application of fundamental symmetry principles and the other half jointly to: Maria Goeppert-Mayer and J. Hans D. Jensen for their discoveries concerning nuclear shell structure.

1964 The prize was divided, one half being awarded to: Charles H. Townes the other half jointly to: Nicolay Gennadiyevich Basov and Aleksaner Mikhailovich Prokhorov for fundamental work in the field of quantum electronics, which has led to the construction of oscillators and amplifiers based on the maser-laser principle.

1965 The prize was awarded jointly to: Sin-Itiro Tomonaga, Julian Schwinger, and Ruichard P. Feynman for their fundamental work in quantum electrodynamics, with deep-ploughing consequences for the physics of elementary particles.

1966 Alfred Kastler for the discovery and development of optical methods for studying hertzian resonances in atoms.

1967 Hans Albrecht Bethe for his contributions to the theory of nuclear reactions, especially his discoveries concerning the energy production in stars.

1968 Luis W. Alvarez for his decisive contributions to elementary particle physics, in particular the discovery of a large number of resonance states, made possible through his development of the technique of using hydrogen bubble chambers and data analysis.

1969 Murray Gell-Mann for his contributions and discoveries concerning the classification of elementary particles and their interactions.

1970 The prize was divided equally between: Hannes Alfvén for fundamental work and discoveries in magneto-hydrodynamics with fruitful applications in different parts of plasma physics and Louis Néel for fundamental work and discoveries concerning antiferromagnetism and ferrimagnetism which have led to important applications in solid state physics.

1971 Dennis Gabor for his invention and development of the holographic method.

1972 The prize was awarded jointly to: John Bardeen, Leon N. Cooper and J. Robert Schrieffer for their jointly developed theory of superconductivity, usually called the BCS-theory.

1973 The prize was divided, one half being equally shared between: Leo Esaki and Ivar Giaever, for their experimental discoveries regarding tunneling phenomena in semiconductors and superconductors, respectively, and the other half to Brian D. Josephson for his theoretical predictions of the properties of a supercurrent through a tunnel barrier, in particular those phenomena which are generally known as the Josephson effects.

1974 The prize was awarded jointly to: Sir Martin Ryle and Antony Hewish for their pioneering research in radio astrophysics Ryle for his observations and inventions, in particular of the aperture synthesis technique, and Hewish for his decisive role in the discovery of pulsars.

1975 The prize was awarded jointly to: Aage Bohr, Ben Mottleson and James Rainwater for the discovery of the connection between collective motion and particle motion in atomic nuclei and the development of the theory of the structure of the atomic nucleus based on this connection.

1976 The prize was divided equally between: Burton Richter and Samuel C. C. Ting for their pioneering work in the discovery of a heavy elementary particle of a new kind.

1977 The prize was divided equally between: Philip W. Andeson, Sir Neville F. Mott and John H. van Vleck for their fundamental theoretical investigations of the electronic structure of magnetic and disordered systems.

1978 The prize was divided, one half being awarded to: Pytor Leonidovich Kapitsa for his basic inventions and discoveries in the area of low-temperature physics and the other half divided equally between: Arno A. Penzias and Robert W. Wilson for their discovery of cosmic microwave background radiation.

1979 The prize was divided equally between: Sheldon L. Glashow, Abdus Salam, and Steven Weinberg for their contributions to the theory of the unified weak and electromagnetic interaction between elementary particles, including inter alia the prediction of the weak neutral current.

1980 The prize was divided equally between: James W. Cronin and Val L. Fitch for the discovery of violations of fundamental symmetry principles in the decay of neutral K-mesons.

1981 The prize was awarded by one half jointly to: Nicolaas Bloembergen and Arthur L. Schawlow for their contribution to the development of laser spectroscopy and the other half to: Kai M. Siegbahn for his contribution to the development of high-resolution electron spectroscopy.

1982 Kenneth G. Wilson for his theory for critical phenomena in connection with phase transitions.

1983 The prize was divided equally between: Subramanyan Chandrasekhar for his theoretical studies of the physical processes of importance to the structure and evolution of the stars; William A. Fowler for his theoretical and experimental studies of the nuclear reactions of importance in the formation of the chemical elements in the universe.

1984 The prize was awarded jointly to: Carlo Rubbia and Simon van der

Meer for their decisive contributions to the large project, which led to the discovery of the field particles W and Z, communicators of weak interaction.

1985 Klaus von Klitzing for the discovery of the quantized Hall effect.

1986 The prize was awarded by one half to: Ernst Ruska for his fundamental work in electron optics, and for the design of the first electron microscope; Gerd Binnig and Heinrich Rohrer for their design of the scanning tunneling microscope.

1987 The prize was awarded jointly to: J. Georg Bednorz and K. Alexander Müller for their important breakthrough in the discovery of superconductivity in ceramic materials.

1988 The prize was awarded jointly to: Leon M. Lederman, Melvin Schwartz and Jack Steinberger for the neutrino beam method and the demonstration of the doublet structure of the leptons through the discovery of the muon neutrino.

1989 One half of the award was given to: Norman F. Ramsey for the invention of the separated oscillatory fields method and its use in the hydrogen maser and other atomic clocks. And the other half jointly to: Hans G. DEehemlt and Wolfgang Paul for the development of the ion trap technique.

1990 The prize was awarded jointly to: Jerome I. Friedman, Henry W. Kendall and Richard E. Taylor for their pioneering investigations concerning deep inelastic scattering of electrons on protons and bound neutrons, which have been of essential importance for the development of the quark model in particle physics.

1991 Pierre-Gilles de Gennes for discovering that methods developed for studying order phenomena in simple systems can be generalized to more complex forms of matter, in particular to liquid crystals and polymers.

1992 Georges Charpak for his

Albert Einstein

invention and development of particle detectors, in particular the multiwire proportional chamber.

1993 The prize was awarded jointly to: Russell A. Hulse and Joseph H. Taylor JR. for the discovery of a new type of pulsar, a discovery that has opened up new possibilities for the study of gravitation.

1994 The prize was awarded for pioneering contributions to the development of neutron scattering techniques for studies of condensed matter to: Bertam N. Brockhouse for the development of neutron spectroscopy, and Clifford G. Shull for the development of the neutron diffraction technique.

1995 awarded for pioneering

experimental contributions to lepton physics, with half to Martin L. Perl for the discovery of the tau lepton and the other half to Frederick Reines for detection of the neutrino.

1996 awarded jointly to: David M. Lee, Douglas D. Osheroff and Robert C. Richardson for their discovery of superfluidity in helium-3.

1997 awarded jointly to: Steven Chu, Claude Cohen-Tannoudji and William D. Phillips for development of methods to cool and trap atoms with laser light.

1998 awarded jointly to: Robert B Laughlin, Horst L Stormer and Daniel C. Tsui for their discovery of a new form of quantum fluid with fractionally charged excitations.

Economics

1969 The prize was awarded jointly to: Ragnar Frisch and Jan Tinbergen for having developed dynamic models for the analysis of economic processes.

1970 Paul A. Samuelson for the scientific work through which he developed static and dynamic economic theory and his contributions to economic analysis.

1971 Simon Kuznets for his empirically founded interpretation of economic growth which has led to new and deepened insight into the economic and social structure and process of development.

1972 The prize was awarded jointly to: Sir John R. Hicks and Kenneth J. Arrow for their pioneering contributions to general economic equilibrium theory and welfare theory.

1973 Wassily Leontief for the development of the input-output method and for its application to important economic problems.

1974 The prize was divided equally between: Gunnar Myrdal and Friedrich August von Hayek for their pioneering work in the theory of money and economic fluctuations and for their penetrating analysis of the interdependence of economic, social, and institutional phenomena.

1975 The prize was awarded jointly to: Leonid Vitaliyevich Kantorovich and Tjalling C. Koopmans for their contributions to the theory of optimum allocation of resources.

1976 Milton Friedman for his achievements in the fields of consumption analysis, monetary history, and theory and for his demonstration of the complexity of stabilization policy.

1977 The prize was divided equally between Bertil Ohlin and James E. Meade for their contribution to the theory of international trade and international capital movements.

1978 Herbert A. Simon for his research

into the decision-making process within economic organizations.

1979 The prize was divided equally between: Theodore W. Schultz and Sir Arthur Lewis for their pioneering research into economic development research with particular consideration of the problems of developing countries.

1980 Lawrence R. Klein for the creation of econometric models and the application to the analysis of economic fluctuations and economic policies.

1981 James Tobin for his analysis of financial markets in relation to expenditure, employment, production and prices; Lawrence R. Klein for the creation of econometric models and the application to the analysis of economic fluctuations and economic policies.

1982 George J. Stigler for his seminal studies of industrial structures, functioning of markets and causes, and effects of public regulation.

1983 Gerard Debreu for having incorporated new analytical methods into economic theory and for his rigorous reformulation of the theory of general equilibrium.

1984 Sir Richard Stone for having made fundamental contributions to the development of systems of national accounts and hence greatly improved the basis for empirical economic analysis.

1985 Franco Modigliani for his pioneering analyses of saving and of financial markets.

1986 James M. Buchanan, JR. for his development of the contractual and constitutional bases for the theory of economic and political decision-making.

1987 Robert M. Solow for his contributions to the theory of economic growth.

1988 Maurice Allais for his pioneering contributions to the theory of markets and efficient utilization of resources.

1989 Trygve Haavelmo for his clarification of the probability theory foundations of econometrics and his analyses of simultaneous economic structures.

1990 The prize was awarded with one third each to: Harry M. Markowitz, Merton M. Miller, and William F. Sharpe for their pioneering work in the theory of financial economics.

1991 Ronald H. Coase for his discovery and clarification of the significance of transaction costs and property rights for the institutional structure and functioning of the economy.

1992 Gary S. Becker for having extended the domain of microeconomic analysis to a wide range of human behavior and interaction, including non-market behavior.

1993 The prize was awarded jointly to: Robert W. Fogel and Douglass C. North for having research in economic history by applying economic theory and quantitative methods in order to explain economic and institutional change.

1994 The prize was awarded jointly to: John C. Harsanyi, John F. Nash and Reinhard Selten for their pioneering analysis of equilibria in the theory of non-cooperative games.

1995 Robert Lucas for having developed and applied the hypothesis of rational expectations, and thereby having transformed macroeconomic analysis and deepened our understanding of economic policy.

1996 James A. Mirrlees and William Vickerey for their fundamental contributions to the economic theory of incentives under asymmetric information.

1997 Robert C. Merton and Myrons S. Scholes for a new method to determine the value of derivatives.

1998 Amartya Sen for his contributions to welfare economics.

Literature

William Bulter Yeats

1901 Sully Prudhomme (pen-name of René François Armand), in special recognition of his poetic composition, which gives evidence of lofty idealism, artistic perfection and a rare combination of the qualities of both heart and intellect.

1902 Christian Matthias Theodor Mommsen the greatest living master of the art of historical writing, with special reference to his monumental work, *A History of Rome*.

1903 Bjørnstjerne Martinus Bjørnson as a tribute to his noble, magnificent, and versatile poetry, which has always been distinguished by both the freshness of its inspiration and the rare purity of its spirit.

1904 The prize was divided equally between: Frédéric Mistral in recognition of the fresh originality and true inspiration of his poetic production, which faithfully reflects the natural scenery and native spirit of his people, and, in addition, his significant work as a Provençal philologist; José Echegaray Y. Eizaguirre in recognition of the numerous and brilliant compositions which, in an individual and original manner, have revived the great traditions of the Spanish drama.

1905 Henryk Sienryk Sienkiewicz

because of his outstanding merits as an epic writer.

1906 Giosuè Carducci not only in consideration of his deep learning and critical research, but above all as a tribute to the creative energy, freshness of style, and lyrical force which characterize his poetic masterpieces.

1907 Rudyard Kipling in consideration of the power of observation, originality of imagination, virility of ideas, and remarkable talent for narration which characterize the creations of this world-famous author.

1908 Rudolf Christoph Eucken in recognition of his earnest search for truth, his penetrating power of thought, his wide range of vision, and the warmth and strength in presentation with which in his numerous works he has vindicated and developed an idealistic philosophy of life.

1909 Selma Ottilia Lovisa Lagerlöf in appreciation of the lofty idealism, vivid imagination and spiritual perception that characterize her writings.

1910 Paul Johann Ludwig Heyse as a tribute to the consummate artistry, permeated with idealism, which he has demonstrated during his long productive career as a lyric poet, dramatist, novelist, and writer of world-renowned short stories.

1911 Count Maurice (Morris) Polidore Marie Bernhard Maeterlinck, in appreciation of his many sided literary activities, and especially of his dramatic works, which are distinguished by a wealth of imagination and by a poetic fancy, which reveals, sometimes in the guise of a fairy tale, a deep inspiration, while in a mysterious way they appeal to the readers' own feelings and stimulate their imaginations.

1912 Gerhart Johann Robert Hauptmann primarily in recognition of his fruitful, varied, and outstanding production in the realm of dramatic art.

1913 Rabinranath Tagore because of his profoundly sensitive, fresh, and beautiful verse, by which, with consummate skill, he has made his poetic thought, expressed in his own English words, a part of the literature of the West.

1914 The prize money for 1914 was allocated to the Special Fund of this prize section.

1915 Romain Rolland as a tribute to the lofty idealism of his literary production and to the sympathy and love of truth with which he has described different types of human beings.

1916 Carl Gustav Verner von Heidenstam in recognition of his significance as the leading representative of a new era in our literature.

1917 The prize was divided equally between: Karl Adolph Gjellerup for his varied and rich poetry, which is inspired by lofty ideals; Henrik Pontoppidan for his authentic descriptions of present-day life in Denmark.

1918 The prize money for 1918 was allocated to the Special Fund of this prize section.

1919 Carl Friedrich Georg Spitteler in special appreciation of his epic, *Olympian Spring*.

1920 Knut Pedersen Hamsun for his monumental work, *Growth of the Soil*.

1921 Anatole France (pen-name of Jacques Anatole Thibault), in recognition of his brilliant literary achievements, characterized as they are by a nobility of style, a profound human sympathy, grace, and a true

NOBEL PRIZES

Gallic temperament.

1922 Jacinto Benavente for the happy manner in which he has continued the illustrious traditions of the Spanish drama.

1923 William Bulter Yeats for his always inspired poetry, which in a highly artistic form gives expression to the spirit of a whole nation.

1924 Wladyslaw Stainslaw Reymont (pen-name of Reyment), for his great national epic, *The Peasants*.

1925 George Bernard Shaw for his work which is marked by both idealism and humanity, its stimulating satire often being infused with a singular poetic beauty.

1926 Grazia Deledda (pen-name of Grazia Madesani née Deladda), for her idealistically inspired writings which with plastic clarity picture the life on her native island and with depth and sympathy deal with human problems in general.

1927 Henri Bergson in recognition of his rich and vitalizing ideas and the brilliant skill with which they have been presented.

1928 Sigrid Undset principally for her powerful descriptions of *Northern life During the Middle Ages*.

1929 Thomas Mann principally for his

Thomas Stearns Eliot

great novel, *Buddenbrooks*, which has won steadily increased recognition as one of the classic works of contemporary literature.

1930 Sinclair Lewis for his vigorous and graphic art of description and his ability to create, with wit and humor, new types of characters.

1931 Erik Axel Karlfeldt *The poetry of Erik Axel Karlfeldt*.

1932 John Glasworthy for his distinguished art of narration which takes its highest form in *The Forsythe Saga*.

1933 Ivan Alekseyevich Bunin for the strict artistry with which he has carried on the classical Russian traditions in prose writing.

1934 Luigi Pirandello for his bold and ingenious revival of dramatic and scenic art.

1935 The prize money was allocated to the Main Fund (1/3) and to the Special Fund (2/3) of this prize section.

1936 Eugene Gladston O'Neill for the power, honesty, and deep-felt emotions of his dramatic works, which embody an original concept of tragedy.

1937 Roger Martin du Gard for the artistic power and truth with which he has depicted human conflict as well as some fundamental aspects of contemporary life in his novel cycle *Les Thibault*.

1938 Pearl Buck (pen-name of Pearl Wlash [nee Sydenstricker]), for her rich and truly epic descriptions of peasant life in China and for her biographical masterpieces.

1939 Frnas Eemil Silanpää for his deep understanding of his country's peasantry and the exquisite art with which he has portrayed their way of life and their relationship with nature.

1940-1943 The prize money was allocated to the Main Fund (1/3) and to the Special Fund (2/3) of this prize section.

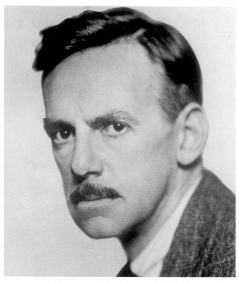

Eugene Gladston O'Neill

1944 Johannes Vilhelm Jensen for the rare strength and fertility of his poetic imagination with which is combined an intellectual curiosity of wide scope and a bold, freshly creative style.

1945 Gabriela Mistral (pen-name of Lucila Godoy Y.Alca-Yaga), for her lyric poetry which, inspired by powerful emotions, has made her name a symbol of the idealistic aspirations of the entire Latin American world.

1946 Hermann Hesse for his inspired writings which, while growing in boldness and penetration, exemplify the classical humanitarian ideals and high qualities of style.

1947 André Paul Guillaume Gide for his comprehensive and artistically significant writings, in which human problems and conditions have been presented with a fearless love of truth and keen psychological insight.

1948 Thomas Stearns Eliot for his outstanding, pioneer contribution to present-day poetry.

1949 William Faulkner for his powerful and artistically unique contribution to the modern American novel.

1950 Earl Bertand Arthur William Russell in recognition of his varied and significant writings in which he champions humanitarian ideals and freedom of thought.

NOBEL PRIZES

1951 Pär Fabain Lagerkvist for the artistic vigor and true independence of mind with which he endeavors in his poetry to find answers to the eternal questions confronting mankind.

1952 François Mauriac for the deep spiritual insight and the artistic intensity with which he has in his novels penetrated the drama of human life.

1953 Sir Winston Leonard Spencer Churchill for his mastery of historical and biographical description as well as for brilliant oratory in defending exalted human values.

1954 Ernest Miller Hemingway for his mastery of the art of narrative, most recently demonstrated in *The Old Man and the Sea* ,and for the influence that he has exerted on contemporary style.

1955 Halldór Kiljan Laxness for his vivid epic power which has renewed the great narrative art of Iceland.

1956 Juan Ramón Jiménez for his lyrical poetry, which in Spanish language constitutes an example of high spirit and artistic purity.

1957 Albert Camus for his important literary production, which with clear-sighted earnestness illuminates the problems of the human conscience in our times.

1958 Boris Leonidovich Pasternak for his important achievement both in contemporary lyrical poetry and in the field of the great Russian epic tradition. (Accepted first, later caused by the authorities of his country to decline the prize.)

1959 Salvatore Quasimodo for his lyrical poetry, which with classical fire expresses the tragic experience of life in our own times.

1960 Saint-John Perse (pen-name of Alexis Léger), for the soaring flight and the evocative imagery of his poetry which in a visionary fashion reflects the conditions of our time.

1961 Ivo Andric for the epic force with which he has traced themes and depicted human destinies drawn from the history of his country.

1962 John Steinbeck for his realistic and imaginative writings, combining as they do sympathetic humor and keen social perception.

1963 Giorgos Seferis (pen-name of Giorgos Seferiadis), for his eminent lyrical writing, inspired by a deep feeling for the Hellenic world of culture.

1964 Jean-Paul Sartre for his work which, rich in ideas and filled with the spirit of freedom and the quest for truth, has exerted a far-reaching influence on our age. (Declined the prize.)

1965 Michail Aleksandrovich Sholokhov for the artistic power and integrity with which, in his epic of the Don, he has given expression to a historic phase in the life of the Russian people.

1966 The prize was divided equally between: Shmuel Yosef Agnon for his profoundly characteristic narrative art with motifs from the life of the Jewish people; Nelly Sachs for her outstanding lyrical and dramatic writing, which interprets Israel's destiny with touching strength.

1967 Miguel Angel Asturias for his vivid literary achievement, deep-rooted in the national traits and traditions of Indian peoples of Latin America.

1968 Yasunari Kawabata for his narrative mastery, which with great sensibility expresses the essence of the Japanese mind.

1969 Samual Beckett for his writing, which — in new forms for the novel and drama — in the destitution of modern man acquires its elevation.

1970 Aleksander Iasevich Solzhenitsyn for the ethical force with which he has pursued the indispensable traditions of Russian literature.

1971 Pablo Neruda for a poetry that with the action of an elemental force brings alive a continent's destiny and dreams.

1972 Heinrch Böll for his writing which through its combination of a broad perspective on his time and a sensitive skill in characterization has contributed to a renewal of German literature.

1973 Patrick White for an epic and psychological narrative art which has introduced a new continent into literature.

1974 The prize was divided equally between: Eyvind Johnson for a narrative art, farseeing in lands and ages, in the service of freedom; Harry Martinson for writings that catch the dewdrop and reflect the cosmos.

1975 Eugenio Montale for his distinctive poetry which, with great artistic sensitivity, has interpreted human values under the sign of an outlook on life with no illusions.

1976 Saul Bellow for the human understanding and subtle analysis of contemporary culture that are combined in his work.

1977 Vincente Alexandre for a creative poetic writing which illuminates man's condition in the cosmos and in present-day society, at the same time representing the great renewal of the

Sir Winston Leonard Spencer Churchill

traditions of Spanish poetry between the wars.

1978 Isaac Bashevis Singer for his impassioned narrative art which, with roots in a Polish-Jewish cultural tradition, brings universal human conditions to life.

1979 Odysseus Elytis (pen-name of Odyssues Alepoudhelis), for his poetry, which, against the background of Greek tradition, depicts with sensuous strength and intellectual clear-sightedness modern man's struggle for freedom and creativeness.

1980 Czeslaw Milosz who with uncompromising clear-sightedness voices man's exposed condition in a world of severe conflicts.

1981 Elias Canetti for writings marked by a broad outlook, a wealth of ideas and artistic power.

1982 Gabriel Garcîa Márquez for his novels and short stories, in which the fantastic and the realistic are combined in a richly composed world of imagination, reflecting a continent's life and conflicts.

1983 Sir William Golding for his novels which, with the perspicuity of realistic narrative art and the diversity and universality of myth, illuminate the human condition in the world of today.

1984 Jaroslav Seifert for his poetry which endowed with freshness, sensuality and rich inventiveness provides a liberating image of the indomitable spirit and versatility of man.

1985 Claude Simon who in his novel combines the poet's and the painter's creativeness with a deepened awareness of time in the depiction of the human condition.

1986 Wole Soyinka who in a wide cultural perspective and with poetic overtones fashions the drama of existence.

1987 Joseph Brodsky for an all-embracing authorship, imbued with clarity of thought and poetic intensity.

1988 Naguib Mafouz who, through works rich in nuance – now clear – sightedly realistic, now evocatively ambiguous-has formed an Arabian narrative art that applies to all mankind.

1989 Camilo José Cela for a rich and intensive prose, which with restrained compassion forms a challenging vision of man's vulnerability.

1990 Ocatvio Paz for impassioned writing with wide horizons, characterized by sensuous intelligence and humanistic integrity.

1991 Nadine Gordimer who through her magnificent epic writing has – in the words of Alfred Nobel – been of very great benefit to humanity.

1992 Derek Walcott for a poetic oeuvre of great luminosity, sustained by a historical vision, the outcome of a multicultural commitment.

1993 Toni Morrison who in novels characterized by visionary force and poetic import, gives life to an essential aspect of American reality.

1994 Kenzaburo Oe who with poetic force creates an imagined world, where life and myth condense to form a disconcerting picture of the human predicament today.

1995 Seamus Heaney for works of lyrical beauty and ethical depth, which exalt everyday miracles and the living past.

1996 Wislawa Szymborska for poetry that with ironic precision allows the historical and biological context to come to light in fragments of human reality.

1997 Dario Fo who emulates the jesters of the Middle Ages in scourging authority and upholding the dignity of the downtrodden.

1998 Jose Saramago who with parables sustained by imagination, compassion and irony continually enables us once again to apprehend an elusory reality.

Peace

1901 The prize was divided equally between: Jean Henri Dunant, Switzerland. Founder of the International Committee of the Red Cross, Geneva; initiator of the Geneva Convention; Frédéric Passy, France. Founder and President of the first French peace society (since 1889 it has been called the Société Francaise pour l'arbitrage entre nations).

1902 The prize was divided equally between: Elie Ducommun, Switzerland. Honorary Secretary of the Permanent International Peace Bureau, Berne and Charles Albert Gobat, Switzerland. Secretary General of the Inter-Parliamentary Union, Berne. Honorary Secretary of the Permanent International Peace Bureau, Berne.

1903 Sir William Randal Cremer, Great Britain. Member of the British Parliament. Secretary of the International Arbitration League.

1904 Institute de droit Internationale (Institute of International Law), Gent, Belgium. A scientific society.

1905 Baroness Bertha Sophie Felicita von Suttner née Countess Kinsky von Chinic und Tettau Austria. Writer. Hon. President of the Permanent International Peace Bureau, Berne. Author of *Die Waffen Nieder* (*Lay Down Your Arms*).

1906 Theodore Roosevelt, USA. President of the United States of America. Drew up the 1905 peace treaty between Russia and Japan.

1907 The prize was divided equally between: Ernesto Teodoro Moneta, Italy. President of the Lombard League of Peace and Louis Renault, France. Professor International Law, Sorbonne University, Paris.

1908 The prize was divided equally between: Kalus Pontius Arnoldson, Sweden. Writer. Former Member of the Swedish Parliament. Founder of the Swedish Peace and Arbitration League and Fredrik Bajer, Denmark. Member

NOBEL PRIZES

of the Danish Parliament. Honorary President of the Permanent International Peace Bureau, Berne.

1909 The prize was divided equally between: Auguste Marie François Beernaert, Belgium. Former Prime Minister. Member of the Belgian Parliament. Member of the Cour Internationale d'Arbitrage (International Court of Arbitration) at the Hague; Paul Henribenjamin Balluet d'Estournelles de Constant, Baron de Constant de Rebecque, France. Member of the French Parliament (Sénateur). Founder and President of the French parliamentary group for international arbitration (Groupe parlementaire de l'arbitrage international). Founder of the Comité de défense des intérêts nationaux et de conciliation internationale (Committee for the Defense of National Interests and International Conciliation).

1910 Bureau Internationale permanent de la paix (Permanent International Peace Bureau), Bern.

1911 The prize was divided equally between: Tobias Michael Carel Asser, the Netherlands. Cabinet Minister. Member of the Privy Council. Initiator of the International Conferences of Private Law at The Hague; Alfred Hermann Fried Austria. Journalist. Founder of the peace journal *Die Waffen Nieder* (later renamed Die Friedenswarte).

1912 Elihu Root, Initiator of several arbitration agreements.

1913 Henri La Fontaine, Belgium. Member of the Belgian Parliament (Sénateur). President of the Permanent International Peace Bureau, Berne.

1914–1916 The prize money was allocated to the Special Fund of this prize section.

1917 Comité International de la Coix-Rouge (International Committee of the Red Cross) Geneva, founded 1863.

1918 The prize money for 1918 was allocated to the Special Fund of this

Thomas Woodrow Wilson, President of the United States of America.

prize section.

1919 Thomas Woodrow Wilson, President of the United States of America. Founder of the Société des Nations (League of Nations)

1920 Leon Victor Auguste Bourgeois, France. Former Secretary of State. President of the Parliament (Sénat). President of the Conseil de la Société des Nations (Council of the League of Nations).

1921 The prize was divided equally between: Karl Hjalmar Branting, Prime Minister. Swedish Delegate to the Conseil de la Société des Nations (Council of the League of Nations); Christain Louis Lange Secretary General of the Inter-Parliamentary

Union, Brussels.

1922 Fridtjof Nansen, Norway. Scientist. Explorer. Norwegian Delegate to Société des Nations (League of Nations). Originator of the Nansen passports (for refugees).

1924–1923 The prize money for this time was allocated to the Special Fund of this prize section.

1925 The prize was awarded jointly to: Sir Austen Chamberlain, Foreign Minister of Great Britain. Negotiator of the Locarno Treaty; Charles Gates Dawes, Vice-President of the United States of America. Chairman of the Allied Reparation Commission. Originator of the Dawes Plan.

NOBEL PRIZES

1926 The prize was awarded jointly to: Aristide Briand Foreign Minister. Negotiator of the Locarno Treaty and the Briand-Kellogg Pact and Gustave Stesemann Former Lord High Chancellor (Reichs-kanzler). Foreign Minister. Negotiator of the Locarno Treaty.

1927 The prize was divided equally between: Ferdinand Buisson – Former Professor at the Sorbonne University, Paris. Founder and President of the Ligue des Droits de l'Homme (League for Human Rights); Ludwig Quidde Historian. Professor at Berlin University. Member of Germany's constituent assembly 1919. Delegate to numerous peace conferences.

1928 The prize money for 1928 was allocated to the Special Fund of this prize section.

1929 Frank Billings Kellog. Former American Secretary of State. Negotiated the Briand-Kellogg Pact.

1930 Lars Olof Nathan (Jonathan) Söderbloom, Archbishop. Leader of the ecumenical movement.

1931 The prize was divided equally between: Jane Addams, sociologist. International President of the Women's International League for Peace and Freedom; Nicholas Murray Butler President of Columbia University. Promoter of the Briand-Kellogg Pact.

1932 The prize money for 1932 was allocated to the Special Fund of this prize section.

1933 Sir Norman Angell (Ralph Lane) writer. Member of the Commission Exécutive de la Société des Nations (Executive Committee of the League of Nations) and the National Peace Council. Author of the book *The Great Illusion*, among others.

1934 Arthur Henderson Former Foreign Secretary. Chairman of the League of Nations Disarmament Conference 1932-1934.

1935 Carl von Ossietzky Journalist (with *Die Weltbühne,* among others), pacifist.

1936 Carlos Saavedra Lamas, Foreign Minister. President of the Société des Nations (League of Nations), mediator in a conflict between Paraguay and Bolivia in 1935.

1937 Cecil of Chelwoodd, Viscount (Lord Edgar Algernon Robert Gascoyne-Cecil). Writer and former Lord Privy Seal. Founder and President of the International Peace Campaign.

1938 Office International Nansen pour les Réfugiés (Nansen International Office for Refugees) an international relief organization in Geneva started by Fridtjof Nansen in 1921.

1939-1943 The prize money was allocated to the Main Fund (1/3) and to the Special Fund (2/3) of this prize section.

1944 Comité International de la Coix-Rouge (International Committee of the Red Cross) Geneva, founded 1863.

1945 Cordell Hull. Former American Secretary of State. One of the initiators of the United Nations.

1946 The prize was divided equally between: Emily Greene Balch, former Professor of History and Sociology, Honorary International President Women's International League for Peace and Freedom and John Raleigh Mott, Chairman of the first International Missionary Council, and President of the World Alliance of Young Men's Christian Associations.

1947 The prize was awarded jointly to: The Friends Service Council (The Quakers), London. Founded in 1647; The American Friends Service Committee (The Quakers), Washington. The society's first official meeting was held in 1672.

1948 The prize money was allocated to the Main Fund (1/3) and to the Special Fund (2/3) of this prize section.

1949 Lord John Boyd Orr of Brechin, physician, alimentary politician, prominent organizer and director of the General Food and Agricultural Organization. President of the National Peace Council and World Union of Peace Organizations.

1950 Ralph Bunche. Professor Harvard University, Cambridge, MA, Director of the UN Division of Trusteeship, Acting Mediator in Palestine 1948.

1951 Léon Jouhaux, France. President of the trade union C.G.T. Force Ouvrière. President of the International Committee of the European Council, Vice President of the International Confederation of Free Trade Unions, Vice President of the World Federation of Trade Unions, member of the ILO Council, delegate to the UN.

1952 Albert Schweitzer, missionary surgeon. Founder Lambaréné Hospital in République du Gabon.

1953 George Catlett Marshall, General, President American Red Cross, ex-American Secretary of State and of Defense, delegate to the UN, originator of the Marshall Plan.

1954 Office of the High Commissioner for Refugees Geneva, an international relief organization, founded by UN in 1951.

1955-1956 The prize money was allocated to the Main Fund (1/3) and to the Special Fund (2/3) of this prize section.

1957 Lester Bowles Pearson, former Secretary of State for External Affairs of Canada, President 7th Session of the United Nations General Assembly.

1958 Georges Henri Pire, Belgium. Father of the Dominican Order, Leader of the relief organization for refugees, l'Europe du Coeur au Service du Monde.

1959 Philip J. Noel-Baker, Great Britain. Member of Parliament, life long ardent worker for international peace and co-operation .

1960 Albert John Lutuli, President of the South Africa liberation movement, and the African National Congress.

1961 Dag Hjalmar Agne Carl Hammarskjöld, UN Secretary General (awarded posthumously).

NOBEL PRIZES

1962 Linus Carl Pauling, California Institute of Technology, Pasadena, CA. Campaigner especially for an end to nuclear weapons tests.

1963 The prize was divided equally between Comité International de la Coix-Rouge (League of Red Cross Societies) Geneva, founded 1863, and Ligue des Societes de las croix rouge (LRCS) Geneva.

1964 Martin Luther King Jr. Leader of the Southern Christian Leadership Conference, campaigner for civil rights.

1965 United Nations Children's Fund (UNICEF) New York, founded by UN in 1946. An international aid organization.

1966-1967 The prize money was allocated to the Main Fund (1/3) and to the Special Fund (2/3) of this prize section.

1968 Rene Cassin, President of the European Court for Human Rights.

1969 International Labour Organization (ILO) Geneva.

1970 Norman Borlaug. Led researcher at the International Maize and Wheat Improvement Center, Mexico City.

1971 Willy Brandt, Federal Republic of Germany, Chancellor of the Federal Republic of Germany, initiator of West Germany's Ostpolitik, embodying a new attitude towards Eastern Europe and East Germany.

1972 The prize money for 1972 was allocated to the Main Fund.

1973 The prize was awarded jointly to: Henry A. Kissenger, American Secretary of State and Le Duc Tho, Democratic Republic of Viet Nam. (Declined the prize.) for jointly negotiating the Vietnam peace accord in 1973.

1974 The prize was divided equally between: Séan Macbride, President of the International Peace Bureau, Geneva, and the Commission of Namibia, United Nations, New York, and Eisaku Sato, Prime Minister of Japan.

1975 Andrei Dmitrievich Sakharov, Soviet nuclear physicist. Campaigner for human rights.

1976 Betty Williams and Mairead Corrigan and Founders of the Northern Ireland Peace Movement (later renamed Community of Peace People).

1977 Amnesty International London, Great Britain. A world-wide organization for the protection of the rights of prisoners of conscience.

1978 The prize was divided equally between: Mohamed Anwar Al-Sadat President of the Arab Republic of Egypt, and Menachem Begin, Prime Minister of Israel for jointly negotiating peace between Egypt and Israel.

1979 Mother Teresa, India, leader of the Order of the Missionaries of Charity.

1980 Adolfo Perez Esquivel, Argentina, architect, sculptor and human rights leader.

1981 Office of the United Nations High Commissioner for Refugees Geneva, Switzerland.

1982 The prize was awarded jointly to: Alva Myrdal, former cabinet minister, diplomat, delegate to United Nations General Assembly on Disarmament, writer; Alfonso García Robles, diplomat, delegate to the United Nations General Assembly on Disarmament, former Secretary for Foreign Affairs.

1983 Lech Walesa, Poland. Founder of the Polish Solidarity Movement, campaigner for human rights.

1984 Desmond Mpilo Tutu, South Africa, Bishop of Johannesburg, former Secretary General South African Council of Churches (SACC). For his work against apartheid.

1985 International Physicians for the prevention of Nuclear War Boston, MA, USA.

1986 Elie Wiesel, USA, Chairman of 'The President's Commission on the Holocaust.' Author, humanitarian.

1987 Oscar Arias Sanchez, Costa Rica, President of Costa Rica, initiator of peace negotiations in Central America.

1988 The United Nations Peace-Keeping Forces New York, USA.

1989 The 14th Dalai Lama (Tenzin Gyatso), Tibet. Religious and political leader of the Tibetan people.

1990 Mikhail Sergeyevich Gorbachev, President of the USSR, helped to bring the Cold War to an end.

1991 Aung San Suu Kyi, Burma. Opposition leader, human rights advocate.

1992 Rigoberta Menchu-Tum, Guatemala. Campaigner for human rights, especially for indigenous peoples.

1993 The prize was awarded jointly to: Nelson Mandela, leader of the ANC and Frederik Willem de Klerk, President of the Republic of South Africa.

1994 The prize was awarded jointly to: Yasser Arafat, Chairman of the Executive Committee of the PLO, President of the Palestinian National Authority, and Shimon Peres, Foreign Minister of Israel, and Yitzhak Rabin, Prime Minister of Israel for their efforts to create peace in the Middle East.

1995 The prize was awarded jointly to: Joseph Rotblat and to the PUGWASH Conferences on science and world affairs for their efforts to diminish the part played by nuclear arms in international politics and in the longer run to eliminate such arms.

1996 The prize was awarded jointly to: Carlos Felipe Ximenes Belo and Jose Ramos-Horta for their work towards a just and peaceful solution to the conflict in East Timor.

1997 The prize was awarded jointly to: International Campaign to Ban Landmines (ICBL) and Jody Williams for their work for the banning and clearing of anti-personnel mines.

1998 Awarded jointly to: John Hume and David Trimble for efforts to find a peaceful solution to the conflict in Northern Ireland.

PULITZER PRIZES

Drama

1918	*Why Marry?* Jesse Lynch Williams	1959	*J.B.,* Archibald MacLeish
1919	No award given	1960	*Fiorello!,* George Abbott, Jerome Weidman,
1920	*Beyond the Horizon,* Eugene O'Neill		Sheldon Harnick, and Jerry Bock
1921	*Miss Lulu Bett,* Zona Gale	1961	*All the Way Home,* Tad Mosel
1922	*Anna Christie,* Eugene O'Neill	1962	*How to Succeed in Business Without Really Trying,*
1923	*Icebound,* Owen Davis		Abe Burrows and Frank Loesser
1924	*Hell-Bent for Heaven,* Hatcher Hughes	1963	No award given
1925	*They Knew What They Wanted,* Sidney Howard	1964	No award given
1926	*Craig's Wife,* George Kelly	1965	*The Subject Was Roses,* Frank D. Gilroy
1927	*In Abraham's Bosom,* Paul Green	1966	No award given
1928	*Strange Interlude,* Eugene O'Neill	1967	*A Delicate Balance,* Edward Albee
1929	*Street Scene,* Elmer L. Rice	1968	No award given
1930	*The Green Pastures,* Marc Connelly	1969	*The Great White Hope,* Howard Sackler
1931	*Alison's House,* Susan Glaspell	1970	*No Place to Be Somebody,* Charles Gordone
1932	*Of Thee I Sing,* George S. Kaufman,	1971	*The Effect of Gamma Rays on Man-in-the-Moon*
	Morrie Ryskind, and Ira Gershwin		*Marigolds,* Paul Zindel
1933	*Both Your Houses,* Maxwell Anderson	1972	No award given
1934	*Men in White,* Sidney Kingsley	1973	*That Championship Season,* Jason Miller
1935	*The Old Maid,* Zoe Akins	1974	No award given
1936	*Idiot's Delight,* Robert E. Sherwood	1975	*Seascape,* Edward Albee
1937	*You Can't Take It With You,* Moss Hart and	1976	*A Chorus Line,* Michael Bennett, James
	George S. Kaufman		Kirkwood, Nicholas Dante, and Edward Kleban
1938	*Our Town,* Thornton Wilder	1977	*The Shadow Box,* Michael Cristofer
1939	*Abe Lincoln in Illinois,* Robert E. Sherwood	1978	*The Gin Game,* Donald L. Coburn
1940	*The Time of Your Life,* William Saroyan	1979	*Buried Child,* Sam Shepard
	(award declined)	1980	*Talley's Folly,* Lanford Wilson
1941	*There Shall Be No Night,* Robert E. Sherwood	1981	*Crimes of the Heart,* Beth Henley
1942	No award given	1982	*A Soldier's Play,* Charles Fuller
1943	*The Skin of Our Teeth,* Thornton Wilder	1983	*'night, Mother,* Marsha Norman
1944	No award given	1984	*Glengarry Glen Ross,* David Mamet
1945	*Harvey,* Mary Chase	1985	*Sunday in the Park with George,* Stephen
1946	*State of the Union,*		Sondheim and James Lapine
	Russel Crouse and Howard Lindsay	1986	No award given
1947	No award given	1987	*Fences,* August Wilson
1948	*A Streetcar Named Desire,* Tennessee Williams	1988	*Driving Miss Daisy,* Alfred Uhry
1949	*Death of a Salesman,* Arthur Miller	1989	*The Heidi Chronicles,* Wendy Wasserstein
1950	*South Pacific,* Richard Rodgers, Oscar	1990	*The Piano Lesson,* August Wilson
	Hammerstein II, and Joshua Logan	1991	*Lost in Yonkers,* Neil Simon
1951	No award given	1992	*The Kentucky Cycle,* Robert Schenkkan
1952	*The Shrike,* Joseph Kramm	1993	*Angels in America: Millennium Approaches,*
1953	*Picnic,* William Inge		Tony Kushner
1954	*The Teahouse of the August Moon,* John Patrick	1994	*Three Tall Women,* Edward Albee
1955	*Cat on a Hot Tin Roof,* Tennessee Williams	1995	*The Young Man From Atlanta,* Horton Foote
1956	*The Diary of Anne Frank,*	1996	*Rent,* Jonathan Larson
	Frances Goodrich and Albert Hackett	1997	No award given
1957	*Long Day's Journey into Night,* Eugene O'Neill	1998	*How I Learned to Drive* by Paula Vogel
1958	*Look Homeward Angel,* Ketti Frings	1999	*Wit* by Margaret Edson

PULITZER PRIZES

Fiction

1917		1961	*To Kill a Mockingbird*, Harper Lee
1918	*His Family*, Ernest Poole	1962	*The Edge of Sadness*, Edwin O'Connor
1919	*The Magnificent Ambersons*, Booth Tarkington	1963	*The Reivers*, William Faulkner
1920	No award given	1964	No award given
1921	*The Age of Innocence*, Edith Wharton	1965	*The Keepers of the House*, Shirley Ann Grau
1922	*Alice Adams*, Booth Tarkington	1966	*The Collected Stories of Katherine Anne Porter*,
1923	*One of Ours*, Willa Cather		Katherine Anne Porter
1924	*The Able McLaughlins*, Margaret Wilson	1967	*The Fixer*, Bernard Malamud
1925	*So Big*, Edna Ferber	1968	*The Confessions of Nat Turner*, William Styron
1926	*Arrowsmith*, Sinclair Lewis (award declined)	1969	*House Made of Dawn*, N. Scott Momaday
1927	*Early Autumn*, Louis Bromfield	1970	*Collected Stories*, Jean Stafford
1928	*The Bridge of San Luis Rey*, Thornton Wilder	1971	No award given
1929	*Scarlet Sister Mary*, Julia Peterkin	1972	*Angle of Repose*, Wallace Stegner
1930	*Laughing Boy*, Oliver La Farge	1973	*The Optimist's Daughter*, Eudora Welty
1931	*Years of Grace*, Margaret Ayer Barnes	1974	No award given
1932	*The Good Earth*, Pearl S. Buck	1975	*The Killer Angels*, Michael Shaara
1933	*The Store*, T.S. Stribling	1976	*Humboldt's Gift*, Saul Bellow
1934	*Lamb in His Bosom*, Caroline Miller	1977	No award given
1935	*Now in November*, Josephine Winslow Johnson	1978	*Elbow Room*, James Alan McPherson
1936	*Honey in the Horn*, Harold L. Davis	1979	*The Stories of John Cheever*, John Cheever
1937	*Gone with the Wind*, Margaret Mitchell	1980	*The Executioner's Song*, Norman Mailer
1938	*The Late George Apley*, John P. Marquand	1981	*A Confederacy of Dunces*, John Kennedy Toole
1939	*The Yearling*, Marjorie Kinnan Rawlings	1982	*Rabbit is Rich*, John Updike
1940	*The Grapes of Wrath*, John Steinbeck	1983	*The Color Purple*, Alice Walker
1941	No award given	1984	*Ironweed*, William Kennedy
1942	*In This Our Life*, Ellen Glasgow	1985	*Foreign Affairs*, Alison Lurie
1943	*Dragon's Teeth*, Upton Sinclair	1986	*Lonesome Dove*, Larry McMurtry
1944	*Journey in the Dark*, Martin Flavin	1987	*A Summons to Memphis*, Peter Taylor
1945	*A Bell for Adano*, John Hersey	1988	*Beloved*, Toni Morrison
1946	No award given	1989	*Breathing Lessons*, Anne Tyler
1947	*All the King's Men*, Robert Penn Warren	1990	*The Mambo Kings Play Songs of Love*,
1948	*Tales of the South Pacific*, James A. Michener		Oscar Hijuelos
1949	*Guard of Honor*, James Gould Cozzens	1991	*Rabbit at Rest*, John Updike
1950	*The Way West*, A.B. Guthrie, Jr.	1992	*A Thousand Acres*, Jane Smiley
1951	*The Town*, Conrad Richter	1993	*A Good Scent from a Strange Mountain*,
1952	*The Caine Mutiny*, Herman Wouk		Robert Olen Butler
1953	*The Old Man and the Sea*, Ernest Hemingway	1994	*The Shipping News*, E. Annie Proulx
1954	No award given	1995	*The Stone Diaries*, Carol Shields
1955	*A Fable*, William Faulkner	1996	*Independence Day*, Richard Ford
1956	*Andersonville*, MacKinlay Kantor	1997	*Martin Dressler: The Tale of an American Dreamer*,
1957	No award given		Steven Millhauser
1958	*A Death in the Family*, James Agee	1998	*American Pastoral* by Philip Roth
1959	*The Travels of Jamie McPheeters*,		(Houghton Mifflin)
	Robert Lewis Taylor	1999	*The Hours* by Michael Cunningham
1960	*Advise and Consent*, Allen Drury		(Farrar, Straus and Giroux)

OLYMPICS

This information is for the Track and Field events for the Summer Olympics this century.
It is interesting to note that women took part for the first time only in 1928 and that even in 1996
women accounted for only one-third of the overall number of competitors.
Below is a list of some lesser known nation abbreviations.

AHO	Netherlands Antilles	DEN	Denmark	IRL	Ireland	NEP	Nepal	SWE	Sweden
ALG	Algeria	DMA	Dominica	IRN	Iran	NGR	Nigeria	SWZ	Swaziland
ANG	Angola	DOM	Dominican Republic	IRQ	Iraq	NIG	Niger	SYR	Syria
ANT	Antigua	ECU	Ecuador	ISL	Iceland	NOR	Norway	TAN	Tanzania
ARG	Argentina	ESA	El Salvador	ISR	Israel	NZL	New Zealand	TCH	Czechoslovakia
AUS	Australia	ESP	Spain	JAM	Jamaica	OMA	Oman	THA	Thailand
AUT	Austria	EST	Estonia	JOR	Jordan	PAK	Pakistan	TJK	Tajikistan
AZE	Azerbaijan	ETH	Ethiopia	KAZ	Kazakhstan	PAN	Panama	TKM	Turkmenistan
BAH	Bahamas	EUN	Commonwealth of	KEN	Kenya	PAR	Paraguay	TPE	Taipei (formerly
BAR	Barbados		Independent States	KOR	Korea	PER	Peru		Formosa/Taiwan)
BEL	Belgium	FIN	Finland	KSA	Kingdom of Saudi	PHI	Philippines	TRI	Trinidad and Tobago
BER	Bermuda	FRA	France		Arabia	POL	Poland	TUN	Tunisia
BIZ	Belarus	FRG	Germany (West)	KUW	Kuwait	POR	Portugal	TUR	Turkey
BOL	Bolivia	GAM	Gambia	LAT	Latvia	PRK	Democratic People's	UAE	United Arab Emirates
BRN	Bahrain	GBR	Great Britain	LBA	Libya		Republic of Korea	UKR	Ukraine
BRU	Brunei	GDR	Germany (East)	LBR	Liberia	QAT	Qatar	URS	Soviet Union
BUL	Bulgaria	GER	Germany	LCA	Saint Lucia	ROM	Romania	URU	Uruguay
CAN	Canada	GHA	Ghana	LIT	Liechtenstein	RSA	South Africa	UZB	Uzbekistan
CAY	Cayman Islands	GRE	Greece	LTU	Lithuania	RUS	Russian Federation	VAN	Vanuatu
CHA	Chad	GUA	Guatemala	LUX	Luxembourg	RWA	Rwanda	VEN	Venezuela
CHI	Chile	GUI	Guinea	MAD	Madagascar	SAF	South Africa	VIE	Vietnam
CHN	China	GUM	Guam	MAL	Malaysia	SER	Serbia	VIN	St Vincent and the
COL	Colombia	GUY	Guyana	MAR	Morocco	SIN	Singapore		Grenadines
COM	Comoros	HAI	Haiti	MAW	Malawi	SLE	Sierra Leone	VOL	Upper Volta
CPV	Cape Verde	HKG	Hong Kong	MOZ	Mozambique	SLO	Slovenia	YEM	Yemen
CRC	Costa Rica	HUN	Hungary	MRI	Mauritius	SOL	Solomon Islands	YUG	Yugoslavia
CRO	Croatia	INA	Indonesia	MTN	Mauritania	SRI	Sri Lanka	ZAI	Zaire
CUB	Cuba	IND	India	NAM	Namibia	SUD	Sudan	ZAM	Zambia
CYP	Cyprus	IOP	Independent Olympic	NCA	Nicaragua	SUI	Switzerland	ZIM	Zimbabwe
CZE	Czech Republic		Participants	NED	Netherlands	SVK	Slovakia		

Paris 1900

Participants:1,225
Men: 206
Women: 9
Countries 26
Sports: 24
Events: 166

Top Five Medal Winners — By Country

PLACE	COUNTRY	GOLD	SILVER	BRONZE
1	France	29	41	32
2	USA	20	14	9
3	Great Britain	17	8	10
4	Belgium	8	7	5
5	Switzerland	6	2	1

Athletics — Men

EVENT	GOLD		SILVER	BRONZE
100 m	Francis Jarvis (USA)	11.0	Walter Tewksbury (USA)	Stanley Rowley (AUS)
200 m	Walter Tewksbury (USA)	22.2	Norman Pritchard (IND)	Stanley Rowley (AUS)
400 m	Maxwell Long (USA)	49.4	William Holland (USA)	Ernst Schultz (DEN)
800 m	Alfred Tysoe (GBR)	22.2	John Cregan (USA)	David Hall (USA)
1,500 m	Charles Bennet (GBR)	4:06.2	Henri Deloge (FRA)	John Bray (USA)
5,000 m Team Event	Great Britain	26	France	
Marathon	Michel Theato (FRA)	2:59:45	Emile Champion (FRA)	Ernst Fast
110 m Hurdles	Alvin Kraenzlein (USA)	15.4	John McLean (USA)	Fred Moloney (USA)
400 m Hurdles	Walter Tewksbury (USA)	57.6	Henri Tauzin (FRA)	George Orton (CAN)
High Jump	Irving Baxter (USA)	6'2"	Patrick Leahy (GBR/IRL)	Lajos Gonczy (HUN)
Standing High Jump	Ray Ewry (USA)	5'5"	Irving Baxter (USA)	Lewis Sheldon (USA)
Pole Vault	Irving Baxter (USA)	10'9"	Meredith Colkett (USA)	Carl-Albert Andersen(NOR)
Long Jump	Alvin Kraenzlin (USA)	23'6"	Myer Prinstein (USA)	Patrick Leahy (GBR/IRL)
Triple Jump	Myer Prinstein (USA)	47'5	James Connolly (USA)	Lewis Sheldon (USA)
Shot	Richard Sheldon (USA)	46'3"	Josiah McCracken (USA)	Robert Garrett (USA)
Discus	Rudolph Bauer (HUN)	118'2"	Frantisek Janda-Suk (BOH)	Richard Sheld (USA)
Hammer	John Flanagan (USA)	163'1"	Truxton Hare (USA)	Josiah McCracken (USA)

St. Louis 1904

Participants: 687
Men: 681
Women: 6
Countries: 13
Sports: 6
Events:104

Top Five Medal Winners — By Country

PLACE	COUNTRY	GOLD	SILVER	BRONZE
1	USA	80	86	72
2	Germany	5	4	6
3	Cuba	5	3	3
4	Canada	4	1	1
5	Hungary	2	1	1

Athletics — Men

EVENT	GOLD		SILVER	BRONZE
100 m	Archie Hahn (USA)	11.0	Nathaniel Cartmell (USA)	William Hogenson (USA)
200 m	Archie Hahn (USA)	21.6	Nathaniel Cartmell (USA)	William Hogensonon (USA)
400 m	Harry Hillman (USA)	49.2	Frank Waller (USA)	Herman Groman (USA)
800 m	James Lightbody (USA)	1:56.0	Howard Valentine (USA)	Emil Breitkreuz (USA)
1,500 m	James Lightbody (USA)	4:05.4	W. Frank Verner (USA)	Lacey Hearn (USA)
Marathon	Thomas Hicks (USA)	3:28:35	Albert Coray (FRA)	Arthur Newton (USA)
110 m Hurdles	Frederick Schule (USA)	16.0	Thaddeus Shideler (USA)	Lesley Ashburner (USA)
Pole Vault	Charles Dvorak (USA)	11'6"	LeRoy Samse (USA)	Louis Wilkins (USA)
Long Jump	Myer Prinstein (USA)	24'1"	Daniel Frank (USA)	Robert Stangland (USA)
Triple Jump	Myer Prinstein (USA)	47'1"	Frederick Englehardt (USA)	Robert Stangland (USA)
Shot	Ralph Rose (USA)	48'7"	William W. Coe (USA)	Leon Feuerbach (USA)
Discus	Martin Sheridan (USA)	128'10"	Ralph Rose (USA)	Nicolaos Georgantas (GRE)
Hammer	John Flanagan (USA)	168'0"	John DeWitt (USA)	Ralph Rose (USA)

London 1908

Participants: 2,035
Men:1,999
Women: 36
Countries: 22
Sports: 21
Events: 110

Top Five Medal Winners — By Country

PLACE	COUNTRY	GOLD	SILVER	BRONZE
1	Great Britain	56	50	39
2	USA	23	12	12
3	Sweden	7	5	10
4	France	5	5	9
5	Germany	3	5	5

Athletics — Men

EVENT	GOLD		SILVER	BRONZE
100 m	Reginald Walker (SAF)	10.8	James Rector (USA)	Robert Kerr (CAN)
200 m	Robert Kerr (CAN)	22.6	Robert Cloughen (USA)	Nathaniel Cartmell (USA)
400 m	Wyndham Halswelle (GBR)	50.0		
800 m	Melvin Sheppard (USA)	1:52.8	Emilio Lunghi (ITA)	Hanns Braun (GER)
1,500 m	Melvin Sheppard (USA)	4:03.4	Harold Wilson (GBR)	Norman Hallows (GBR)
Marathon	John Joseph Hayes (USA)	2:55.18.4	Charles Hefferon (SAF)	Joseph Forshaw (USA)
110 m Hurdles	Forrest Smithson (USA)	15.0	John Garrels (USA)	Arthur Shaw (USA)
High Jump	Harry Porter (USA)	6'3"	Con Leahy (GBR/IRL)	
			Istvan Somody (HUN)	
			Georges Andre (FRA)	
Pole Vault	Edward Cooke(USA)	12'2"	Ed Archibald(CAN)	
	Alfred Gilbert (USA)	12'2"	Charles Jacobs (USA)	
			Bruno Soderstrom (SWE)	
Long Jump	Francis Irons (USA)	24'6"	Daniel Kelly (USA)	Calvin Bricker (CAN)
Triple Jump	Timothy Ahearne (GBR/IRL)	48'11"	J. Garfield McDonald(CAN)	Edvard Larsen (NOR)
Shot	Ralph Rose (USA)	46'7"	Dennis Horgan (GBR)	John Garrels (USA)
Discus	Martin Sheridan (USA)	134'2"	Merritt Giffin (USA)	Marquis Horr (USA)

Stockholm 1912

Participants: 2,547
Men: 2,490
Women: 57
Countries: 28
Sports: 13
Events: 102

Top Five Medal Winners — By Country				
PLACE	COUNTRY	GOLD	SILVER	BRONZE
1	Sweden	24	24	17
2	USA	23	19	1
3	Great Britain	10	15	16
4	Finland	9	8	9
5	France	7	4	3

Athletics — Men

EVENT	GOLD		SILVER	BRONZE
100 m	Ralph Cook Craig (USA)	10.8	Alvah Meyer (USA)	Donald Lippincott (USA)
200m	Ralph Cook Craig (USA)	21.7	Donald Lippincott (USA)	William Applegarth (GBR)
400 m	Charles Reidpath (USA)	48.2	Hanns Braun (GER)	Edward Lindberg (USA)
800 m	James Meredith (USA)	1:51.9	Melvin Sheppard (USA)	Ira Davenport (USA)
1,500 m	Arnold Jackson (GBR)	3:56.8	Abel Kiviat (USA)	Norman Taber (USA)
5,000 m	Hannes Kolehmainen (FIN)	14:36.6	Jean Bouin (FRA)	George Hutson (GBR)
10,000 m	Hannes Kolehmainen (FIN)	31:20.8	Louis Tewanima (USA)	Albin Stinroos (FIN)
Marathon	Kenneth McArthur (SAF)	2:36:54.8	Christian Gitsham (SAF)	Gaston Strobino (USA)
110 Hurdles	Frederick Kelly (USA)	15.1	James Wendell (USA)	Martin Hawkins (USA)
4x100 m	Great Britain	42.4	Sweden	
4x400 m	USA	3:16.6	France	Great Britain
High Jump	Alma Richards (USA)	6'4"	Hans Liesche (GER)	George Horine (USA)
Pole Vault	Harry Babcock (USA)	12'11"	Marcus Wright (USA)	Frank Nelson (USA)
Long Jump	Albert Gutterson (USA)	24'11"	Calvin Bricker (CAN)	Georg Aberg (SWE)
Triple Jump	Gustaf Lindblom (SWE)	48'5"	Georg Aberg (SWE)	Erik Almlof (SWE)
Shot	Patrick McDonald (USA)	50'4"	Ralph Rose (USA)	Lawrence Whitney (USA)
Discus	Armas Taipale (FIN)	148'3"	Richard Byrd (USA)	James Duncan (USA)
Hammer	Matthe McGrath (USA)	179'7"	Duncan Gillis (CAN)	Clarence Childs (USA)
Javelin	Erik Lemming (SWE)	198'11"	Juho Saaristo (FIN)	Mor Koczan (HUN)
Decathlon	Hugo Wieslander (SWE)	7,724.495	Charles Lomberg (SWE)	Gosta Holmer (SWE)

Antwerp 1920

Participants: 2,668
Men: 2,591
Women: 77
Countries: 29
Sports: 21
Events: 154

Top Five Medal Winners — By Country				
PLACE	COUNTRY	GOLD	SILVER	BRONZE
1	USA	41	26	27
2	Sweden	17	19	26
3	Great Britain	15	15	13
4	Belgium	14	11	10
5	Finland	14	10	8

Athletics — Men

EVENT	GOLD		SILVER	BRONZE
100 m	Charles Paddock (USA)	10.8	Morris Kirksey (USA)	Harry Edward (GBR)
200 m	Allen Woodring (USA)	22.0	Charles Paddock (USA)	Harry Edward (GBR)
400 m	Bevil Rudd (SAF)	49.6	Guy Butler (GBR)	Nils Engdahl (SWE)
800 m	Albert Hill (GBR)	1:53.4	Earl Eby (USA)	Bevil Rudd (SAF)
1,500 m	Albert Hill (GBR)	4:01.8	Philip Noel-Baker (GBR)	Lawrence Shields (USA)
5,000 m	Joseph Guillemot (FRA)	14:55.6	Paavo Nurmi (FIN)	Erik Backman (SWE)
10,000 m	Paavo Nurmi (FIN)	31:45.8	Joseph Guillemot (FRA)	James Wilson(GBR) 31:50.8
Marathon	Hannes Kolehmainen (FIN)	2:32:35.8	Juri Lossmun (EST)	Valerio Arri (ITA)
110 m Hurdles	Earl Thomson (CAN)	14.8	Harold Barron (USA)	Frederick Murray(USA)
400 m Hurdles	Frank Loomis (USA)	54.0	John Norton (USA)	August Desch (USA)

Athletics — Men continued

EVENT	GOLD		SILVER	BRONZE
4x100 m	USA	42.2	France	Sweden
4x400 m	Great Britain	3:22.2	South Africa	France
High Jump	Richmond Landon (USA)	6'4"	Harold Muller (USA)	Bo Ekelund (SWE)
Pole Vault	Frank Foss (USA)	13'5"	Henry Petersen (DAN)	Edwin Myers (USA)
Long Jump	William Pettersson (SWE)	23'5"	Carl Johnson (USA)	ErikAbrahamsson (SWE)
Triple Jump	Vilho Tuulos (FIN)	47'7"	Folke Jansson (SWE)	Erik Almlof (SWE)
Shot	Ville Porhola (FIN)	48'7"	Elmer Niklander (FIN)	Harry Liversedge (USA)
Discus	Elmer Niklander (FIN)	146'7"	Armus Taipale (FIN)	Augustus Pope (USA)
Hammer	Patrick Ryan (USA)	173'5"	Carl Johan Lind (SWE)	Basil Bennet (USA)
Javelin	Jonni Myyra (FIN)	215'9"	Urho Peltonen (FIN)	Paavo Jaale-Johansson (FIN)
Decathlon	Helge Lovland (NOR)	6,804.355	Brutus Hamilton (USA)	Bertil Ohlson (SWE)

Paris 1924

Participants: 3,092
Men: 2,956
Women: 136
Countries: 44
Sports: 17
Events: 126

Top Five Medal Winners — By Country

PLACE	COUNTRY	GOLD	SILVER	BRONZE
1	USA	45	27	27
2	Finland	14	13	10
3	France	13	15	10
4	Great Britain	9	13	12
5	Italy	8	3	5

Athletics — Men

EVENT	GOLD		SILVER	BRONZE
100 m	Harold Abrahams (GBR)	10.6	Jackson Scholz (USA)	Arthur Porritt (NZL)
200 m	Jackson Scholz (USA)	21.6	Charles Paddock (USA)	Eric Liddell (GBR)
400 m	Eric Liddell (GBR)	47.6	Horatio Fitch (USA)	Guy Buder (GBR)
800 m	Douglas Lowe (GBR)	1:52.4	Paul Martin (SUI)	Schuyler Enck (USA)
1,500 m	Paavo Nurmi (FIN)	3:53.6	Willy Scharer (SUI)	Henry Stallard (GBR)
5,000 m	Paavo Nurmi (FIN)	14:31.2	Ville Ritola (FIN)	Edvin Wide (SWE)
10,000 m	Ville Ritola (FIN)	30:23.2	Edvin Wide (SWE)	Eero Berg (FIN)
Marathon	Albin Stenroos (FIN)	2:41:22.6	Romeo Bertini (ITA)	Clarence DeMar (USA)
110 m Hurdles	Daniel Kinsey (USA)	15.0	Sidney Atkinson (SAF)	Sten Pettersson (SWE)
400 m Hurdles	F. Morgan Taylor (USA)	52.6	Erik Vilen (FIN)	Ivan Riley (USA)
4x100 m Relay	USA	41.0	Great Britain	Netherlands
4x400 m Relay	USA	3:16.0	Sweden	Great Britain
High Jump	Harold Osborn (USA)	6'6"	Leroy Brown (USA)	Pierre Lewden (FRA)
Pole Vault	Lee Barnes (USA)	12'11"	Glen Graham(USA)	James Brooker(USA)
Long Jump	William DeHart Hubbard (USA)	24'5"	Edward Gourdin (USA)	Sverre Hansen (NOR)
Triple Jump	Anthony Winter (AUS)	50'11"	Luis Bruneto (ARG)	Vilho Tuulos (FIN)
Shot	Clarence Houser (USA)	49'2"	Glenn Hartranft (USA)	Ralph Hills (USA)
Discus	Clarence Houser (USA)	151'5"	Vilho Niittymaa (FIN)	Thomas Lieb (USA)'
Hammer	Frederick Tootell (USA)	174'1"	Matthew McGrath (USA)	Malcolm Nokes (GBR)
Javelin	Jonni Myyra(FIN)	206'6"	Gunnar Lindstrom (SWE)	Eugene Oberst (USA)
Decathlon	Harold Osborn (USA)	7710.775	Emerson Norton (USA)	Alexander Klumberg (EST)

Amsterdam 1928

Participants: 3,014
Men: 2,724
Women: 290
Countries: 46
Sports: 14
Events: 109

Top Five Medal Winners — By Country

PLACE	COUNTRY	GOLD	SILVER	BRONZE
1	USA	22	18	16
2	Germany	10	7	14
3	Finland	8	8	9
4	Sweden	7	6	12
5	Italy	7	5	7

Athletics — Men

EVENT	GOLD		SILVER	BRONZE
100 m	Percy Williams (CAN)	10.8	Jack London(GBR)	Georg Lammers (GER)
200 m	Percy Williams (CAN)	21.8	Walter Placeeley (GBR)	Helmut Kornig (GER)
400 m	Raymond Barbun (USA)	47.8	James Ball (CAN)	Joachim Buchner (GER)
800 m	Douglas Lowe (GBR)	1:51.8	Erik Bylehn (SWE)	Hermann Engelhard (GER)
1,500 m	Harry Larva (FIN)	3:53.2	Jules Ladoumegue (FRA)	Eino Purje (FIN)
5,000 m	Ville Ritola (FIN)	14:38.0	Paavo Nurmi (FIN)	Edvin Wide (SWE)
10,000 m	Paavo Nurmi (FIN)	30:18.8	Ville Ritola (FIN)	Edvin Wide (SWE)
Marathon	Mohammed El Quafi (FRA)	2:32:57	Miguel Plaza (CHI)	Martti Marttelin (FIN)
110 m Hurdles	Sidney Atkinson (SAF)	14.8	Stephen Anderson (USA)	John Collier (USA)
400 m Hurdles	David Burghley (GBR)	53.4	Frank Cuhel (USA)	F. Morgan Taylor (USA)
4x100 m	USA	41.0	Germany	Great Britain
4x400 m	USA	3:14.2	Germany	Canada
High Jump	Robert King (USA)	6'4"	Benjamin Hedges (USA)	Claude Menard (FRA)
Pole Vault	Sabin William Carr (USA)	13'9"	William Droegemueller (USA)	Charles McGinnis(USA)
Long Jump	Edward Hamm (USA)	25'4"	Silvio Cator (HAI)	Alfred Bates (USA)
Triple Jump	Mikio Oda (JPN)	49'10"	Levi Casey (USA)	Vilho Tuulos (FIN)
Shot	John Kuck (USA)	52'0"	Herman Brix (USA)	Emil Hirschfeld (GER)
Discus	Clarence Houser (USA)	155'2"	Antero Kivi (FIN)	James Corson (USA)
Hammer	Patrick O'Callaghan (IRL)	168'7"	Ossian Skiold (SWE)	Edmund Black (USA)
Javelin	Erik Lundkvist (SWE)	218'6"	Bela Szepes (HUN)	Olav Sunde (NOR)
Decathlon	Paavo Yrjola (FIN)	8,053	Akilles Jarvinen (FIN)	John Kenneth Doherty (USA)

Athletics — Women

EVENT	GOLD		SILVER	BRONZE
100 m	Elizabeth Robinson (USA)	12.2	Fanny Rosenfeld (CAN)	Ethel Smith (CAN)
800 m	Lina Radke-Batschauer (GER)	2:16.8	Kinue Hitomi (JPN)	Inga Gentzel (SWE)
4x100 m	Canada	48.4	USA	Germany
High Jump	Ethel Catherwood (CAN)	5'2"	Carolina Gisolf (HOL)	Mildred Wiley (USA)
Discus	Halina Konopacka(POL)	129'11"	Lillian Copeland (USA)	Ruth Svedberg(SWE)

Los Angeles 1932

Participants: 1,408
Men: 1,281
Women: 127
Countries: 37
Sports: 14
Events: 117

Top Five Medal Winners — By Country

PLACE	COUNTRY	GOLD	SILVER	BRONZE
1	USA	41	32	30
2	Italy	12	12	12
3	France	10	5	4
4	Sweden	9	5	9
5	Japan	7	7	4

Athletics — Men

EVENT	GOLD		SILVER	BRONZE
100 m	Eddie Tolan (USA)	10.38	Ralph Metcalfe (USA)	Arthur Jonath (GER)
200 m	Eddie Tolan (USA)	21.2	George Simpson (USA)	Ralph Metcalfe (USA)
400 m	William Carr (USA)	46.2	Benjanin Eastman (USA)	Alexander Wilson (CAN)
800 m	Thomas Hampson (GBR)	1:49.7	Alexander Wilson (CAN)	Philip Edwards (CAN)
1,500 m	Luigi Beccali (ITA)	3:51.2	John Cornes (GBR)	Philip Edwards (CAN)
5,000 m	Lauri Lehtinen (FIN)	14:30.0	Ralph Hill (USA)	Lauri Virtanen (FIN)
10,000	Janusz Kusocinski (POL)	30:11.4	Volmari Iso-Hollo (FIN)	Lauri Virtanen (FIN)
Marathon	Juan Carlos Zabala (ARG)	2:31:36.0	Samuel Ferris (GBR)	Armas Toivonen (FIN)
110 m Hurdles	George Saling (USA)	14.6	Percy Beard (USA)	
400 m Hurdles	Robert Tisdall (IRL)	51.7	Glenn Hardin (USA)	Morgan Taylor (USA)
4x100 m	USA	40.0	Germany	Italy
4x400 m	USA	3:08.2	Great Britain	Canada
High Jump	Duncan McNaughton (CAN)	6'5"	Robert Van Osdel (USA)	Simeon Toribio (PHI)
Pole Vault	William Miller (USA)	14'1"	Shuhei Nishida (JPN)	George Jefferson (USA)
Long Jump	Edward Gordon (USA)	25'0"	Charles L. Redd (USA)	Chuhei Nambu (JPN)
Triple Jump	Chuhei Nambu (JPN)	51'7"	Erik Svensson (SWE)	Kenkichi Oshima (JPN)
Shot	Leo Sextol (USA)	52'5"	Harlow Rothert (USA)	Frantisek Douda (TCH)
Discus	John Anderson (USA)	162'4.5"	Henri J. Laborde (USA)	Paul Winter (FRA)
Hammer	Patrick O'Callaghan (IRL)	176'11"	Ville Porhola (FIN)	Peter Zaremba (USA)
Javelin	Matti Jarvinen (FIN)	238'6"	Matti Sippala (FIN)	Eino Penttila (FIN)
Decathlon	James Bausch (USA)		Akilles Jarvinen (FIN)	Wolrad Eberle (GER)

Athletics — Women

EVENT	GOLD		SILVER	BRONZE
100 m	Stanislawa Walasiewicz (POL)	11.9	Hilda Strike (CAN)	Wilhelmina Bremen (USA)
80 m Hurdles	Mildred Didrikson (USA)	11.7	Evelyne Hall (USA)	Marjorie Clark (SAF)
4x100 m	USA	47.0	Canada	Great Britain
High Jump	Jean Shiley (USA)	5'5"	Mildred Didrikson (USA)	Eva Dawes (CAN)
Discus	Lillian Copeland (USA)	133'1"	Ruth Osburn (USA)	Jadwiga Wajsowila (POL)
Javelin	Mildred Didrikson (USA)	143'4"	Ellen Braumuller (GER)	Tilly Fleischer (GER)

OLYMPICS

Berlin 1936

Participants: 4,066
Men: 3,738
Women: 328
Countries: 49
Sports: 19
Events: 129

Top Five Medal Winners — By Country

PLACE	COUNTRY	GOLD	SILVER	BRONZE
1	USA	38	27	19
2	Sweden	16	11	17
3	France	10	6	13
4	Hungary	10	5	12
5	Italy	8	12	9

Athletics — Men

EVENT	GOLD		SILVER	BRONZE
100 m	Jesse Owens (USA)	10.3	Ralph Metcalfe (USA)	Martinus Osendarp (HOL)
200 m	Jesse Owens (USA)	20.7	Mathew Robinson (USA)	Martinus Osendarp (HOL)
400 m	Archie Williams (USA)	46.5	Godfrey Brown (GBR)	James Luvalle (USA)
800 m	John Woodruff (USA)	1:52.9	Mario Lanzi (ITA)	Philip Edwards (CAN)
1,500 m	John Lovelock (NZL)	3:47.8	Glenn Cunningham (USA)	Luigi Beccali (ITA)
5,000 m	Gunnar Hoeckert (FIN)	14:22.2	Lauri Lehtinen (FIN)	Henry Jonsson (SWE)
10,000 m	Ilmari Salminen (FIN)	30:15.4	Arvo Askola (FIN)	Volmari Iso-Hollo (FIN)
Marathon	Kitei Son (JPN)	2:29:19.2	Ernest Harper (GBR)	Shoryu Nan (JPN)
110 m Hurdles	Forrest Towns (USA)	14.2	Donald Finlay (GBR)	Frederick Pollard (USA)
400 m Hurdles	Glenn Hardin (USA)	52.4	John Loaring (CAN)	Miguel White (PHI)
4x100 m	USA	39.8	Italy	Germany
4x400m	Great Britain	3:09.0	USA	Germany
High Jump	Cornelius Johnson (USA)	6'7.75"	David Albritton (USA)	Delos Thurber (USA)
Pole Vault	Earle Meadows (USA)	14'3"	Shuhei Nishida (JPN)	Sueo Oe (JPN)
Long Jump	Jesse Owens (USA)	26'5"	Luz Long (GER)	Naoto Tajima (JPN)
Triple Jump	Naoto Tajima (JPN)	52'10.5"	Masao Harada (JPN)	John P Metcalfe (AUS)
Shot	Hans Woellke (GER)	53'1.25"	Sulo Barlund (FIN)	Gerhard Stock (GER)
Discus	Kenneth Carpenter (USA)	165'7"	Gordon Dunn (USA)	Giorgio Oberweger (ITA)
Hammer	Karl Hein (GER)	185'4"	Erwin Blask (GER)	Fred Warngard (SWE)
Javelin	Gerhard Stock (GER)	235'8"	Yrjo Nikkanen (FIN)	Kalervo Toivonen (FIN)
Decathlon	Glenn Morris (USA)	7,900	Robert Clark (USA)	Jack Parker (USA)

Athletics — Women

EVENT	GOLD		SILVER	BRONZE
100 m	Helen Stephens (USA)	11.5	S. Walasiewicz (POL)	Kathe Kraub (GER)
80 m Hurdles	Trebisonda Valla (ITA)	11.7	Ann Steuer (GER)	Elizabeth Taylor (CAN)
4x100 m	USA	46.9	Great Britain	Canada
High Jump	Ibolya Csak (HUN)	5'3"	Dorothy Odam (GBR)	Elfriede Kaun (GER)
Discus	Gisela Mauermayer (GER)	156'3"	Jadwiga Wajswna (POL)	Paula Mollenhauer (GER)
Javelin	Tilly Fleischer (GER)	148'2.5"	Luise Kruger (GER)	Maria Kwasniewska (POL)

OLYMPICS

London 1948

Participants: 4,099
Men: 3,714
Women: 385
Countries: 59
Sports: 17
Events: 136

\multicolumn{5}{c}{Top Five Medal Winners — By Country}				
PLACE	COUNTRY	GOLD	SILVER	BRONZE
1	USA	38	27	19
2	Sweden	16	11	17
3	France	10	6	13
4	Hungary	10	5	12
5	Italy	8	12	9

Athletics — Men

EVENT	GOLD		SILVER	BRONZE
100 m	Harrison Dillard (USA)	10.3	Norwood Ewell (USA)	Lloyd LaBeach (PAN)
200 m	Melvin Patton (USA)	21.1	Norwood Ewell (USA)	Lloyd LaBeach (PAN)
400 m	Arthur Wint (JAM)	46.2	Herbert McKenley (JAM)	Malvin Whitfield (USA)
800 m	Malvin Whitfield (USA)	1:49.2	Arthur Wint (JAM)	Marcel Hansenne (FRA)
1,500 m	Henry Eriksson (SWE)	3:49.8	Lennart Strand (SWE)	Willem Slijkhuis (HOL)
5,000 m	Gaston Reiff (BEL)	14:17.6	Emil Zatopek (TCH)	Willem Slijkhuis (HOL)
10,000 m	Emil Zatopek (TCH)	29:59.6	Alain Mimoun (FRA)	Bertil Albertsson (SWE)
Marathon	Delfo Cabrera (ARG)	2:34:51.6	Thomas Richards (GBR)	Etienne Gailly (BEL)
110 m Hurdles	William Porter (USA)	13.9	Clyde Scott (USA)	Craig Dixon (USA)
400 m Hurdles	Leroy Cochran (USA)	51.1	Duncan White (CEY)	Rune Larsson (SWE)
4x100 m	USA	40.6	Great Britain	Italy
4x400 m	USA	3:10.4	France	Sweden
High Jump	John Winter (AUS)	6'6"	Bjorn Paulson (NOR)	George Stanich (USA)
Pole Vault	Guinn Smith (USA)	14'1"	Erkki Kataja (FIN)	Robert Richards (USA)
Long Jump	Willie Steele (USA)	25'7.75"	Thomas Bruce (AUS)	Herbert Douglas (USA)
Triple Jump	Arne Ahman (SWE)	50'6.25"	George Avery (AUS)	Ruhi Sarialp (TUR)
Shot	Wilbur Thomson (USA)	56'2"	Francis Delaney (USA)	James Fuchs (USA)
Discus	Adolfo Consolini (IRA)	1731.5"	Giuseppe Tosi (ITA)	Fortune Gordien (USA)
Hammer	Imre Nemeth (HUN)	183'11"	Ivan Gubijan (YUG)	Robert Bennett (USA)
Javelin	Tapio Rautavaara (FIN)	228'10.5"	Steve Seymour (USA)	Jozsef Varszegi (HUN)
Decathlon	Robert Mathias (USA)	7,139	Ignace Heinrich (FRA)	Floyd Simmons (USA)

Athletics — Women

EVENT	GOLD		SILVER	BRONZE
100 m	Fanny Blankers-Koen (HOL)	11.9	Dorothy Manley (GBR)	Shirley Strickland (AUS)
200 m	Fanny Blankers-Koen (HOL)	24.4	Audrey Williamson (GBR)	Audrey Patterson (USA)
80 m Hurdles	Fanny Blankers-Koen (HOL)	11.2	Maureen Gardner (GBR)	Shirley Strickland (AUS)
4x100 m	Netherlands	47.5	Australia	Canada
High Jump	Alice Coachman (USA)	5'6"	Dorothy Tyler-Odam (GBR)	Micheline Ostermeyer (FRA)
Long Jump	Olga Gyarmati (HUN)	18'8"	Noemi Simonetto De Portela (ARG)	Ann-Britt Leyman (SWE)
Shot	Micheline Ostermeyer (FRA)	45'1.25"	Amelia Piccinini (ITA)	Ine Schaffer (AUT)
Discus	Micheline Ostermeyer (FRA)	137'6"	Edera Gentile-Cordiale (ITA)	Jacqueline Mazeas (FRA)
Javelin	Herma Bauma (AUT)	149'6"	Kaisa Parviainen (FIN)	Lily Carlstedt (DEN)

Helsinki 1952

Participants: 4,925
Men: 4,407
Women: 518
Countries: 69
Sports: 17
Events: 149

Top Five Medal Winners — By Country

PLACE	COUNTRY	GOLD	SILVER	BRONZE
1	USA	40	19	17
2	USSR	22	30	19
3	Hungary	16	10	16
4	Sweden	2	12	10
5	Italy	8	9	4

Athletics — Men

EVENT	GOLD		SILVER	BRONZE
100 m	Lindy Remigino (USA)	10.4	Herbert McKenley (JAM)	Emmanuel McDonald-Bailey (GBR)
200 m	Andrew Stanfield (USA)	20.7	Thane Baker (USA)	James Gathers (USA)
400 m	George Rhoden (JAM)	45.9	Herbert McKenley (JAM)	Ollie Matson (USA)
800 m	Malvin Whitfidd (USA)	1:49.2	Arthur Wint (JAM)	Heinz Ulzheimer (GER)
1,500 m	Josy Barthel (LUX)	3:45.1	Bob McMillen (USA)	Werner Lueg (GER)
5,000 m	Emil Zatopek (TCH)	14:06 6	Alain Mimoun (FRA)	Herbert Schade (GER)
10,000 m	Emil Zatopek (TCH)	29:17.0	Alain Mimoun (FRA)	Alexander Anufriyev (URS)
Marathon	Emil Zatopek (TCH)	2:23.03.2	Reinaldo Gorno (ARG)	Gustaf Jansson (SWE)
110 m Hurdles	Harrison Dillard (USA)	13.7	Jack Davis (USA)	Arthur Barnard (USA)
400 m Hurdles	Charles Moore (USA)	50.8	Yuriy Lituyev (URS)	John Holland (NZL)
4x100 ml	USA	40.1	USSR	Hungary
4x400 m	Jamaica	3:03.9	USA	Germany
High Jump	Walter Davis (USA)	6'8.25"	Ken Wiesner (USA)	J. Telles da Conceiceaiao (BRA)
Pole Vault	Bob Richards (USA)	14'11"	Donald Laz (USA)	Ragnar Lundberg (SWE)
Long Jump	Jerome Biffle (USA)	24'10"	Meredith Gourdine (USA)	Odon Foldessy (HUN)
Triple Jump	Adhemar Ferreira da Silva (BRA)	53'2.5"	Leonid Shcherbakov (URS)	Arnoldo Devonish (VEN)
Shot	Parry O'Brien (USA)	57'1.25"	Darrow Hooper (USA)	Jim Fuchs (USA)
Discus	Sim Iness (USA)	180'6.5"	Adolfo Consolini (ITA)	James Dillion (USA)
Hammer	Jozsef Csermak (HUN)	197'11.5"	Karl Storch (GER)	Imre Nemeth (HUN)
Javelin	Cyrus Young (USA)	242'0.5"	William Miller (USA)	Toivo Hyytiainen (FIN)
Decathlon	Robert Mathias (USA)	7,887	Milton Campbell (USA)	Floyd Simmons (USA)

Athletics — Women

EVENT	GOLD		SILVER	BRONZE
100 m	Marjorie Jackson (AUS)	11.5	Daphne Hasenjager-Robb (SAF)	Shirley de la Hunty-Strickland (AUS)
200 m	Marjorie Jackson (AUS)	23.7	Bertha Brouwer (HOL)	Nadyezda Khnykhina (URS)
80 m Hurdles	Shirley de la Hunty-Strickland	10.9	Maria Golubnichaya (URS)	Maria Sander (GER)
4x100 m Relay	USA	45.9	Germany	Great Britain
High Jump	Esther Brand (SAF)	5'5.5"	Sheila Lerwill (GBR)	Aleksandra Chudina (URS)
Long Jump	Yvette Williams (NZL)	20'5.5"	Aleksandra Chudina (URS)	Shirley Cawley (GBR)
Shot	Galina Zybina (URS)	50'1.5"	Marianne Werner (GER)	Klavdiya Tochenova (URS)
Discus	Nina Romashrova (URS)	168'8"	Elizaveta Bagriantseva (URS)	Nina Dumbadze (URS)
Javelin	Dana Zatopkova (TCH)	165'7"	Aleksandra Chudina (URS)	Yelena Gorchakova (URS)

Melbourne 1956

Participants: 3,184
Men: 2,813
Women: 371
Countries 67
Sports: 17
Events: 151

Top Five Medal Winners — By Country

PLACE	COUNTRY	GOLD	SILVER	BRONZE
1	USSR	37	29	32
2	USA	32	25	17
3	Australia	13	8	14
4	Hungary	9	10	7
5	Italy	8	8	9

Athletics — Men

EVENT	GOLD		SILVER	BRONZE
100 m	Robert Morrow (USA)	10.5	Thane Baker (USA)	Hector Hogan (AUS)
200 m	Robert Morrow (USA)	20.6	Andrew Stanfield (USA)	Thane Baker (USA)
400 m	Charles Jenkins (USA)	46.7	Karl-Friedrich Haas (GER)	Voitto Hellsten (FIN)
800 m	Tom Courtney (USA)	1:47.7	Derek Johnson (GBR)	Andun Boysen (NOR)
1,500 m	Ronaid Delany (IRL)	3:41.2	Klaus Richtzenhain (GER)	John Landy (AUS)
5,000 m	Vladimir Kuts (URS)	13:39.6	Gordon Pirie (GBR)	Derek Ibbotson (GBR)
10,000m	Vladimir Kuts (URS)	28:45.6	Jozsef Kovacs (HUN)	Allan Lawrence (AUS)
Marathon	Alain Mimoun (FRA)	2:25:00.0	Franjo Mihalic (YUG)	Veikko Karvonen (FIN)
110 m Hurdles	Lee Calhoun (USA)	13.5	Jack Davis (USA)	Joel Shankle (USA)
400 m Hurdles	Glenn Davis (USA)	50.1	Eddie Southern (USA)	Joshua Culbreath (USA)
4x100 m	USA	39 5	USSR	Germany
4x400 m	USA	3:04.8	Australia	Great Britain
High Jump	Charles Dumas (USA)	6'11"	Charles Porter (AUS)	Igor Kashkarov (URS)
Pole Vault	Bob Richards (USA)	14'11.5"	Bob Gutowski (USA)	Georgios Roubanis (GRE)
Long Jump	Greg Bell (USA)	25'8.25"	John Bennett (USA)	Jorma Valkama (FIN)
Triple Jump	Adhemar Ferreira da Silva (BRA)	53'7"	Vilhjamur Einarsson (ISL)	Vitold Kreyer (URS)
Shot	Parry O'Brien (USA)	60'11"	Bill Nieder (USA)	Jiri Skobla (TCH)
Discus	Al Oerter (USA)	184'10.5"	Fortune Gordien (USA)	Desmond Koch (USA)
Hammer	Harold Connolly (USA)	207'3"	Michail Krivonosov (URS)	Anatoliy Samotsvetov (URS)
Javelin	Egil Danielsen (NOR)	281'2"	Janusz Sidlo (POL)	Viktor Tsibulenko (URS)
Decathlon	Milton Campbell (USA)	7,937	Rafer Johnson (USA)	Vassily Kusnetsov (URS)

Athletics — Women

EVENT	GOLD		SILVER	BRONZE
100 m	Betry Cuthbert (AUS)	11.5	Christa Stubnick (GER)	Marlene Matthews (AUS)
200m	Betty Cuthbert (AUS)	23.4	Christa Stubnick (GER)	Marlene Matthews (AUS)
80 m Hurdle	S de la Hunty-Strickland (AUS)	10.7	Gisela Kohler (GER)	Norma Thrower (AUS)
4x100 m	Australia	44.5	Great Britain	USA
High Jump	Mildred McDaniel (USA)	5'9"	Maria Pisaryeva (URS)	Thelma Hopkilns (GBR)
Long Jump	Elzbieta Krzesinska (POL)	20'10"	Willye White (USA)	Nadyezda Dhavalishev (URS)
Shot	Tamara Tyshkevich (URS)	54'5"	Gailna Zybina (URS)	Marianne Werner (GER)
Discus	Olga Fikotova (TCH)	176'1.5"	Irina Beglyakova (URS)	Nina Ponomaryeva (URS)
Javelin	Inese Jaunzeme(URS)	176'8"	Marlene Ahrens (CHI)	Nadyezda Kollyayeva (URS)

Rome 1960

Participants: 5,346
Men: 4,736
Women: 610
Countries: 83
Sports 17
Events:150

PLACE	COUNTRY	GOLD	SILVER	BRONZE
1	USSR	42	28	29
2	USA	34	21	16
3	Italy	13	10	13
4	Germany	12	19	11
5	Australia	8	8	6

Top Five Medal Winners — By Country

Athletics — Men

EVENT	GOLD		SILVER	BRONZE
100 m	Armin Hary (GER)	10.2	David Sime (USA)	Peter Radford (GBR)
200 m	Livio Berutti (ITA)	20 5	Lester Carney (USA)	Abdoulaye Seye (FRA)
400 m	Otis Davis (USA	44.9	Carl Kauffmann (GER)	Malcolm Spence (SAF)
800 m	Peter Snell (NZL)	146.3	Roger Moens (BEL)	George Kerr (ANT)
1,500 m	Herbert Elliott (AUS)	3:35 6	Michel Jazy (FRA)	Istvan Rozsavolgyi (HUN)
5,000 m	Murray Halberg (NZL)	13:43.4	Hans Grodotzki (GER)	Kasimierz Zimny (POL)
10,000 m	Pjotr Bolotnikov (URS)	28:32.2	Hans Grodotzki (GER)	David Power (AUS)
Marathon	Abebe Bikula (ETH)	2:15:16.2	Rhadi Ben Abdesselam (MAR)	Barry Magee (NZL)
110 m Hurdles	Lee Calhoun (USA)	13. 8	Willie May (USA)	Hayes Jones (USA)
400 m Hurdles	Glenn Davis (USA)	49.3	Clifton Cushman (USA)	Richard Howard (USA)
4x100 m	Germany	39.5	USSR	Great Britain
4X400 m	USA	3:02.2	Germany	Antilles
High Jump	Robert Shavlakadze(URS)	7'1"	Valeriy Brumel (URS)	John Thomas (USA)
Pole Vault	Donald Bragg (USA)	15'5"	Ron Morns (USA)	Eeles Landstrom (FIN)
Long Jump	Ralph Boston (USA)	26'7"	Irvin Roberson (USA)	Igor Ter-Ovanesian (URS)
Triple Jump	Jozef Schmidt (POL)	55'1"	Vladimir Goryayev (URS)	Vitold Kreyer (URS)
Shot	Bill Nieder (USA)	64'6"	Parry O'Brien (USA)	Dallas Long (USA)
Discus	Al Oerter (USA)	194'1"	Richard Babka (USA)	Dick Cochran (USA)
Hammer	Vasiliy Rudenkov (URS)	220'1"	Gyula Zsivotzky (HUN)	Tadeusz Rut (POL)
Javelin	Viktor Tsibulenko (URS)	277'8"	Walter Kruger (GER)	Gergely Kulscsar (HUN)
Decathlon	Rafer Johnson (USA)	8,392	Chuan-Kwang Yang (TPE)	Vassily Kusnetsov (URS)

Athletics — Women

EVENT	GOLD		SILVER	BRONZE
100 m	Wilma Rudolph (USA)	11.0	Dorothy Hyman (GBR)	Giuseppina Leone (ITA)
200 m	Wilma Rudolph (USA)	24.0	Juta Heine (GER)	Dorothy Hyman (GBR)
800 m	Ludmilla Schevtsova (URS)	2:04.3	Brenda Jones (AUS)	Ursula Donath (GER)
80 m Hurdles	Irina Press (URS)	10.8	Carol Quinton (GBR)	Gisela Birkemeyer-Kohler (GER)
4x100 m	USA	44.5	Germany	Poland
High Jump	Yolanda Balas (ROM)	6'0"	Jaroslawa Jozwiakowska (POL)	
			Dorothy Shirley (GBR)	
Long Jump	Vera Krepkina (URS)	20'10"	Elzbieta Krzesinska (POL)	Hildrun Claus (GER)
Shot	Tamara Press (URS)	56'9"	Johanna Luttge (GER)	Earlene Brown (USA)
Discus	Nina Ponomaryeva (URS)	180'9"	Tamara Press (URS)	Lia Manoliu (ROM)
Javelin	Elvira Ozolina (URS)	183'7"	Dana Zatopkova (TCH)	Birute Kalediena (URS)

OLYMPICS

Tokyo 1964

Participants: 5,140
Men: 4,457
Women: 683
Countries: 93
Sports: 19
Events: 163

Top Five Medal Winners — By Country

PLACE	COUNTRY	GOLD	SILVER	BRONZE
1	USA	36	28	28
2	USSR	30	31	35
3	Italy	16	5	8
4	Germany	10	21	19
5	Australia	10	10	7

Athletics — Men

EVENT	GOLD		SILVER	BRONZE
100 m	Robert Hayes (USA)	10.0	Enrique Figuerola (CUB)	Harry Jerome (CAN)
200 m	Henry Carr (USA)	20.3	Otis Paul Drayton (USA)	Edwin Roberts (TRI)
400 m	Michael Larrabee (USA)	45.1	Wendell Mottley (TRI)	Andrzej Badenski (POL)
800 m	Peter Snell (NZL)	1:45.1	William Crothers (CAN)	Wilson Kiprugut (KEN)
1,500m	Peter Snell (NZL)	3:38.1	Josef Odlozil (TCH)	John Davies (NZL)
5,000 m	Robert Schul (USA)	13:48.8	Harald Norpoth (GER)	William Dellinger (USA)
10,000 m	William Mills (USA)	28:24.4	Mohamed Gammoudi (TUN)	Ronald Clarke (AUS)
Marathon	Abebe Bikila (ETH)	2:12:11.2	Basil Heatley (GBR)	Kokichi Tsubaraya (JPN)
110 m Hurdles	Hayes Jones (USA)	13.6	Blaine Lindgren (USA)	Anatoliy Mikhailov (URS)
400 m Hurdles	"Rex" Cawley (USA)	49.6	John Cooper (GBR)	Salvatore Morale (ITA)
3,000 m Steeplechase	Gaston Roelants (BEL)	8:30.8	Maurice Herriott (GBR)	Ivan Belyayev (URS)
4x100 m	USA	39.0	Poland	France
4x400 m	USA	3:00.7	Great Britain	Trinidad
20 km Walk	Kenneth Matthews (GBR)	1:29:34.0	Dieter Lindner (GER)	Vladimir Golubinichy (URS)
50 km Walk	Abdon Pamich (ITA)	4:11:12.4	Paul V. Nihill (GBR)	Ingvar Pettersson (SWE)
High Jump	Valeriy Brumel (URS)	7'1"	John Thomas (USA)	John Rambo (USA)
Pole Vault	Fred Hansen (USA)	16'8"	Wolfgang Reinhardt (GER)	Klaus Lehnertz (GER)
Long Jump	Lynn Davies (GBR)	26'5"	Ralph Boston (USA)	Igor Ter-Ovanesyan (URS)
Triple Jump	Jozef Schmidt (POL)	55'3"	Oleg Fedoseyev (URS)	Viktor Kravchenko (URS)
Shot	Dallas Long (USA)	66'8.1"	Randy Matson (USA)	Vilmos Varju (HUN)
Discus	Al Oerter (USA)	200'1.5"	Ludvik Danek (TCH)	David Weill (USA)
Hammer	Romuald Klim (URS)	228'9"	Gyula Zsivatzky (HUN)	Uwe Beyer (GER)
Javelin	Pauli Nevala (FIN)	271'2"	Gergely Kulcsar (HUN)	Janis Lusis (URS)
Decathlon	Willi Holdorf (GER)*	7,887	Rein Aun (URS)	Hans-Joachim Walde (GER)

Athletics — Women

EVENT	GOLD		SILVER	BRONZE
100 m	Wyomia Tyus (USA)	11.4	Edith McGuire (USA)	Ewa Klobukowska (POL)1
200 m	Edith McGuire (USA)	23.0	Irena Kirszenstein (POL)	Marilyn Black (AUS)
400 m	Betty Cuthbert (AUS)	52.0	Ann Packer (GBR)	Judith Amoore (AUS)
800 m	Ann Packer (GBR)	2:01.1	Maryvonne Dupureur (FRA)	Ann Chamberlain (NZL)
80 m Hurdles	Karin Balzer (GER)	10.5	Tereza Ciepla (POL)	Pamela Kilborn (AUS)
4x100 m	Poland	43.6	USA	Great Britain
High Jump	Iolanda Balas (ROM)	6'2"	Michele Brown-Mason (AUS)	Taisia Chenchik (URS)
Long Jump	Mary Rald (GBR)	22'2"	Irena Kirszenstein (POL)	Tatyana Schelkanova (URS)
Shot	Tamara Press (URS)	59'6"	Renate Garisch (GER)	Galina Zybina (URS)
Discus	Tamara Press (URS)	187'10"	Ingrid Lotz (GER)	Lia Manoliu (ROM)
Javelin	Mihaela Penes (ROM)	187'7"	Marta Rudas (HUN)	Yelena Gorchakova (URS)
Pentathlon	Irina Press (URS)	5,246	Mary Rand (GBR)	Galina Bystrova (URS)

OLYMPICS

Mexico 1968

Participants: 5,530
Men: 4,749
Women: 781
Countries: 112
Sports: 18
Events: 172

Top Five Medal Winners — By Country				
PLACE	COUNTRY	GOLD	SILVER	BRONZE
1	USA	45	28	34
2	USSR	29	32	30
3	Japan	11	7	7
4	Hungary	10	10	12
5	GDR	9	9	7

Athletics — Men

EVENT	GOLD		SILVER	BRONZE
100 m	Jim Hines (USA)	9.9	Lennox Miller (JAM)	Charlie Greene (USA)
200 m	Tommie Smith (USA)	19.8	Peter Norman (AUS)	John Carlos (USA)
400 m	Lee Evans (USA)	43.8	Larry James (USA)	Ronald Freeman (USA)
800 m	Ralph Doubell (AUS)	1:44.3	Wilson Kiprugut (KEN)	Thomas Farrell (USA)
1,500 m	Kipchoge Keino (KEN)	3:34.9	Jim Ryun (USA)	Bodo Tummler (FRG)
5,000 m	Mohamed Gammoudi (TUN)	14:05.0	Kipchoge Keino (KEN)	Naftali Temu (KEN)
10,000 m	Naftali Temu (KEN)	29:27.4	Mamo Wolde (ETH)	Mohmed Gammoudi (TUN)
Marathon	Mamo Wolde (ETH)	2:20:26.4	Kenji Kimihara (JPN)	Michael Ryan (NZL)
110 m Hurdles	Willie Davenport (USA)	13.3	Ervin Hall (USA)	Eddy Ottoz (ITA)
400 m Hurdles	David Hemery (GBR)	48.12	Gerhard Hennige (FRG)	John Sherwood (GBR)
4x100 m	USA	38.2	Cuba	France
4x400 m	USA	2:56.1	Kenya	FRG
High Jump	Dick Fosbury (USA)	7'4.6"	Edward Caruthers (USA)	Valentin Gavrilov (URS)
Pole Vault	Robert Seagren (USA)	17'8.5"	Claus Schiprowski (FRG)	Wolfgang Nordwig (GDR)
Long Jump	Bob Beamon (USA)	29'2"	Klaus Beer (GDR)	Ralph Boston (USA)
Triple Jump	Viktor Saneyev (URS)	57'0"	Nelson Prudencio (BRA)	Giuseppe Gentile (ITA)
Shot	Randy Matson (USA)	67'4.5"	George Woods (USA)	Eduard Grischin (URS)
Hammer	Gyula Zsivotzky (HUN)	240'8"	Romuald Klim (URS)	Lazar Lovasz (HUN)
Javelin	Janis Lusis (URS)	295'7"	Jorma Kinneunen (FIN)	Gergely Kulcsar (HUN)
Decathlon	William Toomey (USA)	8,193	Hans-Joachim Walde (FRG)	Kurt Bendlin (FRG)

Athletics — Women

EVENT	GOLD		SILVER	BRONZE
100m	Wyomia Tyus (USA)	11.0	Barbara Ferrell (USA)	Irena Szewinska-Kirszenstein (POL)
200 m	Irena Szewinska-Kirszenstein (POL)	22.5	Raelene Boyle (AUS)	Jennifer Lamy (AUS)
400 m	Collette Besson (FRA)	52.0	Lillian Board (GBR)	Natalya Pechenkina (URS)
800 m	Madeline Manning (USA)	2:00.9	Ilona Silai (ROM)	Maria Gommers (HOL)
80 m Hurdles	Maureen Gird (AUS)	10.3	Pam Kilborn (AUS)	Chi Cheng (TAI)
4x100 m	USA	42.8	Cuba	USSR
High Jump	Miloslava Rezkova (TCH)	5'11"	Antonina Okorokova (URS)	Valentina Kozyr (URS)
Long Jump	Viorica Viscopoleanu (ROM)	22'4.5"	Sheila Sherwood (GBR)	Tatyana Talysheva (URS)
Shot	Margitta Hehmboldt (GDR)	64'4"	Marita Lange (GDR)	Nadyezda Chizhova (URS)
Discus	Lia Manoliu (ROM)	191'2"	Liesel Westermann (FRG)	Jolan Kleiber (HUN)
Javelin	Angela Nemeth (HUN)	198'0"	Mihaela Penes (ROM)	Eva Janko (HUN)
Pentathlon	Ingrid Becker (FRG)	5,098	Lise Prokop (AUT)	Annamaria Toth (HUN)

OLYMPICS

Munich 1972

Participants: 7,123
Men: 6,065
Women: 1,058
Countries: 121
Sports 21
Events: 195

\multicolumn{5}{c}{Top Five Medal Winners — By Country}
PLACE	COUNTRY	GOLD	SILVER	BRONZE
1	USSR	50	27	22
2	USA	33	31	30
3	DDR	20	23	23
4	West Germany	13	11	16
5	Japan	13	8	8

Athletics — Men

EVENT	GOLD		SILVER	BRONZE
100 m	Valeriy Borsov (URS)	10.14	Robert Taylor (USA)	Lennox Miller (JAM)
200 m	Valeriy Borsov (URS)	20.00	Larry Black (USA)	Pietro Mennea (ITA)
400 m	Vincent Matthews (USA)	44.66	Wayne Collett (USA)	Julius Sang (KEN)
800 m	Dave Wottle (USA)	1:45.9	Yewgeniy Arzhanov (URS)	Mike Boitt (KEN)
1,500 m	Pekka Vasala (FIN)	3:36.3	Kipchoge Keino (KEN)	Rodney Dixon (NZL)
5,000 m	Lasse Viren (FIN)	13:26.4	Mohamed Gammoudi (TUN)	Ian Stewart (GBR)
10,000 m	Lasse Viren (FIN)	27:38.4	Emiel Puttemans (BEL)	Miruts Yifter (ETH)
Marathon	Frank Shorter (USA)	2:12:19.8	Karel Lismont (BEL)	Mamo Wolde (ETH)
110 m Hurdles	Rodney Milburn (USA)	13.24	Guy Drut (FRA)	Thomas Hill (USA)
400 m Hurdles	John Akii-Bua (UGA)	47.82	Ralph Mann (USA)	David Hemery (GBR)
3,000 m Steeplechase	Kipchoge Keino (KEN)	8:23.6	Benjamin Jipcho (KEN)	Tapio Kantanen (FIN)
4x100 m	USA	38.19	USSR	FRG
4x400 m	Kenya	2:59.8	Great Britain	France
20 km Walk	Peter Frenkel (GDR)	1:26:42.4	Vladimir Golubnichiy (URS)	Hans Reimann (GDR)
50 km Walk	Bernd Kannenberg (FRG)	3:56:11.6	Venjamin Soldatenko (URS)	Larry Young (USA)
High Jump	Yury Tarmak (URS)	7'3"	Stefan Junge (GDR)	Dwight Stones (USA)
Pole Vault	Wolfgang Nordwig (GDR)	18'0.5"	Robert Seagren (USA)	Jan Johnson (USA)
Long Jump	Randy Williams (USA)	27'0"	Hans Baumgartner (FRG)	Arnie Robinson (USA)
Triple Jump	Viktor Sanqev (URS)	56'11"	Jorg Drehmel (GDR)	Nelson Prudencio (BRA)
Shot	Wladyslaw Komar (POL)	69'6"	George Woods (USA)	Hartmut Briesenick (GDR)
Discus	Ludvik Danek (TCH)	211'3"	Jay Silvester (USA)	Rickard Bruch (SWE)
Hammer	Anatoliy Bondarchuk (URS)	247'8"	Jochen Sachse (GDR)	Vasiliy Khmelevski (URS)
Javelin	Klaus Wolfermann (FRG)	296'10"	Janis Lusis (URS)	William Schmidt (USA)
Decathlon	Nikolai Avilov (URS)	8,454	Leonid Litvinenko (URS)	Ryszard Katus (POL)

Athletics — Women

EVENT	GOLD		SILVER	BRONZE
100 m	Renate Stecher (GDR)	11.07	Raelene Boyle (AUS)	Silvia Chivas (CUB)
200 m	Renate Stecher (GDR)	22.40	Raelene Boyle (AUS)	Irena Szewinska-Kirszenstein (POL)
400 m	Monika Zehrt (GDR)	51.08	Rita Wilden (FRG)	Kathy Hammond (USA)
800 m	Hildegard Falck (FRG)	1:58.6	Niole Sabaite (URS)	Gunhild Hoffmeister (GDR)
1,500 m	Ludmila Bragina (URS)	4:01.4	Gunhild Hoffmeister (GDR)	Paola Cacchi (ITA)
100 m Hurdles	Annelie Ehrhardt (GDR)	12.59	Valeria Bufanu (ROM)	Karin Balzer (GDR)
4x100 m	FRG	42.81	GDR	Cuba
4x400 m	GDR	3:23.0	USA	FRG
High Jump	Ulrike Meyfarth (FRG)	6'3.5"	Yordanka Blagoyeva (BUL)	Ilona Gusenbauer (AUT)
Long Jump	Heide Rosendahl (FRG)	22'3"	Diana Yorgova (BUL)	Eva Suranova (TCH)
Shot	Nadyezda Chizhova (URS)	60'0"	Margitta Gummel (GDR)	Ivanka Khristova (BUL)
Discus	Faina Melnik (URS)	218'7"	Argentina Menis (ROM)	Vassilka Stoyeva (BUL)
Javelin	Ruth Fuchs (GDR)	209'7"	Jacqueline Todten (GDR)	Kathy Schmidt (USA)
Pentathlon	Mary Peters (GBR)	4,801	Heide Rosendahl (FRG)	Burglinde Pollak (GDR)

Montreal 1976

Participants: 6,028
Men: 4,781
Women: 1,247
Countries: 92
Sports: 21
Events: 98

Top Five Medal Winners — By Country

PLACE	COUNTRY	GOLD	SILVER	BRONZE
1	USSR	49	41	35
2	GDR	40	25	25
3	USA	34	35	25
4	FRG	10	12	17
5	Japan	9	6	10

Athletics — Men

EVENT	GOLD		SILVER	BRONZE
100 m	Hasely Crawford (TRI)	10.06	Donald Quarrie (JAM)	Valeriy Borsov (URS)
200 m	Donald Quarrie (JAM)	20.23	Millard Hampton (USA)	Dwayne Evans (USA)
400 m	Alberto Juantorena (CUB)	44.26	Fred Newhouse (USA)	Herman Frazier (USA)
800 m	Alberto Juantorena (CUB)	1:43.5	Ivo van Damme (BEL)	Richard Wohlhuter (USA)
1,500 m	John Walker (NZL)	3:39.2	Ivo van Damme (BEL)	Paul-Heinz Wellmann (FRG)
5,000 m	Lasse Viren (FIN)	13:24.8	Dick Quax (NZL)	Klaus-P. Hildenbrand (FRG)
10,000 m	Lasse Viren (FIN)	27:44.4	Carlos Lopez (POR)	Brendan Foster (GBR)
Marathon	Waldermar Cierpinski (GDR)	2:09:55.0	Frank Shorter (USA)	Karel Lismont (BEL)
110 m Hurdles	Guy Drut (FRA)	13.30	Alejandro Casanas (CUB)	Willie Davenport (USA)
400 m Hurdles	Edwin Moses (USA)	47.64	Michael Shine (USA)	Yevgeniy Gavrilenko (URS)
4x100 m	USA	38.33	GDR	USSR
4x400 m	USA	2:58.65	Poland	FRG
High Jump	Jacek Wszola (POL)	7'4.5"	Gregory Joy (CAN)	Dwight Stones (USA)
Pole Vault	Tadeusz Slusarski (POL)	18'0.5"	Antti Kalliomaki (FIN)	David Roberts (USA)
Long Jump	Arnie Robinson (USA)	27'4.25"	Randy Williams (USA)	Frank Wartenberg (GDR)
Triple Jump	Viktor Saneyev (URS)	56'8.74"	James Butts (USA)	Joao de Oliveira (BRA)
Shot	Udo Beyer (GDR)	69'0.75"	Yevgeniy Mironov (URS)	Alexander Baryshnikov (URS)
Discus	Mac Wilkins (USA)	221'5"	Wolfgang Schmidt (GDR)	John Powell (USA)
Hammer	Yuriy Sedykh (URS)	254'4"	Alexey Spiridonov (URS)	Anatoliy Bondarchuk (URS)
Javelin	Miklos Nemeth (HUN)	310'4"	Hannu Siitonen (FIN)	Gheorghe Megelea (ROM)
Decathlon	Bruce Jenner (USA)	8,617	Guido Kratschmer (FRG)	Nikolai Avilov (URS)

Athletics — Women

EVENT	GOLD		SILVER	BRONZE
100 m	Annegret Richter (FRG)	11.08	Renate Stecher (GDR)	Inge Helten (FRG)
200 m	Barbel Eckert (GDR)	22.37	Annegret Richter (FRG)	Renate Stecher (GDR)
400 m	Irena Szewinska (POL)	49.29	Christina Brehmer (GDR)	Ellen Streidt (GDR)
800 m	Tatyana Kazankina URS)	1:54.9	Nikolina Shtereva (BUL)	Elfie Zinn (GDR)
1,500 m	Tatyana Kazankina (URS)	4:05.5	Gunhild Hoffmeister (GDR)	Ulrike Klapezynski (GDR)
100 m Hurdles	Johanna Schaller (GDR)	12.77	Tatyana Anisimova (URS)	Natalya Lebedeva (URS)
4x100 m	GDR	42.55	FRG	USSR
4x400 m	GDR	3:19.2	USA	USSR
High Jump	Rosemarie Ackermann (GDR)	6'4"	Sara Simeoni (ITA)	Yordanka Blagoyeva (BUL)
Long Jump	Angela Voight (GDR)	22'0.75"	Kathy McMillan (USA)	Lidia Alfeyeva (USR)
Shot	Ivanka Khristova (BUL)	69'5.25"	Nadyezda Chizhova (URS)	Helena Fibingerova (TCH)
Discus	Evelin Schlaak (GDR)	226'4"	Maria Vergova (BUL)	Gabriele Hinzmann (GDR)
Javelin	Ruth Fuchs (GDR)	209'7"	Marion Becker (FRG)	Kathy Schmidt (USA)
Pentathlon	Siegrun Siegl (GDR)	4,745	Christine Laser (GDR)	Burglinde Polak (GDR)

Moscow 1980

Partidpants: 5,217
Men: 4,043
Women: 1,124
Countries: 80
Sports: 21
Events: 204

Top Five Medal Winners — By Country

PLACE	COUNTRY	GOLD	SILVER	BRONZE
1	USSR	80	69	46
2	GDR	47	37	42
3	Bulgaria	8	16	17
4	Cuba	8	7	5
5	Italy	8	3	4

Athletics — Men

EVENT	GOLD		SILVER	BRONZE
100 m	Allan Wells (GBR)	10.25	Silvio Leonard (CUB)	Petar Perrov (BUL)
200 m	Pictro Mennea (ITA)	20.19	Allan Wells (GBR)	Donald Quarrie (JAM)
400 m	Viktor Markin (URS)	44.60	Richard Mitchell (AUS)	Frank Schaffer (GDR)
800 m	Steve Ovett (GBR)	1:45.4	Sebastian Coe (GBR)	Nikolai Kirov (URS)
1,500 m	Sebastian Coe (GBR)	3:38.4	Jurgen Straub (GDR)	Steven Ovett (GBR)
5,000 m	Miruts Yifter (ETH)	13:21.0	Suleiman Nyambui (TAN)	Kaarlo Maaninka (FIN)
10,000 m	Miruts Yifter (ETH)	27:42.7	Kaarlo Maaninka (FIN)	Mohammed Kedir (ETH)
Marathon	Waldemar Cierpinsh (GDR)	2:11:03	Gerard Nijboer(HOL)	Sat Dzhumanazarov (URS)
110 m Hurdles	Thomas Munkelt (GDR)	13.39	Alejandro Casanas (CUB)	Alexander Puchkov (URS)
400 m Hurdles	Volker Beck (GDR)	48.70	Vasiliy Arkhipenko (URS)	Gary Oakes (GBR)
3,000 m Steeplechase	Bronislaw Malinowski (POL)	8:09.7	Filbert Bayi (TAN)	Eshetu Tura (ETH)
4x100 m	USSR	38.26	Poland	France
4x400 m	USSR	3:01.1	GDR	Italy
20 km Walk	Maurizio Damilano (ITA)	1:23:35.5	Pyotr Pochenchuk (URS)	Roland Wieser (GDR)
50 km Walk	Hartwig Gander (GDR)	3:49:24	Jorge Llopart (ESP)	Yevgeniy Ivchenko (URS)
High Jump	Gerd Wessig (GDR)	7'8"	Jacek Wszola (POL)	Jorg Freimuth (GDR)
Pole Vault	Wladislaw Kozakiewicz (POL)	18'11"	Konstantin Volkov (URS) Tadeusz Slusarski (POL)	
Long Jump	Lutz Dombrowki (GDR)	28'0"	Frank Paschek (GDR)	Valeri Podluzhniy (URS)
Triple Jump	Jaak Uudmae (URS)	56'11"	Viktor Saneyev(URS)	Joao de Oliveira (BRA)
Shot	Vladimir Kiselyev (URS)	70'0.5"	Alexander Baryshnikov (URS)	Udo Beyer (GDR)
Discus	Viktor Rashchupkin (URS)	218'7"	Imrich Bugar (TCH)	Luis Delis (CUB)
Hammer	Yuriy Sedykh (URS)	268'4"	Sergey Litvinov (URS)	Yuriy Tamm (URS)
Javelin	Dainis Kula (URS)	299'2"	Alexander Makarov (URS)	Wolfgang Hanisch (GDR)
Decathlon	Daley Thompson (GBR)	8,495	Yuriy Kutsenko (URS)	Sergey Zhelanov (URS)

Athletics — Women

EVENT	GOLD		SILVER	BRONZE
100 m	Ludmila Kondratyeva(URS)	11.06	Marlies Gohr (GDR)	Ingrid Auerswald (GDR)
200 m	Barbel Wockel (GDR)	22.03	Natalya Bochina (URS)	Merlene Ortey (JAM)
400 m	Marita Koch (GDR)	48.88	Jarmila Kratochvilova (TCH)	Christina Lathan (GDR)
800 m	Nadyezda Olizarenko (URS)	1:53.2	Olga Mineyeva (URS)	Tatyana Providokhina (URS)
1,500 m	Tatyana Kasankina (URS)	3:56.6	Christiane Wartenberg (GDR)	Nadyezda Olizarenko (URS)
100 m Hurdles	Vera Komisova (URS)	12.56	Johanna Klier (GDR)	Lucyna Langer (POL)
4x100 m	GDR	41.60	USSR	Great Britain
4x400 m	USSR	3:20.2	GDR	Great Britain
High Jump	Sara Simeoni (ITA)	6'5"	Urszula Kielan (POL)	Jutta Kirst (GDR)
Long Jump	Tatyana Kolpakova (URS)	23'2"	Brigitte Wujak (GDR)	Tatyana Skachko (URS)
Shot	Ilona Slupianek (GDR)	73'6.5"	Svetlana Krachevskaya (URS)	Margitta Pufe (GDR)
Discus	Evelin Jahl (GDR)	229'6"	Maria Petkova-Vergova (BUL)	Tatyana Lesovaya (URS)
Javelin	Maria Caridad-Colon (CUB)	224'5"	Saida Gunba (URS)	Ute Hommola (GDR)
Pentathlon	Nadyezda Tkachenko (URS)	5,083	Olga Rukavishnikova (URS)	Olga Kuragina (URS)

Los Angeles 1984

Particpants: 6,797
Men: 5,230
Women: 1,567
Countries: 40
Sports: 21
Events: 221

Top Five Medal Winners — By Country

PLACE	COUNTRY	GOLD	SILVER	BRONZE
1	USA	83	61	30
2	Romania	20	16	17
3	FRG	17	19	23
4	China	15	8	9
5	Italy	14	6	12

Athletics — Men

EVENT	GOLD		SILVER	BRONZE
100 m	Carl Lewis (USA)	9.99	Sam Graddy (USA)	Ben Johnson (CAN)
200 m	Carl Lewis (USA)	19.80	Kirk Baptiste (USA)	Thomas Jefferson (USA)
400 m	Alonzo Babers (USA)	44.27	Gabriel Tiacoh (CIV)	Antonio McKay (USA)
800 m	Joaquim Cruz (BRA)	1:43.00	Sebastian Coe (GBR)	Earl Jones (USA)
1,500 m	Sebastian Coe (GBR)	3:32.53	Steve Cram (GBR)	Jose Abascal (ESP)
5,000m	Said Aouita (MAR)	13:05.59	Markus Ryffel (SUI)	Antoaio Leitao (POR)
10,000 m	Alberto Cova (ITA)	27:47.54	Michael McLeod (GBR)	Mike Musyoki (KEN)
Marathon	Carlos Lopes (POR)	2:09:21	John Treacy (IRL)	Charles Spedding (GBR)
110 m Hurdles	Roger Kingdom (USA)	13.20	Greg Foster (USA)	Arto Bryggare (FIN)
400 m Hurdles	Edwin Moses (USA)	47.75	Danny Harris (USA)	Harald Schmid (FRG)
4x100 m	USA	37.83	Jamaica	Canada
4x400 m	USA	2:57.91	Great Britain	Nigeria
Long Jump	Carl Lewis (USA)	28'0.25	Gary Honey (AUS)	Giovanni Enngelisti (ITA)
High Jump	Dietmar Mogenburg (FRG)	7'81.5"	Patrik Sjoberg (SWE)	Jianhua Zhu (CHN)
Pole Vault	Pierre Quinon (FRA)	18'0.25"	Mike Tully (USA)	Earl Bell (USA)
Triple Jump	Al Joyner (USA)	56'7.5"	Mike Conley (USA)	Keith Connor (GBR)
Shot	Allessandro Andrei (ITA)	69'9"	Michael Carter (USA)	Dave Laut (USA)
Discus	Rolf Danneberg (FRG)	218'6"	Mac Wilkins (USA)	John Powell (USA)
Hammer	Juha Tiainen (FIN)	256'2"	Karl-Hans Riehm (FRG)	Klaus Ploghaus (FRG)
Javelin	Aro Harkonen (FIN)	284'8"	David Ottley (GBR)	Kenth Eldebrink (SWE)
Decathlon	Daley Thompson (GBR)	8,798	Jurgen Hingsen (FRG)	Siegfried Wentz (FRG)

Athletics — Women

EVENT	GOLD		SILVER	BRONZE
100 m	Evelyn Ashford (USA)	10.97	Alice Brown (USA)	Merlene Ottey (JAM)
200 m	Valerie Brisco-Hooks (USA)	21.81	Florence Griffth (USA)	Merlene Ottey (JAM)
400 m	Valerie Brisco-Hooks (USA)	48.83	Chandra Cheeseborough (USA)	Kathryn Cook (GBR)
800 m	Doina Melinte (ROM)	1:57.60	Kim Gallagher (USA)	Fita Lovin (ROM)
1,500 m	Gabriella Dorio (ITA)	4:03.25	Doina Melinte (ROM)	Maricica Puica (ROM)
3,000 m	Maricica Puica (ROM)	8:35.96	Wendy Sly (GBR)	Lynn Williams (CAN)
Marathon	Joan Benoit (USA)	2:24:52	Grete Waitz (NOR)	Rosa Mota (POR)
100 m Hurdles	Benita Fitzgerald-Brown (USA)	12.84	Shirley Strong (GBR)	Kim Turner (USA)
				Michele Chardonet (FRA)
400 m Hurdles	Nawal El Moutawakel (MAR)	54.61	Judi Brown (USA)	Cristina Cojocaru (ROM)
4x100 m	USA	41.65	Canada	Great Britain
4x400m	USA	3:18.29	Canada	FRG
High Jump	Ulrike Meyfarth (FRG)	67'2.25	Sara Simeoni (ITA)	Joni Huntley (USA)
Long Jump	Anis Stanciu-Cusmir (ROM)	22'10"	Vali Ionescu (ROM)	Susan Hearnshaw (GBR)
Shot	Claudia Losch (FRG)	67'2.25"	Mihaela Loghin (ROM)	Gael Martin (AUS)
Discus	Ria Stalman (HOL)	214'5"	Leslie Deniz (USA)	Florenta Craciunescu (ROM)
Javelin	Tessa Sanderson (GBR)	228'2"	Tiina Lillak (FIN)	Fatima Whitbread (GBR)
Heptathlon	Glynis Nunn (AUS)	6,390	Jackie Joyner (USA)	Sabine Everts (FRG)

OLYMPICS

Seoul 1988

Participants: 8,465
Men: 6,279
Women: 2,186
Countries: 159
Sports: 23
Events: 237

Top Five Medal Winners — By Country				
PLACE	COUNTRY	GOLD	SILVER	BRONZE
1	USSR	55	31	46
2	GDR	37	35	30
3	USA	36	31	27
4	South Korea	12	11	10
5	FRG	11	14	15

Athletics — Men

EVENT	GOLD		SILVER	BRONZE
100 m*	Carl Lewis (USA)	9.92	Linford Christie (GBR)	Calvin Smith (USA)
200 m	Joe DeLoach (USA)	19.75	Carl Lewis (USA)	Robson da Silva (BRA)
400 m	Steven Lewis (USA)	43.87	Butch Reynolds (USA)	Danny Everett (USA)
800m	Paul Ereng (KEN)	1:43.45	Joaquim Cruz (BRA)	Said Aouita (MAR)
1,500 m	Peter Rono (KEN)	3:35.96	Peter Elliott (GBR)	Jens-Peter Herold (GDR)
5,000 m	John Ngugi (KEN)	13:11.70	Dieter Baumann (FRG)	Hansjorg Kunze (GDR)
10,000 m	Brahim Boutaib (MAR)	27:21.44	Salvatore Antibo (ITA)	Kipkemboy Kimeli (KEN)
Marathon	Gelindo Bordin (ITA)	2:10:32	Douglas Wakihuriu (KEN)	Ahmed Saleh (DIJ)
110 m Hurdles	Roger Kingdom (USA)	12.98	Colin Jackson (GBR)	Anthony Campbell (USA)
400 m Hurdles	Andre Philipps (USA)	47.19	Amadou Dia Ba (SEN)	Edwin Moses (USA)
4X100 m	USSR	38.19	Great Britain	France
4X400 m	USA	2:56.16	Jamaica	FRG
High Jump	Gennadi Avdeyenko (URS)	7'9"	Hollis Conway (USA)	Rudolf Povarnitsin (URS)
				Patrick Sjoberg (SWE)
Pole Vault	Sergei Bubka (URS)	19'4"	Rodion Gataulin (URS)	Grigori Yegorov (URS)
Long Jump	Carl Lewis (USA)	28'7.5"	Mike Powell (USA)	Larry Myricks (USA)
Triple Jump	Khristo Markov (BUL)	57'9"	Igor Lapshin (URS)	Alexander Kovalenko (URS)
Shot	Ulf Timmermann (GDR)	73'8"	Randy Barnes (USA)	Werner Gunthor (SUI)
Discus	Jurgen Schult (GDR)	225'9"	Romas Ubartas (URS)	Rolf Danneberg (FRG)
Hammer	Sergeiy Litinov (URS)	278'2"	Yuriy Sedych (URS)	Yuriy Tamm (URS)
Javelin	Tapio Korjus (FIN)	276'6"	Jan Zelezny (TCH)	Seppo Raty (FIN)
Decathlon	Christian Schenk (GDR)	8,488	Torsten Voss (GDR)	Dave Steen (CAN)

Athletics — Women

EVENT	GOLD		SILVER	BRONZE
100 m	Florence Griffith-Joyner (USA)	10.54	Evelyn Ashford (USA)	Heike Drechsler (GDR)
200 m	Florence Griffith-Joyner (USA)	21.34	Grace Jackson (JAM)	Heike Drechsler (GDR)
400 m	Olga Brizgina (URS)	48.65	Petra Muller (GDR)	Olga Nasarova (URS)
800 m	Sigrun Wodars (GDR)	1:56.10	Christine Wachtel (GDR)	Kim Gallagher (USA)
1,500 m	Paula Ivan (ROM)	3:53.96	Lelute Baikauskaite (URS)	Tatyana Samolenko (URS)
3,000 m	Tatyana Samolenko (URS)	8:26.53	Paula Ivan (ROM)	Yvonne Murray (GBR)
10,000 m	Olga Bondarenko (URS)	31:05.21	Elizabeth McColgan (GBR)	Yelena Yupiveva (URS)
Marathon	Rosa Mota (POR)	2:25:40	Lisa Martin (AUS)	Katrin Dorre (GDR)
100 m Hurdles	Yordanka Donkova (BUL)	12.38	Gloria Siebert (GDR)	Claudia Zaczkewicz (FRG)
400 m Hurdless	Debra Flintoff-King (AUS)	53.17	Tatyana Ledovskaya (URS)	Ellen Fiedler (GDR)
4x100 m	USA	41.98	GDR	USSR
4x400 m	USSR	3:15.18	USA	GDR
High Jump	Louise Ritter (USA)	6'8"	Stefka Kostadinova (BUL)	Tamara Bykova (URS)
Long Jump	Jackie Joyner-Kersee (USA)	24'3"	Heike Drechsler (GDR)	Galina Chistyakova (URS)
Shot	Natalia Lisovskaya (URS)	72'11"	Kathrin Neimke (GDR)	Meisu Li (CHN)
Discus	Martina Hellmann (GDR)	237'2"	Diana Gansky (GDR)	Szvetanka Christova (BUL)
Javelin	Petra Felke (GDR)	245'0"	Fatima Whitbread (GBR)	Beate Koch (GDR)
Heptathlon	Jackie Joyner-Kersee (USA)	7,291	Sabine John (GDR)	Anke Behiner (GDR)

Barcelona 1992

Participants: 9,364
Men: 6,657
Women: 2,707
Countries: 169.
Sports: 24
Events: 257

Top Five Medal Winners — By Country

PLACE	COUNTRY	GOLD	SILVER	BRONZE
1	Unified Team	45	38	28
2	USA	37	34	37
3	Germany	33	21	28
4	China	16	22	16
5	Cuba	14	6	11

Athletics — Men

EVENT	GOLD		SILVER	BRONZE
100 m	Linford Christie (GBR)	9.96	Frank Fredericks (NAM)	Dennis Mitchell (USA)
200 m	Mike Marsh (USA)	20.01	Frank Fredericks (NAM)	Michael Bates (USA)
400 m	Quincy Watts (USA)	43.50	Steve Lewis (USA)	Samson Kitur (KEN)
800 m	William Tanui (KEN)	1:43.66	Nixon Kiprotich (KEN)	Johnny Gray (USA)
1,500 m	Fermin Ruiz (ESP)	3:40.12	Rachid El Basir (ESP)	Mohamed Sulaiman (QAT)
5,000 m	Dieter Baumann (GER)	13:12.52	Paul Bitok (KEN)	Fita Bayisa (ETH)
10,000 m	Khalid Skah (MAR)	27:46.70	Richard Chelimo (KEN)	Addis Abebe (ETH)
Marathon	Young-Cho Hwang (KOR)	2:13:23	Koichi Morishita (JPN)	Stephan Freigang (GER)
110 m Hurdles	Mark McKoy (CAN)	13.12	Tony Dees (USA)	Jack Pierce (USA)
400 m Hurdles	Kevin Young (USA)	46.78	Winthrop Graham (JAM)	Kriss Akabusi (GBR)
4x100 m	USA	37.40	Nigeria	Cuba
4x400 m	USA	2:55.74	Cuba	Great Britain
High Jump	Javier Sotomayor (CUB)	7'8"	Patrick Sjoberg (SWE)	Artur Partyka (POL)
				Timothy Forsyth (AUS)
				Hollis Conway (GBR)
Pole Vault	Maxim Tarrassov (EUN)	19'0"	Igor Trandellkow (EUN)	Javier Garcia (ESP)
Long Jump	Carl Lewis (USA)	28'5 "	Mike Powell (USA)	Joe Greene (USA)
Triple Jump	Michael Conley (USA)	59'7"	Charles Simpkins (USA)	Frank Rutherford (BAH)
Shot	Michael Stulce (USA)	71'2"	James Doehring (USA)	Vyacheslav Lycho (EUN)
Discus	Romas Ubartas (LIT)	213'7"	Jurgen Schult (GER)	Roberto Moya (CUB)
Javelin	Jan Zelezny (TCH)	294'2"	Seppo Raty (FIN)	Steve Backley (GBR)
Hammer	Andrey Abdulvalyev (EUN)	270'96"	Igor Astapkovich (EUN)	Igor Nikulin (EUN)
Decathlon	Robert ZIllelik (TCH)	8,611	Antonio Penalver (ESP)	David Johnson (USA)

Athletics — Women

EVENT	GOLD		SILVER	BRONZE
100 m	Gail Devers (USA)	10.52	Juliet Cuthbert (JAM)	Irina Privalova (EUN)
200 m	Gwen Torrence (USA)	21.81	Juliet Cuthbert (JAM)	Merlene Ottey (JAM)
400 m	Marie-Jose Perec (FRA)	48.83	Olga Brysgina (EUN)	Ximena Gaviria (COL)
800 m	Ellen Van Langen (HOL)	1:55.54	Lilia Nurutdinova (EUN)	Ana Quirot (CUB)
1,500 m	Hassiba Boulmerka (ALG)	3:55.30	Ludmilla Rogacheva (EUN)	Yunxia Qu (CHN)
3,000 m	Yelena Romanova (EUN)	8:46.04	Tatyana Dorovskich (EUN)	Angela Chalmers (CAN)
10,000 m	Derartu Tulu (ETH)	31:06.02	Elena Meyer (RSA)	Lynn Jennings (USA)
Marathon	Valentina Yegorova (EUN)	2:32:41	Yuko Arimori (JPN)	Lorraine Moller (NZL)
100 m Hurdles	Paraskevi Patoulidou (GRE)	12.64	Lavonna Martin (USA)	Jordanka Donkova (BUL)
400 m Hurdles	Sally Gunnell (GBR)	53.23	Sandra Farmer-Patrick (USA)	Janeene Vickers (USA)
4x100 m	USA	42.11	Unified Team	Nigeria
4x400 m	Unified Team	3:20.20	USA	Great Britain
High Jump	Heike Henkel (GER)	6'7"	Galina Astafei (ROM)	Joanet Quintero (CUB)
Long Jump	HeikeDrechler (GER)	23'5"	Inessa Kravets (EUN)	Jackie Joyner-Kersee (USA)
Shot	Svetlana Kriveleova (EUN)	69'1"	Zhihong Huang (CHN)	Kathrin Neimke (GER)
Discus	Maritza Marten (CUB)	229'10"	Zvetanka Christova (BUL)	Daniela Costian (AUS)
Javelin	Silke Renke (GER)	224'2.5"	Natalya Shikolenko (EUN)	Karen Forkel (GER)
Heptathlon	Jackie Joyner-Kersee (USA)	7,044	Irina Belova (EUN)	Sabine Braun (GER)

OLYMPICS

Atlanta 1996

Participants: 10,310
Men: 6,797
Women: 3,513
Countries: 197
Sports: 26
Events: 271

Top Five Medal Winners — By Country

PLACE	COUNTRY	GOLD	SILVER	BRONZE
1	USA	44	32	25
2	Russia	26	21	16
3	Germany	20	18	27
4	China	16	22	12
5	France	15	7	15

Athletics — Men

EVENT	GOLD		SILVER	BRONZE
100 m	Donovan Bailey (CAN)	9 84	Frankie Fredericks (NAM)	Ato Boldon (TRI)
200 m	Michael Johnson (USA)	19.32	Frankie Fredericks (NAM)	Ato Boldon (TRI)
400 m	Michael Johnson (USA)	43.49	Roger Black (GBR)	Davis Kamoga (UGA)
800 m	Vebjorn Rodal (NOR)	142.58	Hezekiel Sepeng (RSA)	Fred Onyancha (KEN)
1,500 m	Noureddine Morceli (ALG)	3:35.78	Fermin Cacho (ESP)	Stephen Kipkorir (KEN)
5,000 m	Venuste Nyongabo (BUR)	13:07.96	Paul Bitok (KEN)	Khalid Boulami (MAR)
10,000 m	Haile Gebrselassie (ETH)	27:07.34	Paul Tergat (KEN)	Salah Hissou (MAR)
Marathon	Josiah Thugwane(RSA)	2:12.36	Lee Bong-Ju (KOR)	Eric Wainaina (KEN)
110 m Hurdles	Allen Johnson (USA)	12.95	Mark Crear (USA)	Florian Schwarthoff (GER)
400 m Hurdles	Derrick Adkins (USA)	47.55	Samuel Matete (ZAM)	Calvin Davis (USA)
4x100 m	Canada	37.69	USA	Brazil
4x400 m	USA	2:55.99	Great Britain	Jamaica
High Jump	Charles Austin (USA)	7'10.25"	Artur Partyka (POL)	Steve Smith (GBR)
Pole Vault	Jean Galfione (FRA)	19'5.25"	Igor Trandenkow (UKR)	Andrei Tiwonchik (GER)
Long Jump	Carl Lewis (USA)	27'10"	Jaunes Beckford (JAM)	Joe Greene (USA)
Triple Jump	Kenny Harrison (USA)	59'4"	Jonathan Edwards (GBR)	Yoelvis Quesada (CUB)
Shot	Randy Barnes (USA)	70'11.25"	John Godina (USA)	Oleksandr Bagach (UKR)
Discus	Lars Aiedel (GER)	227'8"	Vladimir Dubrovchik (BLR)	Vassili Kapryukh (BLR)
Javelin	Jan Zelezny (CZE)	289'3"	Steve Backley (GBR)	Seppo Raty (FIN)
Hammer	Balazs Kiss (HUN)	266'6"	Lance Deal (USA)	Oleksiy Krykun (UKR)
Decathlon	Dan O'Brien (USA)	8,824	Frank Busemann (GER)	Tomas Dvorak (CZE)

Athletics — Women

EVENT	GOLD		SILVER	BRONZE
100 m	Gail Devers (USA)	10.94	Merlene Ottey (JAM)	Gwen Torrence (USA)
200 m	Marie-Jose Perec (FRA)	22.12	Merlene Ottey (JAM)	Mary Onyali (NGR)
400 m	Marie-Jose Perec (FRA)	48.25	Cathy Freeman (AUS)	Falilat Ogunkoya (NGR)
800 m	Svetlana Masterkova (RUS)	1:57 73	Ana Quirot (CUB)	Maria Mutola (MOZ)
1,500 m	Svetlana Masterkova (RUS)	4:00.83	Gabriela Szabo (ROM)	Theresia Kiesel (AUT)
5,000 m	Wang Junxia (CHN)	14:59.88	Pauline Konga (KEN)	Roberta Brunet (ITA)
10,000 m	Fernanda Ribeiro (POR)	31:01.63	Wang Junxia (CHN)	Gete Wami (ETH)
Marathon	Fatima Roba (ETH)	2:26:05	Valentina Yegorova (RUS)	Yuko Arimori (JPN)
100 m Hurdles	Lyudmila Engquist (SWE)	12.58	Brigita Bukovec (SLO)	Patricia Girard (FRA)
400 m Hurdles	Deon Hemmings (JAM)	52:82	Kim Batten (USA)	Tonja Buford-Bailey (USA)
4x100 m	USA	41.95	Bahamas	Jamaica
4x400 m	USA	3:20.91	Nigeria	Germany
High Jump	Stefka Kostadinova (BUL)	6'8.75"	Niki Bakogianni (GRE)	Inga Babakova (UKR)
Long Jump	Chioma Anjunwa (NGR)	23'4.5"	Fiona May (ITA)	Jackie Joyner-Kersee(USA)
Triple Jump	Inessa Kravets (UKR)	50'3.5"	Inna Lisovskaya (RUS)	Sarka Kasparkova (CZE)
Shot	Astrid Kumbernuss (GER)	67'5.5"	Sun Xinmei (CHN)	Irina Khudorozkhina (RUS)
Discus	Iike Wyludda (GER)	228'6"	Natalya Sadova (RUS)	Ellina Zvereva (BLR)
Javelin	Heli Rantanen(NOR)	222'11"	Louise McPaul (AUS)	Trine Hattestad (NOR)
Heptathlon	Ghada Shouaa (SYR)	6,780	Natasha Sazonovich (BLR)	Denise Lewis (GBR)

CHRONOLOGY

1900's

At the dawn of the new century the British Empire sprawled across a quarter of the world and though it would linger throughout the first few decades, the first stirrings of change could be felt. The United States economy, fuelled by a massive industrial base, overtook Britain's, while Germany began an armament program that would escalate as the decade matured, bringing unease and suspicion to Europe. In Russia, strikes and riots brought death to the streets and in South Africa the Boer War revealed Britain's army to be hopelessly out of date and needlessly brutal.

However, the 1900s were a period marked by relative peace and stability as well as rapid progress in the arts, sciences, and technology. In France the *Belle Epoque* (Beautiful Era) initiated a period of innovative design — Art Nouveau, which influenced artists worldwide and Picasso reached maturity, creating cubism with Georges Braque. The Wright brothers took to the air in the US, while human understanding of the universe took an enormous leap with the publication of Einstein's *Theory of Relativity*. The first trans-Atlantic wireless signal heralded a new era of communication and the foundation of the Ford Motor Company pointed the way forward in terms of industry and transport.

The second Olympic Games open in Paris.

Count von Zeppelin's airship takes to the skies for its maiden flight.

The death of German intellectual Friedrich Nietzsche.

McKinley elected President in the U.S..

Oscar Wilde dies in Paris.

Max Planck publishes his revolutionary paper on quantum theory.

Claude Monet paints *Water Lilies*.

1904

Henry Ford smashes the car speed record, traveling at 91.37 mph.

In Britain, Charles Rolls and Henry Royce join forces to found a car manufacturing business.

The U.S. hosts the opening of the third Olympic games in St Louis.

Deaf, dumb, and blind student Helen Keller graduates from Radcliffe College.

Theodore Roosevelt wins a second term in office.

In the U.S., Charles W. Follis becomes the first professional African-American football player.

1905

Albert Einstein publishes his special theory of relativity.

American May Sutton becomes the first non-British player to win the Wimbledon tennis championship.

The first double-sided record appears in the shops.

1906

Russian Revolutionary, Leon Trotsky, is exiled to Siberia.

Paul Cézanne, lauded as the greatest impressionist painter dies at the age of 67.

CHRONOLOGY

1901

The death of Queen Victoria and the ascension of Edward VII in Great Britain.

The work of unknown Spanish artist Pablo Picasso is given its first public display in Paris.

William McKinley, the 25th president of the United States is gunned down by an anarchist, Leon Czolosz in Buffalo, New York on September 6. The assassin, who shot McKinley in the stomach at point blank range, is executed on October 29.

Following the McKinley assassination, Vice-President Theodore Roosevelt becomes President.

The death of French artist Toulouse-Lautrec.

The first Nobel Prize award ceremony.

In Newfoundland, Marconi receives the first trans-Atlantic radio signal from Cornwall, England.

Woodrow Wilson publishes *The History of the American People*.

1902

Arthur Balfour elected Conservative Prime Minister of Britain following the retirement of his uncle, Lord Salisbury.

The coronation of Edward VII and Queen Alexandra at Westminster Abbey.

Arthur Conan Doyle publishes *The Hound of the Baskervilles*.

"Teddy Bears," enjoy popularity after President Roosevelt refuses to shoot a bear cub.

Pierre and Marie Curie succeed in isolating radium salt.

1903

Emmeline Pankhurst together with her daughters Christabel and Sylvia found the Women's Political and Social Union in Great Britain.

Coronation of Pope Pius X at the Vatican in Rome.

Boston Red Sox are triumphant at the first baseball World Series.

Ford Motor Company founded.

Built by brothers Orville and Wilbur Wright, the first heavier than air machine to manage a sustained flight takes to the skies.

1907

Robert Baden-Powell, a veteran of the Boer War, founds the Boy Scouts in Great Britain.

Georges Braque becomes the first artist to exhibit a painting in the cubist style. Picasso's first cubist painting *Les Demoiselles d'Avignon* was also completed in this year.

Leo Baekeland invents the first plastic, which he names Bakelite.

1908

Henry Ford markets the first "Model T" Fords.

William Taft is elected President of the United States.

The two-year-old Pu Yi ascends the imperial throne of China.

The Cullinan diamond, the largest diamond in the world, is cut to make jewelry for Queen Alexandra.

World Series won by Chicago Cubs.

The fourth Olympic Games opens in London, England.

Jack Johnson is the first African-American to win the World Heavyweight Boxing Championship.

1909

US naval officer Robert Peary is the first man to stand at the North Pole.

Joan of Arc becomes a saint, nearly 500 years after being burned at the stake by the English.

First flight across the English Channel by Louis Blériot.

Apache Chief Geronimo, who led the last Native American uprising in 1882, dies.

CHRONOLOGY

1910

1910's

The teens of the 20th century were dominated by the Great War, the war to end all wars, a cataclysmic conflict that cost the lives of some ten million. The aftermath of the struggle shifted political power toward America, which was less effected by the carnage and subsequent economic turmoil than the European powers.

In Russia, the conflict sparked a revolution that had been waiting to happen for many years. This would also make an enormous impact on the political map of the world.

A decade marked by tragedy, 1912 also saw the sinking of *Titanic* on her maiden voyage and the death of Robert Falcon Scott during an expedition to reach the South Pole.

The Boy Scout movement reaches the U.S..

Marie Curie isolates radium and publishes *Treatise on Radium* in France.

W. E. B. Du Bois edits *Crisis* written by African-American intellectuals of the National Association for the Advancement of Colored People.

Mark Twain dies aged 74.

E. M. Forster publishes *Howard's End*.

Dr Crippen murders his wife in London and flees for the U.S..

King Edward VII of England dies suddenly of pneumonia to be succeeded by his son George V.

The death of the great Russian novelist Leo Tolstoy, author of *War and Peace*.

1914

Archduke Franz Ferdinand of Austria is assassinated, sparking World War I.

Edgar Rice Burroughs' novel *Tarzan of the Apes* is published.

Holst composes *The Planets*.

1915

British nurse Edith Cavell is executed by a German firing squad after being found guilty of helping British prisoners escape. She had been treating both Allied and German patients.

D. W. Griffith's directs *The Birth of a Nation*.

D. H. Lawrence publishes *The Rainbow*.

1916

Woodrow Wilson re-elected as U.S. President.

David Lloyd George becomes Prime Minister of Great Britain.

General Sir Douglas Haig takes command of British forces and immediately pursues a strategy of all out offensives which leads to the loss of many more British troops at the Somme. Tens of thousands of soldiers are sent "over the top" to be slaughtered by German machine guns.

Charlie Chaplin appears in *The Pawn Shop*.

U.S. scientist A. Michelson proves the existence of the Earth's molten core.

The Olympic Games are cancelled.

CHRONOLOGY

1911

Irving Berlin writes "Alexander's Ragtime Band."

The first Hollywood film studio is opened by David Horsley.

Norwegian explorer Roald Amundsen becomes the first man to set foot on the South Pole.

1912

Woodrow Wilson elected U.S. President.

First news film produced by Charles Pathé.

Scott reaches the South Pole to find that Amundsen has beaten him. The expedition fails to return and the bodies of the team are eventually found, only 11 miles from a food deposit that would have saved their lives.

The Titanic hits an iceburg in the North Atlantic and sinks, killing 1,523 crew and passengers.

1913

Geiger counter invented by Hans Geiger, Germany.

Death of J. Pierpont Morgan, American industrialist and financier of *Titanic* aged 75.

Louis Blériot achieves the first "loop the loop" in an aircraft.

In Britain, Emily Davidson, a suffragette protester, dies beneath the hooves of horses running in the Derby.

C. J. Jung publishes *The Psychology of The Unconcious*.

1917

Vladimir Ilich Lenin publishes *The State and Revolution*.

Tsar Nicholas of Russia abdicates but is arrested with his family soon after. They are exiled to Siberia.

All German titles are renounced by the German descended British Royal family.

Winston Churchill becomes Minister for Munitions in Britain.

The death of American legend W. F. Cody, better known as "Buffalo Bill."

Pulitzer Prizes are first awarded.

1918

Execution of the Russian Royal Family.

The abdication of German Kaiser Wilhelm II.

Peace talks commence in Paris with the arrival of President Wilson.

The armistice is signed on November 11, bringing an end to the war.

1919

Treaty of Versailles signed.

The first Trans-Atlanic flight by British flyers J. W. Alcock and A. W. Brown.

The death of former president Theodore Roosevelt.

In Italy, Benito Mussolini founds the Fascist Party, while in Germany the National Socialist, or Nazi as it becomes known, Party is formed.

Lady Nancy Astor becomes the first woman in Britain to take a seat in Parliament.

Walter Gropius founds the Bauhaus School of Design, Building, and Crafts in Germany.

United Artists founded by Charlie Chaplin, Douglas Fairbanks, D. W. Griffith and Mary Pickford.

CHRONOLOGY

1920's

The "Jazz Age" or "Roaring Twenties" is commonly seen as time of freedom, decadence, and economic stability. But beneath the surface, the forces that were to plunge the world once more into catastrophe were at work. The Fascist Party, led by Benito Mussolini made great gains in Italy, in Germany the failed artist Adolf Hitler took control of the Nazi Party and rapidly gained popular support, and in Russia Josef Stalin purged his enemies and opponents ruthlessly. In the last months of the decade an overstretched global economy finally crashed, bringing an abrupt end to the party.

However, great strides continued to be made in science, technology, and the arts. The discovery of penicillin by Alexander Fleming would cure many illnesses around the world, John Logie Baird brought the moving image to the small screen for the first time with television, the first movie with sound was a massive success, and T. S. Eliot produced *The Waste Land*, his masterful poem that has come to exemplify the modern age.

1920

Warren Harding elected president in the U.S..

World press attention focuses on the marriage of Hollywood stars Douglas Fairbanks and Mary Pickford.

Hollywood comedian Fatty Arbuckle charged with rape and murder.

Alcohol is banned throughout the U.S..

The invention of the machine-gun by J. T. Thompson.

"Crazy Blues" is the first record to be made by a female Africa-American singer.

Margaret Gorman is the first winner of the U.S. beauty pagent "Miss America."

7th Olympic Games open in Antwerp.

1924

Former U.S. president Woodrow Wilson dies.

Mahatma Ghandi released from jail after serving less than two years of a six year sentence, later in the year he begins a fast in an effort to quell anti-British rioting.

Hitler sentenced to five years in prison, but later released on parole.

The first Winter Olympics are held in Chamonix, France, and Paris hosts the 8th Olympic Games.

Clavin Coolidge elected president in the U.S., while in Britain Ramsay MacDonald becomes the first Labour prime minister.

Lenin dies at age 53 and is embalmed.

The first performances of Gershwin's *Lady Be Good* and *Rhapsody in Blue*.

J. Edgar Hoover takes charge at the Bureau of Investigation.

1925

Mussolini takes dictatorial power in Italy.

Hitler publishes *Mein Kampf (My Struggle)*.

Louis Armstrong forms Hot Five in Chicago, a band playing Dixieland jazz.

F. Scott Fitzgerald publishes *The Great Gatsby*, perhaps the greatest novel of the Jazz Age.

The Gold Rush starring Charlie Chaplin is released.

African-American dancer Josephine Baker takes to the stage in Paris and is an immediate success.

1926

Death of Houdini the great escapologist.

Death of Rudolph Valentino the greatest star of silent movies aged 31.

John Logie Baird demonstrates television for the first time in Britain. His invention is seen as a novelty that will never catch on.

The first round the world flight by aviator Alan Cobham.

Hirohito becomes emperor of Japan.

Robert H. Goddard develops a rocket powered by liquid fuel.

British crime novelist Agatha Christie disappears from her home and is never seen again.

Charles Atlas opens a gymnasium in New York City.

Fritz Lang makes the science fiction movie *Metropolis*.

U.S. swimmer Gertrude Ederle becomes the first woman to swim the English Channel.

CHRONOLOGY

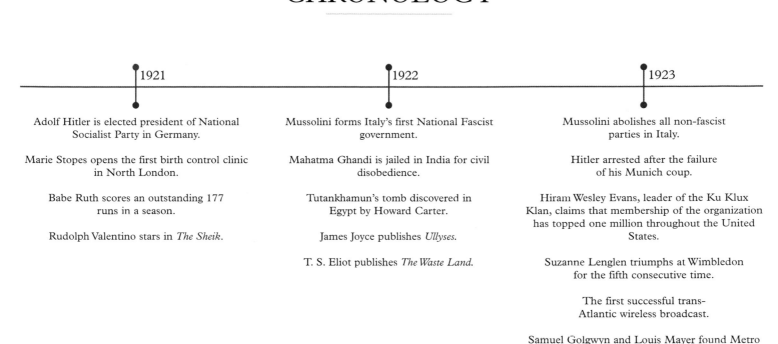

1921

Adolf Hitler is elected president of National Socialist Party in Germany.

Marie Stopes opens the first birth control clinic in North London.

Babe Ruth scores an outstanding 177 runs in a season.

Rudolph Valentino stars in *The Sheik*.

1922

Mussolini forms Italy's first National Fascist government.

Mahatma Ghandi is jailed in India for civil disobedience.

Tutankhamun's tomb discovered in Egypt by Howard Carter.

James Joyce publishes *Ullyses*.

T. S. Eliot publishes *The Waste Land*.

1923

Mussolini abolishes all non-fascist parties in Italy.

Hitler arrested after the failure of his Munich coup.

Hiram Wesley Evans, leader of the Ku Klux Klan, claims that membership of the organization has topped one million throughout the United States.

Suzanne Lenglen triumphs at Wimbledon for the fifth consecutive time.

The first successful trans-Atlantic wireless broadcast.

Samuel Golgwyn and Louis Mayer found Metro Goldwyn Mayer film studios in Hollywood.

Henry A. Luce and Briton Haddon found *Time* magazine in the U.S..

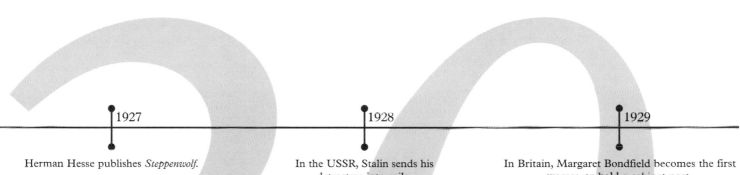

1927

Herman Hesse publishes *Steppenwolf*.

Charles Lindbergh makes solo flight across the Atlantic in his aircraft *Spirit of St Louis*.

Malcolm Campbell achieves a new land speed record of 174 mph in one of a series of ever-faster cars named *Bluebird*.

The first talkie is released, *The Jazz Singer* starring Al Jolson.

In China the Nationalist Party, led by Chiang Kai-shek, take Shanghai while the Communist Party are victorious in Nanking.

1928

In the USSR, Stalin sends his detractors into exile.

Amelia Earhart becomes the first woman to fly across the Atlantic.

Alexander Fleming announces the accidental discovery of penicillin, earning him a Nobel Prize.

Chiang Kai-shek becomes President of China.

Margaret Mead publishes *Coming of Age in Samoa*.

Herbert Hoover elected president in the U.S..

The coronation of Ras Tafari in Ethiopia.

Disney creation Mickey Mouse makes his first appearance in *Steamboat Willie*.

British poet and novelist Thomas Hardy dies.

The first color movies are pioneered by George Eastman.

Stan Laurel and Oliver Hardy star in four hit movies together.

1929

In Britain, Margaret Bondfield becomes the first woman to hold a cabinet post.

Ernest Hemingway publishes *A Farewell to Arms*.

First Academy Awards ceremony.

Edwin Powell Hubble announces that the universe is expanding.

Panic on Wall Street as the stock market crashes after a decade of steady growth.

CHRONOLOGY

1930's

Characterized by economic depression throughout the Western world and the build up of tensions that would lead to the second catastrophic war of the century, this was a decade of gloom, turmoil, and widespread poverty.

Franco was swept to power during the Spanish Revolution and proved a cruel and ruthless dictator, while Hitler achieved dictatorial power in Germany and fostered a return to military might. In Russia, Stalin's regime equalled any atrocities that were to come in Nazi Germany, and Japan and China were locked into conflict that cost the lives of thousands. China also suffered internal struggle between opposing Nationalist and Communist factions while the British Empire began a gradual disintegration as the Indian people, led by Mahatma Ghandi, demanded liberation from British rule.

1930

Amy Johnson becomes the first woman to fly from Britain to Australia.

In India, Ghandi is arrested again by the British following the start of his peaceful disobedience campaign.

Stalin orders the collectivisation of all Soviet farms.

Hitler's Nazi Party makes great gains in German elections although he is banned from taking his seat due to his Austrian nationality.

Haile Selassie crowned emperor in Ethiopia.

Revolution begins in Spain.

Marlene Diertich stars in *The Blue Angel*.

Chinese rebels, led by Yen Hsi-chan sieze power in Peking.

1934

Oswald Mosely, Britain's fascist politician enjoys growing support from British voters. In New York City, a Nazi demonstration attracts some 9,000 followers.

Bonnie and Clyde, legendary U.S. criminals are shot dead by police.

Hitler and Mussolini convene talks in Venice, Mussolini orders the invasion of Albania a week later. Hitler becomes dictator in Germany the following month.

King Alexander I of Yugoslavia is assassinated in France.

The "Long March" lead by Mao Tse-tung begins in China.

Ghandi resigns from Indian Congress Party and ends his campaign of civil disobedience.

Marie Curie dies aged 66.

1935

Mary Pickford and Douglas Fairbanks divorce.

An incredible five world records are broken in a single day by one athlete, American Jesse Owens.

Stanley Baldwin elected Prime Minister in Great Britain.

George Gershwin's *Porgy and Bess* opens in New York.

Charles B. Darrow markets the first "Monopoly" board game.

Alfred Hitchcock directs *The 39 Steps*.

Anna Karenina starring Greta Garbo is released.

Ginger Rogers and Fred Astaire star in *Top Hat*.

The Marx Brothers appear in *A Night at the Opera*.

1936

King George V of England dies. Nine months later his successor, Edward VII abdicates in order to marry American divorcee Wallis Simpson.

Hitler opens the 11th Olympic Games in Berlin and has his theories of an Aryan "master race" confounded by African-American athlete Jessie Owens who wins four gold medals. The German dictator also launches the Voltswagen motor company.

The Axis pact between Rome and Berlin is announced by Mussolini.

Chiang Kai-shek takes Canton and declares war on Japan.

Margaret Mitchell's *Gone With the Wind* is published.

Civil war erupts in Spain. Franco becomes supreme ruler.

U.S. photographer Ansel Adams opens his first exhibition.

The New York Yankees purchase Joe DiMaggio from the San Francisco Seals.

CHRONOLOGY

1931

Ghandi is released from prison and attends talks with the British government. Indians riot in protest to British rule.

Malcolm Campbell smashes the land speed record again in another *Bluebird*.

Communists in northern China are ousted by Chiang Kai-shek.

Following the resignation of King Alfonso, Spain is declared a republic.

U.S. gangster Al Capone is arrested and sentenced to 11 years for tax evasion.

The Empire State Building is completed in New York City.

Inventor Thomas Edison dies.

James Cagney appears in *The Public Enemy*.

1932

Ghandi is arrested yet again in India after leading more protests over the treatment of Indian people.

Hitler is nominated by the Nazi Party as presidential candidate but is beaten in elections by Hindenburg. However the year sees him making great political strides, culminating in his refusing the position of Chancellor.

French President Doumer is assassinated.

Amelia Aerhart completes a solo flight over the Atlantic.

Franklin Roosevelt achieves a landslide victory in U.S. elections with his "New Deal" economic policies.

British scientist John Cockcroft becomes the first to split the atom.

The son of American aviator Charles Lindburgh is kidnapped and murdered.

The first Tarzan movie, starring Johnny Weissmüller as *Tarzan the Ape Man*.

1933

Ghandi returns to jail, found guilty of inciting anti-British riots.

Adolf Hitler accepts the position of Chancellor of Germany from President Hindenburg. His supporters celebrate with a massive procession through Berlin. He assumes almost total control almost immediately and the same year sees the construction of the first concentration camp at Dachau and widespread persecution of Jews and Nazi opponents.

King Kong opens in movie theaters in the U.S..

Frances Perkins becomes the first female member of the cabinet in the U.S..

Hedy Lamarr appears in the nude in the movie *Ecstacy*.

Fred Astaire appears in his first movie *Dancing Lady*.

1937

Neville Chamberlain is elected Prime Minister of Britain.

George Gershwin dies. In Britain, engineer Frank Whittle tests the first jet engine.

Picasso paints his anti-war masterpiece *Guernica*.

Hitler orders the construction of a second concentration camp — Buchenwald.

Jazz singer Bessie Smith dies after being refused entry into a whites-only hospital.

The German airship *Hindenburg* crashes in flames in New Jersey, U.S..

Cary Grant stars in the screwball comedy *The Awful Truth*.

1937

Hitler assumes control of the War Ministry in Germany and mobilises troops. British Prime Minister Chamberlain meets with the German Chancellor and continues to appease him. Chamberlain is attacked at home by Churchill.

Orson Welles's radio production of *War of the Worlds* induces panic in the US.

Disney studios release the first full-length animated feature, *Snow White and the Seven Dwarfs*.

Howard Hughes completes a record breaking round the world flight in under four days in his aircraft, *New York World Fair*.

Bette Davis appears in *Jezebel*.

1939

Hitler orders German troops into Moravia and Bohemia, then Slovakia followed by Lithuania. Six days after Britain signs a pact with Poland, German troops invade, and Britain and France declare war.

Stalin orders the invasion of eastern Poland and Finland.

Pope Pius XII is elected by the conclave of cardinals in Rome.

John Steinbeck publishes *The Grapes of Wrath*.

John Ford's movie *Stagecoach* is released.

J. R. R. Tolkien publishes *The Hobbit*.

Land speed record of 368.85 mph set by John Cobb on the Salt Flats of Bonneville, Utah, U.S..

Sigmund Freud dies aged 83.

The movie of Margaret Mitchell's *Gone With the Wind* is released starring Clark Gable and Vivien Leigh.

CHRONOLOGY

1940's

The 1940s, like the 1910s, were characterized by carnage and chaos. Countless people lost their lives in the second catastrophic war of the century — among the most enduring images of the decade are those of the mushroom clouds created by the two atom bombs dropped on Japan and of the victims of the Nazi concentration camps. At the end of World War II, the political and physical boundaries of the world had shifted irrevocably, with the U.S. and USSR now the undisputed superpowers, while Britain's empire collapsed totally. And the defeat of Hitler only marked the beginning of a new conflict — the Cold War between the massive communist Eastern Bloc and the West. The Middle East too, was to become the site of bitter dispute after the Jewish state of Israel was founded.

In Britain, Chamberlain resigns as prime minister, his popular replacement is Winston Churchill.

Hitler invades France with lightening speed, British forces are evacuated from the beaches of Dunkirk, the bombing of London begins. German forces conquer Holland, Belgium, and Luxembourg and advance on Norway.

Roosevelt wins another term as president.

F. Scott Fitzgerald dies aged 44.

Charlie Chaplin stars in the satiric film, *The Great Dictator*.

Vera Lynn becomes the forces' sweetheart singing "We'll Meet Again and "White Cliffs of Dover."

Bob Hope, Bing Crosby, and Dorothy Lamour star in the first of their "Road" movies, *The Road to Singapore*.

1944

Allied troops under the command of General Eisenhower land in Normandy and begin to push German forces back.

In Japan, General Tojo resigns.

de Gaulle arrives in Paris after Allied troops take the city and begins an inquisition of German collaborators.

German General Rommel commits suicide.

Laurence Olivier stars in the film adaptation of Shakespeare's *Henry V*.

American bandleader Glenn Miller dies in an air crash.

1945

First atomic bomb is exploded in the New Mexico desert.

U.S. President Franklin Delano Roosevelt dies.

Soviet troops take Berlin and Hitler takes his own life. Germany surrenders.

Mussolini executed by Italian partisans, crowds form to mutilate his corpse.

Pétain receives a death sentence in France for collaboration.

American aircraft drop atomic bombs on the Japanese cities of Hiroshima and Nagasaki, forcing Japan to surrender.

Almost immediately after Allied victory Churchill is ousted in the British general election to be replaced by Clement Atlee who announces that India will return to self-rule.

George Orwell publishes *Animal Farm*.

1946

Charles de Gaulle resigns as French leader.

Juan Perón elected president in Argentina.

At the first meeting of the United Nations General Assembly, Norwegian Trygve Lie is elected as Secretary General.

Churchill coins the term "Iron Curtain."

In Germany, Hess goes on trial at Nuremburg while Goering takes his own life.

In China, communist leader Mao Tse-tung declares war on his Nationalist adversary Chiang Kai-shek.

Benjamin Spock publishes *Common Sense Book of Baby and Child Care*.

James Stewart stars in the Frank Capra movie, *It's a Wonderful Life*.

CHRONOLOGY

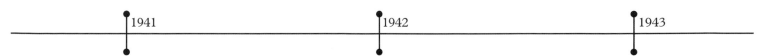

1941

Hitler's deputy Rudolf Hess parachutes into Scotland to attempt negotiations.

Churchill and Roosevelt meet to sign the Atlantic Charter.

General Tojo becomes prime minister in Japan and launches an attack on Pearl Harbor soon after. America joins the war as a consequence.

Orson Welles's masterpiece, *Citizen Kane*, is released.

British novelist Virginia Woolf commits suicide.

1942

Hitler makes the tactical mistake of pushing troops into the Soviet Union, the climate and the prowess of Soviet commanders take a massive toll on the German army.

British General Montgomery, "the Desert Fox" takes control of forces in North Africa and turns the tide against his adversary, Rommel.

US General Dwight Eisenhower lands with troops in North Africa and joins the fray.

Ghandi returns to politics to demand Indian independence.

Ingrid Bergman and Humphrey Bogart star in *Casablanca*.

Frank Lloyd Wright designs Guggenheim Museum.

Bing Crosby sings Irving Berlin's "White Christmas" in the movie *Holiday Inn*.

1943

Allied leaders Churchill, Roosevelt, and de Gaulle meet to discuss tactics.

Beset by Allied troops and facing the hatred of his people, Mussolini resigns and is immediately arrested. Italy surrenders on September 8 and declares war on Germany on October 13.

Churchill and Roosevelt meet with Stalin. Rodgers and Hammerstein's musical *Oklahoma* opens in New York.

Jaques Cousteau and Emile Gagnan invent the aqualung.

1947

The death of auto tycoon Henry Ford.

Nehru becomes Prime Minister of the newly independent India.

In Britain, Princess Elizabeth, the future Queen marries Philip Mountbatten.

Tennessee Williams publishes his new play, *A Streetcar Named Desire*.

John Cobb sets a new land speed record of 634.39 mph.

Howdy Doody makes television debut on NBC.

The Diary of Anne Frank is published.

Al Capone is released from prison and dies soon after.

1948

Engineer and aviator Orville Wright dies.

Mahatma Ghandi is killed by an assassin in India.

Margaret Chase Smith becomes the first woman to be elected senator in the U.S..

Juan Perón again wins elections in Argentina.

Chiang Kai-shek is victorious in Chinese elections and becomes President.

Chaim Weizmann becomes the first president of newly formed Israel.

Harry S. Truman is elected president in the U.S.

The 14th Olympic Games are staged in London.

A hamburger restaurant opens in the U.S. bearing the name of its owners Richard and Maurice McDonald.

Fred Astaire and Judy Garland star in *Easter Parade*, a musical scored by Irving Berlin.

1949

President Truman announces "New Deal" in US.

Chiang Kai-shek resigns as Chinese communists take Peking. Mao Tse-tung declares Communist People's Republic of China.

George Orwell publishes *1984*.

Arthur Miller completes his play *Death of a Salesman*.

New heartthrob Frank Sinatra stars in *On the Town*.

John Wayne stars in the John Ford movie *She Wore a Yellow Ribbon*.

CHRONOLOGY

1950's

From the austerity of the post-war years to the emergence of Rock n' Roll, the 1950s saw the return of a muscular Western economy and the emergence of a new youth culture with Elvis Presley at the forefront. The Cold War reached new levels of intensity and President Truman pledged to combat Communism with military aid while Senator Joseph McCarthy led a "witch hunt" of American citizens with Communist sympathies.

The 50s also saw the emergence of Martin Luther King as a Civil Rights leader in the U.S. and the politics of racial integration became an increasingly difficult issue for politicians to ignore. Science also made great strides — every youngster was a fan of science fiction comics — DNA was discovered, IBM patented the first computer, and the USSR sent the first satellite, Sputnik I, into orbit.

1950

President Truman orders the construction of the H-bomb marking the start of the arms race between the U.S. and USSR.

As the Korean War rages, U.S. General MacArthur is sent to command United Nations forces helping the beleagured South Koreans to resist the Communist forces of North Korea.

Walter Cronkite joins CBS News as the Washington correspondent.

Salvador Dali paints *The Madonna of Port Lligat*.

George Orwell dies.

American cartoonist Charles Schulz invents Charlie Brown.

Bette Davis appears in *All About Eve*, which also features Marilyn Monroe in a minor role.

Color television broadcasting begins in the U.S..

1954

The election of Georgi Malenkov as Soviet premier.

The four minute mile is broken by British athlete Roger Bannister.

Senator McCarthy, whose anti-Communist inquisition reached its peak the preceeding year, is censured by the U.S. Senate.

Evangelist Billy Graham conducts a mass rally in London.

Elvis Presley releases "That's All Right."

Bill Haley and the Comets release "Shake Rattle and Roll."

J. R. R. Tolkien publishes the first two volumes of *Lord of the Rings*.

Marlon Brando stars in *On the Waterfront*.

1955

Churchill resigns due to ill-health to be replaced as Prime Minister by Anthony Eden.

The death of renowned physicist Albert Einstein at the age of 80.

Walt Disney opens the first Disneyland theme park in California.

Juan Perón resigns as President of Argentina.

U.S. actor James Dean is killed in a car crash.

Lolita is published by Vladimir Nabokov.

Bill Haley and the Comets release "Rock Around the Clock."

Chuck Berry releases "Roll Over Beethoven."

1956

Egyptian President Colonel Nasser takes control of the Suez Canal after Britain and the U.S. withdraw financial backing for the Aswan Dam. French and British warships are dispatched to Suez but military action is soon called off when the U.S. fails to support the move.

American actress Grace Kelly marries Prince Rainer III of Monaco.

Elvis Presley storms the charts with "Heartbreak Hotel," Hound Dog," and "Love Me Tender."

American actress Marilyn Monroe marries playwright Arthur Miller.

Laurence Olivier has his portrait painted by Salvador Dali on the set of *Richard III*.

CHRONOLOGY

1951

The death of media tycoon William Randolph Hearst, upon whose life *Citizen Kane* was based.

U.S. Tennis Championships won by 16 year old Maureen Connolly.

Winston Churchill returns to power in Britain.

Eva Perón announces that she will stand as Vice President of Argentina.

Traitors Guy Burgess and Donald MacLean cause a sensation in Britain when they defect to the USSR.

The first long playing records "LPs" are marketed in the U.S.

1952

King George VI of England dies and Elizabeth II ascends the throne.

President Truman withdraws during his re-election campaign.

Eva Perón dies aged 30

The 15th Olympic Games are held in Helsinki..

Dwight Eisenhower becomes U.S. president.

The first successful operation to change a man's sex is performed by K. Hamburger in Denmark.

Gibson market the first solid-bodied electric guitar.

John Steinbeck publishes *East of Eden*.

Katherine Hepburn and Humphrey Bogart star in John Huston's *The African Queen*.

Gary Cooper and Grace Kelly star in *High Noon*.

1953

Churchill meets with president Eisenhower.

Soviet premier Josef stalin dies aged 74 causing convulsions in the USSR and a scramble to replace him.

Mount Everest is conquered by Edmund Hillary and Sherpa Norkey Tenzing.

The execution of Julius and Ethel Rosenburg who are found guilty in the U.S. of passing atomic secrets to the USSR.

Nikita Khrushchev becomes First Secretary in USSR.

Britain's new Queen is crowned, the ceremony is televised.

Dag Hammarskjold is elected Secretary General of the UN.

Korean War ends.

Ian Fleming publishes the first James Bond novel, *Casino Royale*.

Hugh Hefner founds *Playboy* magazine in the U.S.

Gentlemen Prefer Blondes, starring Jane Russell and Marilyn Monroe, is released.

1957

Dwight Eisenhower wins U.S. presidential election again.

Senator Joseph McCarthy dies.

Malenkov is ousted from power in the USSR. He is succeeded by Nikita Khrushchev.

The first satellite, Sputnik I, is sent into space by the USSR to be followed soon after by another carrying a dog, Laika.

President Eisenhower sends 1,000 troops to Little Rock, Arkansas to disperse white demonstrators preventing black students from enrolling in college.

The Leonard Bernstein musical *West Side Story* opens in New York.

Fidel Castro declares war on the Cuban regime of President Batista but the rebels are defeated.

Humphrey Bogart dies aged 56.

1958

Cardinal Ronacalli becomes Pope John XXII following the death of Pope Pius XII.

Charles de Gaulle returns to French politics and is elected president.

Elvis Presley joins the U.S. Army.

Martin Luther King publishes *Stride Towards Freedom* after a strenuous Civil Rights lecture tour of the U.S.

Truman Capote publishes *Breakfast at Tiffany's*.

James Stewart and Kim Novak appear in Hitchcock's *Vertigo*.

1959

Fidel Castro sweeps to power in Cuba after President Batista flees and orders the invasion of Panama.

Film director Cecil B. de Mille dies.

Rock n' Roll star Buddy Holly dies in an air crash.

A U.S. satellite successfully returns to Earth with its passengers — two monkeys alive.

Frank Lloyd Wright dies aged 89, months before his architectural masterpiece — the Guggenheim Museum — opens in New York.

Blues singer Billie Holiday makes her final appearance at a benefit concert in New York and dies of a drug overdose within days.

Charlton Heston stars in the Hollywood epic *Ben Hur*.

William Burroughs publishes *The Naked Lunch*.

Berry Gordy founds the black-owned Motown Records in Detroit.

CHRONOLOGY

1960's

The "Swinging Sixties" saw transformations on a hitherto unimaginable scale. At every level — social, cultural, technological, scientific, political — the rate of progress seemed unstoppable. The tension between East and West fuelled a race into space that became a matter of national pride and by the end of the decade the world watched, stunned, as Neil Armstrong stepped out onto the surface of the moon. The tentative youth rebellion of the 50s became a fully fledged revolution led by the Beatles and The Rolling Stones in Britain and by Bob Dylan and the Doors in the U.S.. Fashions shocked the older generation as women around the world adopted the mini skirt and in art Andy Warhol began a revolution from his studio The Factory. The Civil Rights movement gained a momentum under Martin Luther King, Jr. that witnessed mass rallies in Washington and the passing of legislation that transformed the political standing of African-Americans.

1960

John F. Kennedy is elected president.

Olympic Games open in Rome.

Alfred Hitchcock releases *Psycho*.

In Britain the ban on D. H. Lawrence's *Lady Chatterley's Lover* is lifted.

"The Pill" is approved by the U.S. Food and Drug Administration and goes on general sale.

Andy Warhol's *Superman* begins Pop Art.

The Beatles perform in Hamburg, Germany.

1964

The death of General Douglas MacArthur.

Nelson Mandela is sentenced to life imprisonment in South Africa.

Lyndon Johnson wins U.S. Presidential elections.

The Civil Rights Act is passed in the U.S., giving African-Americans equality in the workplace. A review of the education system also begins.

Leonid Brezhnev stages a coup and siezes control of the USSR from Nikita Khrushchev.

President Johnson sends the first U.S. troops into Vietnam.

The Beatles release their first movie, *A Hard Day's Night*.

Cassius Clay becomes Boxing Heavyweight Champion and announces his conversion to Islam, changing his name to Muhammed Ali.

The Beatles and the Rolling Stones cross the Atlantic to appear in the U.S.

1965

The poet T. S. Eliot dies.

Winston Churchill dies, aged 90, and is the first non-royal to be given a state funeral.

Militant black muslim leader Malcolm X is gunned down in the U.S..

Soviet astronaut Alexei Leonov leaves his space craft to walk in space, three months later U.S. astronaut Edward H. White repeats his feat.

In Arizona, U.S., Lorna Elizabeth Lockwood becomes the first female chief justice of a state supreme court.

The Beatles receive MBEs from Queen Elizabeth II.

The Rolling Stones release "Satisfaction."

The Beach Boys release "California Girls."

Julie Andrews stars in the Rodgers and Hammerstein's *The Sound of Music*.

1966

Mrs Indira Ghandi is elected Prime Minister of India.

Mao Tse-tung begins the Cultural Revolution in China.

Ronald Reagan is elected governor of California.

The militant Black Panthers organization is formed in the U.S..

Andy Warhol goes on tour with *The Velvet Underground*.

Walt Disney dies aged 64.

Truman Capote publishes *In Cold Blood*.

Thomas Pynchon publishes *The Crying of Lot 49*.

Bob Dylan releases *Blonde on Blonde*.

CHRONOLOGY

1961

Kennedy sanctions the doomed "Bay of Pigs" invasion of Cuba.

Ernest Hemmingway takes his own life after years of mental ill-health.

The Berlin Wall is constructed.

"The Pill" is released in Britain.

Ballet dancer Rudolph Nuryev defects to the West.

Yuri Gagarin of the USSR becomes the first man in space.

Bob Dylan takes to the stage for the first time in Greenwich Village, New York.

Marilyn Monroe appears in her last screen role, *The Misfits*, by husband Arthur Miller.

1962

Adolf Eichmann, the notorious Nazi war criminal is executed in Israel.

The Cuban Missile Crisis is diffused.

U.S. writer William Faulkner dies aged 64.

Eleanor Roosevelt dies aged 78.

Marilyn Monroe dies aged 36.

John Glenn becomes the first American in space.

A productive year for Andy Warhol who produces Campbell's Soup cans, 210 Coca-Cola Bottle, and the first in a series of Marilyn Monroe prints.

Sean Connery appears in his first James Bond film, *Dr No*.

1963

Following revelations about an affair with model Christine Keeler, British cabinet minister John Profumo resigns. Keeler is said to have been conducting another relationship with a Soviet naval attache Captain Ivanov.

The death of American poet Robert Frost.

Pope John XXIII dies and Pope Paul VI is elected.

President Kennedy is assassinated in Dallas by Lee Harvey Oswald. Vice-President Lyndon Johnson is sworn in. Oswald is himself shot soon after.

Martin Luther King gives his historic "I have a dream" speech.

Soviet Valentina Tereshkova becomes the first woman in space.

Lecturer Timothy Leary conducts experiments with psychedelic drugs at Harvard University and is dismissed.

The Beatles release their first album, *Please Please Me*.

1967

The first superbowl is played in the U.S., Green Buy packers triumph.

The Beatles release *Segeant Pepper's Lonely Hearts Club Band*.

Dr Christiaan Bernard performs the first successful heart transplant operation.

Record breaking Donald Campbell dies in an attempt to surpass his own water speed record in *Bluebird*.

Che Guevara is shot dead by Bolivian forces.

Svetlana Stalin, daughter of former Soviet Premier Josef defects to the West.

100,000 march on Washington to protest the war in Vietnam.

The Doors release their first album *The Doors*.

The summer months become known as "The Summer of Love" as hippie culture spreads.

1968

Martin Luther King is assassinated by James Earl Ray while attending a Civil rights meeting in Memphis.

Feminists storm into the Miss America beauty contest.

Robert Kennedy is assassinated.

Soviet astronauts orbit the moon foolowed by America astronauts in *Apollo 8*.

Jackie Kennedy and Aristotle Onassis marry.

Philip K. Dick publishes *Do Androids Dream of Electric Sleep?*

Henry Moore exhibition of sculpture travels the world.

Marvin Gaye releases "I Heard It Through The Grapevine."

Clint Eastwood stars in *The Good, The Bad, and The Ugly*.

Charlton Heston stars in *Planet of the Apes*.

1969

Neil Armstrong becomes the first man on the moon.

The death of former president Dwight Eisenhower aged 78.

Concorde takes to the air for the first time.

North Vietnamese Communist leader Ho Chi Minh dies.

Woodstock festival is a massive success, 500,000 people attend the three day event.

Following mass demonstrations the withdrawal of American troops from Vietnam is announced.

Charles Manson murders Sharon Tate and four others in Hollywood.

Richard Nixon elected President.

John Lennon marries Yoko Ono.

Jack Nicholson, Peter Fonda, and Dennis Hopper star in *Easy Rider*.

CHRONOLOGY

1970's

The 70s were the antithesis of the overt optimism and revolutionary activities of the 1960s. Flower Power wilted early on in the decade and was replaced by a cynical political atmosphere that peaked during the Watergate scandal, which saw the first ever presidential resignation. Internationally, various terrorist organizations began a series of violent campaigns that caused worldwide revulsion. And in Uganda, the murderous Idi Amin took control, so beginning a reign of terror that would endure throughout the decade. Following the American withdrawal from Vietnam, hundreds of thousands of South Vietnamese people took to the seas in an attempt to escape the oppressive communist regime. The global economy was also in decline, causing widespread unemployment in many countries.

1970

After the U.S. send troops into Cambodia in an attempt to subdue Communist activities, four students are shot dead by the National Guard during a protest in Ohio.

Riots erupt in Northern Ireland and more British troops are sent in to try and maintain order.

Palestinian terrorists hijack and blow up three airliners in Jordan.

An explosion on board U.S. space ship Apollo 13 halts a planned moon landing.

Rock icons Jimi Hendrix and Janis Joplin both die of drug overdoses.

French President Charles de Gaulle dies.

President Nasser of Egypt dies.

Germaine Greer publishes *The Female Eunuch*.

Andy warhol paints a tin of Cambell's soup. It is sold for $25,000.

The Beatles split up.

IBM researchers develop the floppy disk.

1974

In China, a massive earthquake kills over 200,000, while Honduras is devastated by Cyclone Fifi, which claims 10,000 lives.

Following the Watergate hearings, President Nixon resigns and is replaced by Gerald Ford.

Muhammad Ali becomes world heavyweight boxing champion for the second time, beating George Foreman.

The Eurovision Song Contest is won by Swedish pop group Abba, who dominate the charts for the remainder of the decade.

Argentinia premier Juan Perón dies at the age of 78.

1975

General Francisco Franco of Spain dies and Prince Juan Carlos returns Spain to a monarchy, becoming King Juan Carlos I.

The 19-year-old Bill Gates co-founds the computer software company Microsoft.

Stephen Spielberg directs the blockbuster *Jaws*.

Rock group Queen release the single "Bohemian Rhapsody." It is accompanied by the first video to enjoy widespread success.

Chinese Nationalist leader Chiang Kai-Shek dies aged 87.

1976

Jimmy Carter is elected president of the US.

Chinese Communist Premier Mao Tse-tung dies. As a member of the "Gang of Four," his wife attempts to sieze power.

Steven Jobs and Stephen Wozniak found Apple Computers.

American tycoon and eccentric Howard Hughes dies on board an aircraft at the age of 70.

The Eagles release their classic single "Hotel California."

Alex Haley writes *Roots*.

Sylvester Stallone stars in the movie *Rocky*.

Jim Henson's *The Muppet Show*, is first aired in the U.S.

CHRONOLOGY

● 1971

Idi Amin siezes control of Uganda in a military coup.

American jazz legend Louis Armstrong dies.

Soviet politician Nikita Khrushchez dies aged 77.

Fashion designer Coco Chanel dies aged 87.

The Rolling Stones release the single "Brown Sugar" followed by the album *Sticky Fingers*.

Clint Eastwood stars in *Dirty Harry*.

Francis Ford Coppola directs Marlon Brando and Al Pacino in *The Godfather*.

● 1972

During the Munich Olympic games, 11 Israeli athletes are killed by Arab terrorists.

Violence continues in Northern Ireland. In one incident, British soldiers shot 13 dead after protesters began throwing stones during a civil rights march.

In Germany, the Baader-Meinhof gang, otherwise known as the Red Army Faction are finally caught after carrying out numerous bomb attacks on German cities.

J. Edgar Hoover, the shadowy director of the FBI, dies aged 77.

Edward, Duke of Windsor and former king of England, dies aged 77.

David Bowie releases his masterpiece, *The Rise and Fall of Ziggy Stardust*.

Anthony Burgess publishes *A Clockwork Orange*.

● 1973

President Nixon signs the treaty that ends the Vietnamese War.

In London, two car bombs planted by the IRA kill an innocent civilian and wound over 200 more.

Spanish Prime Minister Luis Carrero Blanca is killed by a car bomb planted by the terrorist organization ETA.

Arab terrorists kill over 30 people at Rome airpot.

The U.S. launches a space station — Skylab 4.

Spanish artist Pablo Picasso dies at the age of 91.

David Ben-Gurion, first premier of Israel, dies aged 87.

Pink Floyd release the album *Dark side of the Moon*.

● 1977

Idi Amin orders the murder of the Archbishop of Uganda and soon after takes over 200 American citizens hostage.

Apple Computers market the world's first personal computer — the Apple II.

Rock and Roll singer Elvis Presley dies at the age of 42.

Stephen Spielberg directs *Close Encounters of the Third Kind*.

George Lucas releases *Star Wars*.

John Travolta stars in *Saturday Night Fever*.

American singer and Actor Bing Crosby dies on the golf course, aged 73.

In the UK the Sex Pistols release the single "God Save the Queen," launching the "punk" movement.

Singer Maria Callas dies at the age of 53.

● 1978

Pope Paul VI dies, to be succeeded by Pope John Paul I, who reigns for just 33 days before he too dies. Pope John Paul II is elected soon after.

The oil tanker Amoco Cadiz is caught on rocks off Brittany, France, causing a huge environmental disaster.

The religious cult, the People's Temple, commit mass suicide under orders from their leader Jim Jones. Over 900 are found dead at their commune in Guyana.

The first "test tube" baby, Louise Brown is born in the UK.

American artist Norman Rockwell dies.

American anthropologist Margaret Mead dies aged 76.

Christopher Reeve stars in the movie *Superman*.

Robert de Niro appears in *The Deer Hunter*.

Grease, starring John Travolta, is released to massive box office success.

The soap opera "Dallas," is first screened in the U.S.

● 1979

Conservative leader Margaret Thatcher becomes the first female Prime Minister of the United Kingdom.

Cambodia is invaded by Vietnam and the Cambodian leader Pol Pot is deposed. The excesses of his regime are exposed as Vietnamese troops discover the remains of countless people in torture camps.

Idi Amin's rule of Uganda is ended by an invasion by neighboring Tanzania.

An accident at the Three Mile Island nuclear power station in Pennsylvania releases radioactivity into the atmosphere.

Mother Theresa is awarded the Nobel Peace Prize.

American actor John Wayne dies aged 72.

Ridley Scott directs *Alien*, starring Sigourney Weaver.

CHRONOLOGY

1980's

The affluent eighties were characterized by the "yuppie." Thanks to the policies of Ronald Reagan in the U.S. and Margaret Thatcher in Britain, economies boomed and "upwardly mobile" young business people enjoyed the financial benefits. The Cold War also ended, with Soviet Premier Mikhail Gorbachev declaring glasnost and perestroika (meaning openess and reconstruction respectively), which were intended to end the political oppression of previous regimes and enliven the flagging Soviet economy. Soon after, the Eastern European states of Poland, Czechoslovakia, Bulgaria, East Germany, and Rumania renounced Communism and mounted democratic elections. By the end of the decade the Berlin Wall was torn down; an event that was symbolically celebrated with a huge rock concert in Potsdamer Platz, an area for so long a wasteland between East and West.

This was also a time of growing concern about environmental issues after it was announced that the use of everyday chemicals was creating a hole in the ozone layer surrounding the earth. Chernobyl was the site of a major nuclear accident the effects of which spread over Europe and a series of major oil spills threatened sea life. There was also grave concern about the felling of the rain forests and pollution from car exhaust fumes and heavy industry.
Perhaps the most emotional moment of the decade was the Live Aid concert of 1985, which saw rock and pop stars on both sides of the Atlantic stage massive benefit events to help relieve famine in Ethiopia. Over $100 million was eventually raised.

Aging Hollywood actor Ronald Reagan enjoys a landslide victory in U.S. presidential elections.

Lech Walesa is elected as the leader of the new Solidarity movement in Poland.

An American attempt to free 53 hostages held at the American Embassy in Iran goes disastrously wrong. Eight of the rescue squad die in an air accident and their bodies are triumphantly displayed at an Iranian press conference.

Iranian terrorists take over the Iranian Embassy in London and hold 26 people hostage. The British SAS storm the embassy, killing all but one of the terrorists and release all of the hostages.

Tennis player Bjorn Borg becomes Wimbledon Champion for the fifth time.

Rock musician and singer John Lennon is shot dead by a demented fan outside his New York home.

Film director Alfred Hitchcock dies aged 80.

American actress Mae West dies aged 88.

1984

Soviet Premier Yuri Andropov dies and is succeeded by Kostantin Chernenko.

Just one year after Sally Ride's trip into space, another female U.S. astronaut, Kathryn Sullivan, becomes the first woman to complete a "space walk."

Indian Prime Minister Indira Ghandi is assassinated.

Television stations across the globe broadcast harrowing images of starvation caused by famine in Ethiopia. In the UK, pop singer Bob Geldof writes and organizes the single "Do They Know It's Christmas?" which tops the charts for weeks on end, raising over a million pounds for famine relief.

The IRA bomb the Grand Hotel in Brighton, England, which is the venue for the Conservative Party's annual conference.

Soul singer Marvin Gaye is shot dead by his father.

Arnold Scharzenegger stars in *Terminator*.

1985

In the USSR, Kostantin Chernenko dies and is replaced by Mikhail Gorbachev.

The wreck of the Titanic is located by marine researcher Robert Ballard.

Actor and Director Oeron Welles dies.

The Live Aid concert is watched by almost every country in the world and raises $100 million for famine relief in Ethiopia.

President Reagan and Premier Gorbachev meet in Geneva.

Natural disasters claim many thousands of lives. In Colombia an erupting volcano kills 25,000, while in Mexico an earthquake kills 20,000.

French security services sink Greenpeace's flagship Rainbow Warrior in New Zealand.

Violence explodes in South African townships following the passing of a new constitution which excludes blacks from political representation. President P.W. Botha declares a state of emergency.

1986

U.S. aircraft carry out bombing missions over Libya.

In the USSR, an accident at the Chernobyl nuclear power station spreads radioactivity over Europe.

The space shuttle Challenger explodes soon after launch and all seven astronauts on board are killed.

In the second British royal wedding of the decade Prince Andrew marries Sarah Ferguson.

American artist Georgia O'Keefe dies aged 98.

Movie star James Cagney dies aged 86.

British sculptor Henry Moore dies 88.

CHRONOLOGY

1981

President Reagan and Pope John Paul II are both the victims of attempted assassinations.

Egyptian President Mohammed Anwar el Sadat is assassinated by an Islamic terrorist in Cairo.

The first space shuttle Columbia is successfully launched.

Prince Charles and Lady Diana Spencer are married at St Paul's Cathedral in London. The ceremony is broadcast around the world.

Race riots break out across the UK.

John McEnroe beats Bjorn Borg to become Wimbledon Champion.

Steven Spielberg directs *Raiders of the Lost Ark*, starring Harrison Ford.

The Hip-hop trend begins after Grandmaster Flash and the Furious Five release their album *The Message*.

1982

Argentina invades the British Falkland Islands, sparking armed conflict.

Princess Grace of Monaco, formerly actress Grace Kelly, dies in a car accident.

Following the death of Soviet leader Leonid Brezhnev, Yuri Andropov becomes the Soviet leader.

The IRA continue their bombing campaign on the British mainland. Deaths and injuries follow the bombing of London's Hyde and Regent's parks.

Charles and Diana, Prince and Princess of Wales rejoice in the birth of William Arthur Philip Louis, their first son and heir to the throne.

American actor Henry Fonda dies soon after winning an Oscar for his last film, *On Golden Pond*.

Steven Spielberg directs *ET, The Extra Terrestrial*.

Michael Jackson releases *Thriller*.

1983

Concern grows over the new disease, AIDS, which is taking more and more lives, particularly in the U.S.

U.S. astronaut Sally Ride becomes the first woman in space.

Tensions in the Middle East focus on Beirut. A bomb attack on the U.S. Embassy kills 60 and injures many more.

The IRA bomb the prestigious Harrods department store in London, killing five and injuring nearly 100 more.

The birthday of Martin Luther King becomes a national holiday in the U.S..

Madonna releases her first album, *Madonna*.

Alice Walker publishes *The Color Purple*.

1987

President Reagan and Premier Gorbachev sign groundbreaking arms treaties. Gorbachev also develops a rapport with British Prime Minister Margaret Thatcher.

Two disasters afflict the UK. The cross channel ferry, Herald of Free Enterprise capsizes in the Engish channel, killing 184, and a fire at King's Cross underground station claims the lives of 30.

Pop Artist Andy Warhol dies aged 57.

American actor and dancer Fred Astaire dies aged 88.

Glenn Close and Michael Douglas star in the thriller *Fatal Attraction*.

1988

General Noriega of Panama is charged with drug offences.

President Reagan makes a historic visit to Moscow further strengthening East/West relations.

A Pan Am aircraft explodes over Lockerbie, Scotland, 270 people are killed.

Canadian athlete Ben Johnson is disqualified and has his gold medal rescinded at the Seoul Olympics after testing positive for drugs.

President Reagan makes further progress in the USSR, reaching agreements on various issues including arms and civil rights.

George Bush wins U.S. Presidential election.

Australia celebrates 200 years as a nation.

Over 100,000 die as an earthquake rocks Armenia.

Mkartin Scorsese's film *The Last Temptation of Christ* is released amid controversy and charges of blasphemy.

1989

In South Africa P.W. Botha, leader of the National Party resigns and is replaced by F.W. de Klerk, sparking hopes for social and political reform.

Emperor Hirohito of Japan dies.

Following the publication of his novel, *The Satanic Verses*, which satirizes Islam, British author Salman Rushdie is sentenced to death by the Ayatollah Khomeini. Muslims in Britain burn effigies of Rushdie on the street and the author is forced into hiding.

An earthquake hits San Francisco, killing 80.

Margaret Thatcher celebrates ten years as British Prime Minister.

British actor Laurence Olivier dies aged 82.

General Noriega is dismissed from power in Panama after U.S. troops invade.

In China, 2,000 students are massacred in Tiananmen Square where they were gathered to demand democratic reform.

Country after country deserts the Soviet bloc until finally — in November — the Berlin Wall, for nearly 40 years a symbol of the East/West divide, is demolished.

CHRONOLOGY

1990's

Beginning with the hope and joy of German reunification and the release from prison of South African leader Nelson Mandela, the last decade of the century has been as beset with conflict and disaster as any preceding it. The Gulf War, fought between the allied powers of the West and Iraq, was thought to have ended in a decisive victory for the allies, and yet the Iraqi leader, Saddam Hussein continues to threaten world peace. In central Europe, ethnic cleansing on a scale not seen since Hitler's massacre of the Jews continues to destabilize the region of Kosovo and in India fighting has once again broken out over the region of Kashmir.

In the White House, President Bill Clinton has been threatened with impeachment following a scandal involving a sexual liaison with intern Monica Lewinsky.

As the human race approaches the millennium there seems no resolution to the problems that have plagued it for thousands of years. War, famine, and pestilence continue to afflict us despite the revolutions in science and technology that have occurred during the last century. Yet there is some measure of hope. There have been genuine efforts made to resolve long-standing problems — for instance the Irish conflict has reached a tenuous but optimistic stage in the peace process and Apartheid has been abolished in South Africa.

The internet has precipitated an unprecedented communications revolution, and some genetic scientists predict a cure for cancer and AIDS within the next five years. Plans for the celebration of the new millennium promise to bring a global unity that would have seemed impossible at the beginning of the century.

African National Congress leader Nelson Mandela is released from prison further spurring the political movement toward a multi-racial society in South Africa.

Iraqi leader Saddam Hussein orders the invasion of Kuwait. In response Western powers place economic sanctions on Iraq and build up troops in the area.

Margaret Thatcher resigns as British Prime Minister and is succeeded by John Major.

Lech Walesa wins a landslide victory in Polish elections.

The Hubble telescope is placed in orbit around earth by the space shuttle Discovery.

Hollywood icon Greta Garbo dies aged 84.

Jodie Foster and Anthony Hopkins star in the thriller *The Silence of the Lambs*.

1994

Nelson Mandela is elected President of South Africa in the first elections open to all races.

Bill and Hillary Clinton face questions about their role in Whitewater Development Corporation in Arkansas after it is alleged that their investment has been improperly used.

President Clinton is accused of sexual harassment by Paula Jones.

The sinking of the car ferry Estonia claims the lives of over 900 passengers and crew.

Singer Kurt Cobain of Nirvana commits suicide.

Former U.S. president Richard Nixon dies aged 81.

David Zemeckis directs Tom Hanks in *Forrest Gump*.

Quentin Tarantino's film *Pulp Fiction* provokes controversy and acclaim.

British pop group Oasis achieve overnight success with their album *Definitely Maybe*.

1995

More than 5,000 die in and around Kobe, Japan after an earthquake hits the region.

A nerve gas attack in Tokyo subway kills eight and injures thousands. The Aum Shinrikyo ("Supreme Truth") cult is to blame

Scores are killed as a terrorist car bomb blows up outside a block-long Oklahoma City federal building. Timothy McVeigh, an American Army veteran, is charged.

Ethnic violence engulfs the African country of Rwanda, the death toll soars into the thousands, and border refugee camps swell as people flee.

Israelis and Palestinians agree on transferring the West Bank to Arabs in a landmark agreement. Soon after, Israeli Prime Minister Yitzhak Rabin is slain by a Jewish extremist at a peace rally.

The crime-of-the-century ends with former football star O.J. Simpson, being aquitted of any involvement in the murder of his ex-wife Nicole and her friend. The case remains unsolved.

The French-speaking province of Quebec narrowly rejects independence from Canada in October.

1996

At least 73 die in a Sri Lankan suicide bombing.

Britain alarmed by a deadly bacteria found in beef, begins a measure that will see the slaughter of all cattle in an effort to eradicate the disease known as "mad cow disease."

After years of terrorising members of academia and the technology industry with unexpected letter bombs, the F.B.I. arrests a suspect in the Unabomber case. The suspect, Ted Kaszynski is found in his remote cabin, after being turned in by his brother.

Israel elects right-wing leader Benjamin Netanyahu as prime minister. Talks between Israel and Arab leaders hit an all-time low after sparks of progress.

Jazz great Ella Fitzgerald dies in June.

After months of speculation and rumors of infidelity, Prince Charles and Princess Diana agree to a divorce

Taliban Muslim fundamentalists capture Afghan capital

CHRONOLOGY

1991

Western powers begin "Operation Desert Storm" air strikes against Iraq.

In South Africa, F.W. de Klerk begins the process of dismantling Arpatheid.

Winnie Mandela, the wife of ANC leader Nelson is sentenced to six years imprisonment for kidnap and assault.

France elects its first female President, Edith Cresson.

Mikhail Gorbachev resigns as President of the USSR. Boris Yeltsin takes power.

Croatia and Slovenia declare independence from Yugoslavia and are followed by Macedonia.

Nirvana release the single "Smells Like Teen Spirit" and their second album *Nevermind*, sparking the "grunge" fashion.

Rock singer Freddie Mercury dies of AIDS.

Dancer Margot Fonteyn dies aged 71.

Ridley Scott directs Susan Sarandon and Gena Davis in *Thelma and Louise*.

1992

Mafia boss John Gotti is convicted of murder in the U.S.

Race riots cause the deaths of over 50 people in Los Angeles after four policemen are acquitted of assaulting Rodney King, despite video evidence confirming the assault.

Bill Clinton wins U.S. Presidential elections.

Prince Charles and Princess Diana announce their separation.

Toni Morrison publishes *Jazz*.

Hollywood siren Marlene Dietrich dies aged 90.

Stars perform at an AIDS benefit concert at Wembley Stadium, London, in honor of Freddie Mercury.

British artist Damien Hirst produces his piece *The Physical Impossibility of Death in the Mind of Someone Living* — a preserved shark floating in a tank.

1993

Bill Clinton instigates the "don't ask, don't tell" policy of the U.S. services toward homosexual recruits.

In Waco, Texas the FBI lay siege to the headquarters of a cult led by David Koresh. The leader and 50 of his followers die in a blaze that consumes the compound.

In a historic meeting Pope John Paul II talks to the Chief Rabbi of Israel at the Vatican.

Boris Yeltsin demands elections in the Russia.

Steven Spielberg directs the year's two hit movies, *Jurassic Park* and *Schindler's List*.

1997

Israeli Prime Minister Netanyahu finds himself at the center of controversy over a failed attempt to assassinate a militant Islamic leader.

The U.S., U.K., and France agree to freeze Nazis' gold loot.

Deng Xiaoping, China's leader, dead at 92

A state of anarchy engulfs Albania when a third of the country's population loses their savings because of a pyramid scheme.

The Hale-Bopp Comet makes its closest spin around the Earth until 4397.

Tiger Woods breaks multiple records in the Masters Golf Tournament

Hong Kong returns to Chinese rule

Princess Diana, 36, is killed with two others in a Paris car crash. An unprecedented display of public mourning marks her funeral.

Mother Teresa, Nobel Peace Prize winner, dies at the age of 87.

1998

Pope John Paul II makes a landmark visit to Cuba for five days. A first for a religious leader in this Communist nation, where Catholicism is practiced secretly.

President Bill Clinton becomes embroiled in a sex scandal and initially denies allegations of an affair with a White House intern named Monica Lewinsky.

A U.S. military plane cuts a ski cable in Italy and sends the car plunging. Twenty holidaymakers die.

Serbs battle ethnic Albanians in Kosovo.

The Vatican announces its regret for inaction during the Holocaust

The F.D.A. approves Viagra, a drug meant to resolve male impotence.

Europeans agree on a single currency: the "Euro."

India conducts three atomic tests despite worldwide disapproval. Pakistan retaliates by staging five nuclear tests of its own.

1999

Freak tornadoes wipe out parts of the American mid-west.

Following reports of ethnic cleansing in Kosova by neighboring Serbs. NATO wages a war — the first done entirely by air strikes — on the region. A peace settlement is reached in the summer although the area remains unstable.

The much-hyped 'prequel,' to the *Star Wars* series — *The Phantom Menace* — is released.

Prince Edward, son of Queen Elizabeth, marries Sophie Ryhs-Jones. The couple opt for a simple ceremony instead of the pomp and pageantry which accompanied Edwards' siblings' marriages — all of which ended in divorce.

President Bill Clinton escapes removal from office, over the Lewinsky Affair.

South Africa's Nelson Mandela completes his term as presdent.